R. F

"YOU USED TO LIVE IN MY HOUSE."

Cuz Sere,
We have great memories from our childhood days (Hoover Dr) and I'm so glad we've reconnected. Best to you, Bill & the family.
Go Get your Snad!
12/11/2007 [signature]

"You Used to Live in My House."

Copyright © 2007 House of 7s LLC
All rights reserved.
ISBN: 1-4196-7651-2
ISBN-13: 9781419676512
Library of Congress Control Number: 2007906548

"You Used to Live in My House."

ACKNOWLEDGEMENTS

Special thanks to my family and friends.
First, to my best friend, **Louisa H. Coons**, and to
Kelly Blood, Chris Coons, Chris Harrison, Dave Harrison,
Virginia Coons, Michael E. Coons, Paul A. Hunter,
Brandy Harrison, Pete Blood, Jamie Harrison,
Bill Michaels, Julie Smallin, Cherie Hudson-Whittlesey,
George Blood, Zac Stoumbaugh, Mark Shearon
and
especially for the hours of editing by
Louisa H. Coons, Stephen A. Taylor, and Steve Little.

Without their support and encouragement and in the ways
they challenged me,
you would not be reading this book.

In Loving Memory of Kevin Todd Coons.

Praise God, Who Never Gave Up On Me.

*A True Story Of
A Shared Romance,
Synchronicity
…linked To The Invisible
…something Inexpressible.
…logic So Inflexible
…yet Nothing Is Invincible. (1)*

BOOK ONE

CHAPTER 1
When you come to a fork in the road, take it. (2)

You've no doubt experienced "defining moments" or "turning points" in your life. Sometimes we don't recognize them as such, until later. At other times they're locked in place like a frozen frame on a roll of film.

"*You used to live in my house*" was said to me on Friday, March 6, 1981. I can tell you, within the hour, exactly where I was, what I was doing, and of course, who said it. Those words created a defining moment in my life. The path that was created has rarely been dull. Like most paths, it has changed from time to time, with its own twists and turns, hills and valleys, and even Grand Canyon-like landscapes. But, as you who have hiked mountains or even the Grand Canyon, know that the journey can be hard, exhausting and exhilarating. The journey has its own rewards.

"You used to live in my house." Those 7 words were the first words that my wife, Louisa, said to me.

My response was immediate, and I have thought about it many times since. I said, "You must be one of the Hunter girls." She replied that she was Louisa Hunter Harrison. I still find my response curious because my former wife and I had lived in a number of rental properties in the years we were married. How did I know that Louisa spoke of *that* house? How did I know that she was one of "the Hunter girls?" I had never even seen a photo of them. I just recall the neighbors referring to *the Hunter girls*.

Her house, 49 Brandon Road, is located in a beautiful neighborhood called Brandon Heights, in Newport News, Virginia. Louisa's Mother designed the house and her father built it in 1950. Her mother had been an architect and her father an aeronautical engineer and is the son of a builder.

Louisa had grown up in it, leaving after high school in 1969 to attend college. From Labor Day weekend, 1975 until Memorial Day weekend, 1977, I lived in that house, "her house," with my former wife, Judi, and our children Kevin, Kelly and Chris. I had heard our neighbors refer to *the Hunter girls*. I hadn't met them and had no knowledge of where they were during those years, and of course, no need to know. I didn't know that I would ever meet either Louisa or sister, Ellen. I don't recall that I even knew their names. I later learned that our paths had crossed in many ways.

When I looked at Louisa I saw those big blue eyes, the curly…almost "Annie"-like hair, and a very attractive body that topped out at 5'2". I knew that she was someone I wanted to know.

At the time I was the marketing director for Newmarket North Mall, in Hampton, Virginia. I met Louisa in my office. She was a part of a group of market researchers whom I had briefed prior to their conducting a mall survey of our shoppers.

After that meeting I went back to work, overseeing the mall's spring fashion show. I also had a date that night, with one of the models in the show. As it turned out, the date was short lived. It was a fact that I was dating a lot of different women during that time, and enjoying it. I'll address that in more detail as it becomes relevant.

I was distracted by Louisa's image in my mind, so I'm sure I wasn't as attentive to my date as I could have been. It was also fact that my date was irritating me by making remarks about stories she'd heard, that I dated a lot of women. Later, while at my beach house, my phone rang. I started to answer it, thinking it could have been my daughter Kelly, and less likely her brother Chris, but I didn't because I thought it was too late for one of them to call. I thought of their older Brother, Kevin. Could his Mother have called me about him? The date, remaining nameless because I have no recollection of her name, made a remark about it being one of my girlfriends. At that point I picked up my car keys. She asked where I was going. I replied, "I'm taking you back to your car. End of date." We rode in silence.

The next week, while having lunch with Phyllis, the supervisor for the research group, I asked whether I could 'hit on Louisa.' She asked me to wait until the survey was completed. On Friday, March 13th, I told Louisa, as she was hurrying to gather interview forms in my office, that I had asked Phyllis about her…and yes, 'hitting on her.' Of course she knew, because Phyllis had already told her. Still, my saying it startled her and added to her frantic day. She was already getting a late start with the interviews on the mall. Friday the 13th had already included a burst radiator hose, and a call to a friend, asking him to help her replace the hose for her. Startled, she said, "I'm running late. I need to go."

At the time, I was involved with three other women, excluding the model I had dated that fateful day. I was not someone you would want your daughter to bring home. It was what I refer to as "binge" behavior. When I smoked, I chain-smoked. When I drank, I drank what I had available. It was the same when I 'dated.' I womanized. In today's terms, I was a player.

I had been single again for less than two years and I was

enjoying it. To say that I had been unfaithful in my marriage is an understatement. I hadn't changed my habits. There were women I truly cared about, and a few that I believed I loved. Some believed that they loved me. However, I wasn't a great catch by any stretch of the imagination.

I felt an attraction to Louisa, and I was aware that she was interested in me too. So, at that point, my behavior was pretty much normal, if not admirable. As you'll see, I didn't act on my thoughts about dating her. I had some other things going on that required my immediate attention.

CHAPTER 2
The best-laid plans…

I had to deal with a couple of those turns in the road; one I had known about. The other, I presumed. My employer, Hahn Property Management, had asked me a month earlier to transfer to Memphis to coordinate the opening of "The Mall of Memphis." I had sought and received permission from my children to do so, or so I thought.

I wasn't looking for a lasting relationship. The reality of it is that I was backing away, or running away, from anything even remotely resembling one, or keeping my distance from anyone who might have represented that possibility. Memphis became an excuse to convince myself not to follow up with Louisa, and others whom I was already dating. One had asked me to stay with her until I moved. She said she was concerned that I'd meet a Memphis belle and get married.

The proposed move to Memphis was real. I had moved out of my beach house and in with my friend Paul Phillips at the end of March, expecting to be at his place for a couple of months. I settled into Paul's house in the Hidenwood neighborhood in Newport News, and almost immediately took a trip to Memphis and on to San Diego for corporate meetings that were called the annual "Hahn School."

My life is filled with events that in some fashion are connected to what has been or will come to be. I don't use the word coincidence. When I studied psychology, I came to believe in Carl Jung's theory of synchronicity. Perhaps you're familiar with the popularized version, recorded by the pop music group, The Police. I like the lyrical definition better than any I could find in a dictionary.

After arriving in San Diego, I was checking in at the Mission Bay Hilton, renewing friendships and acquaintances with people who worked for the Hahn Company throughout the country. I had been with the company since April 1979, and was attending my third "Hahn School." While I was telling several people about my adventures on the way to Memphis, and my impending transfer, a woman who had been with the company for several years, Margaret Fleming, tapped me on the shoulder. As I recall, at that time she was working at a mall in the Los Angeles area. She pulled me aside, and told me that I might not want to talk about Memphis too much, because she had heard that I might not be going there after all...but she couldn't say anymore. I knew that she was close enough to the corporate grapevine that I started to wonder what was going on.

The next morning I was sent to a meeting with ten other marketing directors, from malls in various parts of the country, as well as a handful of mall managers I knew, including David Morgan the manager of our mall, Newmarket North. David and I were close and he hadn't given me any hint of what was about to happen.

I learned that I would *not* be transferred to Memphis, but would stay in Virginia. I would hold the newly formed position of Regional Marketing Director, and continue to serve as the marketing director for Newmarket North Mall. I was also given the responsibilities of overseeing the marketing for the shopping center across the street, and 5 other malls in a four states. It also meant a hefty annual salary increase.

More importantly, I wouldn't be moving away from my children.

I flew back to Memphis after the Hahn School, and picked up my Honda Accord. It had been repaired while I was in California. It needed repairs because the engine had caught fire about 50 miles from Memphis. I was able to put out the engine fire, and surprisingly could drive on into the city. I later regretted that I hadn't let it burn up. My insurance agent had told me that the carrier would cover it, when I left it in Memphis. When I returned to pick it up, their position had been reversed. I had to call my banker in Virginia to arrange a loan to pay for the repairs.

It was about a 5-hour drive north to my hometown of Alton, Illinois and a surprise visit with my mother, over Easter weekend. I stayed another day and visited Grandma Fleming for the last time.

On my way back home, I made a stop in Richmond and went to dinner with a woman I had been dating. She was a senior at the University of Richmond. The difference in our ages was the primary reason we weren't taking our relationship any further. She asked me to stay for the night, but I was anxious to move on and drove to Newport News after dinner.

The next morning I told my friend Paul of the change of plans, and that I hoped to move back to the beach as soon as possible. He said that I was welcome to stay there as long as I wanted to. We had been friends for several years. At some point he had become my insurance agent. At that time he was busy building a thriving business with Amway, in addition to his insurance business.

I visited with my kids after work the next day, to tell them that I wasn't going to move to Memphis after all. I had waited to share that news in person. They were as excited as I.

It wasn't until then that I learned what I should have known, that my daughter Kelly had really been hurt by my plans to move away. She had verbalized her approval or acceptance and hidden her true feelings. She doesn't do that anymore. The next step would be to find my own place, and preferably near the beach. My vacated beach house was not an option. When I was getting ready to move, neighbors told me that my landlady's friends were using it for "nooners" while I was renting it. I felt betrayed. We had dated and I had enjoyed our relationship. I didn't return the keys to her. I left them inside the house. I didn't call her on it and later regretted how I handled it.

Paul had said that my kids were always welcome at his house, even to stay over with me. He was a very generous friend. However, he was focused on building his Amway business, and I became frustrated with his attempts to show it to me. After all, I had just received a big raise in salary, and was climbing the corporate ladder. I had no problem with the products he had shown me and invited me to make use of. I didn't understand why a successful insurance agent would want to sell them. I finally wished him well, and told him that it just wasn't for me. He accepted that and it was never an issue again. Paul went on to create a very successful Amway business without me.

Meanwhile back at the office...Among the changes would be the hiring of an assistant. I would need to delegate responsibilities for many of the daily tasks of marketing Newmarket North Mall, because my new responsibilities would take me to Greenville and Durham, North Carolina, Clearwater, Florida and Kingsport, Tennessee.

I don't recall how many people I interviewed for the newly created position of Assistant Marketing Director. I do know that when we hired Kathy Wescott, a high school teacher, we immediately became friends. As time went on, she became much more like a sister; a close and trusted friend.

CHAPTER 3
You can run, but you can't hide…

It was near the end of April when I saw an ad for a 10K coming up in May. I hadn't run that far in the 3 years that I had toyed with running. I registered for the race anyway. It was challenging to train for it. Running in the Hidenwood area meant running in a lot of traffic. I had to cross major streets and intersections regardless of which direction I ran.

I dated only couple of times in April, spending most of my non-working hours with my kids and my increased running. I hadn't followed up with Louisa because of my concern that she was a lot younger than I, and blah-blah-blah. That was about to change.

On May 2, 1981 I was re-introduced to Louisa Hunter Harrison. I had run the Daily Press newspaper's "Run for the Arts 10k" and stopped by a grocery store on the way home. Louisa was there giving free samples of a new diet drink. I was surprised to see her, and stopped to say hello. She said, 'I thought you were going to call me." I was embarrassed and began to try to explain about the proposed move to Memphis and how I thought she was much younger than me; too young. (It's not easy to back pedal after running a 10k race.) She laughed and explained that she had two sons, one who was celebrating his 7th birthday *that day*, and the other almost 10. I was shocked. I didn't stay long, but on the way back to Paul's house I kept thinking about her. I returned to the store almost immediately, ostensibly to pick up a carton of milk that I'd forgotten on the first trip.

When I saw her again I waved. I stopped at her booth again and said, "Okay, you can go out with me tonight or tomorrow." She said she already had a date for that night and that we could get together the next day. She was hosting a birthday party for her younger son, David, and I was welcome to come to the party. I suggested getting together before that. I planned to run at Mariner's Museum Park. I didn't see a first date in the form of a birthday party for a 7 year old. She agreed to join me, and I agreed to go to David's birthday party. It turned out that, while staying with my friend Paul, I was living only a couple of miles from Louisa. In another brush with synchronicity, I learned that Paul had gone to school with Louisa's sister, Ellen, and knew of Louisa.

The next morning we went to the park to run. She didn't run much due to a bad knee, but we managed to talk, as I ran ahead and then ran back to her.

It's funny to think back to think about the day when I ran into her again. After the Run for the Arts 10k, I ran into a woman with whom I'd had relationship years earlier in Williamsburg. She introduced me to her husband and we talked briefly. I had thought of her from time to time, and usually when I heard the Doobie Brothers' song, "What a Fool Believes". (3) I thought about her on the way to the grocery store. Of course what happened at the grocery store sent me in a different direction all together.

While Louisa and I were running and walking in Mariner's Museum Park, I had told Louisa about my children, Kevin, Kelly and Chris, and that my older son, Kevin, had Cerebral Palsy, and was severely restricted by his handicap. She told me that she had a brother, Bruce, who had had Cerebral Palsy. Bruce died when he was 13.

"YOU USED TO LIVE IN MY HOUSE."

It seemed strange to be going to a birthday party, knowing only the hostess. I became aware that everyone there already knew about me. The kids, David and his older brother Chris, and the others weren't interested in me at all. There was food and drink, and badminton. I actually had a good time. I liked her friends, and accepted that I was being evaluated. I think that's when I met her parents for the first time, too. They came by, having been at a Republican meeting of some sort, wearing quite an array of bling. I thought, 'nice folks…but Republican.' I could *never* vote Republican. That's when I learned that Louisa was in the Amway business with them. I wondered… Amway…Republican…what's next?

On my next visit Louisa produced four records albums… AKA vinyl LP's. The albums jackets each had my name, or a form of my name that I'd written. "Property of Perry Coons," or "Perry Lane." The latter was the name I had used while working as a radio DJ. Louisa had purchased the records from my former wife, at a garage sale when we were still living at 49 Brandon Road. That would have been 4 or 5 years before we met. I had no idea the records were gone, and no recollection of the garage sale.

Louisa and I had been seeing each other virtually everyday for about three weeks when she came to see me at Paul's house. I was anxious to share with her a song that had been on my mind. It's was from the Moody Blues' LP "Long Distant Voyager," a Justin Hayward song, "In My World." I could feel her presence when I heard the lyrics…

…"If you knew…the changes I feel that you put me through, and you do, I see in your eyes that you really do…" (4)

CHAPTER 4
"Happy Days" meets Woodstock…

Louisa had been a single Mom for over 4 years at that time. The boys' Dad wasn't involved in their lives. I was told that he might call and want to take them out, and it turned out to be taking them to where he played pool. They might, or might not hear from him on their birthdays, or holidays. They didn't see him with any regularity or consistency. Chris wasn't quite 10 years old when we met, and he was more mature than many teenage boys. He was very protective of David, and of Mom.

Louisa was making the boys' clothes, and even without any child support from her ex-husband, somehow found the money to send them to a parochial school. She'd been brought up in a safe and conservative environment. I would later describe her childhood, which was very different from mine, as an "Ozzie & Harriet" family life. People my age will remember the Ozzie and Harriet Nelson TV show, a precursor to "The Cleavers."

I've poked fun at her 'safe' childhood environment, and I say it with affection. I could see that her parents had instilled in her, strong moral values that I came to appreciate and learn from through the years. Paul and Carol did that in the face of their own challenges, of course. Losing their son Bruce was one that I would later come to know in a personal way.

We soon discovered that she had almost certainly attended the Warwick High School football and basketball games when they played James Blair High School. I had been the play-by-play announcer for WBCI-FM, for the James Blair High School games.

Even though Louisa graduated from high school in 1969, she was only a part time member of the flower child, or Woodstock, generation. Her values were more often like those of the president of the Young Republicans.

She was also a walking-talking contradiction from all of that. She definitely was ready to party when she had a break from being super Mom. I think the statue of limitations would allow me to tell you that she was growing weed behind her storage shed when we met and drying it in her attic. She hadn't tried pot until only a few years before that. She wasn't a pothead. She is a true Scot and wouldn't spend money on it. She enjoyed it occasionally and it only made sense to her, to grow her own. She didn't sell it or buy it.

When we met she was also a driving force in a local food co-op. She was a "granola-girl," practicing Catholic, Amway distributor and Republican. Why I didn't instinctively run in the other direction, I don't know. I know now that the contradictions were part of the attraction. God knows I have my own behavioral contradictions, and even more so in those days.

I had talked about Louisa to co-workers in my travels. One of them, Brent Merrill, said when he met her, "She's so petite. The way you described her I expected a woman who could kick-start her own vibrator."

In part, Louisa's childhood differed from mine as the 50's differed from the 60's. My childhood was stable in my early years. I don't have clear memories of the same day birth and death of my only sister in 1951. I wasn't quite 9 at the time. We never talked about her, even though she'd lived long enough to be named Brenda Sue. Years later, her birth and death date would appear as yet another piece of synchronicity in my relationship with Louisa.

My life changed dramatically after we moved from my hometown of Alton, Illinois to Tampa/Plant City, Florida in 1955, and back to Alton in 1956. My parents never recovered from those moves. I know they didn't recover financially, and I saw my dad in a different light. He had chased his dream and saw it fall apart. My parents weren't highly educated. Everything they achieved came about from desire, hard work and their love for each other.

What I saw as a downward spiral hit bottom when dad died suddenly, in an automobile accident on June 14, 1958. I have vivid memories of virtually every minute of that day. My mother was left to raise my brothers and me. I was 15 and my brothers were 11, 4 and 2. Mom was not yet 36. I hope God has a special place in mind for her when he calls her home.

We were left with no insurance and dad's employer having successfully defeated the claim of Workers Compensation Insurance. In today's terms we would have been homeless had it not been for my Uncle George "Pitts" and Aunt Frances Campbell, Mom's brother-in-law and sister. A lot of people said that they'd be there for us. Some were. My memory is that Pitts and Frances *were* there for us. They welcomed us into their home, with their son, Darby, while their new home was being built. I don't recall the square footage of that 'row house,' only that it was small. There were 3 adults and 5 kids living in it and it felt like home. We stayed there after the Campbell's moved into their new home.

It took a while for me to realize that others had it worse than I did. Those experiences would come to serve me well through the years. I think of them, in the context of writing this book, more in terms of how different Louisa and I are...or were, and how it played into all of the challenges we had as we learned (begrudgingly) to embrace those differences.

CHAPTER 5
Ch-ch-ch-Changes, Turn and face the strain…(5)

I was entering a period of my life when I would eat enough crow that I should be able to fly. I had been dating around, and successfully avoiding or running from serious relationships. There had been two women whom I loved, and yet deep down inside I knew that I wasn't *in love with*. I had found a way to end those relationships. I did not want to feel love. I didn't trust it. I had said, and have been quoted as saying; I would never fall in love again, or get married again. (Eating Crow, part 2-Did you recognize part 1?) Those are only two items from a list of things that I said I'd never do, but have done and still do, since meeting Louisa.

Louisa had just come out of a serious relationship. Her sons were very close to him, and it would take a very long time before I felt that I was at least as important to them, and in some ways, as important to Louisa, as Steve had been. She hadn't wanted their relationship to end, so I really caught her on the rebound. Steve's loss…a *huge* loss. Thank you, Steve!

We saw quite a bit of each other over the next few weeks. In early June, I was to take my first trip to visit Clearwater Mall, in Clearwater, Florida. For some reason that I've never quite understood, the day before that trip I went home early and changed to go running. I felt so good during the run, that I stretched my mileage. Afterwards I drove the route to check the miles. TEN MILES! I had never run that far before. I was so excited that I called Louisa to tell her that I was coming over with a bottle of wine to celebrate. We drank that wine, and perhaps more. I don't recall. What I do recall is waking up late and missing my flight to Tampa. As you might guess, when I did arrive in Tampa, I received a good bit of kidding from my peers.

Something else occurred on that trip. I was still basking in the glow of my first ten-mile run while flying. I was reading a copy of "Runner's World" magazine. I saw an ad for the first Philadelphia Independence Marathon. I thought of my good friend Ken Kirby who lived there. I thought, 'Why don't I go to Philly and run that marathon. I'm sure that I could stay with Ken.' That sounds incredible, even now. I really was that full of myself about having run ten miles.

Running 10 miles does not equate to running 26.2 miles, which I came to learn all too well. There's a phrase that I've heard attributed to World Class Marathoner Bill Rogers that says, "The first half of a marathon is 20 miles. The other half is 6.2 miles." I have since run *that* marathon more than once.

I did register for the Philadelphia Independence Marathon. However, I told only Louisa about it. A few weeks later while running, I came upon my friend Brian Cole. We talked about the fact that we had each noticed that the other was running longer distances. Finally, we admitted that we had each registered for the marathon in Philadelphia.

Slowly, I began to admit to myself that I was falling in love with Louisa. I recall a particular day when Brian and I were running, and I had rattled off a number of things 'I didn't want.' He stopped running. Then I stopped too, and asked what was wrong. He said, "I'm pretty tired of hearing what you **don't** want. Maybe you'd better figure out what you *do* want." He added, "I hope it isn't just another one of your sexual adventures." He'd gotten to know Louisa by then, and recognized how special she is.

That was a scary moment for me. I knew I wanted Louisa, but I was so afraid to surrender to those feelings. It happened, little by little because of that fear. I wouldn't learn until much later that it was myself that I was afraid of. I didn't trust myself, and with good cause.

Not long after that I shared the details of my previous marriage, and my children.

I wanted Louisa to know about the times that Judi had been separated, and how it came about that we reunited in our marriage. In 1969 and 1970, Judi had lived in Scotland, and England. During that time I had a long distance relationship with a woman in North Carolina. I was also dating women in Williamsburg. Judi wrote to me in 1970, saying that she wanted to call me and talk with me about getting back together. I recall reading the letter at poolside, at the apartment complex where I lived. I wondered why I was even reading it. At the time I was working as a DJ at the radio station, and my brother Pat was living with me. I used Judi's letters to break off my long distance relationship, while still not planning to reunite with her.

It was during that period that I indulged in marijuana for the first time, or so I thought. That occurred at the home of one of my neighbors, an Army helicopter pilot. His wife had invited me to one of their "black-light" parties, where I smoked what I thought was grass. I was later told that it was Hashish… my first high at age 29. I had quit smoking (cigarettes) 5 years earlier and hadn't come close to smoking anything since.

Why then? You probably guessed it. I was interested in the pilot's wife.

My lifestyle was a contradiction too. At times being responsible for my younger brother, and at other times being as wild as you might ever hear about DJ's...a lot of booze and a lot of women.

It was actually during a party at my apartment that Judi called me from England. Somebody at the party answered the phone and called me to it. I had to excuse myself from the woman I was with to take the call. Judi said that she really wanted to comeback to Williamsburg, and to me. I asked, 'Why me?' 'Why now?' She answered that she was pregnant and wanted me to be the child's father. I almost automatically said yes, and that's how Kevin came into my life. I had no idea just how much he would *change* my life.

When I met Judi in New York we picked up where we'd left off. She was upset that I hadn't come alone. I came with another DJ, Joe Thomas, who was from New Jersey and could tell me how to get around in New York City. We returned to Virginia and she and I moved into a cabin in the woods near the Chickahominy River outside of Williamsburg.

Kevin was born January 3, 1971. I learned a lot about myself that day. I was a wreck after being told first that he wouldn't live. Then, if he did live, he'd be severely handicapped, retarded and perhaps blind. I met with the station manager, Don Bentley, and he asked whether I should go on the air for my shift that day. I said that I really needed to. I did and he said it was one of the best shows I'd ever done. I just channeled all that emotion into being more upbeat, loose and a little crazier. I already loved that boy *so much*. He was in the Intense Care Unit. I hadn't even held him yet.

That Kevin had been born significantly disabled with Cerebral Palsy and mental retardation didn't faze Louisa at all.

"YOU USED TO LIVE IN MY HOUSE."

Those who had known us in Williamsburg, where we lived until September 1974, knew that I wasn't Kevin's biological father. However, after moving to Hampton, virtually no one outside of our family had known until I told Louisa. Maybe I wanted to show her that my past wasn't all dark side, that I had some good in me too. I felt the need to tell Louisa everything about myself. Perhaps I was hoping, at some level, to run her off.

I brought out all the ghosts of my past. It was my own Halloween parade. I knew that I didn't want Louisa to hear those stories from others. It was easily one of the best decisions I've ever made.

I also had to tell her that I'd been married briefly when I was a teenager. I broke my mother's heart when I begged her to sign for me. Linda broke my heart when she ended it less than two months later. We were kids. We were married for the reason that kids often do. When we learned that she wasn't pregnant, she didn't want to be married.

I learned that she later went on to have a long-term marriage and family. I hadn't seen her since the early 60's. She has since died.

Louisa and I sat for quite some time, on the peak of her storage shed roof, as I offered up the bright, the not so bright, and even the darkest aspects of my life. I was a little surprised that she embraced me after those stories.

I learned that she had heard some of my reputation. A few years earlier, she had been told some things about the '(expletive) DJ who lived in her house.' I wasn't a DJ at the time I lived on Brandon Road, though I was still working in radio. While the description of me that was told to her was not flattering, it was a pretty accurate description of my behavior.

The contradictions of my behavior weren't lost on me. I loved to sit on the beach and listen to the sounds of the water. I rarely did it without coffee, beer or a bottle of Harvey's Bristol Crème, depending on the time of day. I thought of my excesses and how or why I would cause myself to be in a state where I would be out of control. The question was framed against the image of Kevin who didn't have that choice. I often thought about those contradictions. While I love each of my kids as themselves, and each influence me, even today, it was easy to see that Kevin influenced me in ways that I wouldn't understand for a long time. It was more than 20 years later, and more than 3000 miles from that shore, that I came to understand those contradictions in my behavior.

CHAPTER 6
"We're going to grow old together."

My former neighbors on Lighthouse Drive, Doug and Shirley Quinn had invited me to a July 4th cookout and keg party. By this time I had given in to my feelings for Louisa. That night, as she and I were lying on their lawn, and I heard myself say, "We're going to grow old together." She replied, "You're scaring the hell out of me."

A month later my friend Brian had connected me with a property owner of a cottage a few doors north of his cottage at Buckroe Beach. So I moved from Paul's home and into the cottage at Buckroe Beach at the end of August. I was about six miles from my kids, fourteen miles from Louisa and ten miles from work…and living on the beach of The Chesapeake Bay.

It was great to be back at the beach. The location would become significant for me, and for us. Actually, that cottage and Buckroe Beach hold special memories for a number of reasons, most of which are good memories.

I loved running at sunrise there. I would stop and watch the huge red sphere peek over and then pop up from the horizon.

As Louisa and I continued to date, and as the weeks passed, I told women that I had dated that I was now dating only Louisa. I did not always handle that well. While attending a shopping center conference in Miami, I came face to face with my future. I was with a woman I had dated, and who had visited my beach house at Grand View in 1980. I told her that

I wouldn't be with her anymore that I had met someone special and had been dating exclusively her since June.

It wasn't so much what I told her, as when and where. I saw the thin line between love and hate crossed in a manner of a few seconds. She had a different view of our relationship, hoping that it would one day become permanent. My friend Dave Morgan had told me, when he had met her in 1980, that he saw something in her eyes that said that she was in love with me. He had urged me to let her know that I was not interested in a permanent relationship. I hadn't taken his advice. She lived in another town, so I didn't see her often. I had counted on the Memphis move to help things take care of themselves. I saw her at a few conferences after that, and she would never accept my apologies. It took me a long time to move past that. I trust that she has moved past it as well.

When I got back home, I asked Louisa to sit with me and listen to a song that expressed my feelings to perfectly. The song, our song, is "Waiting For A Girl Like You," by Foreigner.…"It feels so right, so warm and true…I need to know if you feel it too…" (6)

I then described another challenge that I had with our relationship. I told her that I hadn't been with one woman, exclusively, for a very long time, including my infidelities in my previous marriage. I had lied and cheated and had lost my self-respect. I knew that I didn't want to live like that again, or put her through that.

I told Louisa that I needed to know that I could be with her and her only, intimately, before I committed to her. I didn't offer any guarantees. I thought I could just *do* it if I willed it. I still had a lot to learn about myself.

We've been asked how our children got along, being thrown together as they were. Early on they seemed to get along well. We were the sources of the differences and the difficulties.

We constantly challenged each other and reluctantly gave ground in an effort to make up. Later, they dealt with their own differences, in their own ways.

Our children began to spend more time together. They were close in age. We'd taken them to movies together, and they'd been together at my house and Louisa's. One movie, "Time Bandits" brought out verbal responses from both Chris Harrison and Kevin. We thought it was hilarious. However, most people in the audience didn't understand Kevin's sounds. I rolled him out of the auditorium and he got upset with me. So, we went back in and he was less 'verbal' through the remainder of the movie. He understood it.

Then there was the infamous camping trip to the outer banks of North Carolina. When Louisa asked me if I liked to camp, I said 'no.' I'd had my share of camping while serving in the Army at Fort Riley, Kansas. We had gone out into the field for exercises. At the time they were called war games. My first off-post "field trip" was on a convoy from Fort Riley, Kansas to Tarryall, Colorado in November 1961. Tarryall is a section of the southwest side of Pike's Peak, above Colorado Springs, and Manitou Springs. We were there for war games and the word was that we'd be spending Christmas on the Rhein, referring to the Rhein River in Germany. It was during the time of the Berlin Crisis. Of course, we'd "camped" during Basic Training too, in June and July at Fort Leonard Wood, Missouri, and on the plains of Kansas that same summer. That camping would differ significantly from camping in Colorado in November 1961. There's another story for another time about the latter.

I did agree to go camping with Louisa and the children. We took all of the kids, and gear, in my 1979 Honda Accord and headed for Duck and Kill Devil Hills, NC. Louisa had borrowed a tent from a friend, and it was big enough for all of us. The weather turned foul. Correction: We were hit by a monsoon. I put Kevin in the car, believing that he would be safer there. As it turned out, I was the only one who didn't sleep. I held the tent up by using my legs as a prop to keep it from collapsing in the torrential the wind and rain. That night I wasn't any more excited about camping than I had been in the Army.

The weather broke for much of the next day, and the wind returned...just ahead of the rain. My former wife, Judi, had given us some fish that her boyfriend Walter had caught. Louisa, who is a great cook, began to get it ready to cook for dinner. It was so windy that she and the kids took the Coleman stove into the Women's Room nearby to cook it. The process took even longer because the stove wouldn't get hot. We didn't learn until after it was finally cooked, that the salt preservative hadn't been rinsed from it. We snacked for dinner.

It seemed that, suddenly, we had become a couple. There were still snags. We would often disagree and argue about little things, building huge mountains out of barely discernable molehills. I wanted it to be perfect, of course. We hadn't figured out the 'working for it' part yet.

There were no boundaries for our arguments, personal or geographic. Our friends saw us pick at each other and correct each other. I know several of them wondered, at times out loud, *why* we even stayed together. I don't recall what we were arguing about...long distance...while I was on a business trip to Clearwater. However, I had hung up on her in the heat of the moment and regretted it. When I called back, she didn't answer. I cancelled the trip and flew home early to make amends. Louisa is a strong person. She made it clear that she didn't *need* me, and making amends was never easy. It was made even more difficult because I didn't know how to sincerely apologize. I just wanted things to be good.

CHAPTER 7
Road trip!

Not long after I had registered for the Philadelphia Independence Marathon, I called Ken Kirby to ask about our staying with him before and afterwards. It would be Louisa and me, plus Brian, and Kathy Westcott. She had met Brian through me, and they had been dating for a few weeks at the time.

It was a tangled web because Brian's ex-wife, Susan, worked for me, as the marketing secretary, at that time as well. I still have a vivid image of the first time I hurt Louisa enough to see her cry. I had accused her and Kathy of trying to embarrass Susan with comments about Brian. She was so very hurt, "you don't know me at all," she yelled through her tears. "I would *never* do something like that!" I think she came close to canceling her plans for the trip to Philadelphia. Perhaps more.

Something else happened during that period that has become a tradition. I was not open to public affection. Louisa is very open to it. The result is, and I don't recall when it started, we always kiss on elevators…to this day, whether others are there or not. Sometimes I tell other passengers that we're newlyweds.

If you think that shopping malls are hectic during the Christmas season, you haven't seen anything until you see it from the inside. Working in a shopping mall and getting ready for "Santa's arrival," can get pretty crazy. It's very stressful for the merchants because so much of their annual sales are generated over that period from mid-November through mid-January.

It was during that period that I was training for my first marathon. I could not have dedicated enough time to train for it, had it not been for the patience and friendship of David Morgan, and Dwight Rice. Running 100 miles a week takes a lot of time. It's not just the running. It involves changing clothes, stretching, and running, then cooling down, showering and changing clothes again.

The four of us set out for Philadelphia in Kathy's Mercedes on Friday, November 27, 1981…a week after my 39th birthday. Louisa had given me a sterling silver neck chain for my birthday, with the marathon distance of '26.2' as the pendent…along with a number of black balloons. I wouldn't wear the pendent until after I had completed the marathon. We were having a great time on the drive to Philadelphia until the headlights on the Mercedes stopped working as we entered the city. I don't recall how we made it to Ken's house that night, with no headlights. We played tourists the next day, with Ken as our guide, while Kathy's car was repaired.

Telling this story hasn't always been easy to do. I've been a very private person most of my life, and I have a long history of the "looking good" image programs. One of the guys I worked with, a mall manager, Doug O'Brien, once called me the most disciplined degenerate he knew. He has known his share. As it relates to me, he made the comment because I drank too much, and smoked some pot. And yet, I abstained from all of that for the 90 days of training for the marathon. We occasionally enjoyed brownies, commonly known as 'Alice B. Toklas brownies' because they were laced with marijuana.

And now, back to 'the Philadelphia (Marathon) story.' Ken drove us out to the starting area at Fort Washington. The marathon route ran through Germantown near Ken's home at the time, along the Schuylkill River, and into Philadelphia's Center City. If you know that area, you know there are a few hills that are not so gentle.

At some point Brian became very angry with me, saying 'I thought you said this was a flat course.' I made an effort to remind him that we had each registered for the event, without having talked to the other about it.

He was not to be dissuaded from his anger...ok, his fear. When we got out of the car, I asked where we might work our way into the group of about 6,000 somewhere behind the starting line. His response was 'f- you.' He walked away. By the time the race started, he was standing beside me and in a better mood. After about four miles into the marathon, Brian said that the pace was too slow for him. He wanted to pick up his pace and would see me down the road. I understood because he is a few years younger than me, stronger, and a much better athlete.

I was running at a pace between 8 and 8.5 minutes per mile, and feeling pretty good about it. While I've never been accused of being the most outgoing person in the world, I was meeting new people and as runners do, having conversations along the way.

Brian and I connected again at about Mile 18. I think we both enjoyed running through Germantown, near where Ken lived and the long gradual downhill along the Skulkyll River. The people of the Philadelphia area were terrific and made us very welcome every step of the (long) way. Brian and I ran and walked together, and crossed the Finish Line hand-in-hand.

Ken, Louisa and Kathy played mile marker leapfrog to catch up with us at different locations along the way. They greeted us at the Finish Line with beer and 'ABT' brownies that had been baked in Virginia. Ken hadn't been aware of them before then. I'd be remiss if I didn't tell you about 'hitting the wall' as a part of the marathon experience, sort of.

On the way back to Germantown, we drank beer and ate the brownies. Brian was trying to sleep and I was loud and proud. At one point he said, "It looks like you got through that better than I did." That remained to be seen. By the time we arrived at Ken's house, I was well on my way to being in a state of alcohol and marijuana induced euphoria. That led to my joining Louisa in the shower, much to her surprise.

We all discussed dinner, and I voted to have pizza delivered. As 'under the influence' as I was, I was aware enough to know that I did not belong in public. I was out voted, with Brian, who almost never ate beef, saying he wanted a big steak. He was under the same influences as I. We went to a nice, family steak house. I had no business being there. I excused myself to go to the restroom and walked smack into a wall. So, there was much ado about my hitting the wall, as marathoners sometimes do...during the marathon. It's a different wall of course, and I'd have traded walls at that moment. I was helped to the car where I slept, while the others dined. We had a safe and uneventful trip back to Virginia the next day.

Shortly after the Philadelphia Independence Marathon, I began training for another one. The Shamrock Marathon which takes place in Virginia Beach on the Sunday preceding St. Patrick's Day.

CHAPTER 8
The balancing act of family ties

The holiday season was in full swing. One afternoon, while I was in my office, Louisa's son David called and asked whether I could pick him up at home, and take him to the mall to get his mother a Christmas present. I said that I could, and picked him up a while later. As we entered the mall, I asked how much he had to spend. He said, 'nothing.' So he asked me for the money. I went along with it, admiring his initiative and a desire to get his mother a gift.

I had been spending much of my time training for the marathon, and keeping up with the demands of being the marketing director for a mall, during the Christmas season. It meant less time with my three children. I spent more time with Louisa and it often involved her children too. Any parent who has ever been involved in that situation knows about the friction that can happen. One evening I thought that Judi and I had agreed that she would bring the kids to Louisa's house in Newport News, and I would take them back to her house in Hampton, later. A heated exchange followed when she didn't bring them, and I was accused of forgetting about my kids in favor of my 'new family.'

My first visit to Louisa's parents' house was a little scary for me. I had told Louisa that I had no interest in Amway, with her or her parents. I think she had let them know. They didn't mention their business to me. However, my first visit to their house, for dinner on Christmas Eve, was scary because I'd been drinking with the office staff. As best I recall, it worked out okay. They accepted me, and over the years we became very close. Carol and I had a special encounter in 1993 that I'll share in due course. Through the years her father, Paul, has become one of my most important friends. We kid each other quite a bit, enjoying the comfort of a strong friendship and love for one another. We have said, "I love you," to each other. Paul says that he still has a hard time saying that to another man.

After the Christmas season I went resumed my trips to the other malls in my region. In early February I drove to Greenville, North Carolina. I spent the day with the new marketing director. I stayed over night and headed back the next afternoon after lunch. A few of us often measured distances by how much beer it took to get there. Dwight Rice made the trip with me. For whatever reason, the miles were measured by bourbon, as well as beer. Drinking bourbon led to another turn on the path that Louisa and I were sharing.

When I arrived at Louisa's house she was ready to serve dinner. I had eaten a late lunch and wasn't hungry. She was upset because she knew that I had been drinking and driving. We got into a heated argument about it and I stormed out, somehow making it back to my beach cottage some 14 miles away.

The next morning after slowly coming around, I did manage to run. I was in training, so I ran the 10 miles required for that day. It wasn't pretty. With a clearer head, I called Louisa to apologize. She was not happy to hear from me and made it clear that she wouldn't put up with my verbal abuse. I recalled that I had been loud and vulgar with her when we had fought. I vowed to her that I would never drink hard liquor again.

Over the years we've looked back at that argument, in February 1982, and called it the last time I ever drank hard liquor. It really wasn't, as I continued to drink Bloody Mary's,

Screwdrivers, and on too many occasions, tequila. I believe that I never again drank anything with bourbon in it after the hot tub party argument, only a month later, and I had never had a taste for gin.

When The Shamrock Marathon drew near I told Louisa that I wanted to stay at Virginia Beach by myself the night before and then be ready for the run the next morning. I scheduled a post-marathon party at my beach house.

I awoke the morning of the marathon to the sounds of heavy winds and rain. Part of the course was through a nature preserve and the trails were very muddy, especially for those of us who were middle of the pack runners. As we came out of the park, volunteers hosed down our feet. I still loved it, even as the rain blew horizontally along the boardwalk.

My time in The Shamrock Marathon was the best I had run and I loved running in the rain…even the heavy rain. No lightning, thank you. Louisa and Kathy Wescott were waiting for me at the Finish Line with Bloody Marys that Kathy had concocted. I downed two and then went to pick up the refreshments provided by the race organizers, including a few beers.

We went to my hotel room, and then they left so that I could shower and take a nap before returning to my beach cottage, and the party I had planned for that evening. I had planned it, but Louisa had put it together with lots of seafood, including lobster. I slept a few hours and then headed back to the peninsula, with a stop at a convenience store to buy a couple of 12 packs. I drank about 4 or 5 beers while driving back to my cottage. I walked in to the smell of food cooking, and Louisa noticed that I'd been drinking already. She was not happy with me, and didn't get any happier when I passed out as my own party had barely gotten underway. That's when she took a serious look at our relationship, and how much I was drinking.

CHAPTER 9
Not a traditional proposal...

In 1982, a little more than a year after our first date, we were at the lowest point of our relationship. One of us said that we were finished. It was probably her. She took her sons and headed to Florida in her Capri, for a vacation, and I was miserable without her.

I called my friend Brian Cole, expecting to find a sympathetic ear, as I expressed my anger that she hadn't called me while she was on the trip. He said, 'why should she? She doesn't owe you anything. *You want her. You don't want her.* I don't blame her.' I really stewed over that, and the next day I went over to his house and told him to "stay the f—- out of my life." Some close friend, huh.

When she and the boys returned from Florida I couldn't wait to see her. The feeling wasn't mutual. I finally talked her into letting me come by to talk with her.

We didn't get off to a very good start and I started to leave. It was when she didn't try to stop me that I realized that I had to do something to get her back into my life. I got as far as starting my car. The radio came on, playing Chicago's "Hard To Say I'm Sorry". (7)

I went back into the house and said that I wanted to talk about *us*. She essentially said, 'what *us*?' To sum up how our differences showed up in our daily lives, exposed for the world to see, I've told people that we had *decided* to get married. That decision came at the resolution of an argument. It went something like…Louisa saying, "You once said that we are going to grow old together, but you've never asked me to marry you." I responded something like this…"You would never leave this house." She responded with "How would you know? You've never asked." That's a sketch of how we had sparred during our first year…and for many of our years together.

I don't recall after which volley we decided to get married. However we did, setting a date for one year later. The wedding would be on July 16, 1983. We reconsidered that, because my daughter's birthday is July 16th. A couple of days later, we moved the date to June 18, 1983.

In the midst of our euphoria I told Louisa that I didn't want to have any more kids. I love my kids, but enough is enough. She said, "I wouldn't mind having a little Perry." Pointing at myself, I replied, "You've got the only little Perry you're going to get."

After making the "decision" we joined an office party at a Bennigan's restaurant in Hampton. My office was hosting the staff from the Kings Dominion theme park. They were putting on a show that weekend at the mall where I worked. We were excited to share the news, and it was certainly well received there. However, Louisa's eyes showed the effects of her crying during the argument that preceded the "decision."

The next morning I was off to talk with my kids, and my former wife, about it. I was picking up the kids for a trip to King's Dominion. The kids were happy, and Judi said that she wasn't surprised, noting that I'd been with Louisa longer than anyone since she and I had split. She had another comment, asking, "Was I *really* that bad?" I answered, "It's not that you were that bad. It's that I wasn't *that good* with you."

Louisa and I were taking the kids to King's Dominion, north of Richmond for everything a theme park has to offer, and a concert featuring James Taylor and J.D. Souther.

The next day I went to see Brian again. He was on a lounge chair in his backyard...the beach. As I approached, he gave me a look of contempt, and asked, "What'd I do now?" I replied that he hadn't done anything and that I was there to ask him to be my best man. "Your what?" He exclaimed. The he smiled, jumped up and gave me a big hug, and said, "Hot damn! You know I will."

Then Louisa and I went to the mall, to use the WATS line to call David Morgan. David and I had been roommates, while he was the manager of Newmarket North Mall and I was the marketing director. When I first invited him to be my roommate, his reply was, "I don't know if we need to know that much about each other." We had also traveled together a good bit as Regional Manager and Regional Marketing Director. He had since moved to Dallas. I was calling him to ask him to be in the wedding.

All too aware of the roller coaster relationship that Louisa and I had experienced his reply to our marital plans...given over the office speaker phone with the entire staff listening, was..."You stupid son-of-a-bitch!" I know that while many of the people we knew might have agreed with David, no one else voiced it. At least they didn't in such direct terms.

It wasn't the first time that using the WATS line had an unpredicted result. Several months before that, on a Saturday, I stopped by Louisa's house. She was changing the brakes on her Capri, and asked me to help. I really didn't want to. She was struggling with bleeding the lines, and I suggested that she take a break and that we'd go to the mall and use the WATS line to call my old friend Ronnie Meyer, in Illinois, a professional mechanic who also knew Ford products from top to bottom. We did that. While Ronnie was agreeable to giving advice, he also said, "Why doesn't Perry do it? He knows how to do that as well as I do." My cover of ignorance was blown and Louisa was pretty angry with me.

Later that summer we took the kids to Kings Dominion again, catching a Chicago concert. Something I said there would come back to haunt me years later. Louisa and I danced to "Colour My World" and then the kids took their turn on the dance floor, to "25 or 6 to 4." I looked at David, and Chris Coons, and said, "Wonder how many times we'll have to bail those two out of jail." They were too far away to hear my comment...that time. However, Chris pointed out to me years later that he'd heard me repeat it many times, telling others. They were barely 7 years old at the time. *"Wasn't I the clever?"*

CHAPTER 10
Home is where…you create it?

Louisa and I made plans to attend The Shelter Institute at Bath, Maine, for our honeymoon. Ok, so we're different. We wanted to learn how to build a house that would use passive solar heat. We planned to buy property along Buckroe Beach in Hampton, and build our first home together. The office staff even gave me a framing hammer as a gag gift for the wedding. They were aware that *she* is the one with the handyman genes. Have you ever heard of relationships being challenged when a couple builds or remodels a home together? Well, it was probably a good thing that those honeymoon plans fell through.

My assistant, Kathy, had accepted a transfer to Clearwater Mall in 1982. She did so even though she had reconnected with Michael Lehmkuhler at a high school reunion just before making the move. As their relationship became stronger I could foresee another change of marketing directors for the mall.

It was during a trip to Clearwater Mall, in September 1982, that Gary Doyle, a company Sr. Vice President, told me that a change was being considered for the Regional Marketing Director program. He went on to say that I might be asked to move to Denver or Dallas. I told him that I couldn't hear Dallas, and that I had only seen his lips move. I would consider a move to Denver if asked, and only if Louisa and the children agreed.

He told me not to talk with anyone about it until when/if it became official. He promised to call me as soon as a decision was made. I agreed not to mention it to my family or to anyone at the mall until he called me about it. He also said that he thought I should do more to distance myself from the staffs at the malls and spend less time with them over dinner and drinks. We'd just had dinner and drinks with the staff, so I didn't get it.

About two weeks later I heard from one of Gary's assistants, Bob Welanetz. Bob said that he was calling to let me know that I would be transferred to Denver in January 1983. We discussed how that would be handled in terms of expenses, and working around my June wedding date. I told him that I would discuss it with my family, and pending their approval, I would make the move.

I left work to meet and talk with Louisa about it and with the kids and their mother later that afternoon. It met with the approval of all...including, to my surprise, my former wife. She said that she would be ok with a move of her own to end a relationship, and that it would keep the kids close to me. So, the beach house plans, and the honeymoon in Maine were discarded.

However, we didn't change the wedding date. I had been to Colorado in 1961, but my only visit to Denver was on a flight from Memphis to San Diego in 1981. I hadn't left the plane on that trip.

I knew that if I had not accepted the transfer that I would be back to being the marketing director for Newmarket North Mall, and any prospect of being promoted would be dimmed. I don't know how the company would have handled the salary issue. I was being paid a corporate level salary, paid in part out of the Merchants Association budget, and part by corporate.

"YOU USED TO LIVE IN MY HOUSE."

The Merchants Association would not have been able to carry the entire package. That's hindsight. I didn't take that into consideration at the time. I was open to the move.

I was training for the Marine Corps Marathon when the transfer, and replacing myself as mall marketing director, were my priorities at work. I was confident that my assistant, Debbie Moreau would be a good marketing director.

CHAPTER 11
Running on Empty

The events surrounding the Marine Corps Marathon were significantly different from my previous marathons. Louisa and I were engaged to be married. We traveled to Washington, DC the morning before the marathon, and would return home the following day. We wandered through Georgetown the night before the marathon, seeing that all of the Italian restaurants were packed, and opted to 'carbo-load' at an Indian restaurant. Then it was early to bed at a motel near the race start and Finish Lines.

The morning air was cool, which is a blessing for a marathon. However, it warmed up pretty quickly and I had worn a baseball jersey under my Tidewater Striders singlet. Overdressing has been more of an issue for me, than under dressing, in all of my years of running.

I 'hit the wall' for real this time. I had been on a pace that would put me at the Finish Line at about 3 hours and 30 minutes. I was standing on the 14th Street Bridge, admiring the boats when someone stopped to ask if I was okay. I wasn't aware of when I had stopped, or how long I had been standing there. Looking at my Tidewater Striders shirt, he patted me on the back, and said, "Come on Strider, let's finish." I did finish with a time of 4 hours and 5 minutes with the help of that person. To this day, I have no idea who he is.

As the thousands who've run it know, the Marine Corps Marathon has a special challenge at the end of the route. The last .2 miles is uphill to the very familiar statue of the raising of the American flag at Iwo Jima. Somehow, looking at that statue took my mind off of how badly I felt at the time. Louisa had seen me at the 10-mile maker and knew the pace I was running at that point. She had become concerned about me when it had become so much later than she expected for me to reach the Finish Line. She had climbed up onto the statue to look for me in the crowd.

I've always been surprised at how quickly I had recovered from running races. It's led me to believe that my reserve of energy is higher than the strength of my will to endure physical pain. Unlike the other post marathon experiences, I settled for one beer with an Italian dinner.

As planned, we returned to Virginia the next day. I took Louisa home and drove back to the beach house. I knew something was wrong as soon as I entered. My house had been burglarized. The refrigerator was empty, my stereo was gone, and along with it, my vast record collection. I called the police, then Louisa and then Brian.

I went to Louisa's house after filing the police report. We decided that I would move in with her and the boys until I left for Colorado in January. The Hampton Police called the next day. They had found everything but the food and beer, in a storage shed a few houses from mine. It turned out that my landlady's son had done it, primarily to embarrass his parents. He said that he'd been in my house, which he had lived in as a kid, and had been coming and going at will for some time.

Louisa's mother wasn't keen on our living together because we weren't married.

It was the first time, but not the last, that she would talk with Louisa about moving up our wedding date.

The next time came would occur in March. I had been notified that I had won a cruise for two while attending the ICSC Convention in September. They gave away two cruises in a drawing and the other winner was from Coliseum Mall, our competitor just 3 miles away.

As I've mentioned that the atmosphere around the mall stays in a state of organized frenzy during the Christmas season. I had run the Marine Corps Marathon before "Santa's arrival," unlike the timing of the Philadelphia marathon. None of us on the staff left the mall for very long periods of time just before or after "Santa's Arrival." We arrived early and left late, and more often left early...the next morning. We'd make a quick trip home for naps and showers and be back at the mall early again. There wasn't much time with the families for any of us. I saw Louisa when she came to the mall, sometimes bringing all of the kids for a brief visit or sharing of pizza.

We had an office tradition of taking each other out to lunch as a birthday treat, at the restaurant of the celebrant's choice. My birthday is November 20th and my birthday lunch was usually pizza or some kind of sandwich. In 1982, it included a belly dancer for entertainment. That was part of a set up, too.

The management secretary and the landscape supervisor were married to each other. So I bought into it when it was announced that we would have a staff meeting at their home in the late afternoon. We'd had pizza, although I thought it was a smaller amount than we usually ordered, and we'd been entertained by the belly dancer. I did think it was unusual that Dave Morgan would allow all of us to go that far from the mall, and yet I didn't debate it. It was still my birthday, and being off site for any reason was another treat. Dave asked me to check the Santa photo booth and a couple of other things before I left for the meeting. I would be the last to leave. I didn't think that was unusual because the marketing director is the person primarily responsible for everything that happens 'on the mall' during Christmas, or for any mall-wide promotion.

I was the good soldier and left about 30 minutes after everyone else. I arrived at the Starek home to find a surprise 40th birthday party in my honor. Louisa had even invited someone whom I had dated before meeting her.

I learned early on, that Louisa Taliaferro Hunter Harrison is not a predictable person, for which I am eternally grateful…if not always appreciative at a given moment. We had a Christmas dinner at her house that year, with all five of the children, and I (we) would leave for Colorado two weeks later.

CHAPTER 12
Westward Ho…

In January 1983, Louisa and I drove to Denver. Louisa had never driven across the country before and we were excited about taking the trip together.

The Hahn Company allowed a one-way rental car. We planned to sell our cars in Virginia because I would have a company car after moving to Denver. Given that we took the road trip in January, we were very fortunate with the weather. We drove in light snow in Ohio and Indiana and the rest of the trip was precipitation free. We stopped in my hometown, Alton, Illinois. It was Louisa's first visit with my mother. They liked each other immediately. However, after two days of showing her around Alton she commented, "I'm sure glad you don't want to move back home."

I love a lot of people in and around Alton, and that comment will not sit well with some of them. We know that we're not better than anyone else.

I'm glad I moved when I did, in 1967. So, I understood Louisa's comment. Given the circumstances, my childhood in Alton was a good one. The challenges that I faced there would have been much the same anywhere. However, Alton…like so many former 'factory towns'…isn't the same as it was when I was a kid. While I do look forward to going back for brief visits, I have an internal timer that goes off after 3 days, telling me that it's time to leave.

We drove to Lawrence, Kansas the next day and on to Denver the following day. I had told Louisa about my years at Ft. Riley, Kansas, and about the Kansas landscape. Imagine my surprise when she saw it and liked the rolling "hills" and even the flatter plains. She said that she could imagine cowboys riding across the rolling hills and into the sunset. Oh well. Have I mentioned that we see things differently?

We arrived on the eve of the world famous 'National Western Stock Show.' We had no idea what that meant, at least until we checked-in at the Stapleton Plaza Hotel. The reservations had been made for me. The company used it because it was across the street from the airport. While they were, like most hotels and motels, turning away people, they had held onto my reservation. I'm sure it cost them money because my corporate rate was $49 per night. It was the first, and certainly not the last time that the Stapleton Plaza Hotel…and its successive names…would play an important role in our lives.

After a week of driving around Denver and Boulder, and looking at the housing prices, (STICKER SHOCK!) Louisa flew back to Virginia and I flew to Albuquerque. It would be the first stop on my tour of the 10 malls, in 9 states, that had become a part of the new InterMountain Region. Only one of the malls, Pueblo Mall, was in Colorado.

Stan McWhorter and I caught up with each other in Albuquerque. We planned to fly through Denver to Seattle, where I would spend the weekend with him and Janey and visit Capital Mall in Olympia. Because of dense fog in Seattle, our flight from Denver was diverted to Portland. As we landed, the pilot said, "Well, so far so good. Now, if we can locate the terminal." There was a dense fog there, too. Stan rented a car and we drove from Portland, Oregon to Olympia, Washington in heavy fog. We went to Seattle the next day to pick up our bags. It was the first of many trips with Stan, each a new adventure.

I had known Stanley since 1975 when he was an assistant manager at Newmarket North Mall, and I managed a radio station satellite office there. I hadn't met Janey or their sons, before that foggy night. She was a gracious as she is beautiful. Stan knew what a lucky man he was.

Over the next five and a half months, I would visit each of the malls a number of times, and also travel to Virginia to visit my children and Louisa once a month. I often tell people that I pseudo-lived at the Stapleton Plaza Hotel the first six months of 1983. They were kind enough to store my belongings for me while I was away. The entire staff treated me very well.

While I was traveling, during that 6 month period, I was eating in restaurants and/or on airplanes...you may remember when they served food...virtually every day and night. There were occasions when I would eat a home cooked meal with Stanley and Janey McWhorter in Olympia, Washington, or Rick Garcia and Sylvia Tause, in Pueblo. Stanley would be joining me in Denver after their sons' school term ended in June, and Rick was the Manager of Pueblo Mall.

I wasn't all alone in this new landscape. My good friend and secretary, Susan Shelton, had moved to Colorado too. There were some who might have questioned her move, and her role. I believe that Louisa never doubted my relationship with Susan.

Susan had been married to my friend Brian Cole when I met them in 1975. When they parted ways, I maintained friendship with both, having established boundaries for conversations with and about them. Early in that period, Brian said that his daughters thought that Susan and I would end up together. Susan and I became close friends, and that's what we wanted our relationship to be. We had chosen that path, knowing that we were close and having discussed the possibilities. The choice was made easier because Susan had fallen in love with a man she later married.

Shortly after I moved to Denver, Susan did also. We did occasionally go to lunch together, even on the weekends, and to movies. The latter was something we had enjoyed together long before I met Louisa.

When I made the monthly trips to Virginia, I was really looking forward to a home cooked meal with Louisa, and of course being with her and the kids.

Louisa was eating home cooked meals every night, and was anxious to go out to eat when I arrived. Somehow we didn't revert to one of our arguments. It didn't threaten our engagement.

CHAPTER 13
Heading home

It was during that time and during one of my weeks at the Stapleton Plaza Hotel in February that I found the home we would purchase in Denver and still live in today. When I came in from running, someone at the front desk called out to me, asking if I had been running on Quebec Street. I said that I had, and she said that it was one of the busiest streets in Denver. She asked, "Do you have a rental car?" I told her that I did, and she got a map, highlighting the route to a park, called Washington Park. She said that it was a great place to run.

The next day, a Sunday, I drove to Washington Park and while running the 2+ miles of the interior road, I saw a real estate Open House sign with an arrow pointed to a house that I could see from the park. After I finished running, I grabbed a towel and a jacket, and went to the house. I looked through it, discovering that it had enough room for our soon-to-be family, with five bedrooms and two baths. There was a drawback…an in-ground swimming pool in the backyard. Five kids and a pool. I wasn't sold on that combination. However, I told the agent that I'd offer a contract contingent upon Louisa coming out from Virginia to see it, and approve of it.

Louisa flew out a couple of days later, battling a severe case of the flu that probably should have prevented her from flying. I wanted to soften the blow of the ugly box that the owners had built by raising the dormer to make a bedroom for their daughter. At that time, you could drive the interior road in Washington Park, and I did so to sell Louisa on the location. I stopped the car, pointing out the Recreation Center, and she looked the other way, saying "I hope it isn't the house with that ugly box on top of it."

Without saying anything else, I drove to it. We had already offered on a house in Park Hill during her January visit, and didn't get it. So she agreed to look at it. We toured the house with the agent and then she later signed the offer to purchase it. We were told that is was an older, established neighborhood, and knew little else about it. I recall that I was told that the house had been on the market for almost 18 months. We purchased it for about $4,000 less than they were asking, though I initially offered about $8,000 less. The price was set at about $80 per square foot…$128,000. That was a lot more than we had anticipated paying. Our combined payments, for our two places in Virginia, totaled about half of the first mortgage payment of $1200.00 in Denver. It meant that Louisa would be going to work after we were married and moved into the house. It was quite a stretch for us. Louisa signed the contract, 'ugly box on top' and all. I don't think she had been as concerned about the pool as I.

Of course the Denver market has changed since then, including Washington Park. What had been a big stretch for us in 1983 has become a great investment. Someday, hopefully in the very distant future, our children will enjoy the benefits of that investment.

As for me, I don't plan to move out of this house. As I told my friend Steve Little, "You'll know I've moved again when you come to the wake."

In March 1983 I scheduled a visit to Clearwater Mall, as a part of my transition. It happened to coincide with the

"YOU USED TO LIVE IN MY HOUSE."

cruise that Louisa and I were to take. The cruise departed from Tampa. The weather was rough the first night and Louisa was a little sick. She recovered the next day. Our first stop was at Playa del Carmen. As soon as we reached land, I was peeling off clothing to go running. Louisa stopped me, saying something about being in another country and they might not take to my disrobing. There was a soldier patrolling the beach, and the question of 'why?' didn't occur to me. He directed me to a public restroom where I could change clothes. I ran about three miles, dodging traffic. I hadn't been to Mexico before and I wasn't prepared for roads with no shoulders, or drivers who flew by me without giving any ground. I had to stop and step off the road several times.

About the third day we had one of our spats. She was curious about what the adjoining cabin looked like, compared with ours. Understand that Louisa has the perpetual curiosity of a three year old. She wanted to open the door between the cabins and I considered it an invasion of the tenants' privacy. She thinks that I don't have a curious bone in my body. Of course, I do. However, I'll admit that it runs along different paths than hers. We debated and fought about it. I stormed out, knowing that she would do what she wanted (anyway). I think she might have peeked in the other cabin. I didn't ask.

That storm passed quickly and we enjoyed everything about the cruise. We also hooked up with a couple from Chicago, Bruno and Gayle, and toured our next stop, Cozumel on motorbikes. We stopped at a beach bar on the other side of the island, where a monkey tried to steal Gayle's purse. Gayle won the tug of war. Some of the crewmembers put us on to a nightclub in town where the four of us partied late into the night, with some of the crew.

We made a brief stop in Key West, during a downpour, before returning to Tampa.

Sometime later I was told that Louisa's Mother had suggested to her that we have a private wedding ceremony before the cruise. Her reasoning was that Louisa and the boys could be added to my insurance sooner. We didn't do that and referred to the trip as our shakedown cruise.

After I returned to Denver from the cruise, I volunteered to work the Mile High Marathon. I was not in shape to run a marathon at altitude. It would be several years before I learned just how much that decision would mean to me, to my life. The informational meeting for volunteers was held at the Holiday Inn downtown. That's where I met Bill Michaels, the race director. My friendship with Bill was the first that I would develop in Denver, outside of my work environment.

Bill and I had very little in common in 1983, save our passion for running and baseball. Yet, that friendship has meant more to me than I could possibly have known at the time. He became my confidant, privy to much more information than he would ask for through the years, much of it you and others will see for the first time on these pages.

Bill is ten years and two days younger than me. For a long time we'd meet for drinks on the day between our birthdays, or as close to it as family and business obligations allowed. In recent years, the drinks haven't been alcohol, but rather coffee, around our birthdays. No doubt, our families are happier with that change.

CHAPTER 14
Crunch time

Louisa asked me to seek an annulment of my marriage to Judi. I gave it a considerable amount of thought, specifically because in my marriage to Judi I was given the gift of three children. I agreed to do it after the process was explained to me.

I found that writing about the relationship we'd had, and how we sabotaged any chance of a long-term marriage, was very cathartic. I really felt good about it. That is, until my daughter Kelly over heard me talking with someone of the phone about how my marriage to her mother 'never should have happened.' Kelly was crushed, as you and I would be in the same circumstance. While I knew that I meant that the marriage never really had a chance because all of the barriers we placed in the path of its success, it was a long time before I felt that Kelly understood or accepted my explanation.

The Catholic Church did not approve the annulment before our wedding. In addition, the Bishop did not approve of our plans to marry on a public beach, even though the pastor at Mt. Carmel, Louisa's church, wanted to perform the wedding ceremony there. They encouraged us to use a church and we were not willing to change our plans of a beach wedding. We wanted to have the wedding take place at Buckroe Beach, in Hampton, at the home of Brian Cole. I had lived four doors north of Brian and the area still has very sentimental meaning for us.

As I thought about who we could ask to perform the marriage ceremony, I recalled that I had, not long before that, run into a longtime friend, John Harwood...at Newmarket North Mall. John, a Methodist minister, was living in North Carolina. I'd known John since 1969. We'd lost touch a few years later. I don't believe it was any coincidence that John and I reconnected. *More synchronicity.* I called him and he invited us to visit with him in North Carolina to discuss it.

It was at about the same that I had to cancel some long-held plans with my kids. I had planned to take Kelly and Chris to New York City over Easter weekend. The city was buried by a huge blizzard. I contacted my friend Ken Kirby who urged me to cancel the trip, saying that if we could get into the city we wouldn't be able to go anywhere. Everything had been shut down. It wasn't easy to convince the kids that we had to cancel the trip. To them, it was just one more thing I wasn't there for.

Louisa and I made the trip to visit with John. After the introductions, and pleasantries, he asked me..."Why marriage? Why now? Why this person?"

Since I didn't know in advance, what particulars we'd be discussing, I had no opportunity to anticipate the question, or an answer. My answer came quickly, "because being with this person gives me the energy to do the work that I know marriage requires...because the love I feel isn't like any feeling I have ever felt before. I told her not long after we started dating, that we would grow old together." He smiled, saying...'that's good enough for me. Let's get to the details.' So we worked it out as to when he and his wife, Gail, would come to Hampton and who would be involved in the wedding." We still talk every once in a while, and Gail and I exchange email messages. John's input is from over her shoulder, so I'm told. He has retired from the ministry, to the extent that he is no longer pastor of a church.

However, he is teaching. I am hopeful that they will come to Denver in June 2008, to celebrate the 25th year of our marriage.

I was surprised when I learned that my youngest brother, Mike, planned to drive to Virginia for our wedding, along with his wife at the time, and my mother. Mike had lived with me for a while, when I lived in Williamsburg. However, my mother had not been to Virginia. I told Louisa that I wanted to have some ABT brownies for my mother to eat. I thought it would be cool to see her in that particular state of euphoria, and giggling. It didn't happen because they didn't make the trip. On the 25th anniversary of my father's fatal auto accident, Mike crashed his car into a telephone pole. He escaped without serious injury. However, my mother was understandably shaken up, and their trip was cancelled.

Have you ever heard this question? "What comes after the wedding?" I'll tell you, after I tell you about the wedding and the honeymoon.

Growing old together…**gets a temporary setback.** On the eve of the wedding, as is custom, we had a wedding rehearsal, and rehearsal dinner. The dinner took place at the home of Louisa's parents, Paul and Carol. The mood was light and lively with a huge dinner and drinks. John and Gail were there, along with the members of the wedding party, was an assortment of family members and friends, and their children. At some point, I looked at that scene and it suddenly hit me that *my* children were **not** there. I left the room for a while. I just felt empty. My children hadn't been invited, not by me, *or* by Louisa. I was stunned. I began to think about whether I could or should go through with the wedding. Was I so out of touch that I could ignore my own children? Evidently.

When we went home that night, I couldn't sleep and I knew why. I got up at midnight and went for a long run, to the Newport News shipyard and back. I was gone long enough to cause her to worry about me. I had runabout 13 miles in all. When I returned she asked whether everything was all right. I was not honest with her, as I said, "sure.' As far as she knew I was having 'cold feet.' She didn't know why. Unfairly, I buried it inside for years. I didn't say anything about it to Louisa until years later...during one of our arguments. Even after all those years, she's still the only one I've told about that incident and how badly I hurt at the time. I know that my own kids will know it for the first time when they read this story.

I made the right choice...to go through with the wedding. However, I now know that Louisa would have been as upset as I was that my children hadn't been included. It's one of those things that can happen if you get caught up in the moment and aren't focused on *all* of the people you love. When we did discuss it years later, she was very hurt, that I hadn't mentioned it, yes...but also that she hadn't seen it at the time. I still have trouble looking at the pictures of the wedding rehearsal dinner.

The morning of the wedding the weather was questionable. If I were a betting man, I would have bet on rain. Before noon the skies cleared and we were to enjoy a beautiful day at the beach.

The Reverend Mr. Harwood orchestrated the ceremony beautifully. Our families and friends gathered near the beach that was Brian's backyard. The reception took the form of a covered dish lunch and keg party.

I think the party was going strong when Louisa and I left for Norfolk to fly to New Jersey, for a weekend honeymoon in Manhattan. Our friends, Michael and Kathy Lehmkuhler, were from York County and had come from their home on Staten Island, to attend our wedding. They stayed with family in York County while we used their home in New York for our honeymoon. Michael had gone out of his way to make sure our brief stay would begin on a high note. We relaxed and made ourselves at home in their home. We had a terrific, if whirlwind, tour of Manhattan and on Monday morning, Michael arrived to take us to the airport before he went to work on Wall Street.

Recently, I was looking at our wedding album with our grandsons, Brendan and Riley, my daughter Kelly and our son-in-law Pete. Kelly looked at the photo of Louisa and me, and the five children. She asked, "What *were* you thinking?" We did start with a full plate. The kids were ages 8, 9, 10, 11 and 12 on our wedding day. And of course, Kevin then 12 was in his wheel chair. He would be the least of our challenges with the kids. The photo did beckon her question. It made me think of something a flight attendant said on our way to Denver a few days later.

So, what comes after the wedding? The marriage.

BOOK TWO

CHAPTER 1
This Ain't the Brady Bunch

When Louisa and I returned from our honeymoon to Newport News her mother, Carol, was supervising the loading of the moving van. The next day, June 21st, we boarded a United Airlines flight to Denver. The 'we' included 5 children, ages *8, 9, 10, 11 and 12*...a beagle mutt and a black cat. The latter two were confined to kennels in the area where animals are carried during the flight. We had a layover in Chicago to change planes. Our cruise ship friends, Bruno and Gayle, came out to O'Hare Airport to say hello and meet the family.

We all wore our wedding clothes, so we definitely stood out as a unit. One of the flight attendants asked us about our group and we explained about the wedding and the move to Denver. Later she brought us a bottle of champagne, saying, "you'll need it."

We had been under contract to purchase our home since February. We got a VA loan, at 12.75% and were happy to get it. If you weren't around, or aware, 1983 was not a time of fiscal prosperity and many home loans were at 16% and higher.

The loan approval had taken longer, even for a VA loan. It took longer than we see today. There was no Internet, or email at the time. Even the fax was in its neophyte stage. As the loan dragged out, the sellers' agent had been telling them that they should cancel the contract. That resulted in our staying at the

Stapleton Plaza Hotel, with the aforementioned 5 kids and 2 animals, from June 21st, through June 30th. They animals stayed in the kids' room, with a litter box in the bathtub for Gato. We were asked to sneak Spice, the beagle, down the stairs to do her duty. They, very graciously, turned a blind eye, and/or took pity on us. The other result was that our belongings arrived before the sellers' moving van arrived. So we moved all of our stuff into the basement before we closed on the house. We moved in on July 1, 1983. I'm convinced that there are things in the garage that are exactly where we put them in July 1983.

July 2nd being Chris Coons' birthday, we kept a (then new) tradition of taking the birthday person out to eat wherever he/she might want to go. Chris made it easy for us. He just wanted to have pizza, anywhere but in the house. So we went to get our pizzas at the Saucy Noodle, at Bonnie Brae. You may have seen the sign that's still there after all these years..."If you don't like garlic, go home." When I picked up the pizza, the late owner, Mr. Badis, looked at my out-of-state check, smiled and said, "This won't bounce on me will it?" I held up the pizza and said, "This won't make me sick will it?" He laughed and said I was welcome to come back anytime. A few years later Chris Harrison was a pizza cook there while he was in high school.

I had heard about Red Rocks Park and wanted to have Chris' pizza/birthday party there. We didn't know much more about it, than the location. There was a concert going on, and a lot of traffic. We found a place in the southern part of the park, outside the concert venue of course. We could hear the music clearly. So Chris got a picnic *and* concert for his 9th birthday.

A couple of weeks after we moved in I had an accident that haunts me to this day, and then some. I was mowing the front yard with the power mower we'd brought from Virginia.

It hadn't been tuned for altitude and wasn't running good. The front yard is above street level, and as I came up from the sidewalk the mower stalled and all of my weight went up under the handle and I felt everything in my right shoulder ripping apart. I was crazy with pain and had a fast swelling shoulder. I had been hurrying so that we could get on the road to a party in Beulah, outside of Pueblo. I really didn't know how badly I had hurt myself until much later. Yet, on to the party we went. Louisa drove and I rode with an ice pack on my shoulder.

It wasn't until my shoulder began to separate with very little movement that I learned that I'd torn up the rotator cuff. I don't know how many trips we made to Porter Hospital to have the shoulder put back into place. It came out easily and often, and painfully. A trip to the hospital meant that I would be given drugs that would induce the strange sense of not knowing where I was, or why, or that I didn't care.

I had called a moratorium on my business travels for June and July. In between unpacking and sorting through everything, we did take time out to play tourists. I'd taken maps of the Denver area to Louisa on my trips back to Virginia, and she'd learned the area better than I had after being here for 6 months. We saw the Garden of the Gods, in Colorado Springs, the Air Force Academy and a Denver landmark…Casa Bonita. The kids enjoyed the swimming pool from the first day. All in all, it looked like everybody was excited about the move and our new home.

We signed a contract for a food delivery service that included a big upright freezer. That allowed us to buy a lot of food and have it on hand for our new, larger family.

CHAPTER 2
We are family….nuclear that is….

The bottom fell out of the euphoria in early July. We had expected that Judi, the mother of my three children would be moving to Colorado. There was a WATS line at my office, so the kids were able to call her several times a week. They were really enjoying living in Denver, and had fallen in love with Colorado very quickly. It was during one of those calls that she told them she had no intention of moving from Virginia to Colorado. The kids even pleaded with her to do it, to no avail. She'll deny to this day that she ever said that she would do so. So, on July 26, 1983, I faced the toughest moment of my life…to that point.

I was scheduled to go to a 'shopping center school,' at East Lansing, Michigan. The International Council of Shopping Centers (ICSC) sponsored the conference at the Kellogg Center, at Michigan State University. On July 26th I boarded another United Airlines flight…with Kevin, Kelly and Chris Coons. I flew with them to Chicago, where I would change planes and go on to East Lansing, Michigan. The kids would fly on to Virginia. I left a part of my heart in that plane as I left them. We were all crying. We didn't know when we would be together again.

The mental picture of looking back at them as I walked up the aisle of that plane is one that is as clear today as it was on that day in 1983.

Taking that hurt and anger with me to the conference could have led me back to old habits. Many of us would walk from the motel to the classrooms together each day. I knew some of the participants and met others from malls throughout the US and Canada.

There was a toga party announced for the last night of the school and a woman asked me to be her date. We were both married. I told her that a group of us would be going together, and that she'd be welcome to join us. I was actually taken by surprise by the invitation. One of the women I knew said that I'd missed several signals that she saw the woman give me throughout the week. I was still so focused on Louisa, and separation from my kids, that I didn't see or hear anything of a personal nature. Not too long before that, I would have. I liked the new feeling. Actually she and I were the last to leave the campus the next day. We had brunch together and talked about our marriages. We were both happy that we were there as friends and hadn't made a fateful mistake.

I wouldn't know the impact that separation from my kids would have on my life, for several years. I carried a lot of guilt over moving away from my children. I blamed their mother for a long time. I believed she had committed to move when we did. Nonetheless, it was my choice to move to Colorado. I don't regret it today. However, I did second-guess myself about it for a long time. I can see that I really didn't give Chris and David my all during the early years, while I lived apart from Kevin, Kelly and Chris. When I was with them, in their activities or family outings, a part of me was missing. It was still with the other three children in Virginia.

I made trips back to Virginia, to see them in October and December, and in April 1984. Even on those trips I saddled myself with guilt. I would arrive and stop somewhere to eat

"YOU USED TO LIVE IN MY HOUSE."

dinner and have a couple of drinks before going to see them. I didn't rush to them. I wasn't comfortable being at their mother's house. I would sometimes drop off my bags at my friend Brian's house, or at my in-law's. I would typically stay with one or the other. So, I would visit my kids for a few hours before they went to bed and then see them again the next day after school. When I left Kelly and Chris would run beside my car to the end of the block. I could have done more with and for them during those trips. I recall dropping Chris off at baseball practice during one visit. Yes, I said 'dropping him off.' I didn't stay to watch him.

CHAPTER 3
Returning to pre-marital form?

During that time I often lost myself in my long distance running, and in my drinking. That might seem a strange combination to you, but I had done both for several years.

For the most part, Louisa was patient with my volatile mood swings. I could enjoy being with her, and the boys, and yet I would blow up at them, venting my hurt, my guilt and my anger. She could get as angry as I. To her, I was a part-time husband and father. I hadn't opened up fully. No doubt that our neighbors witnessed the loud arguments. We not only yelled, we threw things. I recall turning over a table in the kitchen in the middle of a heated argument, and a time when Louisa threw a screwdriver toward me, breaking a window. She said that if she had really wanted to hit me with it, she could have. I know of only one occasion when the fighting became physical. I was watching TV and she stood in front of it, demanding to be heard. I pushed her down and yelled at her. Then Chris jumped in to defend his Mom. He and I wrestled and threw punches at each other. She separated us and I think he and I both felt embarrassed about it. I was working a lot of hours and when I wanted to kick back to escape it, I didn't want anything to disrupt what *I* chose to do. I did not consider what the family might want or need.

Once, as I was about to storm out, Louisa jumped on my back. I carried her to the street before I relented and went back into the house with her. Like most arguments, ours were rarely about the topic at hand. It was the underlying anger and hurt, and no doubt, my reluctance to accept where I was with my life. Most of the original neighbors are still around, and they must be amazed that we survived that period in our marriage.

Some, but not all of the people we worked with, knew how much at odds we were most of the time. Most of them chalked it up to the step-parenting issues, and others saw just how different, from each other, we were.

It wasn't as though we fought constantly. We weren't without love or passion for each other. Our emotional highs were as passionate as the loud arguments. Recently, when Louisa and I were talking about my writing this story, she asked whether I would tell one story, or another that revealed something about us that no one else knew. I said, as long as I believe it to be relevant to my purpose in writing the story, I'll include anything. Then she brought up the next story. She's immodest and in those days she was more of a risk taker.

She asked specifically about a trip back from Pueblo when she wanted to take a detour into the hills at the foot of the mountains. We had taken Stan's company car, a big Chrysler that he'd brought back from the mall in Montana. Louisa is passionate about life, and that includes being daring beyond peeking into a neighbor's cabin on a cruise ship. We drove into the hills and well into the forest. She said that she wanted to enjoy nature by taking off her top. She did and we ended up making love in the car, parked on a dirt road that had no signs of recent use. An approaching car interrupted us. When we rose up from the back seat they backed down the trail. I could see them laughing. I was immediately going into 'I told you so' mode. I'm much more the private person, and in those days, extremely so. I had been a reluctant participant *initially*. In the end we laughed about it and drove home.

We hosted what seems like a lot of pool parties, always encouraging guests to stay over. I woke up one morning, after one of those parties, to find an empty keg floating in the pool. I had passed out long before two of our friends throwing it in, to see whether it was empty. Leaving my own parties early wasn't new to me.

Stan McWhorter and I hosted a meeting for the managers and marketing directors from our region, at my former psuedo-home, The Stapleton Plaza Hotel.. We were all having cocktails before dinner when Louisa saw me throw a kiss to someone across the room. She asked who she was and I said, "She's Pat, the marketing director at the mall in Billings." I probably had a crush on Pat, but I'd never shown it before that impulsive move. Louisa asked who the guy was sitting with Pat. I said, "That's Ed. He's the mall manager there." She promptly got out of her seat and went over to Ed...planting a big kiss on him. He was shocked and when she walked back to our table, he called out, "WAIT! Don't leave. I love you!"

Louisa stayed for the opening dinner, and then got a ride home with Stan's wife, Janey. I told her that I would have Stan drop me off at home later. We all went from the meeting to the lounge, which is what we did at most company-sponsored meetings I ever attended. After an hour, Stan was ready to leave and I said I'd find a ride home. What I did was stay longer and drink a lot more, and I took a cab home. Louisa was sitting on the front steps when I arrived. She was crying, saying that she had called and woke up Stan, who said he'd left about thirty minutes after she and Janey had, and I had stayed there.

In October while I was unloading a verbal attack on Chris Harrison, I heard our front door open. Then I saw a travel bag being thrown into the living room, and heard someone say, "Stop yelling at that kid!" I looked again and saw my old friend

Brian Cole, from Virginia, standing in the doorway, grinning. I told Chris to get back to what he had been doing. Brian said something like, ' I see that things aren't going so great.'

I was really happy to see a friendly face, even though he was chastising me for yelling at Chris. We hadn't known he was coming, of course. Still, it was great to see him. Louisa wasn't home when he arrived, and she was as excited as I when she came home and saw him there.

We made plans to go out to dinner and Brian suggested that we invite Susan to join us. A phone call later we were making reservations at Mataam Fez, a Moroccan food restaurant we had discovered with Stan and Janey McWhorther. We had some weed, and we took time to ride through the park and indulged before picking up Susan.

I wonder how we ever got away with carrying that stuff, (weed), on planes. I recall leaving San Diego after corporate meetings on one particular trip and sharing a rental car with a manager, whom we'll call Ed. Just as we were parting ways, headed to different concourses, and as I was about to enter the Security check area, he said…"Oh by the way, happy birthday." I started to thank him when he put an envelope in my suit coat pocket and quickly headed off in the opposite direction. We didn't have to empty our pockets of non-metallic items back then. After I'd gone through Security, I went to the Men's Room and checked the envelope. It contained two joints. I stood there in disbelief that I had actually just gone through Security with that stuff in my pockets…regardless of how it got there. It's true that weed can cause paranoia…even before you smoke it.

Oh yeah…Mataam Fez…as always provided a fun atmosphere where you sit on the floor, on big pillows as you eat. The weed and a couple of bottles of wine enhanced dinner.

One of my favorite pictures of Louisa was taken there, with her napping on the pillows after dinner. Somewhere, along the way, that photo disappeared.

We saw our first big snow that year. Stanley, Janey and their son Brandon joined us for Thanksgiving dinner. The temperature was close to 70 degrees, and then the storm rolled in the late afternoon. The McWhorters headed home just before it started snowing. The snowfall totaled 20" from that storm. Then the temperatures dropped dramatically and it stayed very cold for several weeks.

CHAPTER 4
Being away, even at home

When I traveled to the other malls, or to corporate meetings, with few exceptions it involved a lot of drinking. I never left home horny. Stanley laughed when I told him about my send offs. He said, make sure you *come home* horny. We were flying from, and back to, Stapleton Airport during those times. Stanley and I typically carried our bags on board...it was easier to do back then. Walking back into the terminal, he'd ask if Louisa was coming to pick me up, knowing that she'd be mad about the drinking. He'd say 'see ya,' and head off in the other direction, laughing.

Stan and I liked to have a good time. On one road trip I asked Bob Sorensen how often he regretted putting Stan and I in the same office. He said, without blinking, "Everyday."

Did I suddenly morph into the model husband? Not. I didn't begin to re-invent myself until the last part of 1991. The shopping center business is loaded with attractive women. I was traveling a lot. I was feeling guilty about being separated from my kids. I made a terrific victim. I was at my worst when I was drinking, which was often. What I didn't recognize then, and have learned through the years is that I want what we have and can have, in our relationship. I was running on high-octane anger. Even then I knew that I couldn't stand to hurt Louisa or chance losing the most passionate relationship I'd ever had. There were so many times that I could have caused her to leave.

There were times when friends like David Morgan and Stanley McWhorther saved me from blowing it all. I was no less the flirt and no less attracted to other women. The difference was that I was beginning to corral my ego and not pursue the opportunities to be with them. I still had, and have, a lot of growing to do.

Along the way I developed a habit that helped. It was almost ten years ago that I realized what I was doing, I'll share it with you before we part ways.

When I was traveling, I would typically call my kids in Virginia early, given the time differences. I rarely called Louisa until the next morning. No doubt she knew that I was out drinking in the evening. There were times that she called me, and she always asked if I'd been drinking. Even when I lied about it, she knew better. I have what we call the Coons-tongue, because my brothers have it, too.. The tongue seems to swell and impede speaking. There's no hiding it.

Louisa and I were meeting a lot of people around Denver in 1984, and while it didn't take long for it to feel like home, we were still not 'at home' with each other.

We went to counseling, for ourselves, each other, and also for Chris and David. Chris was primarily involved in the counseling for the family transition, with each other and the move from Virginia to Colorado. It was apparent early on that David was having more difficulty with both, than Chris was. David had a lot of individual counseling as well. We were having difficulty with each other as I assumed my parental role and would then leave for another business trip.

We had a couple of specific issues with David's behavior. Spoons kept disappearing. We learned that he'd eat something on the way to school and through away the spoons from Louisa's Revere Ware. The other stemmed from his craving of chocolate.

At one point we decided to lock ice cream, and anything with chocolate, in the basement freezer.

We've since discussed the times when I would be riding the bus home, not really wanting to go there. She wasn't any more excited about my coming home, than I was. What would be the next thing to set off a fight? They were often too loud to simply call arguments

It was on those bus rides that I first began to write. I wrote a short story, a piece of fiction that Louisa would later come across and ask about. It centered on a businessman who, on a bus, struck up a conversation and then a relationship with a woman on the bus. He didn't go home that night. Certainly there were attractive women riding the buses I rode. I didn't go anywhere with any of them. I actually met very few. It was a work a fiction, and as likely a fantasy.

Regardless of what had happened in my workday, I didn't want to share it at home. I carried a briefcase each way and rarely opened it at home. I opened beer more often than the briefcase or only surface conversations.

My moods were so mercurial that no one knew what to expect, including me. There were times when Louisa and I really enjoyed being with each other, and times when we didn't want to be together. She pointed out that we often fought after making love. That got my attention. I wondered if I was becoming sexually dyslexic. We had always enjoyed our intimacy. I recalled having heard that a marriage won't succeed if it's based on sex. It also won't succeed without it. In many ways we'd stack the cards against a successful married and I didn't like the idea of *that* card being added to that stack.

We'd gone to one of the early pre-opening Tivoli parties with Stan and Janey McWhorter, and we'd all had a great time. Louisa and I have always enjoyed dancing with each other. As we were leaving Stan said that we should all go into business together. I laughed and replied that I would *never* want to go into business with my wife. It wasn't just the timing of my remark that was bad, let's say foolish, it was the message that I was sending to Louisa, and to Stan and Janey. Louisa has had occasion(s) to remind me of it. *I* understood what I meant. I wasn't happy in our personal relationship and I didn't want to extend that to a business relationship. I was confused. Deep inside I knew that I loved Louisa. I also knew that I wasn't happy with her. I hadn't forgotten that before we were married, I had told her, and myself that if I couldn't be happy with her I couldn't be happy with anyone.

I don't know what Janey McWhorter thought when she heard me say that. Stan just shrugged, saying, "Well, okay…just a thought." Looking at how our relationship has changed, it would be a very good thing today. I threw away an opportunity to work with Louisa, and with Stan and Janey. That opportunity hasn't been available since 1991.

Louisa had often said to me, in the heat of arguments and during discussions, that she didn't believe I wanted to be happy or that I could ever be happy…period. But there was more to it that I didn't recognize at the time. I didn't see it, or recognize it, or **get it** until May 2003 when the light bulb not only went *on*, it ***flashed like a strobe light***, awakening me to my lack of trust and honesty, with myself.

CHAPTER 5
A bold move

I grew weary of the travel. I could be gone as much as two weeks each month, with two or three days here and another two or three there. When I returned home it was as though I had to reintroduce myself to Louisa, Chris and David. Chris had not been eager to give up his role of man of the house, which his departing father had assigned to him when he was 5 and a half. I'd heard stories of how Chris had walked David to and from school, protective arm around his little brother. I hadn't seen that, but I had seen him being protective of David in other ways. I could relate to that. I had vivid images of being told that I was the man of the house, after my dad died, and that I had to be there for my brothers. They said that it was what my dad would have wanted.

While the circumstances for Chris and David were different from mine, I know they play out daily in thousands of families. Even my own grandsons face it today. Like Chris and David they have a step dad who cares and is more of a father to them, than their biological father has ever been. Unlike Chris and David, their biological father pops in and out of their lives, adding to their confusion about him.

Chris and I weren't at odds. It just took a while for him to accept my role. David and I were at odds. I wouldn't know until later, that he hadn't given up on Claude, his biological father at that point, and that he hadn't wanted to move to Colorado.

There were also constant bouts with the corporate accountants, over expense reports and reimbursements. I still believe they cheated me out of a lot of money that I was due from my travel expenses. Not surprisingly, Louisa became very angry over all of that too. When we married we hadn't planned on her going to work. With a house payment of about $1200 per month, we couldn't afford to have her stay at home. Many of our fights were about money. The money spent on business travel that wasn't completely reimbursed, the high mortgage payments, the lack of a car (more on that in a moment), and my stress with missing my children, and of course, the drinking, all contributed to the struggles of our first year of marriage.

We had each sold our cars before leaving Virginia, because I had been told that I would have a company car in Colorado. I **wasn't** assigned a company car. The explanation was that the VP, who'd promised it, didn't have the authority to do so. At the time, the company had employed me for a little more than four years. Up until that time, I had felt that they had never lied to me.

The battles with accounting, over my expense reports and reimbursements came to a head in April 1984, and helped me make a decision about a career change. As I've told you, I had grown weary of the travel. During my first year in Denver, I had traveled from Boston to Seattle, interviewing people for the position of marketing director at the Tivoli Denver, a 'specialty center,' that was scheduled to open in that fall. I found that marketing director, in April 1984, while visiting Capital Mall in Olympia, Washington.

Bob Sorensen, then a VP with the Hahn Company, was also visiting Capital Mall at the time. He and I were interviewing people there because we had terminated the employment of the market director. I received a call from accounting in San

Diego. I was told that I would not be reimbursed for a rental car that I'd used during my most recent visit to the corporate offices, because I hadn't put enough miles on it.

When I hung up the phone, I turned to Bob and said, "I've found our marketing director for the Tivoli Denver." He asked, "Really? Which one?" I answered, "Me." There was a look of shock on his face. He asked, "Why would you want to do that? Even John doesn't want that project in our portfolio." He was referring to the president of The Hahn Company.

I told Bob what I'd just been told by the accountant on that phone call. He shook his head, saying, "I wish they'd leave you guys alone. I had hoped to have you together for another year." They were riding each of the regional marketing directors in the same way they'd been riding me.

That's when I told Bob that I wouldn't put up with it anymore, that I wanted to resign from the position of regional marketing director to become the marketing director for the Tivoli Denver. I told him, that I wanted a letter from Gary Doyle, the Sr. VP, authorizing my transfer and that I would not accept any pay reduction. I asked that they guarantee my pay for at least the following year. Bob asked me to think it over on the flight home and then contact him about my decision.

On the flight home I drafted my letter to Gary Doyle. I shared it with Louisa when I got home. She was happy with it, but wondered aloud whether I could trust them to live up to any agreement, given the lie about the company car.

Her mention of the company car hit a nerve. There's a story about a company car that is worth digressing back to November 1983.

In the fall of 1983 Stan McWhorter came to me about picking up a company car at Grand Island, Nebraska. The Hahn Company was dropping its contract to manage Conestoga

Mall, and they had a company car there for the manager who was being transferred. I agreed to fly to Grand Island to pick up the car. He said, "Drive it back and hang on to it. Don't mention it to anyone. They don't know what they're going to do with it. We'll deal with it later."

I made the trip and we then were surreptitiously awarded a company car after all. It was a Ford Granada...not the best model Ford ever produced. I had been to Grand Island twice, by air. During one of those trips, I left during a snowstorm. So, I hadn't *seen* Nebraska. The drive home seemed to last an eternity.

In October someone in accounting discovered that I had the car. I wasn't charging taxi fare to the airport any longer and they uncovered the reason. We were told to solicit bids from local dealers. The car really wasn't worth driving back to the company headquarters in California. Louisa offered to visit the car lots, where she was told 'no thanks,' or was given very low offers at every dealership she visited.

On November 19, 1983, I was across the street at the church's gymnasium selling Christmas decorations for David's Cub Scout Troop, while Louisa took him to the dentist. At one point, I looked up to see her and David standing in front of me. They really looked frightened...really shook up.

Before I could say anything, she said, "The good news is we're alright." I asked what the bad news was. She said, "Come with us, it's sitting outside." I got someone to cover for me and went outside with her and David. She pointed to toward our house, and I saw the remains of the gray Granada on a flatbed tow truck.

Louisa had hit a patch of ice on a bridge, coming from the appointment, and the right rear of the car hit the guardrail. The car turned 180 degrees and then the front of the driver's side hit the same guardrail. The Colorado State Trooper and the tow truck driver were amazed that they had lived through it. David didn't like to wear his seatbelt. After leaving the dentist's office David put it on, at his own suggestion. Thankfully he did. I was in shock. I went into the house and called Stan McWhorter. He listened to me and said, "Happy birthday." It was the day before my 41st birthday.

The irony of it was that the company powers that be, gave us a lot of grief about Louisa driving…and wrecking… the company car that I wasn't authorized to have. They hadn't mentioned it when she had been looking for a buyer for it. The company collected more from the insurance company than any dealer had offered for that car. For a brief period we were back to no company car, no car at all.

The next month, we ended up with a company car from Cedar Rapids, Iowa. A manager who was being transferred had dropped it off in Denver. I don't recall the exact circumstances, as to the rationale for that decision. However, someone later drove it to California at the end of January.

After that we learned to live without a car and didn't buy one until 1985. It was an inconvenience that wasn't the biggest issue that we had to deal with. We hauled everything from a ceiling fan to fencing replacement slats, and of course, groceries, on the local transit, RTD.

Back to where I was when I was so rudely interrupted by myself….1984.

As promised, I called Bob Sorensen and told him that I was firm on my decision to ask for the transfer to the Tivoli, pending a commitment from Gary Doyle to honor my requests as I had outlined them. He talked with Gary, who in turn called me. He almost seemed eager to take me up on my offer, asking me to send the letter. I did so, and he subsequently signed off on it.

Then we set about to find my replacement. I liked their choice. Carol Woelber would replace me. I considered Carol a friend, and knew that she was a Denver native. She had been working in the San Diego offices, managing the graphics department. On June 14th I was introduced as the marketing director for the Tivoli at a benefit for the Denver International Film Society. The new multi-screen cinemas at the Tivoli would become the home of their annual film festival.

After reaching agreement with Gary Doyle to leave my position as Regional Marketing Director, I learned that not everyone approved of the change. There was concern that those in the field would see that position in a lesser light since I had initiated the action.

If they had pulled the plug, rather than I, it would have looked better for them That I chose to leave, it was presumed, would make the position less attractive. How about that for pretzel logic? I was asked to visit each of the malls before the end of July, which I did. I was promoting the position I had left, and Carol Woelber. I said only that I wanted to be in Denver with my family rather than travel. I was okay with that. I didn't need to offer anything about the challenges of the position.

That should make things go better at home, right?

CHAPTER 6
No walk in the park…

The pressure played out in a number of ways. On our first anniversary we walked around the block across the street, which houses St. John's Lutheran Church & School. We literally, said to each other…**'if this is how our marriage is going to be, let's stop here and not do this anymore.'**

The arguments weren't always about the step-parenting challenges. We didn't argue over leaving the toothpaste out. However, I was told how much of it to use. I think my hot button was, and to a lesser degree today still is, punctuality. In some fashion we resolved that it didn't have to be as difficult as it had been. We were always really good at making up after an argument.

I believe that neither of us doubted our love for each other. However, I *do* recall wondering whether love was enough reason to keep going. The challenges certainly didn't end there. We still didn't have a car. Louisa had worked for a drafting firm before moving on to Amoco Production, as a temporary employee. My kids were there for the summer.

My brother Bob and niece Shelli paid a surprise visit. Louisa was excited about the opportunity to meet more of my family. During their stay, Bob decided that he and Shelli would move to Denver. That was his decision. Bob had been raising Shelli alone since her Mother left them 8 or 9 years earlier. On the surface, Bob and Louisa had a lot in common. She has 'the handyman genes' and Bob had been working in remodeling, and small job construction such as building kitchen counters for several years. He wanted to move to Denver to start his own business. The Houston economy was in a recession at the time.

Bob and Shelli stayed for about 2 weeks and returned to Houston, planning to move to Denver before the start of the school year. We offered to let them live with us until they found a place to live.

After a rocky first year of marriage, with five, then two, then five kids in the house for the summer, along with a cat and dog, we would add my brother and niece to the mix.

Bob and I hadn't been close as kids. First, he spoiled my party. I was almost 5 years old when Bob came along. The age difference, particularly in adolescence and the teen years, meant that I always thought that he was too young to go with my friends and me, regardless of where we were going. It wasn't until Bob was married, and having his own marital problems in the early 70's, that we connected. He had begun to call and ask for advice. My credentials for giving it must have been based on the fact that Judi and I had reunited and had started a family of our children plus foster children at the time. Bob and I would really get to know each other, and become very close friends, after his move to Denver in 1984.

The kids arrived from Virginia just before Chris Coons' birthday in July. It was an important visit for many reasons. Of course, because we had missed being with each other, and too, it was because they had really enjoyed Denver while they were with us in 1983 when we had time to act as tourists. When they arrived in 1984, I had started working at the Tivoli development, and was making the 'farewell tour.' Louisa was working full time at Amoco. They had a lot of time with each other, and responsibilities for Kevin too. It was no walk in the park for them to be sure. On the up side, they did get to spend some time with Shelli.

She and Bob returned before the kids went back to Virginia. Let's see…that's new jobs for Louisa and me, five kids, add my brother and his daughter, and of course the dog and cat in the house, one rocky year into the marriage.

In 1984 we contracted to have solar heat added to our house, just before the cowboy president killed off the tax credits for it. It was also an event that set the stage for some ill will, some dramatic arguments in the days and years to come. It was Louisa's project, in part because I was gone so often, but moreover because I did not want to work with her. Has anyone ever taken a tool out of your hand while you were using it, because he or she wanted to do it the right way or correct what you were doing? Louisa had been a tomboy and Paul had often called her *his son Louie*. He didn't do me any favors with that. I have always respected her skills and drive, but she can be too damn bossy on projects. I've managed to steer clear of most of them over the years, or leave them when we would argue about how I was doing something.

CHAPTER 7
This is your life, get used to it

One of the Amoco Project Geo-physicists Bill Weber, and his wife Patty, hosted an annual trail run near Boulder, followed by a potluck and keg party. The trail run, along the Mesa Trail was a pretty challenging route, even for the condition that I was in at the time. I reverted back to my old ways of hitting the beer pretty hard and fast following the run. After an hour or more of eating and drinking…and not necessarily in that order…we left to go home. Louisa wanted to stop at a warehouse store, could have been a PACE Membership Warehouse or something like it. I don't recall. I was thinking, 'this is what my life has come to, walking through a warehouse store on a Saturday night.' I pouted and dragged my feet, anger building inside. It was a part of the battle with accepting my new life.

Our second anniversary was different from our first. We were celebrating my decision to live and work in Denver. We had gone to Mexico and had taken Chris and David with us. I even carried some guilt about that…Kevin, Kelly and Chris hadn't been included.

I had earned a lot of Frequent Flyer Miles, while working as a Regional Marketing Director. We had used some of them in 1983, to take Louisa with me to the Hahn School in San Diego, and to an ICSC convention in New Orleans. I wanted to use the remaining bonus miles before I left 'Regional' position, fearing they'd be taken away from me. So, we scheduled a trip to Virginia, with Cancun as an outward-bound stop. Louisa and the boys left a day ahead of me, while I was attending the Hahn School in San Diego. My secretary met me at the airport and we went to lunch to catch up. She then dropped me off at my home where I showered and changed the clothing in my baggage.

I also met our new dog while I was home. Louisa hadn't bothered to tell me that we had inherited a dog that had been dropped in Washington Park. They had named her Ginger, and she didn't want anything to do with me. Mutual I thought, except that I was here first. We later decided that a man had probably beaten her. She was very slow to warm to me, and if I had a broom in my hand she'd run the other way. I headed off to the airport, an overnight stay at an airport hotel in Chicago and an early flight to Cancun the next day.

After arriving at the Cancun Airport, and passing through Customs, I caught a shuttle to Islas Mujeres, north of Cancun. I'd meet Louisa, Chris and David at Puerto Juarez, where we would catch the ferry to Islas Mujeres. It was a sweltering hot day. I was happy to be offered a cold beer for 35 cents American.

While enjoying my cold beer in the warm sun, I began talking with a couple, Paul and Rita Sammons. I couldn't believe it. They were from Olympia, Washington, where I had been when I decided to resign my corporate position. I had also terminated the employment of the marketing director of Capital Mall on that trip. Rita knew the woman, whom she referred to in unpleasant terms, and who many had called the 'wicked witch of the northwest.' Even though I knew that she had been difficult at times, I had found no pleasure in firing her. I liked her, but saw her as a very unhappy person who often made life miserable for everyone around her. Rita saw it that way too. I don't recall how they had known each other.

Louisa and the boys caught up with us before the ferryboat arrived. They'd been on a bus tour to Cancun. They'd met Paul and Rita the day before, and we spent a good bit of time with them that week. Louisa and I rented motorbikes and took Chris and David around the island. The boys also played soccer in the town square with some of the locals.

A couple of months later, while I was in Olympia to interview prospective marketing directors, I invited Paul and Rita to join a number of us for dinner. Paul was out of town, but Rita did join us. We've lost touch over the years, but sometimes recall how we met them, and enjoyed our time with them in Mexico.

We went on to Virginia from Mexico, visiting with Kevin, Kelly and Chris, and celebrating our second anniversary with several friends at an El Toritos Restaurant in Hampton.

We also had a small celebration at the Mt. Carmel Catholic Church. My annulment had been certified, and we had our marriage blessed by the church. I called it, 'getting my parking validated.' Through it all, Louisa was dealing with a case of "Montezuma's Revenge." She had lost a lot of weight and weighed about 100 pounds. I don't know whether Kelly or Chris had given our trip a second thought. However, it was constantly on my mind not to talk about Mexico when they were around.

We headed back to Denver and to my new role as resident husband and parent. The Tivoli grand opening was postponed, to no one's surprise. The developer had committed to building the Tivoli with more shops than its location and the market could support. Then the Denver oil business went south, and with it the Denver economy. As I recall, that delay of the grand opening, was the second of three. We went from announcing a fall 1984 opening to a March 1985 opening to the eventual August 1985 opening. In the interim we did recover some positive publicity hosting several dinners to benefit different non-profit organizations.

I was happy with my move. Jim Adkins was already in place as the Manager, and I liked him a lot. I still believe Jim would have fared better as a stand-up comic. I put together a staff, with an assistant named Tracy, and had hired a woman named Shannon as our secretary. I had met Shannon previously when she was an intern at Pueblo Mall. That would factor into some of the changes that would come about, and into the stress of the work I'd take on.

The Pueblo Mall manager recommended her for the position that we had open at the Tivoli. She had grown up in Littleton, near Denver.

There were other changes too. To my surprise, Stan McWhorter and Dave Morgan were leaving the company. They saw the changes in the company philosophy and decided it was time to move on. What concerned me most about it was Stan's replacement, Jack Boyster. I didn't know him well, having been around him only at The Hahn Schools and the meetings for Regional Managers and Marketing Directors. I felt uneasy around him. I sensed that I shouldn't trust him.

CHAPTER 8
Spreading our wings

I'd made a career change, ostensibly to spend more time with my family. In reality I had spread myself too thin again, and changed the sources of stress on our relationship, rather than to eliminate them. Bob and Shelli had returned to Texas, to finalize their move to Denver. Kevin, Kelly and Chris returned to Virginia in August.

Louisa was now working full time at Amoco and making her own friends. She took a course in wilderness backpacking from Denver Free University. She had signed up with Natalie Hook, a co-worker, and met Kevin Trechter there. Louisa was branching out and introducing me to her friends. My socializing was primarily done with people whom I knew through my new work responsibilities.

After I had been assigned to the Tivoli, Bill Michaels and I would see each other at the meetings of the Downtown Denver Partnership. We'd escape those dreadful meetings and visit over coffee, often with Larry Ambrose, whom I'd met through the Auraria Higher Education Center (AHEC). AHEC managed the multi-college Auraria Campus where the Tivoli was located. The Tivoli had to have a presence at those meetings, among others.

Another new friend, Diana Hanna Boulter, the host of the meetings, welcomed me. She and Larry Ambrose were instrumental in the awareness and civic cooperation that the Tivoli development would enjoy in the Denver business community at that time. They were among my first real friends in Denver. We went out with Larry Ambrose and his wife Jane, for our first visit to El Chapultepec for some great live jazz music.

I'd connected with one person in the Trizec office, a secretary named Carol. Rick and Sylvia were becoming close friends, but they were in Pueblo.

After Bob came back to Denver we began to hang out with each other more. Socializing with Bob generally meant watching baseball or football and drinking beer, and not in that order. Of course, that didn't serve to improve my marriage. I'm sure that Louisa didn't think that I needed another drinking buddy.

Although Louisa had offered our home to Bob and Shelli before I did, and although she had gone out of her way to make them feel welcome, Bob increasingly became at odds with her. He knew that she and I had our problems, and he began to vent his problems about her, expecting my support. It didn't happen. She had invited him to join the Amoco group that played volleyball, in Washington Park, each Thursday. On one such evening, I was sitting on the front porch when Bob drove up to our house. He and Shelli were then living on the block south of us. I was surprised to see him. He was mad as hell about something Louisa had said to him while they were playing volleyball.

He stormed up to the porch where I was relaxing in the hammock. "She's such a bitch!" He almost yelled. I egged him on, asking "Anybody in particular?" Your g—d—- wife, that's who!" Before I could say anything, and I didn't rush to do it, he continued to rant and rave about something—blah blah blah. "Even your kids hate her! She's a bitch!" I said, "You mean the woman who invited you to live with us? The woman who takes my kids, and yours by the way, around Colorado when we're not available or interested in doing it? *That* wife of mine? If you have a problem with her, then you work it out. Don't bring it to me. I've got my own, thank you."

I learned one thing in that moment that always held true thereafter, and another that I wouldn't learn for almost 7 years. The anger that Bob had displayed over what Louisa had said at the volleyball game went deeper than even he knew at the time.

Bob accepted what I said, and apologized. He said, "No hard feelings?" I said, "None." What I learned and would enjoy until the day he died in 1994, and have missed since, was that he and I could say anything to each other. We often exercised that privilege. In that moment, with that harsh exchange, we opened a totally forgiving relationship. We never held anything after it was said, regardless of how much we might have disagreed. I've never had that level of openness with anyone, not before and not since, and not with even with myself. We had grown up in what I considered a pretty sarcastic environment, not one that embraced trust and openness. I know that my parents did the best that they knew how to do as parents, as most parents do…as I did.

When Louisa came home that day she asked what Bob was so angry about. I said that he was okay, that he'd been upset with something she'd said. She told me what she'd said just before he angrily cussed at her and left the game. It was a very innocent remark.

Louisa has a way about her that can unnerve some people. She's the official question-asker in our family. I think it's sometimes easy to misinterpret what she says. I should know, I've done it thousands of times. It took almost 20 years of marriage to see, rather to accept, that she had a pure heart. If you believe The Beatitudes, you'll know why I believe that ultimately she *will* see the face of God. I don't want to get off track, go too far with that. It's too soon. In 1984, I didn't have a clue as to how to more completely appreciate her. And I certainly wasn't familiar with The Beatitudes.

It wasn't as though Louisa and Bob never got along. Au, contraire. The first winter that Bob was living in Denver, he and Louisa rebuilt the framing for the back door of our house. The next summer they tilled the side yard together. Their skills with tools and fix up projects came natural to them and they worked well together. I have to first, make myself take on a project and then analyze the task and move through it. It doesn't come naturally to me.

That October, the Tivoli played host to The Denver International Film Festival. Eventually the films would be shown at the multiplex theater being built at the Tivoli. The event kicked off with a featured film and black-tie gala, of sorts. Combine the laid back attitude that was prevalent in Denver, at the time, and the "arts crowd," and you were likely to find men in tuxedos wearing cowboy boots or running shoes for footwear. Many of the women wore gowns that were avant-garde or throw backs to a century earlier.

The 1984 event served as a world premier for "The Razor's Edge," featuring Bill Murray in a dramatic role. Murray attended the showing at the historic Paramount Theatre, and the gala that followed. The party was held in an unfinished building, what later became the Denver Post offices. We sat at a table with actors, with Sandy Dennis and Eric Roberts.

As we were leaving, Bill Murray and his entourage were coming in. Louisa walked up to him and said, "I never thought you could make me cry."

Murray pulled his arm back as if he was going to punch her, saying "Oh yeah!" Then he laughed and said, "Have a good night."

"YOU USED TO LIVE IN MY HOUSE."

We had those moments when we were having great fun, out on the town. We just couldn't seem to segue from one to another, or put a string of them together. Two nights after the Bill Murray event, we went to one of the several cocktail parties held in conjunction with the film festival, at a restaurant/lounge in the Cherry Creek shopping area.

Louisa mingles easily, open to meeting and socializing with anyone. I am less outgoing and, in those days, was still a very private person, shy around people I didn't know. I relied on alcohol to break down those barriers for me. However, that didn't always work in my favor and I didn't learn why until some nine years after the event we attended that night.

Louisa didn't want to stand in one spot and eat and drink. She wouldn't have wanted to sit in one spot either, had any chairs been available at the tables. The place was packed. She would wander off, talking to anyone and everyone and I would stand there, at the bar and drink, and sulk. I had told her a couple of times that I wanted to leave. She was having a good time and wasn't ready to leave. I left on my own, leaving her there. I didn't tell her that I was leaving. I just called a cab and left.

Actually, I did that to Stan McWhorter one night in Albuquerque, too. Stan's Brother Clay had a band…Clay-Mac, I think…and we went to hear them after dinner. I drank too much and got tired of the scene. So, I left and walked about a mile or so back to the hotel, without saying anything to Stan or the others. Like most things, it didn't bother Stan much at all.

It's easy enough now, to wonder why I didn't talk with Louisa, or my brother Bob. Of course, Bob was ready to hear anything negative about Louisa at that time. I felt so much tension between Louisa and myself that any discussions could erupt into an argument.

There were good times together too. Then again, they frequently resulted in something that we could find to argue about. On my birthday, in November 1984, Louisa, Bob and our friend Gerard, took me to dinner at Gasho of Japan. We'd met Gerard, a psychiatrist, through our friends in Pueblo. In the months that followed, he told me several times, that he thought I should leave Louisa, that our relationship was unhealthy. I later told that to Louisa who felt betrayed. He'd been a guest in our house several times, and had never said anything negative about her or our relationship. We lost touch with Gerard in 1985.

Does a Scorpio change his stripes…or shell? Whatever. During one of the pre-opening public relations dinners at the Tivoli I met someone at that dinner with whom I felt an immediate physical attraction, and I could tell that she felt it too. She was among the guests and I'd never met her before that night. She asked me if I would take her on a tour of the Tivoli. Encouraged by alcohol, I was eager to do so. Whatever might have happened didn't, and likely because Jim Adkins saw the sparks and told me to enjoy my dinner while he took her on a tour with some other guests. He and I never discussed it after that.

We were getting a lot of media coverage around the restoration and development of the former brewery. I received a call from a man in Vail, Bruce Gillie, who wanted to work out a trade that allowed him to advertise the hotel he managed, The Tivoli Lodge, for a weekend package that we could give away. He invited me, along with my family to spend the weekend at The Tivoli Lodge, as his guests. That's when Louisa, Chris and David, and I learned how to ski. We enjoyed getting to know Bruce and his wife Linda, and have stayed in touch over the years.

CHAPTER 9
An historic landmark with a revolving door

Jim Adkins didn't see the project through. He accepted an offer to become the manager of Aurora Mall. It was a good move for him. When Jim gave notice that he was leaving, the new Regional Manager suggested Ed Reid as his replacement. I had clashed with Ed when I supervised his marketing directors at Rimrock Mall in Billings, Montana. Our relationship was more unusual. We could get along outside of the business and not about business. He didn't respect marketing directors, alluding to them as promotions directors. My former immediate supervisors had read about him in my reports.

Before they formalized Ed's transfer I was asked about the relationship he and I had while I was a regional marketing director. I stood by my reports and said that I didn't trust him. I was given the chance to block his transfer. There were a couple of problems with that opportunity. I didn't want that kind of power, or responsibility, and I didn't trust the man who presented that opportunity, Jack Boyster. I was always on guard around him. As I would later learn, I should have been even more cautious.

Ed had been manager at Pueblo Mall years earlier and I knew that he wanted to get back to Colorado. He flew to Denver and we talked for quite a while about our differences. We'd had *one* very difficult experience when he was managing

Rimrock Mall. Stan McWhorter had intervened on my behalf at the time.

Ed and I resolved our most significant issue in 1984 and put it behind us. I didn't block his transfer. I saw him as having two different personalities. Away from work we socialized over drinks, talking sports. On the job, he wanted everyone to know that he was the **boss**, usually reminding us in front of people with whom we interacted in our job functions. He also called me the moodiest man he'd ever known. I didn't argue that point.

No doubt I carried that stress home with me and added it to other stresses that I felt and shared. I joked that I didn't have an ulcer, that I was a carrier. I was a very unhappy person most of the time, and made sure that others felt my pain.

Ed joined my brother Bob and me when we would go to Brooklyn's sports bar near Mile High Stadium. Jim Adkins and I had often gone there for lunch. However, Ed and I more often went after work, or for a couple of hours of drinking before returning to work. Bob often joined us. On one occasion, I looked up to see Louisa standing a few feet away, in her wedding dress. When a guy is out drinking with the boys, it is a surreal experience to look up and see your wife in her wedding dress.

Meanwhile, Ed, Jack and the newly hired Tivoli security chief became even more frequent drinking buddies. It was an association that would eventually doom Ed's career with the company.

I had mentioned previously that we had hired a woman named Shannon who had been an intern at Pueblo Mall. When she learned that Ed was coming to the Tivoli, she disappeared. She just didn't report for work. I tracked her down through some of her friends who'd visited our office. I didn't talk with her, but we relayed messages through her friends. I used FedEx to exchange her final paycheck for her office key. I didn't ask why she had left. When she didn't show up for work I was concerned for her safety. I was happy to learn that she was okay. We had no idea for a couple of days. I was told later that she'd known Ed when he was at Pueblo Mall, and that she didn't want to work for him. He's gone and only she knows if that was true. I never heard from her again.

CHAPTER 10
No pain, No gain? Got it covered.

My responsibilities for the grand opening of the Tivoli, now scheduled for August 1985, were to develop the budget, schedule the events and hire entertainers for the four-day opening. I hired as my assistant, a young woman named Tracy. We worked well together and became close. We weren't as close as some thought or talked about, which was not uncommon in the company at that time. It's probably commonplace in most big companies, even today. I think Tracy would have done anything I asked her to do, within the context of her employment. How much of the chatter Louisa heard or listened to, I never knew. I do know that it all added to my stress, and to the strain on my marriage. Tracy was a good listener. We were close enough that I confided in her, about my struggles within my family, especially with David. She had her own challenges, having been estranged with her father and she was in a difficult relationship with the man she would later marry. I was looking for someone to confide in, to talk to. Tracy played an integral, not an intimate role. There *was* an office affair going on at the time. However, neither Tracy, nor I were involved in it.

Imagine how surprised I was when she…oh, I'm getting ahead of myself again.

As if I wasn't busy enough planning for the grand opening, in January I began training for my fourth marathon. It's been my experience that the most difficult part of running a marathon is the training, rather than the 26.2 miles to be run on the day of the event. The discipline to stay with it during all kinds of weather, family and work related responsibilities, and the time required to run as much as 100 miles per week during the peak period of the training taxes not only the runner, but everyone around him or her.

When you're reading this you might wonder, 'what ever happened to Louisa?' I know I'm writing a lot about my work at the time. That was how we lived…in the same house, but not always together…with me engulfed in my work, my drinking and my running. That was, in large part, serving as my escapism.

Our marriage was under a lot of stress. For my part, I wasn't giving it the time and attention needed to resolve our personal differences, and I was about to give more time to my training and ultimately, to myself. I hadn't bonded with Chris or David; I was still carrying the guilt about not being with my kids in Virginia. Add the almost bizarre work environment, and one other important element, my drinking. Unlike my training for the pervious three marathons, I did not slow down on, or stop drinking during training. I was running, not only on the streets of Denver, but also from everything that I felt was closing in on me.

Louisa and I weren't giving each other attention in many ways. We took turns asking each other if there was somebody else. There wasn't for me and I believed her when she said that she wasn't seeing anybody else either.

The Mayor's Cup Marathon was scheduled for Cinco DeMayo, the 5th of May. I was on schedule with my training too. Then there was that pick up game of basketball just three weeks before it.

We arrived at the New Inter-Continental Hotel in San Diego, for the annual Hahn School on Sunday April 14th. I had planned a rest day in my training schedule, for that travel day. The next morning I ran from the Inter-Continental to Harbor Island and back, which was about 10 miles. It was three weeks before the marathon and I was in the best shape I'd ever been in at that point in my training. I felt that I had flown through the ten miles. When you read *flown*, think of a plane with a propeller, not a jet.

After the meetings that day, I came across a pick up game of basketball, with a lot of the guys from the company. I love the game, so I joined them. In less than five minutes, my world was turned upside down. As I was about to pass the ball, I faked a shot and the (very big) guy guarding me went up and came back down, landing hard on my right shoulder. It was separated traumatically.

I reeled in pain as I tried several times to get it back into place, using the techniques that my chiropractor had shown me. I made it to my room and called Louisa, who talked me through the same steps, to no avail. After an hour or so, I located Bob Sorensen. He was about to sit down to dinner, but instead drove me to a hospital. He said there was a hospital nearby, but we wouldn't go to it because it was next to a post office, and *this was April 15*th. Instead he drove several miles, in traffic to another hospital. It was that hospital trip that caused me to swear off ever going to a hospital and getting drugs to ease the pain of the shoulder separation. They would load me with drugs, then use a towel as a large rope and twist my arm so that my shoulder would go back into place. Of course, when the drugs wore off the pain from all the twisting seemed to be stronger, and last longer, than the pain from the separation.

When I returned to Denver, I saw Dr. Joe, my chiropractor and received several acupuncture treatments to aid the healing of the separation. The marathon was about two weeks away and I was determined to run it. Dr. Joe cautioned me that my body would be trying to heal itself while I was adding the demands made on it during the marathon.

Louisa was very helpful, beyond being sympathetic. She did however; question my decision to play in that basketball game. I wondered too, what had I been I thinking about…a 42 year old man, all of 5'5", playing in a basketball game with guys nearly half my age and twice my size?

Race day came and I felt good enough to take on the demands of 26.2 miles. Louisa drove me downtown to the area where the race would start. It was in the 18th mile that I felt the first signs of dehydration. In the 19th mile I was in Washington Park in a place where I could see our house. I saw Louisa and stopped. I wanted to quit at that point because of leg cramps. Louisa practices Jin Shin Jyutsu and spent some time doing energy work on my legs. She said, "Why don't I meet you over on Logan Street. If you're still hurting, then I'll give you a ride home." I could *see* our house, and I could visualize a hot shower and a cold beer. I don't know why, but I agreed to her suggestion.

I did make it to the spot on Logan Street where she said that she would be waiting. This time, she suggested that I go to Logan and Speer, which would put me within the last two miles of the course finish line. Again, I agreed. I met another guy who was struggling as much as I and somehow we made it to the finish line together.

I tell people that it was then that I learned that Louisa would lie to me. She had no intention of letting me quit. She wanted me to finish so that I would never seriously consider running another marathon. That was 1985. Her plan is still a success.

CHAPTER 11
Role Reversal

Despite our times of supporting each other, such as her help with the last marathon adventure, we were still not in synch as a couple. I knew, even then, that I had ignored her and the kids. I felt that she had been supportive in letting me put in all the time that I did for the Tivoli Grand Opening, as well as the peripheral events. Including the latter, it was not uncommon for me to arrive at the office before 8 AM and leave after midnight or later. Some of that time was spent 'kicking back' with a beer, or several. I really felt that I'd earned the right to do that, and that I needed to do it.

That summer became such a blur of activity. I think that I saw more of all of the kids when there were events at the Tivoli that I could bring them to. I have photos of them, taken at the Tivoli. I look at those, and think 'oh, yeah...I *did* see them that summer.

Because the grand opening of the Tivoli had been postponed so often, there was growing doubt, expressed in the media that it would ever come about. We scheduled a number of public relations events to counter the negative image. If I recall correctly, there were five such events in the thirteen months between my having come on board as the marketing director, and the actual grand opening.

Louisa had chosen that time to be tested for allergies, which resulted in abstaining from several foods. She was experiencing various allergic reactions to a number of foods and drinks. Regarding the latter, coffee would become an issue and at times a major battle ground. Stop laughing. It's true.

At the end of the period wherein Louisa had abstained from eating certain foods, she was supposed to re-introduce them into her diet, gradually. One of the food items was tomato. One of the drinks Louisa enjoyed was a Bloody Mary. Wait a minute; you're getting ahead of me.

We had scheduled a public relations event that served as a fundraiser for the Auraria Higher Education Center (AHEC). It was a formal, or black-tie affair. Louisa always looks pretty to me. I sometimes just look at her and take in her natural beauty. When she is dressed for a formal affair, she's not only pretty, but also beautiful. I look at her and think 'wow, what did I do to deserve her?' I know that others have had the same thought. Some have verbalized it.

She had that elegant, beautiful look on the night of the benefit for AHEC. It was also the night she chose to re-introduce tomatoes to her diet, in the form of Bloody Marys. She didn't do it gradually. Over the first course, that is to say, the appetizers, she had consumed an unknown quantity of those drinks. As the entrees were being served, she leaned to me and whispered, "I need to leave." I asked when and she said, *"Now!"* She knew that she was on the verge of nausea. My admiration quickly changed to exasperation.

There we were, at a black-tie event, with hundreds of guests who could provide the Tivoli with a lot of credibility. I was the nominal host. I was about to leave. We didn't have cell phones in those days. We had intentionally taken a cab, expecting that we, and more likely I, would drink a lot. I hadn't had the opportunity at that point, but Louisa had more than made up for it. I took her arm and led her to the office, quickly called a cab and took her outside...all at her urgent request. She was buzzed and knew it, and didn't want to embarrass me at that moment. Fortunately we didn't have to wait long for a cab to arrive. As I was helping her into the cab, Mayor Pena and his wife were arriving. We'd met often enough that he knew my name at that time, and greeted me. Under other circumstances, I would have asked Louisa to get out of the cab so that I could introduce them to each other. However, by that time she was lying down in the back seat, saying, "You stay. I'll be okay at home. You stay. It's okay."

In the four years that we had been together, dating or married, there had been so many times that she had put up with my drinking, you'd think that I would be understanding on this rare occasion. You probably know better by now. I was not. I was upset and thought that I would not only stay, but also see what woman I could attract. Some habits are just begging for exercise. The good news is that it was a fleeting thought and just an irrational act on the part of my ego. I didn't stay much longer than dinner, explaining that Louisa had become ill and had taken a cab home.

The next day, one of the architects who had been at the event, asked me who the beauty was that I had with me the night before. He'd met Louisa several times. When I told him that it was Louisa, he said, "Wow! You need to take her out more often."

CHAPTER 12
Just as I am. Not no, but hell no.

We had been ready to buy a car and Louisa took charge of finding it. She found the Subaru at a Volkswagen dealership on West Colfax. They tried to play the usual, 'I have to check with the sales manager' game with her. **HA!** She gave them a 'take it or leave it' offer. We got the car for her price, and after a compression check that *they* paid for.

It was in late June that I made a quick trip, with my brother Bob, to Alton, to pick up Kevin, Kelly and Chris for their summer visit. Their mother had gone back to Alton for a visit and I had agreed to pick them up to save the airfare. It was a quick trip, as we spent only one night in Alton, gathered up the kids and headed back to Denver, driving straight through both ways, in a Subaru wagon we'd purchased a couple of weeks before the trip.

Louisa had been taking a backpacking class at Denver Free University. She loves the outdoors and she was being proactive about doing things that didn't include me. That was easy enough to do since I was never around. She told me that she was going on a hike and overnight trip with her class, that it was up to me to work the kids into my schedule, into my life. She was with Natalie Hook and Kevin Trechter on that trip. We can laugh about it now, and Kevin says that Louisa saved his life, carrying his pack up the mountain. Let's say that Kevin is a *big* man. I have an example of how big that I'll share later.

I became involved with Denver Free University, too. I served on the board of directors, and taught a public speaking class.

As the Grand Opening approached, I found an LP by Air Supply that I wanted to give to Louisa. Yes, Air Supply. I've never said she is perfect. The album was titled "Just As I Am." (Arista Records, 1985) I gave it to Louisa, telling her that I appreciated her letting me be myself, and do what I was doing...accepting me "Just As I Am." She refused to accept the album, telling me that she didn't want me as I was. She wouldn't accept my behavior, or me. I was really hurt, and became angry and even more withdrawn from her. She was more distant from me.

As I worked out the events for the grand opening, I hired Bill Michaels to produce a 5k race that would be a fundraiser for the Denver Broncos Youth Foundation. I connected with Randy Gradishar who had become the president of the DBYF after his retirement. For the benefit of those who don't know, Randy had been a superstar linebacker for the Broncos. Those who elect players to the NFL Hall of Fame should be ashamed that he was not inducted *long ago*. Randy simply asked what I/we wanted in return. I told him we wanted his name recognition and that of the Broncos. With the grand opening having been moved to August we had virtually no shot at getting active players to participate on a Sunday; the players' only day off during training camp.

With the grand opening date drawing near, the work hours and tensions grew even more. I rarely saw any of the kids unless they came to the Tivoli, or on the more rare occasion that we all had dinner together.

Also, at that time, I was dealing with representatives from every media outlet, as the primary spokesman for the Tivoli.

"YOU USED TO LIVE IN MY HOUSE."

I dealt with the on-air personalities and columnists, and also with the sales reps because I was responsible for the advertising as well.

It was during that time that I met a group of people that would take my life's journey down a different path a few years later. In addition to being the spokesman to all of the media, coordinating the advertising and public relations campaigns, I was searching for *"the voice"* of the Tivoli. I listened carefully to a number of radio on-air personalities, wanting to find the right sound for our radio and TV commercials.

Keith Riker was working at FM100 at the time. Today Keith's talent can be heard on radio stations in a number of cities around the country, and on even more commercials. I called him and suggested that we meet over lunch to discuss our using his talent for the Tivoli commercials. We did that and found that we had a lot in common. Of course, a part of it was that I too had been an on-air personality. However, Keith's voice and on-air talent are far greater than my own. We both hailed from Illinois, Keith from Springfield, and I from Alton.

We met over lunch a few times and while Keith and I were getting to know each other, I said something about getting back to the office where I would find as many as two-dozen calls to return or people to see, regarding the scheduled 4-day grand opening. He told me that I should come up to the Bucksnort Saloon and hear the band he played with, saying, "It's just a little three piece band, but we have a lot of fun." I had no idea where the Bucksnort Saloon was located. Keith drew out directions on a napkin, saying that they would be playing Sunday afternoon.

That night I told Louisa about Keith, and his invitation. We decided to go and asked my brother Bob to go with us. Our first trip to the Bucksnort Saloon would be the first of many. It was the first time that we heard the band, "Sashay." Along with Keith, it consisted of a couple, Mark Richey and Deanna Webb, who had moved from Florida to Colorado a few years earlier. They were terrific, and I loved the Bucksnort. The date was August 4, 1985, and the grand opening of the Tivoli would take place August 15-18. It was a surreal experience for me. I loved their music, the setting, the people and the fact that I was that far away from the Tivoli, *and* enjoying the day with Louisa. That was the first of several times that we camped near the Bucksnort.

I hadn't been that far away from work since Bob and I drove back to Illinois to pick up my kids in June. I thought, 'my God, I *do* have a life!' We called it an early birthday present for Louisa, whose birthday is August 17th. No doubt, we…or probably I…would be spending her birthday at the Tivoli. I had either allowed, or caused it, to consume me.

CHAPTER 13
Ain't life grand

As it always happens, the days passed and August 14th arrived. We had our own celebration the night before, inaugurating the disco at Club Tivoli. I think I got home around 2 Am, napped and showered, and was back at the Tivoli at 5:45 AM. As I walked in I was told that Channel 9 was on site and that the morning crew wanted to interview me. I still have the tape of that interview. It's hilarious. My hair was still, 'plastered down' wet, and I hadn't even stopped for a cup of coffee. In a later interview, *after* coffee, I looked like a different person.

The crowds weren't great for the ribbon cutting. The Trizec president was there, and asking why that was so. I had a good relationship with him, and I believe that it was in part because I would answer his questions with what I thought to be true. He had surrounded himself with people that would give him answers that they thought he wanted to hear. I told him that the configuration of the Tivoli allowed people to come in on the opposite side of the building, rather than the main entrance. The overall numbers were there. However, there wasn't a big crowd gathered to witness the ribbon cutting, which is normally the case for a mall opening.

We started the event with music by one of Denver's most talented pianists, Rob Mullins. Over the four days, we had live music, and jugglers, etc and then the PosiTivoli 5k on Sunday, to benefit the Broncos' Youth Foundation.

In addition to Harold Milavski, the Trizec president, there were a number of executives from the Hahn Company present as well. Louisa was coming to join me for lunch. She worked in the AMOCO building at the other end of the 16th Street Mall, about a mile and a half away. I got some great news from Bob Sorensen that would make her mall trek worthwhile.

After many of the officials had left, Bob came into my office. He congratulated me on the grand opening, saying, "It's about as good of a grand opening as I've ever seen, or better." That meant a great deal to me. He's seen more than a few, from Newmarket North, which he opened and is where I first met him in 1975, to Horton Plaza in San Diego, which had opened the weekend before the Tivoli.

Bob went on to say that the company wanted to reward me with a trip for Louisa and me, to 'anywhere in the world,' except Virginia. He knew that I had been going back to Virginia periodically to see Kevin, Kelly and Chris. WOW! What a thank you! After about a week of discussion, Louisa and I chose New Zealand as our destination. That put a wrinkle into Bob's gift plans.

When I told Bob about our choice, he said something like, 'let me see what I can do.' It happened that the company had a trade agreement with one of the larger travel agencies and as Bob had it planned, our trip would not be an out of pocket expense for the company. The wrinkle was that the agency either didn't book trips to New Zealand, or didn't want to include it as a part of a trade agreement.

Bob and I talked about it, and we struck a deal. We were pretty set on New Zealand, so I offered to use my accumulated miles on my United Airlines Mileage Plus program, to defer costs. Thanks to Dr. Stephen Covey, I did know something about win-win. The company came up with the cash for the week that we would spend in New Zealand. The next step would be to decide when we would go.

That fall both Paul and Carol, Louisa's parents, came to visit for the first time. Carol had come alone in March on her way to an Amway function in California. We had the Subaru wagon, but Paul rented a car and asked me to be the driver on their tour of the mountains. The highlight of that tour may have been Trail Ridge Road in the Rocky Mountain National Park, or the homemade pie at Jenny's in Empire. They also enjoyed the Indian cuisine at Viceroy of India, one of the better restaurants at the Tivoli. I was sitting with them at the Viceroy Restaurant when the Cardinals were being robbed of a World Series victory in Kansas City.

The Subaru had been a dependable workhorse for us. Louisa had joined a food co-op and I recall loading the Subaru with bulk foods at a warehouse in northeast Denver. We had the use of a garage at the home of a Gary and Connie Dolezal. For the life of me, I don't recall how Louisa got hooked up with the group. As Louisa had done in Virginia, she became an integral part of the co-op. I helped, from time to time, with the distribution, too.

Brian Cole appeared again in December. He came out to ski and I lined him up with a place at the Tivoli Lodge in Vail. I was set to drive him there in the Subaru when a clutch cable broke. Louisa and I changed those several times on that car. Brian took the bus to and from Vail.

After he came back to Denver we went to see a movie, which we all agreed was horrible. On the way home it was snowing and we drove through Washington Park. He said, "I'll buy the coffee if you'll drive all night." As much as I like coffee, I declined his generous offer.

I saw him, and Paul and Carol the next month when I went back to see Kevin, Kelly and Chris before Christmas. Louisa didn't make those trips with me because she had Chris and David to take care of, and of course, her job at Amoco.

CHAPTER 14
After changes upon changes we are more or less the same (8)

After a series of events involving drinking, one of the company superiors had told Ed Reid, that Club Tivoli was off limits for him.

On February 15, 1986 I arrived at the office at the normal hour of 8:30 AM. Immediately, I received a call from Carol Woelber asking what I knew about Ed having been at Club Tivoli the night before. I told her that I didn't know what she was talking about because Louisa and I had been out to dinner for Valentine's Day, and not at Club Tivoli.. Minutes later, I received a call from Bob Sorensen, in San Diego, asking the same question. I gave him the same answer and asked what had happened. Apparently Ed had been to Club Tivoli the night before and actually got into a fight with someone. I was shocked. In my experience with Ed, I had never known him to even argue angrily, much less want to fight anyone. It was later that morning that Ed came to the office and packed up his personal possessions. His employment with the company had been terminated. I don't recall that I ever saw him again.

Some people, including myself, thought that I should replace him as manager. I had the primary role as spokesman and coordinator for the grand opening. I had been on the project since arriving in Denver 2 years earlier. It was not to be. The company transferred Terry Willey from Capital Mall, in Olympia, to Denver to become the manager of the Tivoli. I then had the added responsibility of educating Terry about Denver and of course, the Tivoli. I knew Terry from my trips to Olympia. He was a likeable guy. However, I was stung by what I felt as being passed over. No one knew the project as well as I did at that point. As far as Louisa was concerned the company had screwed me again. She began to use an altered version of the company name, referring to them as "F—-Hahn." That should be taken in context of how she felt that the company was being run, not the family name. The Hahn family members I had met were good and generous people. I felt that what I saw as the demise of the company, was an injustice to everything that Ernie Hahn and his family had built.

CHAPTER 15
A week, give or take, down under

Why would anyone go all the way to New Zealand for only a week? Glad you asked.

Louisa was taking a few courses at UC-Denver at the time, thinking that she might go back to her pursuit of a degree in architecture. So we scheduled the trip for February 1986, during her spring break. We would be in New Zealand at the end of their summer…barely.

My brother Bob had agreed to watch over, or keep track of Chris and David. He and Shelli lived on the block south of us and he said it wouldn't be a problem. With that we headed off to New Zealand. Those who have flown in and/or out of Denver will at some point experience what the winds can do to a plane. The winds were so strong, as we left the Stapleton airport that we thought ever nut and bolt on that plane was going to come loose. After we got high enough over the Rockies, things settled down and we thought it could only get better after that.

We had a layover at Honolulu, in the middle of the night. Then we were back in the air for the ten-hour flight to New Zealand. That's a long time in the tube. I slept for a while, but spent most of my time reading. I had recently discovered John D. McDonald and had three of his books with me. I love to read, and at that time I was reading two books a week; by authors such as Robert Ludlum and Lawrence Sanders.

We'll get back to New Zealand in a moment. First, I must share with you an example of my passion for reading. It's something I developed while I was serving in the Army. My duties, through most of my three years, were those as a driver for the battalion commander. I was fortunate to work for Lt. Colonel Harry P. Schoenman, a terrific man and officer. Anyway, I spent a lot of time waiting for the colonel, and I developed a passion for reading during those hours. Oh yeah, I'm wandering aren't I.

In 1983, while on a flight from Denver to Las Vegas, I was reading one of Robert Ludlum's books. I was engrossed. I read through the landing and I was almost finished when we arrived at the gate. I knew there would be a couple of people from the staff of Fashion Show Mall waiting for me at curbside, to go to dinner. I had about a dozen pages left to read, so I diverted to the Men's Room and finished reading the book in a stall. I had carry-on luggage, so I didn't need to go to Baggage Claim. When I finally walked outside, I was greeted with 'what happened to you? Did you get lost between the gate and the door?' I explained that I had made a stop at the Men's Room. They were embarrassed that they'd asked. For years I used the reading to escape from the people I lived with, too.

So, anyway, I read my way to New Zealand. We landed in Auckland and caught another plane over to the South Island, to Christchurch. It was an easy hop if you don't mind looking down and seeing nothing but treetops around you while you're landing. It was pretty painless to get through Customs and then to a cab and on to the rental car agency. We had reserved a camper, wanting to see as much of the island as possible and not spend time checking into and out of hotels. We were dropped at the Hertz office in Christchurch. I knew then that I was going to enjoy the New Zealand scenery. A young woman who was a dead ringer for Jacqueline Bissett greeted us. It seemed almost too soon that we were on the road in a six berth Toyota camper…on the *opposite* side of the road, of course.

I didn't find it difficult to stay on the correct side of the road, so much as it felt strange sitting on the opposite side of the cab and turning on the windshield wipers when I wanted to turn. We probably could have made it all week without an argument, but we didn't. We got testy with each other when Louisa wanted me to stop so that she could take a picture, and I didn't stop exactly at that moment or place. While we did manage not to let it spoil the whole trip, there was the long drive from Queenstown to Invercargill in total silence. We had a great time, although too brief a visit. We were particularly drawn to Christchurch, Invercargill and Dunedin, and to the Kiwi people. Driving through the rain forest to Milford Sound, and then seeing 'Milford' for the first time is almost indescribable. Everything that you've ever heard about New Zealand is true, as long as you've only heard great things.

We wrapped up the New Zealand visit with a lunch in Auckland before catching our flight. Louisa had read about the "Hard To Find Café." Indeed it was, because it had been moved several times. We did find it down an alleyway and to our surprise we also found great Mexican food. Then the cabbie took us past "One Tree Hill" before returning to the airport. On the long flight home, I got into trouble by waking Louisa to see a volcano miles below.

Bob said that he hadn't had any trouble with the boys, so I offered him the job full time. I hadn't experienced any jetlag on the trip *to* New Zealand. However, I did on the return trip. When we finally got to our house, distributed gifts and visited with Bob, and with Chris and David, I called Virginia to let Kevin, Kelly and Chris know that we'd returned safely. I begged off from a real conversation because of the jetlag. There was a major event going on at the Tivoli, in conjunction with the Native American Pow-Wow, but I knew that Tracy could handle it. I took a can of beer and walked over to the park and sat under a tree for a long time.

Not long afterwards we told Chris and David that we were going to move to Dunedin. They were upset, and even more so after they had heard us tell all about it and then tell them that we were kidding.

CHAPTER 16
Let's all sing the chorus of "HAIR"? (9)

April brought more surprises. My Mother and her sister Doris came to Denver for a visit, arriving just before Easter. I think that Doris had never been farther from Alton than St. Louis, or perhaps to Kentucky to visit relatives. They'd talked about making the trip and we all thought that it was just that, talk.

They enjoyed going to "Daddy Bruce's" barbeque restaurant, and to the Air Force Academy, but the highlight was more than a foot of snow that fell…and went away over the next couple of days. Neither of them had ever seen that much snow go away so quickly. Back in Alton, we'd see it change colors once or twice before going away. Mom liked it here so much that she came back for Christmas.

Another surprise occurred when I decided to shave my beard that I had worn since Christmas of 1978. Louisa had never seen me without it. She'd seen photos of course, and in those photos I looked significantly heavier with a very round face.

Easter Sunday Louisa, Chris and David had gone to church. I wasn't going to church at the time. I awoke and got ready for my daily run. I had the urge to shave, so I did. I was running south about two blocks from our house when I saw Louisa and the boys coming in my direction in the Subaru. There was a distinct look of shock as I passed by them and waved, while I continued to run.

When I finished my run, I was not met with open arms. My Mom liked the look and Doris was complimentary. Chris and David were frozen in shock and offered no opinion. Louisa however, did have an opinion. It wasn't positive. She was upset that she wasn't consulted. She said that when they initially saw me running down the street, they thought it was somebody else 'running in dad's clothes.' I had the beard for a little more than two years when we met. The next day she said that she felt like she'd been sleeping with a stranger. I asked her if it was good for her. She was not amused. She would just *look* at me. She said that it was weird hearing my voice come out of *that* face. Her brain just couldn't adjust to it. I started growing the beard again that day.

It was the onset of spring. I was enjoying the running, and looking forward to June when the kids would come out from Virginia.

In April, along with Terry and Tracy, I went back to San Diego for the annual Hahn School. It was special for Tracy because it was her first trip there. Terry had flown out ahead of us and picked up an RV somewhere along the way. It would become party-central.

The location was the historic and grand Hotel Del Coronado, on Coronado Island. The grand opening events for both Horton Plaza and the Tivoli were featured that week. I was recognized as "Marketing Director of the Year" for the success of the Tivoli grand opening and given a rather elegant glass trophy. We were all shocked, having thought that the marketing director for Horton Plaza would win. Horton Plaza was a terrific development and had been the grand finale for Ernie Hahn. He was a great person to be associated with and loved by all of us who worked for him. I had been lucky enough to spend some time with him.

We had champagne and more that night. I was told that I won the award in large part because of what we did at the Tivoli without a lot of corporate support. I received a lot of praise and was excited that Tracy was there because she had worked so hard on the project, too.

CHAPTER 17
Those crazy days of summer…a sequel?

June ushered in some crazy days of summer in 1986.

One of the suburban newspapers had been soliciting our advertising business for some time. The newest approach came in the form of a beautiful young woman who was also a student at Denver University. She took me to lunch at Club Tivoli, along with her sales manager. The owner of the club was as taken by her beauty as I. He insisted that the wine would be complimentary and we each drank a lot of it. Finally, the sales manager excused himself and the sales rep suggested that we find her mother who was taking part in a political convention at one of the downtown hotels. I agreed and I followed her, parking in the hotel garage a few minutes later.

We spent that afternoon going from one suite to another, and consuming more wine…a lot more wine. At some point I left and went to the parking garage. No doubt, the best news of the day was that I couldn't find my car. I took a cab back to the Tivoli. One of the security guards spotted me getting out of the cab and ushered me up to my office through the back of the building. He called Louisa and told her that I was in no condition to drive, and that she should come to pick me up. She told him that I had driven the car to work, and that I could sleep in my office, which I did.

It was after that occasion that I gave up drinking wine… for good. Really.

A week or so later, Louisa and I took a camping trip that included Taos, Santa Fe, Chimayo and Chaco Canyon. There were three events that make that trip stand out in my memories. We had an horrendous fight at Chimayo and even threw around the word *divorce* into the mix. What could spark that kind of fight? It began as a debate over how long we'd be there and escalated over how often we disagreed about even the smallest things. I knew that I was tired of it and that after all that time together I was tired of things not changing for the better. That had become a familiar theme.

We finally cooled down and regained some of our emotional equilibrium. We were on the road for the long trip across New Mexico to Chaco Canyon. Those who've been there know how foolish I was not to have stopped for gas long before we headed down the rutty road into the canyon. The Subaru wagon was loaded, full of everything except gas. We arrived at dusk without advance knowledge or planning, at the time of Solstice, *and* a full moon. There were no camping spots open. One couple allowed us to squeeze our small dome tent into their space, and partially into the space of some others who were out somewhere, believing they wouldn't mind. Gratefully, they didn't.

Chaco Canyon is an incredibly spirit-filled area. Yes, there is beauty and history and there was a full moon the first night. We were in awe of the spirit that lives there.

That was the second major event of the trip. The third was the stark realization that I didn't want to go back to the Tivoli…not at the end of the week…not ever. I felt that I had done what I could do for the Tivoli. There wasn't any challenge for me there any longer. Right now, this week, as I am writing, I am also reading Dr. Wayne Dyer's Power of Intention. I see now, how I set the table for what was to come in the months ahead.

"YOU USED TO LIVE IN MY HOUSE."

As far apart as we had been at Chimayo, we became as one at Chaco Canyon. Somehow the Subaru had enough gas to get to the first gas station we saw. I think we willed it to make it. On the way back to Denver, we stopped overnight at The Great Sand Dunes near Alamosa, Colorado and the Sangre de Cristo Mountains. We'd been there before and it's an awesome sight in it's own right. However, the mosquitoes were out in force and we snacked inside the tent, not wanting to be outside even long enough to cook dinner.

We were feeling very close to each other at that point, and having open dialogue about what I would do about my feelings about returning to the Tivoli. Not long after that I received a job offer that wasn't too good to refuse. Actually there were two. I was back to that space where I knew what I *didn't* want, and not what I *did* want.

Of course, as was the norm, that closeness didn't last long. I had a self-destructive behavior pattern that I didn't see then, and even for years.

A couple of my favorite relatives, and their children came to town. They were headed back home to Alton, returning from a trip to California in their van. I decided that we should host a pool party for them. We invited a few friends, and of course, my brothers Bob and Mike, and my niece, Shelli, too.

One measure of having had too much to drink was that I tried to throw our friend Kevin Trechter into the pool by sneaking up on him. I had mentioned previously that Kevin is a big man. He's also athletic, and he's no dummy. I served the latter role. When I thought I was sneaking up on him, I reached out to push him into the pool and he grabbed me, actually *throwing* me into the pool. I had to experience that twice before I realized that it wasn't going to work.

If you take time to listen to Brad Paisley's song, "Alcohol," you'll understand the next story completely. For instance… "You had some of the best times you'll never remember with me: Alcohol…."

Then I got the bright idea that my brothers and I should take my visiting uncle to a strip bar, Shotgun Willie's.

While others were having a good time in the pool and on the patio, I left my own party. My brother Mike and I "snuck" out and laid down in the bed of Bob's pick up truck. We had conspired with my uncle. He and Bob were to leave together to get more beer. I recall his daughter, crying and pleading with him not to go. That image stayed with me long after the event.

My youngest brother, Mike, had moved to Colorado. He had recently divorced and had come out from Illinois for a visit, and stayed. Our other brother, Pat, was somewhere in the south. Pat spent a number of years on the road, and staying in touch is not in his nature.

We did go and at the bar things were getting out of hand. One of the other guys, Terry Willey, left the party and found us at the bar. I became concerned, and was sobering up when I started trying to get them to leave with me. They refused and I left, ready to walk the 2+ miles to my home. I had gone about a mile when I saw Bob's truck coming. They stopped to pick me up. Suddenly it was the next morning and I knew things would turn ugly.

I made coffee and walked over to the park. My uncle and aunt joined me. He was in some kind of doghouse and said something about riding all the way home with her pissed at him. I said, "I never thought I'd say this, but I would love to ride across Kansas with you…all the way to Alton today." She managed a laugh, saying that she didn't blame me, but that I wasn't welcome to join them. She had talked with Louisa.

We didn't have a big fight about it. However, you could have used our house as a storage locker for freshly cut beef for quite a while. Bob and Mike didn't come around for over a week either.

At the end of June, Mike and I took his truck; with its camper shell on the back and headed to Alton to pick up my kids. Once again, Judi had taken them there and I was to pick them up. It worked out well and saved money that would have been spent on airfare.

I was driving when we passed Fort Riley, on I-70. I had spent most of my three years of active duty with the Army, at Fort Riley. I told Mike, "If you see the turn signal on, shoot me. Don't even ask any questions."

It was a rough trip for Kevin and Chris because it was so hot in the camper shell, with so little breeze through it. We stopped more often than we had on other trips. Kelly followed later on a flight to Denver.

That year the visit was different…it became permanent. Their mother was going to move to Denver in the fall. I was excited about all of the kids being in Colorado. I had no idea about how the dynamics would affect my marriage.

BOOK THREE

CHAPTER 1
Should I stay or should I go?

The success of the Tivoli opening had spread throughout the shopping center industry. I received a phone call from a developer from Houston, asking that I meet with him for dinner and a discussion of a business development.

We met and toured the Tivoli in the afternoon and agreed to meet again for dinner. He said that one of his partners would be joining us. He talked about his project, the redevelopment of an old brewery in the Houston area. That evening we met at Club Tivoli. The partner who joined us was a huge man. I don't recall his name. However, I do recall that he played on the offensive line for the (then) St. Louis football Cardinals. I recall too, that he ordered…and ate…two entrees that consisted of a Porter House steak, baked potato and assorted vegetables.

We talked about their project and I made it clear that I wasn't open to moving to Houston. I had been there, visiting my brother Bob, a few years earlier. I was open to consulting, from Denver, and that was not an acceptable option for them.

Not long after that I met an executive in one of the airport private lounges reserved for the airlines' exclusive clientele. He was a VP with a shopping center developer based in Ohio. We talked about the position of corporate vice president of marketing, and whether I might be interested in going to Ohio to meet the president of the company, tour the corporate headquarters, etc. That was all very flattering stuff. However, I knew that I didn't want to leave Denver...only the Tivoli. It was 1986 and after being apart from Kevin, Kelly and Chris since 1983, I wasn't about to move anywhere. They were moving to Denver. When they came out for the summer they stayed, and their mother followed a few months later.

I told Louisa about the interview that wasn't quite an offer, other than the trip to Ohio. She told me something like, '*Doubling* your salary, a house on the river, a yacht and two Mercedes, won't get me to move from Denver to Youngstown, Ohio.' So now, the people of Youngstown can feel offended along with those in Alton, Illinois.

I had to do something, so I told Carol Woelber, Jack Boyster and Terry Willey, that I wanted to become an assistant manager and no longer wanted to be the marketing director for the Tivoli. I felt that I'd done all that I could do in that role. The Tivoli is located on the Auraria campus, which is home to Metropolitan State University (Metro State), the University of Colorado at Denver and the Community College of Denver. As I recall there were plus or minus 35,000 students on the campus each day. I was frustrated that I could not convince the powers that be to target the leasing to the student population.

The leasing efforts were focused on bringing people to high-end shops and restaurants, from the office buildings downtown. Many of those buildings were called "see though" buildings at that time. Denver's economy had gone south. The oil boom had become a bust and many of the people with whom Louisa had worked, were being transferred or had already been transferred to Amoco facilities in Houston.

CHAPTER 2
How many changes can you handle at one time?

We also had a houseguest that summer, a young girl from Mazatlan, Mexico. Annabela Gavica was with us for about six weeks. was 14 years old, and shared a bedroom with Kelly. Louisa took Annabela and the other kids, except Kelly and Kevin, to various places through Colorado, such as the Great Sand Dunes. Kelly didn't want to go and she was very helpful to me, in taking care of Kevin, while I worked and played.

Louisa and Chris Coons were picking at each other more often than not. They really tested each other. Even on that trip to the Great Sand Dunes, they had a confrontation. Louisa had told each of the kids to stay in sight, that it was all too easy to become lost in the 50 square miles of dunes. At one point, she looked around for each of the kids and there was no sign of Chris Coons. She said she then looked to a small figure on top of dune. Just as quickly, it disappeared. The small figure reappeared in the person of Chris Coons.

All too often I felt like a referee. Fortunately for me, I hadn't been with them on that trip. I felt that I, or my loyalty, was being challenged by both of them.

It didn't take Carol Woelber long to name my replacement. Evidently she had been approached by the marketing director at Rimrock Mall in Billings, Montana, regarding any possibility of being assigned to the Tivoli. Nicole's husband was from the greater Denver area. I had met Nicole and seemed nice enough. I had no problem with Carol's choice. Nicole wanted the job and I didn't.

I spent about two weeks working with Nicole to transition to the Tivoli. It quickly became obvious that she didn't want my help. I was eager to get on with my new assignment, so I started working closely with Terry Willey to get up to speed as the assistant manager.

Kevin, Kelly and Chris had made their move to Denver. They were with us full time for nine months. Their mother moved that fall. She stayed with my brother Bob, and his daughter Shelli for a little while, before finding her own place. When we made our move in 1983 it was our understanding that Judi would move at that time. I had an opportunity to put her things in the moving van with ours, and had offered to help her move the rest of her items. In 1986 she felt that I was still obligated to pay for her move. There were three reasons that I agreed to do so. I didn't want her to take them back to Virginia, Louisa agreed with my decision and I reverted to my behavior of the years that I had lived with Judi: acquiescing to her wishes.

While all of the kids were living with us, they became responsible for getting Kevin off his school bus while we were at work. We have neighbors that still talk about how great the kids were about doing that.

When it was finally done, I was very happy that they settled about a mile away, northwest of the park. There was another adjustment to be made when Kevin, Kelly and Chris moved in with her that fall. We'd had everything running pretty smoothly with the seven of us in our home. I had reached a point of being as happy or happier than I had been in several years.

Somehow, Louisa was dodging the bullet called lay-offs at Amoco. There were people to her left and right who were being laid off or transferred, weekly. She had been a full time employee for only one year, so we weren't sure whether she'd avoid being laid off. She was happy enough being there. Of course, she would have preferred to not have to work. However, it's her nature to be happy. It seemed that only I, and/or the Hahn Company could make her unhappy in those days.

We still knew how to laugh together, at each other and ourselves. I picked up Louisa for lunch one day, and pulled to the curb in front of the AMOCO building. She slid into the seat in a hurry and said, "Oh shit! I just ripped the crotch in my panty hose." I said, "Hopefully, no one will notice."

Maybe that was when and where I decided to take a shot at a long held dream. A friend, Kathy De Francis was working with the Comedy Works, downtown. Once I told her that I wanted to do stand up comedy, there was no backing out. I signed up for Amateur's Night. I told Louisa that I'd have 5 minutes on stage. She felt that 5 minutes would be a long time. I added that to my routine…how lucky I am to have a wife who thinks five minutes is a long time. The hardest part was the waiting. One couple got into a major fight back stage before going on. Maybe it was because that was all too familiar to me that I was ready to bail when I heard my name being introduced.

Louisa had been right. 5 minutes in the bright lights was a long time. Kathy said I'd been 'okay,' but should do it again later and be more relaxed…have fun with it. I thought it would be a lot more fun to just watch others do it. So, I went back to my day job.

There were times when I could actually manage my drinking. Randy Gradishar had invited us to see a Broncos' pre-season game, as the guest of Bronco's owner, Pat Bowlen, in his suite at Mile High Stadium. I was very aware of the company we were keeping and drank very little. My marathon training served me well.

In the late fall and early winter of 1986, I was spending more time working closely with Terry Willey. During Christmas week that year, Terry took me to lunch at La Loma, a Mexican food restaurant that we frequented fairly often. I recall the day so clearly for a couple of reasons. We were there a long time and the wait staff was anxious for us to leave so that they could get the place ready for their company party that evening. The other was that Terry dropped a bomb. He told me that I would be trained to assume his role at the first of the new year because the company was going to transfer him, most likely to Texas.

I was really excited about the news, and anxious to share the news with Louisa. I was going to get to manage the property that I felt I should have been managing since Ed Reid had left. I would have a good job and not have to leave Denver to be promoted. I had been firm with the company in that I would not accept a transfer outside of Denver. If I had any trepidation, it was about working directly for Jack Boyster. Never the less, I was very happy that day.

It was Christmas and it seemed that I was getting all the presents. It appeared that everything was going my way. I was getting what I wanted with my job, Kevin, Kelly and Chris had moved to Denver and even the Broncos were winning. On New Year's Day we took the Subaru on a ride through the mountains, along the Palmer Divide north of Colorado Springs.

CHAPTER 3
Chicken Little was a prophet.

On Sunday, January 11, 1987, Louisa, Chris Coons and I watched John Elway lead the Broncos on "the Drive," and win over Cleveland in the AFC Championship game. We were yelling and screaming because the Broncos were on their way to the Super Bowl.

We all raced outside to the front porch to yell and scream our excitement, as so many of our neighbors were doing. Joy turned ugly in a nano-second, as I watch Chris and Louisa fight over who could ring the ship's bell on the front porch. Reality sometimes has a way of kicking you in the gut. It was one of many of their confrontations that were draining the euphoria of having all of the kids in Denver. It sure as hell drained it quickly on that day.

The next Sunday we all went to a pep rally at Mile High Stadium to see the Broncos off for their Super Bowl game in Pasadena. The place was filled to capacity. We were all there with the Tivoli staff, watching from one of the club section boxes. There was food and it was exciting, and yet something was gnawing at me. I felt really uncomfortable around Terry Willey for some reason. Jack wasn't as friendly as he had been, at the office, during the preceding week. Even Carol wasn't all that friendly.

As we were walking back to the car I said to Louisa, "Sometimes I wish they'd just all go away, or even fire me. One day I'm up, the next I'm down." Louisa had, on many occasions, told me that she thought I could never really be happy; that I didn't really want to be happy.

The sky fell on January 12, 1987. No, that wasn't the day when the Broncos lost to the Giants in Super Bowl XXI. When that happened, a couple of weeks later, I was low enough that it only seemed natural. My downward spiral had begun.

When I went to work on Monday, January 12, 1987, I was still feeling the funk from the previous day, feeling that the rest of the staff was distant. I didn't have to wait long to learn that it was real and not just my imagination.

Terry Willey and Jack Boyster asked me to join them in Terry's office. I did and Terry closed the door. Jack simply said 'we're going to let you go.' Terry added that the company was prepared to give me until the end of February to find something else. At any rate, that would be the termination date for my employment. They would also give me a week's pay for each year with the company, which was a little less than eight years. My eight-year anniversary would have been in April. I asked for reasons, any reasons, since I had not ever a blemish on my annual review and had, less than ten months earlier, been named "Marketing Director of the Year." I had copies of each annual review.

Jack was quick to point out that the award was for marketing and I had resigned that position. Terry said that I had made it clear that I would not accept a transfer to any place outside of Denver, and the Tivoli was the only property the company had in the Denver area. Jack added that I was one of several assistant managers that would be given termination notice on that day and that I was getting a better deal than most. He said the company could no long afford to pay me what amounted to the salary of a regional marketing director, for being an assistant manager. I had done nothing wrong;

professionally and personally. I made that statement and they agreed, saying that it was a decision based on numbers. So, who had known about this? They had, obviously, as well as (at least) Carol Woelber, as well as Terry's secretary and Jack's secretary. Next they asked that I not discuss it with anyone on the staff, and that they would tell the staff at the right time.

In less than twenty minutes, I saw a career growth spanning almost eight years, simply evaporate. I was being paid $42,500*, plus benefits, at the time. When you add in the benefits package we had just lost about 70% of our income. *Putting it into perspective, it equates to about $125,000 today.

I left Terry's office and went to my own, passing Terry's secretary Carol Hodapp. It appeared, by her expression that she knew and was waiting to see my reaction.

Without closing my office door, I called Louisa at her office. I wanted everyone, including the marketing secretary, Mary, whom I had hired, to hear what was going on. Of course, Louisa's response was predictable…"***they what?!***"

When I ended the call Terry came into my office and closed the door, saying that I agreed not to tell anyone what was going on and the entire office just heard my conversation. I fired back that I had agreed to nothing of the sort. They had asked me not to, but I had not agreed to their request. "What are you afraid of?" I asked. With that he stood and left.

Of course, I *now* know that I am only one of millions of people who have been treated that way. Many have been treated worse and lost more. In 1987, I was at the leading edge of "downsizing." When you're the one being cut, it's more like what I call "cap-sizing." I still refuse to say that I lost my job. I knew exactly where it was. It was taken from me. I did not lose it.

It's also likely that millions of others have had that experience under similar circumstances…tenuous marital relationship, responsibility for the welfare of five children, and child-support payments, house payments...blah-blah-blah. It has happened so often since it happened to me that our society has become desensitized about it. How many marriages didn't make it through it? How many families have been broken up because of boardroom incompetence and office politics?

I stopped Tracy, and we talked outside the office. I told her that I would beat it. They would *not* keep me down. I didn't know then, that she was no longer a friend or ally.

Next I went to Carol Woelber's office and learned two things; one of them was subtle and profound. Carol asked me to speak softly, because she didn't want to be on record as having talked with me about it. *Say, what?* I told her exactly what had happened and she said that she had been told that there was much more to it. Whatever it was, they were supposedly going to discuss it further detail. I was at a loss. Secondly, the profound thing that I didn't pounce on when she said it was that she was surprised that I didn't have *one friend* in the chain of command that was willing to standup for me and protest what was happening.

Remember back when, referring to Tracy, I said... 'Imagine how surprised I was when she...' Carol also told me that my assistant had complained that I was 'coming on' to her all the time. I asked why there hadn't been any claim filed for harassment? Why wasn't that on any of my records? Why hadn't I been given a warning by management?

I had not been unemployed since I was fifteen years old. The last job I had actually applied for was in 1974, when I left WBCI radio to become a sale rep for WGH-FM.

I wondered what else could go wrong, and then I realized that I hadn't even gone home for the day to face my family.

Months later I understood what Carol had said in that simple phrase. It was so clear when I finally got it. *She* hadn't been friend enough to stand up for me or protest what was happening. *Bob Sorensen* hadn't been friend enough. Not surprisingly, Terry and Tracy hadn't been friend enough. In the next month, only my friend Dwight Rice, then still a Hahn employee would barely discuss it with me. He said word had gone out through the company that no one was to talk with me or there could be repercussions.

At dinner I explained to David and Chris (Harrison) what had happened. I would later venture to Judi's house to talk with her and Kelly and Chris. David and I were already struggling with each other, while Chris and I had been enjoying a good relationship. The impact on David had been more apparent than on the other kids. David was a kid who wanted everything that he saw in advertising and on TV commercials. He didn't understand that we would suddenly have so much less money. I think that, initially it had a stronger effect on his self esteem… that we were suddenly *poor*.

Louisa and I had no idea as to how we would get by, or whether we would. I mentioned the food co-op earlier. Having that available became an important part of how we would get by with so much less money.

I recall one instance while we were driving David to a basketball game at the Cook Park Recreation Center a few days later, Louisa and I were arguing about money. She yelled, "That's just great. Now we can lose the house and you'll be free. You'll get exactly what you've been wanting." I hadn't been thinking that way; not for at least a year.

The next week I had lunch with my friend Rick Garcia. He had left The Hahn Company, moved from Pueblo to Denver. He was managing the small business incubator. He was shocked at my story. He said, "you're Mr. Tivoli" to most of the people in Denver. How could they be so stupid?" I didn't have an answer for that.

CHAPTER 4
It's Big, Old, Goofy World (11)

A couple of weeks later I had breakfast with Randy Gradishar to tell him what had happened, and specifically to ask whether I could use him as a reference. He said, 'sure.' He urged me to get out the resumes quickly. I recall his exact words, "When you stop playing, they stop calling." I thought, WOW! If they weren't calling *Randy*, they wouldn't be calling *me*.

I believed that I could get a job offer with no trouble at all. I had been in the limelight for over two years. I had helped coordinate public relations events and dinners, met dozens of business leaders. I sent out about 300 resumes. I got 5 interviews, 2-second interviews and 1 job offer. I was offered the opportunity to move to Colorado Springs to oversee the closing of a mall. That's the story of the initial job search, beginning to end.

I filed for and was awarded unemployment insurance. The counselor assigned to me told me that the company had initially denied the request, and then reversed its position.

In that fateful meeting with Terry and Jack, I was told that I would not be replaced as assistant manager, for budget reasons. I didn't believe them. I had been in meetings at the corporate level as a regional marketing director, and I knew that they could hire someone fresh out of college, for half the salary that I had been paid.

A month later I asked a friend from the media to call and ask for me. He was told that the company no longer employed me. He asked to speak to the new assistant manager, and was told that the new assistant manager would be joining the Tivoli at the end of (that) month.

We hired an attorney, but when we learned that the attorney handling the file was a friend of a local employee of The Hahn Company, Carol Woelber, I fired him. We hired another attorney who filed a suit based on age discrimination. The Department of Labor investigated the claim and dismissed the suit. It wasn't until much later that I was told about my former fellow employees getting instructions that they were not to talk with me. I'm guessing that it was a violation of my civil rights, and theirs.

After months of paper chasing, it was time to move on and to stop spending money chasing any kind of justice. That doesn't mean that I suddenly got over it.

Louisa, Chris and David went back to Virginia for her grandfather's funeral. I didn't go because I felt that I couldn't justify the expense. Her trip opened a door to an entrepreneurial opportunity, and awakened that spirit in me that I had never acknowledged.

Louisa's Mother took her across the peninsula, to Poquoson, to buy crabs. Somehow in their conversation with the owner, the possibility of shipping fresh seafood to Denver came up.

Louisa called me to ask whether I was interested in brokering seafood, shipped direct from Virginia to Denver. I liked the idea and called the fisherman the next day.

We set up a great arrangement. He would have the catch out of the water before dawn and put it on an early flight with Piedmont Airlines, direct to Denver. I had 90-day contracts with three Denver restaurants and was negotiating with

Alfalfa's market to supply them. The bottom fell out when my supplier became seriously ill just after a break-in at his business. He said that he had to close his business. It was then end of my seafood business.

Looking for any opportunity to make money, I delivered flowers over Mother's Day in 1987. My brother Mike had gotten back together with his ex-wife and moved her to Colorado. She worked for a floral shop and set up both my brother Bob and me to deliver flowers, as needed.

Larry Mostrom, one of the guys I had met while working race events, put me in touch with a guy that he worked for part time, when he wasn't painting houses. The part time job was cleaning carpets in office buildings. Those jobs proved to be my sources of income in 1987.

Another thing was happening, as my world turned into the darkness that everyone who has experienced depression, knows all too well.

My dad had taught me that any work that is legal and ethical is good work. He taught me to work for whatever wage that I had agreed to. I made an effort to live by that advice and actually enjoyed those jobs at times.

The reality is that I had let myself be defeated by those people who terminated my employment. I know there are millions of men who have dealt with the same blow. I grew up in an era where, right or wrong, our work defined us. My self-esteem was fading fast. That didn't lessen the tension at home.

CHAPTER 5
Run, Run, Runaway…(12)

I hadn't run a marathon since May 1985 and I had no desire to run another. However, the pattern that developed was that I would get up and run ten to twelve miles a day, then shower, eat and return to bed. When I wasn't running, or hiding in bed, I spent hours looking out the front window and watching the world go by without me. Any lead for gainful employment became harder and harder to prepare for mentally, or be enthusiastic about. I was in great shape physically, piling up seventy to 100 miles a week on Denver's streets and bike trails. I called them my 'frequent Asics miles.'

It took years before I could get past June 14th without feeling the heavy burden of loss. That's the day, in 1958, that my dad had died in an auto accident. He was 6 weeks shy of his 38th birthday when it happened. My own 38th birthday was very challenging for me. Turning 40, 50 and 60 were so much easier. Louisa didn't really understand how it could still have a significant impact on me so many years later. I didn't either. On June 14, 1987, I was drinking a beer and eating peanuts while lying in a hammock on the front porch. I was sullen. When Louisa came outside and saw me crying, she didn't understand what was going on.

As I was telling her, Bob and Mike pulled up. Bob said, bring the peanuts and we'll buy the tickets and beer. We're going to see a Zephyrs' game. While Louisa may have been concerned about the drinking part, she encouraged me to go. I did. Bob, Mike and I didn't talk about it. I think that silence was my mother's influence.

Running took on another meaning in 1987. I ran away. I loaded the Subaru with camping gear, and a variety of clothing. I didn't know where I was going, only that I was desperate to get away. I spent the first night parked above Georgetown in a place where I'd gone just after the Tivoli grand opening. The situation was different. In 1985 I'd taken a week off, with Louisa's knowledge and blessing, just to unwind. In 1987 she had no advance notice. I just left. She didn't know where I was or how long I'd be gone. I think that she was angry enough with me and tired enough of me, that she just accepted it. I spent about a week away and I did visit a couple of people I knew, but for the most part it was just the Subaru and me. I hadn't been with another woman. Most of what might have happened with any other woman was all in my mind. When I came back we had a heated argument about why and how I left, and where I had gone. When Louisa reconciled the checkbook, she added *Perry's Runaway* in the Memo section on the checks I had used. I'd been predictable and dependable most of my life. At that point I was unstable at best.

CHAPTER 6
Another fork in the road

Because I had hired Sashay to play at the Tivoli, and we often went the Bucksnort Saloon to hear them, I stayed in touch with them. They had approached me, even before I left the Tivoli, to become their manager or booking agent. I had booked a lot of talent while I was the marketing director at the Tivoli. I turned down Sashay. I think I just didn't believe in myself at that time. Keith Riker kept after me, and that fall told me about a young woman whom he'd seen playing music with Don Folguerus, AKA Don Lewis. I had booked Don at the Tivoli as well. He's a good musician who is easy going and easy to be around. Keith had mentioned that her name was Mary…that she played several instruments well and sang with Don too. And, oh by the way, she was great looking. *That's* a great sales pitch. She actually plays and sings so well, that Keith listed her credentials in the right order. He offered to buy the beer if I would go with him to hear them. I did and I met Maree McRae, who has been a friend since.

On November 19, 1987, the day before my 45th birthday, Louisa and I ate lunch together at a fast food restaurant. That may not sound so unusual to most people, but it will to those who know us. We were doing that because she was leaving town on a project for Amoco Production. She would be gone through Thanksgiving, to Gulnare, Colorado where Amoco was conducting coal degas exploration. She would be gone over my birthday and Thanksgiving. I felt like I'd been punched in the gut.

To me, there was irony in Louisa's news about being gone over my birthday and Thanksgiving. I thought about the times when I had to go to California, for corporate meetings over my birthday and on one occasion I was told to fly out there on July 4th because the meetings had to start at 8 AM the next day. We had switched roles, and it was she who was in the position of having to do what the company said, and when.

The next week, my mother came out for Thanksgiving and Bob and Shelli hosted it.

When Louisa returned she confronted me with a question that I hadn't considered. I had been working for the carpet cleaning crew the first day that she was home. When I came home that night she asked, "Who is Diane?" I responded that I didn't know anyone named Diane and asked why she was asking. She said that she answered a call from a female who said that I was cheating on her with someone named Diane. The caller said, "Ask him. He'll know." The caller, whomever and for whatever reason, was dead wrong. I hadn't been cheating on her with anyone. I told Louisa that the only person I could even think of with a name close to Diane was Diana Boulter. Diana had called our house when Louisa and I both were there, and there was never anything between us but a good, more business-related friendship. The caller never called again to the best of my knowledge and Louisa either accepted my explanation, or decided to live with the possibility that I had lied to her about it.

There were other times through the early years when, because we weren't getting along, we weren't intimate. It ran contrary to our attraction to each other. The physical relationship had been good from the start. Yet, with the strains on us, we had each asked at one time or another, 'Are you seeing someone else?'

CHAPTER 7
'Tis the season to be on edge

As Christmas drew nearer, I started delivering flowers again. I gave a portion of what I made, to Judi, for child support. I wasn't giving the amount required by the divorce decree, 20% of my annual income. I was buying some of the clothing for the kids, too, but it caused angry words between Judi and me. I don't know that she and Louisa ever faced off about it.

I was told about one conversation that they'd had, talking about me. Somewhere in that conversation Judi was to have said that I never showed my emotions, but rather that I buried them. Louisa's response was something like, 'Are you kidding? He wears them on his sleeve.' Of course, they were both right, based on their experiences with me.

At that time, my emotions were always on edge. I was very defensive and the anger was never very far below the surface. I could summon it at the drop of a challenging word.

Because we had so little cash flow, Louisa made Christmas presents. Chris and David had been through that before. They had each wanted the popular "powder" jackets and she made them. She probably made them for a lot less than they would cost at retail prices. She made a serape for Kevin that would cover him and his chair. She also made a serape for Kelly, which I really thought she would like. I guess I was wrong. I don't recall ever seeing her with it on. Chris Coons had wanted a University of Colorado jersey, so Louisa got a black jersey and cut out iron-on letters spelling Colorado. I'm quite sure he never wore it. Their reactions, from four of the kids, to the gifts really felt like a low blow to me and I was hurt for Louisa. I know that she created those gifts from her heart. Kevin's reaction was really positive and his smile helped me over come my anger towards the other kids. It wasn't the first or last time I learned from him.

Shortly after Christmas Louisa returned to Gulnare. I don't recall whether it was on the initial trip, or the second one, that she wrecked the company vehicle. You won't be surprised to learn that she took a lot of kidding about wrecking company-owned vehicles. On this occasion, she had lost control while driving on an icy road *and* crossing a cattle guard, driving a Chevrolet Blazer. Fortunately, in this instance too, the Blazer took the biggest hit and she was okay. She really is a good driver. *Really*.

I went out with my brother Bob, while Louisa was gone that week, to hear Sashay. We also connected with Don and Maree. Considering my behavior while drinking, I somehow made the good decision not to go out later with Don and Maree, and a group of people who had been following the band. I recognized my attraction to Maree and I didn't want to deal with it. I think at least two things influenced that decision; I really did miss Louisa and my self-esteem was very low.

Christmas and New Year's passed and I returned to my black hole. I dug in even deeper. Louisa continued to go to and from Gulnare. I was at home with the kids with no work in sight. I was still running a lot. You really can do that year-round in Denver. I was still going back to bed often as well. I recall hearing one of the boys coming in the house in the middle of the school day and I hurried to get dressed so that I wouldn't be caught sleeping during the day.

CHAPTER 8
Is that a light at the end of the tunnel, or…?

I had grown comfortable in my rut of self-pity. My routine was simple. Then, in January Louisa called me from her hotel room in Trinidad and announced that she was going to build an Amway business with or without me. She told me later she wanted me to build it with her, but felt that I wouldn't consider it. She said that she wasn't going to tell her parents just yet. She was so excited that right after she hung up from talking to me she called them.

Paul and Carol were ecstatic and asked what they could do to help, from Virginia. They had been a lot more successful with their Amway business than I knew because I hadn't wanted to know anything about it. Paul had taken an early retirement from NASA because of the income they earned from their Amway business.

After Louisa and I were married we were using a lot of Amway products. I had no problem with that. The quality was good and I'd had some exposure to the products when I had lived with Paul Phillips. Louisa also said that we saved money by buying at wholesale prices. Then a few months after we were married she asked me to sign her renewal card, saying, "You don't have to *do* anything but sign. We're married and I want your name on the registration, too." So I signed the form.

I didn't know much about what she meant by building an Amway business, except my brief exposure to it when I roomed with Paul. To me, it meant inviting a lot of people to some kind of party. It wasn't meant as a reflection of Paul, but I envisioned a room full of guys like Herb Tarlek, the salesman character on the TV show, "WKRP in Cincinnati."

Louisa next told me that there was an annual event held at Snowmass, Colorado near Aspen, and that her parents wanted to send us there for the first few days. It was a weeklong event, and they felt they could afford to pay for our registration and room for three nights. When Louisa told me what they wanted to do for us, the word *our* caught my attention. Louisa went on to say, "You don't have to participate or *do* anything. Just go as my partner, and you can go into Aspen to book the band."

I had been booking Sashay at a few places. Mark Richey, the lead singer had been handling that, and like many artists, not asking for enough money from the clubs where they played. Addressing that was the first order of business. They were playing sports bars, etc for about $75 each for the night…and of course, free beer. The latter's not unimportant in the life of the working musicians I've come to know. It's not uncommon for some of them to drink enough to dig well into their nightly pay. The opportunity to book Sashay in Aspen closed the deal.

The trip to Snowmass wasn't going to take place until mid-March, so I delivered flowers again over the week of Valentine's Day.

CHAPTER 9
You like me. You really like me.

About a week before we left for Snowmass, Bill Michaels called and asked me to meet with him regarding some work that he wanted me to do. I explained that I'd be leaving for the trip to Snowmass soon and he said that wasn't a problem for him. He outlined some public relations work that he needed help with, because of his schedule, and I could start when I got backing town. Bill asked where we were staying at Snowmass. He said 'wow' when I told him. He said that the Wildwood Inn was high end and expensive.

Bob had already agreed to keep track of Chris and David again, so we packed the Subaru for the trip to Snowmass, loading it with winter clothing and gear…and food. We knew we couldn't afford to eat at any high-end resort. Louisa is great at creating meals, good meals, in ways and places that almost no one else would dare to consider. Skis weren't in the budget.

We hadn't been on Colorado's western slope before and enjoyed driving into Aspen Valley for the first time. The Wildwood Inn was easy enough to find. I'd been at The Homestead, at Hot Springs, VA years ago, and what I saw that day didn't look like a high-end resort to me. It's nice enough, it just didn't compare with my frame of reference. If you judge by the cost of the rooms, *then* I'd agree that it's high-end. Anyway, we registered and I met some of the other attendees in the lobby, including the hosts, Chuck and Jean Strehli. Their company was called CLS International, and the event was called SkiGlo.

I had heard about them from Louisa. She had known them since she was sixteen.

Everybody seemed nice enough, and no one was dressed like Herb Tarlek. I had been personally invited to their wine and cheese, and beer, party, so I agreed to go.

One of the things we have always enjoyed about Colorado is the relaxed dress code. I wore a sweater, jeans and western boots to their party. I expected them all to have changed to business dress, and look like 'Herb.' Still, no one did.

There were probably sixty some people at the party. In addition to the free food and beer, I was actually enjoying the people. At some point someone made an announcement that everyone should take a seat. Louisa found me, and told me that I was free to go. I think that when I said that I was enjoying the people and wanted to stay, my response was received first with a look of shock, that became one of pleasantly surprised.

We weren't the only people there who weren't skiing. We may have been the only ones who weren't because we couldn't afford it. However, there were groups meeting during lunch and "après-ski." So, I spent some time with several of those whom I'd met Sunday.

We were only going to be there through Tuesday. That turned out to be significant. Monday we joined the hosts, the Strehli's, at an après ski social hour. They invited us to dinner. However, Louisa had contacted some long-lost high school friend, Haden Gregg, whom she had heard had moved to Aspen years ago…a musician who had followed John Denver to Aspen right after high school twenty years earlier. He had invited us to hear him play with a band that night.

I had been to Aspen Monday afternoon, making attempts to book Sashay, so I knew where he was playing. We did go, and Haden was there, playing with the Bobby Mason Band.

"YOU USED TO LIVE IN MY HOUSE."

I later learned that they're both Aspen Valley legends. We've been friends with Haden and his family since.

When we saw the Strehli's on Monday they told us of an event the next evening that they wanted us attend. It had a name I didn't get, "Diamonds Dine Around" or something. It was a potluck dinner. Some of the people attending the seminar had rented houses rather than stay at the hotel. That part made sense to me. I hurt for Paul and Carol when I saw the shoebox they'd paid for us to stay in. So, we agreed to attend the potluck. I think Louisa had packed enough food to feed them all, but since we had a car there, we were asked only to give someone a ride to a store to pick up ice cream.

It seemed that almost half of the people attending were at the potluck hosted by the Strehli's. I had talked to Chuck and Jean Strehli a good bit, and probably more with Chuck. I had enjoyed and been impressed with virtually everyone I had met, but especially Chuck and Jean. I think one of the things I enjoyed most about them is the lack of pretentiousness. It had been made very clear to me, by others, that they were very high achievers in the Amway business and were very wealthy.

Chuck gathered people and asked each one to share something about his or her experience thus far with the conference. I had been talking with him and was sitting beside him. So, he asked me to go first. I think I surprised Louisa, as much with my comments, as I had that July night when I said we'd grow old together.

At Chuck's request I stood, and said, "I've really enjoyed myself with all of you since we arrived Sunday. I think what has impressed me most is how you treat each other. I have never heard people speak so favorably to or about anyone, as you do, outside of a eulogy." That brought a wave of laughter, but I meant it. I had spent almost eight years in a business atmosphere where company officials talked about transferring people, and even firing people, as "the spring trades," akin to baseball teams trading players. I think the only time I ever heard what I believed was a sincere compliment, by anyone I had worked for, outside of Dave Morgan, was Bob Sorensen's comment about the Tivoli grand opening. And yet he went on to at least approve the termination of my employment. This group of "Amway distributors" was a collection of people from many different geographical locations and careers or professions. I was absolutely amazed. So was Louisa, with regards to my remarks.

I further confounded Louisa by saying that they were people that I wanted to spend my life hanging around. It had been a long time since she had heard me say anything that was that positive or uplifting.

Louisa didn't know that I had sat down with one of the participants, Harry Mauer, an executive with Motorola, that afternoon and asked him to show me how the business worked. They called it "Showing the Plan." I had never seen anyone 'draw the circles,' because I hadn't wanted to know anything about the Amway business. You may have heard the more common pronunciation, **AM**-way. Say it again, with more emphasis on the *AM* and nasal tone. I thought I'd just stumbled on to the Holy Grail. I couldn't wait to get back to Denver to talk to people about my discovery. I just didn't know what to focus on. They had so many products to sell, as I saw it. There was of course, the soap, new vacuum cleaners…we'd already purchased one of them…long distance phone service, voice mail, and on and on. I'd been drinking their coffee for a couple of years.

Louisa had gone off to Snowmass to develop a business she'd had since she was 16, but had let lay dormant since

"YOU USED TO LIVE IN MY HOUSE."

meeting me. She had not expected to come home with a business partner. I had made contacts in Snowmass and Aspen, on behalf of Sashay too. They later played in both locations.

We arrived back in Denver and to reality that afternoon. I didn't get on with my new sales career immediately. It was how I saw the business. I really hadn't gotten the point of those circles that Harry had drawn.

CHAPTER 10
Welcome back to the real world

I also had an appointment to meet with Bill Michaels the day after we got home. He had some *real* work for me to do. While I was excited about the people I had met and the opportunity I thought I had seen, it was all like silly putty to me. Okay, here it is. How do I make something of it? My mind couldn't shape it at that moment, so it would have to wait.

Bill had a contract to handle public relations for Eastern Mountain Sports (EMS) and he had just been awarded the contract to produce the People's Fair. The latter is one of, if not *the*, longest running street festival in Denver, and perhaps in Colorado.

We met and he asked me to work at his office two or three days a week, handling the EMS account. The opportunity to do something productive meant as much as what Bill would pay me. He couldn't afford a lot, but it was all very welcome. One thing I learned very quickly, and believe today, is that Bill Michaels is one of the most generous people to walk the face of the earth. He's almost generous to a fault, usually taking care of himself last.

So Bill, almost single-handedly, helped me get back on track…sort of.

We weren't out of the woods, personally or financially. When I look back at the financial aspect of it, the fact that we were never late on our bills and didn't lose the house stands out.

I call it ***Louisanomics***. The cowboy president had nothing on her. When my salary disappeared we didn't have a car payment or credit card debt.

Most of our arguments centered around how we treated each other on the parenting issues. Our habits, from eating to discipline were different for my kids, from those that their mother practiced. Finding a level playing field was nearly impossible. The divides between David and me, and between Louisa and Chris Coons, became huge crevasses.

Fortunately we can laugh at it now. However, we remember the struggles around the dinner table, over Chris Coons not eating his rice, or piling it in so that he could go with us. I was so harsh with Chris on one occasion that Kelly stood up abruptly and walked out. She'd had enough of how I was siding with Louisa about Chris, as she saw it.

I was still booking Sashay. Keith Riker, the percussionist, was the first to ask about my trip to Aspen. I told him about meeting Haden, and that I'd made contact with managers of a couple of lounges, and the person who booked the Snowmass resort entertainment.

Keith asked me to remind him why it was we had gone there. He didn't recall the reason. So, I told him all about finding the Holy Grail. He asked me to sign him up, wanting to have products shipped direct to his home in Evergreen, but definitely not to sell anything. I didn't care. I had my FIRST DISTRIBUTOR!

CHAPTER 11
Home again, home again

The home front wasn't terribly different. Louisa was back to traveling to Gulnare, and I was at odds with the kids all too often. The two younger ones, David Harrison and Chris Coons, whose birthdays are exactly eight weeks apart, were the more difficult ones.

They were both, ostensibly, attending Merrill Middle School.

I recall one evening when we pulled out of the driveway to go to a parent-teacher conference event. I asked David something about his work and he said he hadn't turned in any of it. Louisa was driving and I asked her to stop less than a block away. I got out, saying "What in the hell am I wasting my time going to the school to hear a teacher tell me what you just old me." I slammed the door and walked back to the house. Of course, in my anger, I became a no-show for Chris Coons too. I rationalized it by telling myself that they weren't showing up for classes, so why should I bother.

You might not want to believe it, but we later had teachers tell us they were passing them on to South High School because they were tired of dealing with them. I have friends in public education that won't like reading that. However, they know it goes on.

It wasn't as though every day was filled with anger and tension, just most. A couple of humorous notes are in order.

I recall that David once asked, "Dad, are you using my deodorant?" I replied that I wasn't and asked why he asked about it. He said his deodorant had hair marks on it.

We live across the street from a church and school. They offer day care, and the school is K through 8th grade, so we have a lot of traffic, especially in the mornings and afternoons.

I think the fastest I ever saw Chris Harrison move happened one morning when I went out to go running and saw his car in the middle of the street. I went back in, and down to Chris' bedroom. He was still asleep until I told him that his car was in the middle of the street. The next site was a blur wearing only blue jeans headed out to move his car. Evidently he didn't have it in gear when he parked the night before.

Even today, one of Kelly's closest friend's is Michelle Trujillo. When they were in high school together, they were inseparable...until one day when Kelly came home with tears streaming down her face. She's cried out, "Michelle and I aren't best friends anymore!" I had a hard time not laughing. It wasn't long before that day was erased from her memory.

It was also at this time that we saw Chris Coons appearance and behavior go south. It was as though someone had thrown a switch. His behavior and appearance changed dramatically; almost overnight. He wanted to look like somebody in the band Guns & Roses. So, his hair was long and often covered his face. It wasn't about the long hair; it was as though he was hiding behind it. My anger and his anger created incredible dynamics. He was also constantly at odds with his Mother at the time.

I didn't understand his anger. I had expected him to be happy after they moved to Colorado. I misread what was going on for him. I knew, but wasn't sensitive enough to the fact that Chris had lost a close friend before they moved from Virginia.

"YOU USED TO LIVE IN MY HOUSE."

Kirk was 11 years old when he died form Leukemia. As I look back on it, I'm sure that I didn't talk with, or more importantly listen to him about Kirk's death. I thought a lot of his anger came from that experience. I later learned that he felt differently; that his anger was about not fitting in with his peers.

Many parents might think about their kids being too invested in sports. The common interest that Chris and I share in sports, specifically the St. Louis Cardinals and the Denver Broncos, served as a line communication for us even in the most estranged of times.

CHAPTER 12
The high cost of learn as you go education

I booked Sashay for the People's Fair and pretty much spent the weekend drinking with them. Louisa was in southern Colorado over that weekend. It was the first weekend in June 1988 and we were headed toward our 5th anniversary. Whoopee! Unlike the previous anniversaries, I don't recall what we did or whether we did it together.

At the same time there was a growing demand for Sashay to play a lot of different and larger clubs. Mark Richey's brother, Mike, was the assistant sports editor for the Denver Post, and because of Mike's contacts, other writers came to see, and then write about Sashay. They were booked in a number of mountain resorts, including Snowmass and Copper Mountain, as well as performing for wedding parties virtually every weekend that spring, and sometimes even two or three.

I booked Sashay at the Steamboat Yacht Club over the 4th of July weekend. It was great weekend for them, and for Louisa and me. The contract included the use of a condo and their meals…as well as their beer…and the highest rate of pay to that point. Louisa and I camped near Rabbit Ears Pass. We all tubed the Yampa River and discovered ice water flows in July.

After that hugely successful 4th of July weekend gig at Steamboat Springs, we started to seriously consider a recording project. Locally produced CD's were not commonplace. The quality of them wasn't consistent. We decided to put together a cassette tape to sell at their gigs and on consignment in local record stores.

I talked with of number of prospective investors, and came up empty. We, who were Louisa and I, took the remainder of the money that I'd been paid as severance and moved forward.

A few weeks after the Steamboat Springs gig, Brian Cole came to town again. This time he and I went camping near the Bucksnort Saloon. When he saw the crowd on Saturday night when Sashay played, he was amazed. He enjoyed their music too. He and I had been camping for two nights and Louisa stayed with me on Saturday night. We all drove back to Denver on Sunday.

We hired an attorney who had worked with entertainers, to write a contract whereby the members of the band would underwrite the money that had been put up for the cost of the project. The band members would pay what monies that weren't recovered by the sales of the cassettes. A fourth member, Mike Reid, who played bass, had been added. We hired a photographer, a graphic artist for the cover and headed into the studio in September.

I knew the studio and the producer from having had Keith Riker record Tivoli commercials there. Keith had done a lot of other voice-over work in the studio as well. The members of Sashay, as musicians, were classic under achievers. I saw a gloomy picture begin to emerge when the studio project began. They weren't prepared in terms of actual material that was ready to record, and hadn't rehearsed enough to get right into recording the tracks. A lot of time and money went into actually rehearsing and re- recording while the studio meter was running. I was not savvy about it and we paid dearly for it.

Other musicians where brought in. Roy Patrick, who played piano, was sort of an unofficial member of the band.

Gordon Burt...the hottest fiddle player in the Denver area at the time, Scott Bennett who was and is a virtuoso musician, and Gannon Kashawa who played base to cover the mistakes made by Mike Reid. We added some Cajun Music with John Magnie, harmonic with Greg Cooperman, also a part time member of the band, and even a cello player. As you can see, it grew rapidly from the three members of Sashay whom I'd met in August 1985.

If we had any misgivings about the product it was that it was too '"tight." The studio was a commercial factory and I thought that much of the tape sounded like a top-notch jingle package. However, the public liked it.

We hadn't always gone with the band when they played. It was different after the project was finished. The only member of the band, who was willing to sell the cassette during their performances, was Keith. So, Louisa took over. The project had created about a $10,000 debt. It could have meant that we'd have to borrow against our home to pay that debt. Louisa hawked tapes before, during and after each performance.

Louisa was still working at Amoco, I was working for Bill, booking Sashay and a few other acts, and delivering flowers when the opportunity arose.

There were many nights and early morning when we would come home from Sashay's gigs, undress on the back patio and shower before going to bed. Almost every place they played was filled with cigarette smoke.

Without Louisa having done that, we would have lost much more money on the project, than we did. I was as deeply invested in second-guessing myself about it, as I was financially.

I also sent tapes to outside sources looking for a chance to get Sashay's talent in front of real recording executives. In

1968, when I was working as a DJ in Williamsburg, Virginia, I'd met and developed a friendship with Austin Roberts who had gone on to enjoy a very successful career as singer and songwriter. At my request he listened to the tape and said that he heard the talent. However, he didn't hear it as a commercially successful sound. Louisa and I had discovered more evidence of synchronicity when I told her about Austin. Her sister, Ellen, had gone to school with him and their parents were friends with his parents. I met Paul Phillips a year after I'd met Austin. I discovered that he and Austin were friends, and for some time, brothers-in-law.

While working for the Williamsburg radio station, I came to know the parents of a very talented young musician named Bruce Hornsby. Bruce's father, Robert, had owned Hornsby Oil Co. and I later learned that Louisa's parents were his clients and acquaintances.

At my request, Lois, Bruce's mother got the Sashay tape to him. Our project came along about two and a half years after he had won the Grammy for "The Way It Is." It was exciting that he would listen to the tape. The word came back to me that Bruce liked some of the writing and offered to talk with Mark Richey about it. When he learned that Louisa and Keith had sold about 600 cassettes, Bruce said that they were at a critical point where they could break through to a different level of success. Have I mentioned that they were under achievers?

Mark never pursued that lead. I, and others, felt that he was afraid of success. Right or wrong it's my value judgment. There's no way to know what might have been. Of course, that's a universal truth, isn't it?

Sashay got a lot of press locally and packed every venue they played at that time. We were inching our way back towards the black ink, or so it seemed. The future had a pretty rosy look to it.

CHAPTER 13
Do you remember your first night?

Handling the PR for EMS, on Bill Michaels' behalf continued well after the People's Fair, and I also began working on other events for him. I could have done it as a volunteer, but he always wanted to pay me something. There were road races more often then than there are these days. So, we kept busy and that was good medicine for me.

I also worked for Bill, on a cross-country ski race in Vail. For some reason, I had my brother Mike's GMC truck over that event and we used it to go to Vail. There was a group of people that Bill pulled together for that and other events. We all roomed at one condo, or another, around Vail. Bill and I spent a lot of time together and he was getting an earful of what was going on with the kids and me, particularly to two younger ones.

Kevin was a delight to be with, and Chris Harrison and Kelly were pretty low maintenance in those days. David Harrison and Chris Coons were incorrigible. Unlike David, who had the consistent support of his mother, Chris Coons was as much at odds with his mother, as with Louisa and me. Their behavior patterns lent to that. David was quiet and seemingly unaffected by any form of discipline. Chris Coons had his dad's temper and the sharp tongue genes from both parents.

In late September, while we were still busy working on the cassette project for Sashay, Bill Michaels put together a plan to bring "First Night" to Colorado. The event was billed as a non-alcohol festival of the arts, held at various cities around the country on New Year's Eve. It had been founded in Boston at the end of the 1976 as the last of the bi-centennial celebrations. Bill wanted me to work with him on that event, too. I think the title of this chapter should be credited to Steve Metcalf. I met him through Bill and then we discovered that our paths had crossed in Elizabeth, Colorado years earlier.

Bill suggested and arranged a meeting with the legendary Barry Fey, to run the idea of bringing First Night to Denver. He's a great resource, the guru for anyone wanting to do special events.

We met with Barry and Bill has referred to Barry's initial comment several times through the years. Paraphrasing, 'I've learned not to do anything on New Year's Eve that doesn't include alcohol.'

First Night was, and may still be a franchised name. First Night Denver had already been registered, so Bill registered "First Night, Colorado," (FNC) as the official name of the event. He set out to gain corporate financing, as he had done with the various sports events through the years. It was near the end of October 1988 when he had rounded up enough financing to produce the initial First Night, Colorado. We had great support from District Attorney Norm Early and David French…a highly respected Denver businessman.

Louisa had wrapped up the sojourns to southern Colorado and was available to help. Bill's sister-in-law, Carol, and a friend of hers from California, rounded out the staff. With five people on staff and roughly 8 weeks to put the event together, we began calling it the First Night fire drill.

I was being paid to line up the entertainment for FNC, for which Bill continuously apologized, in that it wasn't much

"YOU USED TO LIVE IN MY HOUSE."

money. However, it paid better than delivering flowers. Louisa offered to pursue other funding through contracting with street vendors, etc. Bill's sister-in-law, Carol and her friend from California, helped Bill with PR and logistics.

The event began in phases. There was an early celebration at (then) United Bank, for the youngsters, and beginning at 6 pm, 3 different venues near the 16th Street Mall, featuring 14 different acts, including Sashay, at the Paramount Theatre. Admission to the events required the purchase of a FNC button. Everything was to culminate at midnight with fireworks set off from nearby railroad tracks in an area about where the Pepsi Center and Elitch's sit today.

The five of us, along with a legion of volunteers pulled off a pretty good event, particularly with the limited lead-time we had. Bill did a great job of getting the media involved, including live TV coverage by KUSA-TV, 9News.

A few things come to mind, when I think about that inaugural FNC event. For the most part, Louisa and I worked pretty well together, with an occasional spat thrown in, such as 'whose territory is this, yours or mine?' Another was a conversation that Carol and I had, which began with a question about what other kind of work had I done. After my dissertation on my checkered past, she said something like, "You've had an interesting life." 'Yeah,' I thought, and it isn't over yet. I was barely 46 at the time. Of course to Carol, I was way over 30. Later, I learned to laugh about it. Maybe someday I'll write a tell-all book about my checkered past and we'll let the lawyers have at it.

Another thing that happened shouldn't have happened that night. I saw some people connected with the event popping tops on alcoholic beverages. As you no doubt have learned, I was into drinking. However, I got very upset, afraid that it could spell an early death for the non-alcohol event. I didn't keep my anger to myself. I walked away from the event shortly after making all of them angry. I wasn't so angry that I wouldn't grab a couple of beers for myself, hiding them under my coat.

I had booked Sashay at Kailua's Hawaii Restaurant, at the Tivoli, for New Year's Eve, following their earlier appearance at the Paramount Theatre. They were being paid about 30% more, each, than when we started earlier in the year. I wanted to celebrate New Year's Eve there, with them. Louisa had gone to Kailua's about an hour before me. I literally ran over there at about 11: 45 PM, somehow drinking both beers along the way.

The party was well underway as was the countdown to midnight when I arrived. I was immediately given several shots to drink. I don't know what kind of liquor they contained. However, I do know the effect they had on me. I should have taken the warning from The Talking Heads, and their song "Once in a Lifetime"….. "Same as it ever was…same as it ever was" *That* was not a good thing. At some point, for unknown reasons, I unloaded a vicious verbal attack on Louisa. Yes, right there in front of God and everybody at Kailua's on that festive event.

We had just pulled off a successful event, doing a lot of work together, and were having a great time at a wild party and I went bananas in the most negative way. *THAT* became the last time I ever drank anything with hard liquor in it. That having been said, it didn't undo the damage of my verbal assault. I never understood how it had happened. I never escaped the fact that it had. I only learned to accept that it had. Then some four years and four and a half months later, on a ranch in northern California I came face to face with why it had happened.

CHAPTER 14
Caution—Sharp turn ahead

1989: For starters, FNC the staff was to meet for breakfast at a Village Inn. I didn't make it.

During the next week another sharp turn in the path of life. How could I have been so blind? Have you ever had one of those moments when you smack yourself on the forehead with an open palm?

I had missed the early signs that my departure from The Hahn Company was coming, two years earlier. This time it was the revelation that the two lead singers for Sashay, Mark Richey & Deanna Webb, had been living separately during the entire recording project and their split was imminent. It's not uncommon for bands to implode, especially when they're formed around personal and intimate relationships. That news was how my 1989 started.

We had traveled miles together in 1988 and spent many hours in and around the recording studio and I hadn't seen it. They had even dropped me off at home after a recording session, and Mark would drop off Deanna where she was staying.

Mark worked to convince everyone that he was going back to Jacksonville, Florida, where he and Deanna had met, but only for a visit and to rest his voice. He's even a better actor than singer. Some of us actually bought into his story initially. His brother Mike, and his family, had moved there a few months earlier. By the time Mark left, I don't know anyone who believed he'd be back. We all knew that once he was gone, leaving whatever he was running from, he wouldn't be back. The band played a finale at the Bucksnort Saloon in February, and was never together again.

My attention turned to collecting money from each of the band members, for their share of the cost of the recording project, and to working more events with Bill Michaels. I started counting up the failed business ventures, brokering seafood and promoting bands and wondering just what the future had in store.

Deanna had crawled into a dark hole after Mark left. Whether she was suicidal I am not qualified to say. I know that Louisa took food to her and when Deanna wouldn't answer the door, Louisa left it for her. Later Louisa was able to coax Deanna to open up and then invited her to stay with us, which she did until she moved to Steamboat Springs that spring.

I want to point out, to clear the record about the recording project, that Keith did pay his entire share of the unpaid balance. Deanna did also, part of it paid in cash and part of it with items such as furniture, etc that she left behind. Mark paid part of it and then stopped paying anything, a year or so later. Mike fought me in court, over the contract and won his case. It was the judge's opinion that he should pay nothing. In my opinion that mirrored his contribution to the group, so I guess we were even.

In May, Bill and I attended a conference for cities hosting a First Night event. The conference was held at Springfield, Illinois. Bill and I flew to St. Louis, which allowed me to start my return trip from there, and gave me the opportunity to visit my mother after the conference. Bill and I were supposed to have made a connection from St. Louis to Springfield, but due to severe electrical storms our flight was cancelled. We rented a car and shared it with others whom we had met at the airport, and drove on to Springfield. After the conference I rode the train from Springfield to Alton and had a couple of days with my Mother before returning to Denver. Of course that gave me an opportunity to go out drinking with my relative who had been our "house guest" when I left my own party in 1986. At some point, I'm sure his wife wanted to disconnect the phone when my brothers or I were back in Alton.

Louisa and I had some real bouts during that period and I began to think that we weren't going to make the relationship work long enough to grow any older together. During that period that I really began to wonder if I had it in me to persevere in a relationship, or business venture that involved working with her.

My friend Rick Garcia and I were eating lunch at Tosh's one-day and I was explaining to him that I was frustrated and that I felt stalled with my Amway business. I knew that it was because I didn't feel so committed to my marriage at the time, that I really didn't know if I *wanted* to build a business with Louisa. Rick just said, "I don't get it." It took a while for me to realize that he didn't know the nature of the Amway business.

I was wondering 'how do I talk with couples about building *their* business, when I'm not sold on *our* business.' It wasn't the business, but our relationship that I was questioning.

CHAPTER 15
Put on a happy face

Somehow we shelved the tension long enough for a trip to Virginia, for her twenty-year class reunion. I enjoyed visiting with her family and various friends. Even though I'm 9 years older than Louisa we found that we had many friends and acquaintances in common. It was probably at that reunion when I discovered that I had, a year before meeting her, dated one of her classmates. I also knew her longtime friends Bill and Mary Kay. They'd participated in the antique shows at Newmarket north.

I was searching for some spark to generate some positive activity, professionally and personally. I was hiding my inner torment and self doubts that were becoming so active in my thoughts.

I hadn't done much with our Amway business after signing up Keith Riker in 1988. Paul and Carol encouraged me to give more time and energy to that business, for our long-term future. They weren't aware that I was questioning whether Louisa and I even *had* a long-term future. Even though 1988 had been a productive year for me, I had badly slipped back to my poor attitude of 1987 by the time we went back to Virginia in 1989.

The trip to Virginia was good for me, and for us. I always enjoyed the time with Louisa's parents, and the chance to get to know her sister, brother-in-law and their family a little better. We spent some time with or friends, David and Julia

Scoggins, too. Louisa and Julia had known each other since early childhood, and Louisa had known David since he and Julia started dating in high school. When I met them, while Louisa and I were dating, I developed my own friendship with them. I had visited them on my trips back to Virginia when Kevin, Kelly and Chris still lived there. It turned out that Kelly, and Melanie Scoggins, their daughter, had once had dance lessons together.

I had found that I could talk with David about my challenges with Louisa and he always had a way of tweaking my perspective in a positive way that made sense to me. What I saw, and still see in that couple, has always been good for me in terms of the give and take that I perceive in their relationship.

Once we were back in Colorado, it was time to start planning for the next First Night, Colorado. We would establish more venues, featuring more entertainers, and offer better transportation to and from them with a cooperative effort in partnership with RTD, the area transit system. Bill had done a great job of expanding the funding base.

The idea that my marriage was failing became a constant cloud over my head. I didn't see any light at the end of the tunnel that we had built. I felt that Louisa was challenging me more often, even in public, and around the staff and volunteers for FNC. As I've mentioned, Bill was my number one sounding board through all of this. That's not to say that he agreed with me on everything that I was complaining about. He would always ask how things were going. I know that he did it out of caring and hoping that he'd hear something positive.

On one occasion Louisa and I had gone to dinner with Bill and Laura Michaels at the Wazee Supper Club. We rarely socialized with them, for no particular reason that I've ever known. We had a good time with them, except that it became one of those occasions when I would drink too much. When we left, Louisa asked to drive. I was belligerent in my refusal, and after a few blocks of my driving, she demanded to be let out of the car…to the extent that she opened her door and said that she would jump even while the car was moving if she had to. In a drunken rage, I yelled and pulled over to let her out. She walked home that night…a four-mile walk.

First Night, Colorado and the PR for Eastern Mountain Sports kept Bill and me busy. However, it was becoming more obvious that working special events was never going to create financial prosperity, or for that matter, pay the bills.

New Years Eve rolled around and we had a bigger and better event, with fireworks from the D & F Tower on the 16th Street Mall. That was an idea that was not well received by the Denver Fire Department at its inception. We got a lot of help from the pyro-tech expert Bill had found. Mike Carlisle, who somebody nicknamed Boom Boom, had been a fireman in Vail and was able to present his plan in such a way that the DFD could support it, and us.

That wasn't as much of a concern as the two men we had hired to set up and wire the big lights display that would change from 1989 to 1990. I had found them and, looking back on it, I don't know what I was thinking when I brought them into the event. The two brothers had locked themselves into the space where they were to wire the lights and we had every reason to believe they were drinking. Everything about the event was coming together smoothly. However, after making several attempts to get them to open the door, we just had to wait until the clock struck midnight before we would know whether the lights would work. They did and the crowd, numbered in the thousands, according to the police, roared with excitement. I was on a stage with a local band and not with Louisa. For me, it was just a case of working up until the last second. She got her New Year's kiss from a friend. We did find each other a few minutes later and helped with the clean up. Then several of us did get together at the Village Inn in Cherry Creek.

The next week I met with Bill and a couple of others who were working for him at the time, to lay out plans for the annual Governor's Cup Cross Country Ski Race at Devil's Thumb near Fraser, Colorado. He had something else to share.

Bill had a Request For Proposal, (RFP), from the Wyoming Centennial Commission, to submit a bid to coordinate their centennial celebration. That possibility seemed exciting from the outset. Bill, Tracy Ulmer, who'd joined Bill's staff, and I put the proposal together prior to the Governor's Cup, which would take place the first weekend in February. Collectively we had a pretty good resume for an event of that size. However, we were concerned that being from Colorado could be somewhat of an issue.

When we went to Devil's Thumb, Louisa went along, as well as Chris, Chris and David. Bill had arranged for us to have a condo so that the family could come along. That was good for us. However, nothing stands out in my recollection of that event like the incredible cold weather. It was my second trip to Devil's Thumb for that event and by far the coldest I had ever been, anywhere. It wasn't safe for small animals or brass monkeys.

CHAPTER 16
A statewide love affair

I think the only reason I ever watched the TV show, "Cheyenne," was that Clint Walker hailed from the Alton area, specifically Hartford, as I recall. The theme song has stayed in my head all these years.

Shortly after we returned from Devil's Thumb, which couldn't have happened too soon, Bill called to say that he had been invited to Cheyenne to meet with the chairman and director of the centennial commission. He wanted a strong presence, and wanted Tracy and me to go with him. We had a couple of strategy sessions and only a few days after the Governor's Cup event, we were off to Wyoming. I had only been to Cheyenne once before that day, when Louisa, Chris, David and I toured some museums there, shortly after moving to Denver.

In Cheyenne, we met with the director for the Wyoming Centennial Commission, Jeannie Bryant, along Dick Hartman, a railroad executive who served as chairman of the commission, Dennis Frobisch, a PhD historian on leave from the University of Wyoming and Becky Evans who served on the commission staff. Bill presented his plans for the centennial's festival events, which would take place on the capitol grounds over four days in July. Tracy and I were asked to brief them on our backgrounds.

After the initial meeting in Jeannie's office, they took us on a tour of the areas of the Capitol grounds where the events would take place. I suggested some changes based on where the sun would hit those who would be performing on the stages, traffic flow, ingress and egress, etc.

When we returned to Jeannie's office they conferred with Bill only. After a while Bill emerged and talked with Tracy and me and then with me alone. He had told us that they were leaning toward hiring us. They knew they would take some heat for hiring a company from out of state, and wanted to have someone in Cheyenne on a full-time basis, February through mid-July.

When Bill and I met alone he said they might go for it if one of us was there most days of the week. He knew that it wouldn't work for him to be away from home for so long, with his daughter Anna being a baby. He knew that I was struggling with the stress of my home life and wondered whether it might be good for me to be away for a while. He applied no pressure on me, saying "I want you to do it only if that works for you. I'd rather pass on the event than to cause more difficulties for you at home." I told him that I would do it and that it might be more stressful to be at 'home.'

He told Dick and Jeannie that I had agreed to office in their space if we were awarded the contract. Next, I had to tell Louisa.

That evening I talked with Louisa and Chris about my new venture. She wasn't at all opposed and I don't recall that Chris offered an opinion. No doubt, she was looking for a break from me, and from my anger. David wasn't there and that had become the norm. He wanted to move out and was only a few months away from being able to do so legally.

In Colorado, kids are legally allowed to move out at age 16. I don't agree with it, not that *that* had any effect on it. I even more strongly oppose the legal system's use of the term, emancipation, to describe it. When I think of emancipation, I think of The Emancipation Proclamation and I see the use of it for teenagers to leave home, as an affront to those who were legally freed from slavery on January 1, 1863. I was getting ahead of myself before I got to that, so I'll get back on track now.

My first trip to Cheyenne, as the Statehood Festival Coordinator, was by bus. Jeannie Bryant met me at the bus station and took me to The Hitching Post Inn where she had reserved a room for me. Since none of us knew what my stay would look like, there was some disagreement as to whether I should stay at the motel while in town each week, or rent a small apartment. The powers that be finally decided that The Hitching Post Inn would be my home. I spent the next several days getting introduced to and acquainted with people from various state departments who would be involved in the four-day festival.

I fell in love with Wyoming and it's people in pretty quick order, even though some did tease me about my being a "Greenie." The centennial commission did get some negative hits from the media over hiring outsiders to coordinate the state's 100th birthday party. For the benefit of those who haven't heard Coloradoans called "Greenies," it comes from the license plates that have the mountain range outlined in green. They were standard issue back then, as opposed to the wide variety of plates available today.

Staying and working in Cheyenne, three to seven days in a given week provided the break from the daily tensions that I felt at home. It also meant that I wasn't there for the good times, or to support Louisa and the kids when they needed it. Chris Harrison and Kelly rarely caused any problems. Kevin was never a problem for me. However, by working out of state it also meant that I wasn't there for him, or to carry my share of the responsibilities for him. I got what I wanted. However, it didn't always look like I thought it would. So much for having it all go my way.

We had only one car at the time. We had sold the old Subaru in 1989 and picked up at 1981 Volvo 240DL at an auction. I wasn't going to take that to Cheyenne and leave Louisa without a car all week. Once I got to Cheyenne, it was easy enough to walk to and from the office, and to most places I wanted to go to. The hotel shuttle was available also.

I learned that I could ride the airport shuttle bus to Cheyenne and get there faster and quicker. It also would drop me at the hotel where I stayed. I just had to get to the Stapleton Airport to make the connection.

During a March trip to Cheyenne, while we made the usual the stop in Fort Collins to pick up other passengers, it began to snow. As we waited for a connecting shuttle to bring more passengers, the snowfall became heavy. By the time they arrived the snowfall was fierce. Our driver was convinced that we had time to get to Cheyenne before the roads were closed. It's not uncommon to have highways closed in that part of the country during blizzards, and suddenly we were in one. There were about 12 people packed in the shuttle van as we moved slowly up I-25.

We were moving at a slow and steady pace when the line of vehicles came to a stop. There were two items of interest to me, about where we stopped. One I would learn later when the snow cleared, and the other caused us to be there until it did. A state trooper had stopped us to tell us that it was snowing heavier just north of us. He had stopped us on a small hill. However, it was enough of a hill that we couldn't get going again. We were forced to spend the night right there, in the van. We were told not to venture out in the blizzard, though a couple of people did, to smoke. The driver was smart enough to have filled both gas tanks on the shuttle van, and he could keep the engine running all night.

When day broke the next morning, and the snow stopped, a plow cleared enough snow for us to continue the 7 miles to Cheyenne. That's how close we had come before being stopped…at the Perry Ranch Exit.

I got to Cheyenne a day later than my room reservation, but the room had been held for me. I called Louisa at my first opportunity. She had no way of knowing that we were stranded. 1990 was a pre-cell phone era for me. After calling her and telling her about my great overnight adventure, I settled in the restaurant for a meal. I spent the day watching TV because everything in town was closed. There were piles and drifts of snow.

It wasn't until I arrived at work the next day that I learned that I had missed a snow-bound party. I was told that they were not uncommon in Cheyenne. I think, at least back then, no parties were uncommon in Cheyenne. The Wild West was alive in 1990. I was told that they had called the Hitching Post, *after* I had arrived and told that I wasn't in. So they assumed that I had stayed in Denver because of the storm. The more I learned about the party, the angrier I got. They would have come out in a 4-wheel to pick me up, too. I didn't miss many Cheyenne parties after that.

Working on the 4-day statehood festival was a lot more fun than work. It was the first time that I had felt passionate about my work since my early days in radio. I had a lot of freedom, and yet reported to and interacted with dozens of people. Dennis and Becky very helpful and became good friends. My office cubicle was located in an area where attractive women surrounded me.

CHAPTER 17
Boom-Boom and the bike

The situation created some interesting personal as well as professional dynamics for me. I was a hundred miles from home and the everyday challenges…and pleasantries it encompassed. I was drinking a lot, having fun with some great people and doing work that I really enjoyed. Yes, there were tempting situations and opportunities, some more so than others. Of course, many of those with whom I was interacting were women, and I had lunch, or drinks or dinner with some of them. There was every opportunity to cross the line back into my old ways. I did meet attractive women who showed a personal interest in me. Looking back I believe that some force that was watching out for me guided me. I had the opportunities and the urge. I danced and drank, and somehow didn't cross that line. I didn't have sex, by my description or Bill Clinton's, with anyone but Louisa.

No doubt, there were stories to the contrary because of the flirting and the opportunities. It's just that I don't have to worry about it because I know what I lived.

In late April, Boom-Boom arrived on the scene, as Bill had sub-contracted with him to handle the fireworks at the festival finale. It was great because Mike could talk the talk that the Cheyenne Fire Chief could relate to. If my recollection is correct, he or someone in the department, and Mike, had worked together in Colorado at some point.

A significant aspect to Mike's presence came about when he told me that he had a 1975 Honda 55 Super Sport in his garage in Pueblo, Colorado. He offered to deliver it to my house, in Denver, the next week when he returned to Cheyenne. He said, "Ride it and if you like it, you can buy it." It would allow me to ride to Cheyenne, rather than ride the shuttle and the weather was turning favorable for it.

True to his word, Mike delivered the motorcycle the following week. I rode it around the neighborhood for my first motorcycle ride in almost 20 years. I loved it!

When Louisa came home and saw the motorcycle, I told her about Mike's offer and an argument followed. She was dead set against my riding it, or any cycle.

The next morning when she was leaving for work, knowing that I was heading back to Cheyenne, she asked me not to ride it to Wyoming. I told her that I'd take the shuttle again. I lied. I loaded the bike with a coffee maker for my hotel room…they were not common amenities in those days…and other items and headed off to Cheyenne. I had called to arrange insurance, but I didn't have a motorcycle driver's license, which Colorado requires. So imagine the paranoia when, stopped at my first traffic light of the trip, there was a police car behind me. I could almost hear David Crosby singing, "…this increases my paranoia. Yeah, like looking in my mirror and seeing a police car." (16) The good news was that, when the light changed, I controlled the bike successfully and was off to Cheyenne, via Highway 85. I did not want to get on I-25 on the bike.

When Louisa came home and saw the bike was gone, she called to share her fury. I knew that I had done the wrong thing and my lying had made it worse. That, plus riding the bike, had hurt her and damaged our relationship. The fact that I had made it safely or that I had secured insurance was of little consequence to her. I understood that and I offered no defense. I was told, 'don't bother to come home this weekend if you're going to ride that motorcycle!'

By the end of the week Louisa and I had talked several times and while her anger had diminished, she was no less emphatic about my riding the bike to Denver. So, I stayed in Cheyenne over that weekend.

It was a great looking bike and in great shape, with only about 25,000 miles on it. It had been an easy ride to Cheyenne the day before. I left the office early that first day and riding out toward Laramie. I turned around at Curt Gowdy State Park because of the high winds. No surprise there.

I talked with the kids fairly often, and did so that weekend explaining that I would be in Cheyenne all weekend. The kids were basically ok with that. However, the ex-wife was not. She felt that I was neglecting Kevin by not spending more time with him, and reminded me that I was not providing the child support that I was obligated to. She was right on both counts. I felt that I was not there for Kevin, or the other kids. As for the child support, I wasn't sending the full amount per my divorce decree, but what I thought was an amount that I could send to help the kids, and still have something to live on. I wasn't making a lot of money coordinating the Wyoming Centennial Statehood Festival. Of course, I signed for all of the billing, and was well aware that Bill wasn't making a lot either. When someone takes on a project such as the centennial, it's more for the challenge and resume, than the money. I also rationalized about what I sent because I knew that Louisa never received any child support from her ex-husband.

I did ride to Denver the following weekend and then twice in May. Louisa surprised me on Mother's Day, appearing when I answered a knock on the motel room door. I hadn't expected anyone, so I'm glad it was she. I was wearing only a sweat suit, and then only for a little while at that.

We drove to Laramie for lunch that day and then she headed back to Denver that evening.

CHAPTER 18
Pain makes the heart grow fonder

I went back to Denver over Memorial Day weekend, as all of the state offices were closed. It was then that we learned that a friend Bob Hook had died unexpectedly while on a fishing trip with his brother-in-law. Natalie and Louisa worked together and we had socialized with her and Bob several times. We hurt for her, and their two sons, Andrew and Lee. Natalie was younger than my Mom had been when my dad died and she was left with the four of us. Andrew was probably not quite three and Lee was a baby.

It was now even more difficult for Louisa to accept that I would be riding the bike back to Cheyenne. We had just been given a dramatic reminder of our mortality. She had begrudgingly accepted it and I promised to call as soon as I got to Cheyenne. I was about 25 miles from Cheyenne when I saw huge dark clouds in that direction. It was already getting cold, so I had put the rubber suit over the heavy clothes I was wearing. I got to Cheyenne and drove straight to the underground parking. I went to the office, called for the hotel shuttle and then called Louisa. I didn't tell her about the storm that I had been racing, or that Cheyenne was getting freezing rain and some snow at the time.

Mike Carlisle was back in town the next week and I told him that I wanted to buy the bike. I loved it. He offered it for only $425.00. I told him that I needed to run it by Louisa first and he was agreeable to that.

While I was in Cheyenne, Bill had a crew putting together the grand opening of the new Colorado Convention Center, scheduled for June. He asked if I wanted to come to Denver to help. I had already heard him talk about all of the red tape and bureaucracy he was dealing with. I told him thanks, but I'd pass on the invitation. I had also told him about the virtual non-existence of red tape or bureaucratic hoops in Wyoming. I did offer to come to celebrate with him and drink his beer.

I went to Denver and enjoyed the grand opening celebration. Then on Saturday, I took Louisa with me to look at the convention center. While we were walking from the car I told her that I wanted to buy Mike's bike...for only $425. She cried and through her tears told me that she didn't want me to have it at any price. She said it was the saddest day of her life. She begged me not to do it. She feared for my safety. I had seen her cry like that only twice before. I had caused it early on in our relationship, which I've described, and one of our neighbors once brought her to tears with his harsh words.

Thinking back to it, I wonder how I could have gone through with it, seeing her in that state. My thinking has changed a lot since then. Yes, I bought the bike.

When I made my trips back to Denver it reminded me of the first six months of 1983, with what I felt were the many demands made of my time. It was a challenge to juggle the responsibilities of the statehood festival at the risk of ignoring my family in Denver. I loved my work. I loved my family... even more from a distance.

I interfaced with the Governor, Jim Sullivan, primarily through his liaison Leonard Bucsayne, although more directly as the event grew nearer. I also interfaced with the centennial commissioners, various state officials, local civic organizations, and representatives from each of the 50 counties as well as the law enforcement authorities at every level from the Cheyenne Police to the ATF agency. To make matters more complicated President George Bush would be visiting Cheyenne shortly after the festival, so the Secret Service had representatives at some of the briefings as well. When I say it became more complicated, I mean only in terms of how I used my time. In every instance, people were cooperative and straight to the point.

I was spread thin, but always had time for happy hour, and in Cheyenne happy hour was not only from 4 to 7 or 8 PM, in many bars it was revived at 10 PM.

Throughout the planning and execution of the statehood festival, we got a lot of help and cooperation from the people who put together Cheyenne Frontier Days. They had very few paid employees and knew exactly how to get things done. They had been doing it for almost the same length of time that Wyoming had been a state. As the statehood festival drew near, the group from the Frontier Days staff asked how long I would be in Cheyenne following the festival. I told them that I had planned a trip with my wife, to Jackson, accepting an invitation from a centennial commissioner, Mary Meade to stay at her ranch and then would be back to Cheyenne to wrap up. They made an offer that I couldn't refuse…free passes to the Frontier Days events. I decided then that it would take at least until the end of July to finish my reports, etc.

I made trips back to Denver for the graduation exercises for both Chris Harrison and Kelly. Chris had graduated from South High School and initially didn't want to go to the ceremony, to be held at the Boettcher Hall at the Denver Performing Arts Center. Louisa made it clear to him that he was going, that it was as much for her as for him. As it ended we saw his excitement. He waved his hands in the air as he received his diploma.

Before her graduation, we gave Kelly a new set of tires for her Volkswagen Sirocco. I recall running from our home in Washington Park to Alameda High School to pick up the car and then back home after I brought it back to the school. I was in great shape in those days, in spite of all the late hours and drinking while in Cheyenne. We went to her graduation too. There was never a doubt that Kelly would enjoy her graduation.

In July I, offered to have Chris Coons ride to Cheyenne with me to celebrate his 16th birthday. David and Kelly had each ridden on the bike with me, although not that kind of distance. Chris was all for it, not realizing that it was a little more than 100 miles to Cheyenne.

On the Friday before his birthday, I picked up Chris at his mother's house. She greeted me with an outburst about money. Chris intervened, saying that whatever the money issues were, he felt that I had always been there for him. It didn't really resolve the issue, but we did manage to get on the road to Cheyenne without much more delay. He had ridden on motorcycles before, but not that far. I don't think he enjoyed the ride very much. In Cheyenne we went to dinner and a movie and spent the next day riding around Cheyenne and watching TV. He rode the shuttle back to Denver on Sunday. I watched the shuttle leave and I felt empty. It was too little, too late. I was desperately seeking to connect with him. When he left, I felt that I had failed again.

At that point we were about a week away from the Wyoming Statehood Festival. Louisa came to Cheyenne the next weekend to help coordinate the volunteer assignments, staying with me through the events.

I didn't return to Denver before Kelly's birthday on the 16th. However, I was able to see her before then, because she

"YOU USED TO LIVE IN MY HOUSE."

accepted my invitation to drive to Cheyenne, with a friend, to see the centennial finale, featuring Chris LeDoux and The Western Underground, followed by the best fireworks show I've ever seen.

It's worth a diversion to share with you how it was to work with Chris LeDoux. You can read his biography easily enough on the Internet, and learn that he was a living legend in Wyoming. He died in March 2005. I'd learned enough about Chris LeDoux from Dennis Frobisch to convince me that he was not only the best choice, but also the only choice for the finale concert.

I had already enjoyed the friendship of celebrities such as Austin Roberts, Chad Stuart, Bob Eubanks, and Randy Gradishar. They're each as humble as they are talented. I was about to get to see homegrown humility that approached "aw shucks."

I hadn't heard of Chris LeDoux before joining the centennial staff. It was Dennis who offered to loan me several cassettes. I couldn't believe the sound, and more over that it hadn't caught national attention. That was changing because of Garth Brooks' 1989 hit song, "Much Too Young To Feel This Damn Old," that mentioned LeDoux.

When I set my sights on getting Chris LeDoux to perform for the finale I was told that he would be too expensive for our budget. I finally reached him by phone at his ranch and talked with him about our plans. He was quick to accept my invitation. Chris was so easy to deal with. He wanted to take care of his band and be a part of the centennial celebration. What a treat to be able to bring him to Cheyenne, and what a performance they gave!

After the clearing of the capitol grounds, Louisa and I left for Jackson and a few days of just being with each other. Mary

Meade showed us around her ranch and opened the guesthouse cabin for us. She had business to attend to and we were off to play tourist in Jackson Hole. The time together was good for us. I felt more connected with Louisa than I had in months, perhaps longer.

Louisa dropped me off in Cheyenne and headed back to Denver. She planned to return to Cheyenne for the opening of Frontier Days. I began the task of wrapping up my work in Cheyenne, but I was in no hurry to leave. I even thought about looking into job openings at the radio and TV stations and staying there.

The Wyoming Centennial and Statehood Festival celebration had been an overwhelming success. Governor Sullivan presented us with a proclamation for "Bill Michaels & Co. Day." It just was anti-climactic to wrap up and face leaving the people I had come to enjoy so much. Yet, I was optimistic about going back to Denver, to be with Louisa.

CHAPTER 19
From Living Legacy to The Grand-daddy of them all…

Louisa was back in Cheyenne on the 20th of July for the opening of Frontier Days parade and a concert featuring Chicago. I have never seen a parade that compares with the parades that take place during Cheyenne Frontier Days.

Louisa headed back to Denver the next morning. I followed a few hours later on the bike. I went back to Cheyenne on Monday, ostensibly to wrap up the paperwork, and more so to take advantage of the free pass to Frontier Days. It was remarkable. I saw The Judds and Clint Black that week, and I was just learning who they were.

There was one day during Frontier Days that the state offices closed. What follows is one hell of a party. For several months I had socialized with members of a local band, "Avenue," and their families. I spent much of that day and night with them, bar hopping and listening to dozens of bands. Since my transportation was a motorcycle, I left it for the day and we walked from one end of that town to another. Later, in the evening, I took the hotel shuttle to and from other restaurants and bars. I had never seen anything like it. I noticed that no bars were selling anything in glass. You got a plastic cup for whatever you were drinking. I know that must have come from some hard lessons.

On the last morning there, I rode to the Herschler Building, where I had officed. I picked up Dennis Frobisch, to go to the pancake breakfast served up each morning of the event, in a parking lot downtown. Riding a motorcycle while drinking was something I had not done to that point in my life. Riding a motorcycle with a hang over may be as bad. I was very unstable until I had eaten and had several cups of coffee.

It was difficult to leave Cheyenne that day. I felt so at home there. I had enjoyed the work immensely and the people even more. However, it was time to begin another chapter in my life, and I was anxious to go home to Louisa and the kids. So, after having a drink with Dennis that afternoon, I bid happy trails, to Cheyenne.

CHAPTER 20
Regrets, I have a few (17)

The following week I picked up Kevin after school and had him with me all weekend. I caught up with Kelly and Chris briefly. The next weekend Louisa and I took Kelly to dinner, as a belated birthday gift.

Not long after that, I realized that I still wasn't happy with my family life. Louisa's parents had traded one of their timeshares so that we could go to St. George, Utah and the Grand Canyon. Regrets come from bad decisions that can't be undone, and I made one at that time. I told Louisa that I didn't want to go to St. George, and that I wasn't sure about our relationship. I didn't know what else to tell her, but that I didn't feel good or confident about it. She cancelled the reservation and wanted to repay her parents for the deposit, but they wouldn't allow it. Suffice to say that we were entering a new period of doubt and uncertainty about our marriage.

Instead of going to Utah with Louisa, I packed up the motorcycle and headed to the mountains, camping near Deckers, about 60 miles southwest of Denver. It rained hard during most of that weekend.

Also, while I was gone we had a visit from the mother of Anabella Gavica, the young girl who'd been our houseguest 4 years earlier. She was on her way to Kansas with Anabella's brother.

When I got back to Denver I found a note from Louisa asking me to come downtown because she had tickets to the Grand Prix time trials. Louisa is nothing, if not resilient.

Another week later I added another regret to what seemed to be a growing list. My brothers, Bob and Mike, had been talking and had connected with our brother Pat...that was no mean task...about hooking up in Alton. The four of us had not been together in many years.

Two regrets in one...

I didn't invite Louisa and we didn't take Kevin. Judi had offered the use of her mini-van if we would take Kevin. I don't recall my excuse. However, it would have also provided room for Louisa. I took the Volvo, carrying Kelly, Chris Coons, Mike and his son Michael J and drove to Illinois. I still look at the photos of my brothers and me with my Mom, from that visit and feel hurt and shame that I did not include Louisa and Kevin. I should add that Chris and David had shown no interest making the trip. I hadn't seen David much since returning from Wyoming.

I've been able to let go of a lot of things from the past over the years. That event isn't among them.

Mike was going to drive a car back to Denver from Alton, so Michael J and Chris stayed to ride with him. Kelly and I headed back in the Volvo. It was the first time she ever drove it and I had to slow her down a few times early on.

The homecoming was cool at best. Louisa has a forgiving way of working through things that hurt her, or that she doesn't agree with.

CHAPTER 21
I do remember my last…First Night

It was suddenly the fall of 1990 and I was involved in the planning of First Night, Colorado again.

The event was going to be much larger, with more venues and entertainment in this its third year. That was well and good, but I told Louisa that it didn't feel the same. It didn't hold the same excitement for me. She said, 'no wonder. They practically canonized you in Wyoming.' That may be true, but another aspect was the movement towards planning the entertainment by committee. Even before the event took place, I knew that I wouldn't be back for event the following year. FNC would officially become a non-profit organization and committees would make the decisions that I had been allowed to make. I had reported to so many people in Wyoming that I knew it wasn't about reporting to anyone or being accountable to others. From what I could tell, none of the people I met, who would be a part of the new FNC, had experience in booking entertainment. And several of them thought the entertainers should perform for free.

I headed towards the end of 1990 with growing uncertainty about my marriage and what I would be doing for work in the future.

There was enough work to do with First Night, Colorado to keep me busy. We would have fourteen stages, and a total of eighty-five acts running simultaneously, or concurrently over a twelve-hour period, with the finale once again showcased by fireworks from the D & F Tower.

BOOK FOUR

CHAPTER 1
A profound act of cowardice…

In mid-December my friend, Don Folguerus, asked me if I knew of anyone who could house sit his apartment the first three months of 1991. He was going to be living and working in Summit County for the first quarter of the new year. I think I surprised myself as much as I surprised him when I said that I would do it. The next day he showed me the apartment, about 2 miles from our home in Washington Park. Once I had committed to it, I became consumed with fear. I was about to take a huge step and maybe make a huge mistake. Inside I knew that I loved Louisa. I thought about it constantly and wondered whether love was ever going to be enough to make us happy.

I recalled a time when I was storming out of the house during an argument, years earlier, and Louisa jumped on my back to stop me from leaving. So, I rationalized that the only way I could leave was to do so without telling her in advance.

We were so out of touch with each other that she wasn't aware that each day, over the last two weeks of the year, I had been taking clothing and personal items to Don's apartment. There was no thrill in it. Each trip I made, I questioned whether or how I could do what I was doing. I had committed to Don. So what? I had committed to Louisa.

Only Don knew anything about what was going on. I did not even confide in Bill, who had become my confidante. Don had met Louisa, but didn't know her well. He is very much a 'live and let live' person and wasn't really involved in my decision.

January 3, 1991 was Kevin's twentieth birthday. Instead of being with him, I moved the last of my personal items to the apartment after I had taken Louisa to work, and Chris had gone to work. It was not uncommon for me to take Louisa to work, the drop off the car later and run home.

Early in the afternoon, I wrote notes to Louisa, and to Chris and David, explaining why I had left. I parked the car near Louisa's office, and ran to the apartment. I called her, and sighed in relief as I heard her voice mail greeting. I left a message stating *only* where I had left the car.

Louisa had no idea what I had done until she got home and read the note. I called Judi and told her that I wouldn't be there for Kevin that night, and I told Kelly what I had done. Chris Coons had exercised *his* "emancipation," and he wasn't there. I didn't want Kelly to know where I was because I didn't want her to feel pressured into telling Louisa, or to lie to her. My note to Louisa did not state where I had gone.

In November 2004 I was visiting with our friend, Tanya Avedovech, in California and related that story to her. I felt the shame of my cowardice wash over me and she urged me to let it go. She said, "That isn't who you are today. You need to let that go completely." Maybe that will happen after I've written it here, for all the world to see.

There I was in the apartment, fully furnished, with some of my belongings added. It was January 1991, and I was starting over…again…at 48. I had virtually no money. I didn't have a job, and no prospect of one.

I was out. I was "free." I had what I wanted. Or, did I?

The next day I called Bill to tell him what I had done. He was shocked. I met with him and we talked about it, and about First Night, Colorado. He and I knew that I wouldn't be coming back to work on it. He was more concerned about me and what was next for me. He was concerned about Louisa, and the kids. I didn't have any answers. He wondered if it was because I had spent so much time away, in Wyoming. I told him it wasn't his fault because I thought that's where he was heading.

By the weekend Louisa had found me. I shouldn't have been surprised, but I was. She wanted to come by to talk with me. I didn't want that yet. I told her that I'd call in a day or two. She didn't want to wait. We agreed to meet somewhere to talk. I don't recall where that took place. I just recall that the first thing I did was apologize for the way I left.

It was difficult to leave and go back to the apartment but I felt that I had to. She had wanted to schedule something, a date, for the weekend but I wanted to spend it with Kevin, and to visit with Kelly and Chris, if I could find him.

A few nights later I met my friend Ben Levek, whom I'd come to know through Bill Michaels, at the Wynkoop Brewery Bar, for drinks. It's easy to recall that night because we sat there watching President Bush announce the beginning of the Operation Desert Storm.

Louisa and I did go out to a movie the next weekend and she came home with me. She didn't stay the night. We went out again a week later, and she did spend the night.

The following week Chris Coons came to stay with me. Initially it was for a few nights, then every night.

CHAPTER 2
Life goes on, ready or not

On February first, I got a call from Larry Quartuccio, a former co-worker with The Hahn Company. Larry had called my home number and talked with Louisa, who told him where to reach me. He called to tell me that my friend and former traveling partner with The Hahn Company, Stan McWhorter had died.

I felt as though someone had thrown a rock and hit me in the chest…a big rock. Larry went on to say that Stanley had been shopping for groceries and had purchased some off the shelf medicine for a cold that he was fighting. When he got home, he was unloading groceries and told Janey that he needed to sit down and rest. When he sat down, he died. You've likely read or heard of the story of the cold medicine tampering near Seattle, WA. Stanley and Janey had returned to Washington after he left The Hahn Company. They were living in Lacey at the time of his death. As I recall, Stan was one of two people killed after someone else tampered with several boxes of medicine to hide poison he was to have given his wife. There was no other connection between the accused offender and the McWhorter's.

Larry gave me the number where I could reach Janey. I called and could barely talk. I was crying with her so much. Stanley was one of the most likeable and loveable people I'd ever met. I tell people about him and how he got so much out of life. He just didn't hold back. Often, when we rode together in an elevator, he would turn his back to the door and face anyone else riding with us. He'd smile, and say, "Howdy! Havin' a great day?" Anyone who has ever ridden an elevator with others knows how funny that had to be…and was. Knowing him and working with him was great for me.

I was so angry about his death. I was mad at God. I got on the bike and rode like a crazy man. I went to Panama Red's, a bar that catered to the over 40 crowd. I drank and drank and then I left and went to the strip bar, Shotgun Willie's and drank some more. When I left there I took Cherry Creek Drive north, headed back to the apartment, screaming and daring God to take me, too. Obviously he had other plans for me.

When I got back to the apartment, Chris was sitting on the front steps, waiting for me. I had trouble putting the kickstand down, he came to help me and put me to bed.

A few weeks later I went back to Devil's Thumb Ranch to work on the Governor's Cup Cross Country Ski Race again, with Bill. He'd had some car trouble so he rented a new Subaru all wheel drive wagon. He paid the extra money for the rental to allow me to drive. That was good for me because, as I mentioned a few years later when we 'roasted' Bill for his 40th birthday…I love the guy, but I told the other guests, "If you ever travel with him, make sure that *you're* the driver."

I was aware that some of the people, with whom I'd worked on previous events, including this one, were talking about my separation. Even if they weren't I imagined that they were. I roomed with Phil Perington, a frequent volunteer for Bill's events.

Phil and I went out the first night, in the new Subaru…just for a few drinks. We made it back just in time for the opening dinner, hosted by Eastern Mountain Sports' Roy Johnson. We made it in spite of some unplanned delays.

"YOU USED TO LIVE IN MY HOUSE."

The first delay came in the form of two women we danced with a lot, and who invited us to make a longer evening of it. We did manage to 'do the right thing,' in heading back to the ranch. I had been drinking, but fortunately stopped short of losing my ability to react in a timely fashion.

I was driving in a very focused manner, aware that I needed to be careful and really pay attention. I did not allow myself to relax. That probably saved a couple of lives.

As we rounded a curve about a mile from the ranch facilities, I looked up to see two people walking down the middle of the road. I honked and they jumped and I put the new Subaru...the rental car...into a ditch that even all-wheel drive wasn't going be able to pull us out of.

When we got out of the car the couple came over, apologizing profusely and asking if we were ok. "We shouldn't have been in the middle of the road," the woman said, crying. "It's our fault." I just said that we were all lucky that no one was hurt.

Phil and I hurried down the road to the restaurant and told Bill what had happened. Then we called for a tow truck.

The car was ok and Phil and I were back at that bar the next night. The same two women were there and we danced until closing. Then we went our separate ways. The rest of the event went off without any other accidents or problems. I hadn't done anything to make myself feel any better about where my life was going at that point.

CHAPTER 3
Let's add a little wood to the fire

In the third week of February I got another call about another former co-worker who had died. Ed Reid, part friend, part nemesis, in my years with Hahn. He had been killed in a plane crash over Los Angeles. I wasn't angry in the sense that I was when I learned of Stan's death. They were different people and my relationship was different with each of them. But I hurt for Ed, his wife and daughters. I knew that he loved those girls.

I actually made a call to Jim Adkins, Ed's predecessor at the Tivoli. He and his wife, Sarah were living in the Atlanta area. I wanted to make sure he was okay. Somewhere in my mind, things were happening to those of us who had been connected through Hahn or the Tivoli.

It was nearing the end of February, and I had to find some kind of employment.

Neighbors had told Louisa that they had seen me coming and going while she was at work.

I had done that to check the mail because I hadn't changed my permanent address, and to do laundry. She asked me to stay away as long as I lived away. I knew she was right. I had no case to plead, except that I didn't change my mailing address. She said that she'd drop my mail by the apartment. That didn't resolve the laundry issue, but it wasn't her problem.

I looked at job ads in the newspaper and answered an ad for AVIS Car Rental. I applied and was hired, to move cars around their lot at the airport. I thought that eventually I could work my way up to driving a shuttle or working with customers checking in. I sat in the apartment after my first workday there and was amazed at what little I expected of myself. I rationalized that it was something I could go *do* and leave behind when I clocked out...not take it home. I hadn't done anything like that in many years.

I worked the early shift at AVIS, from 6:30 AM to 3 PM. Shortly after going to work there; I got another jolt when I came home one afternoon. Judi called to say that Kevin had been hospitalized. He had a bronchial infection and the doctor wanted to insert a feeding tube into his stomach. I really lost it. I told her I'd come to the hospital right away. I called Louisa, who'd just gotten home from work and told her about it. She said, "You're in no condition to ride the motorcycle, I'll pick you up in a few minutes." Louisa has never written me off. She's always been there for me...mad as hell and deeply hurt at times, but *always* there for me.

Kevin had the feeding tube placed in his stomach, and for the first time in a long time, we saw his mortality. When he was born, the doctors gave him no more than 24 hours to live. He had been transferred from Williamsburg Hospital to Riverside Hospital, in Newport News, and was in ICU for three weeks before going home. After moving to Denver in 1983, I had taken him to Dr. McCartney, who told me back then that Kevin might have another eight to ten years to live, and that his digestive system would be the cause of his death. None of that made it any easier to watch his demise. I felt that my heart was being ripped out, very slowly.

It was also during that time that I enrolled in two classes at Metropolitan State College (now Metro State University). I made another run at Algebra, with the old results. I was missing classes…and not doing the homework while Kevin was in the hospital. I dropped the Algebra class.

However, I did make the time to stay up to date with my Introduction to Business Systems (computer) classes. I wish I could recall the name of the instructor. He helped me develop a keen interest in using computers, I now enjoy. His exams were multiple choice exams and I had a multiple choice exam phobia. I called my former instructor and long time friend Ken Kirby, in Philadelphia, asking how to overcome that phobia. He told me to prepare thoroughly and go with my first sense about the answer, not to over think it. He went on to say that when I was in his classes he knew that he could find out what I really knew with an essay question, and mess with me by using a multiple choice exam. His advice was good and I earned a high B grade in the course.

It was about a week later when I got a call from the woman I'd been dancing with at Fraser, when Phil and I were there. She was going to be in Denver and wanted to meet for lunch. I really did have too much to drink that night. I say that not because she was unattractive, to the contrary, she was very attractive. I must have said something like 'if you get to Denver, give me a call,' and gave her the phone number for Don's apartment. We did go to lunch and we talked and I told her that while I found her very attractive, I shouldn't have invited her to call me. I told her about my recent separation, and that I knew that I wasn't finished with that relationship. It was not a problem for her. She didn't want to get in the middle of that situation.

About a week after that I got a call from one of the entertainers I had booked for First Night, Colorado, asking me to go out with her. She had expressed an interest while Louisa and I were together. When she heard that we were separated, she asked again. We did have lunch. She was someone I found very attractive and I think, under other circumstances we could have enjoyed each other. She was closer to my age, and looking for something I couldn't offer. We went our separate ways. I was free.

Or, was I? What had I accomplished? The question was on my mind constantly. I thought of Stanley McWhorter, and of Ed Reid, of their wives and families, and questioned what I was trying to accomplish.

I did have some space. I really *could* do what I wanted, with whom and when I wanted. I just didn't know *what* I wanted. I found that my freedom didn't mean dating other women. I became close with one of my neighbors, too. We weren't intimate, but the attraction was there. She was involved with someone that Louisa and I both knew. We were more coffee buddies than anything. There was some flirting, but neither of us called the other's bluff.

I was still applying for jobs that had more career promise that schlepping cars at AVIS. I recall going to an interview that I rode the bike to. It was about 10 or 12 miles to Denver Tech Center, to meet with a professional "head hunter." The temperature...before the wind chill, or motorcycle speed factor, was 20 degrees. I wore a suit with running tights under the pants, my suit coat and an overcoat and still thought I'd freeze do death before I got there and back.

The interview offered only an opportunity to pay money I didn't have, so that they would conduct a job search for me.

CHAPTER 4
Just a place to call home

My routine became pretty...well, routine. Then at the end of March, Don was ready to move home and I wasn't. I was homeless...for a week.

I learned that an apartment in the building next door would become available a week later. Don was back and I had to leave. Our friend Natalie invited me to house sit for a week while she and her brother took the boys on a trip. The timing was working out perfectly...until they came back a day early. I spent the next night in a sleeping bag, in Judi's mini-van, in her driveway.

I moved into the apartment and Chris Coons moved with me. He enrolled at East High School and didn't attend classes. I didn't understand why he even bothered at that point. Maybe he just wanted to please me and didn't know how to do it. He hadn't fallen too far from the tree. There were other similarities that would concern me even more. Not long after that Chris moved to *my* hometown...Alton. I never would have seen that coming.

At some point, I think it was in May, David moved back in with Louisa and Chris. He had a paper route that Louisa helped him with. When he moved out again she took over the paper route. I was making just enough money to pay my rent and food costs. However, I wasn't contributing to the household bills I'd left behind. So, Louisa used the newspaper delivery to help her pay the bills.

It was that spring that Louisa and I started counseling. I think it was initially lined up through our Kaiser Insurance plan, which Louisa had available as an AMOCO employee. We met with a counselor, who has since retired, named Pat Blauth. I don't know whether Pat had ever expected us to make it this far, and doubt that she thought she'd ever hear me thank her for her role in it.

I walked out of most of the sessions at one point or another, throwing out obscenities along the way. Pat, I'm told, would tell Louisa not to go after me, but that I would come back and take part if I wanted to. I usually did show up for the next session, but not always. Louisa and I had been going out to movies and had even gone on a camping trip to Kenosha Pass. We had camped several times in the 80's, with better results than we'd had when we lived on the east coast.

It was inevitable that men would make their presence known to Louisa. A couple of them from within the neighborhood started coming around. One of them offered to help Chris Harrison get a job, and loaned her tools to work on the kitchen flooring. I don't think she would have ever gone out with him because he was pretty full of himself. The district manager for the newspaper route was someone that she did like, and did go out with. It turned out that he was married. However, he still came around and was probably someone she would have been interested in under other circumstances. Others made their interest known, although she didn't go out with them.

We did spend our 8th wedding anniversary together. We drove up through the Fort Collins area and out towards Ted's Place on highway 287, expecting to find something like the Bucksnort Saloon along the way. We didn't. However, we did enjoy the ride, the time together and an anniversary dinner. The reality was that we didn't live together. When we spent time together, outside of the counseling, we enjoyed each other. No one would have enjoyed me during the counseling.

During that period David was living at "Third Way," a group home for kids who have trouble living at home for their reasons and/or their parents'. As a part of being allowed to live there, he was in counseling. We went to some of his counseling sessions together, even though we lived apart.

By late July, I was ready to quit AVIS and I didn't know what else I would do. I decided that I would quit in mid-August and take a motorcycle trip. My last day at work was also Louisa's birthday. In contrast to how she had always been there for me, I wasn't there for her. On *my* 40th birthday, she had thrown a surprise party for me. On *her* 40th birthday, she was surprised, but not in a good way. She really thought I'd come by. I didn't. I went drinking with some of the managers from AVIS, leaving early enough that I was still able to ride the bike safely. At least I thought so. I did know that I'd had enough to drink that I shouldn't go to see Louisa.

CHAPTER 5
Headin' down that long, lonesome highway…(18)

I moved out of the apartment that weekend, took some things back to our house in Washington Park and packed the bike for my trip. I planned to go through Steamboat Springs where our friend Deanna Webb lived, then though Utah, and on out to Sacramento to visit my friend Dave Morgan. We'd played softball on the same team in 1978 and he had hired me as marketing director for Newmarket North Mall in 1979. He later became my roommate. We had traveled together and he was in our wedding. I felt that he knew me almost as well as Louisa did. I believed that David could help me sort things out.

I over packed the bike and it had no balance. I waited until Louisa came home from work and asked her to repack it for me. She has this great spatial relations thing going for her.

She took care of it and I saw how she did it so that I could do it the same way after I stopped in Steamboat.

I stayed at Deanna's house for one night. When I was ready to leave the next morning, I discovered a flat rear tire on the bike. I had the bike towed to a shop and the tube was replaced. I was on my way in fairly short order.

My route took me through Craig on US 40 and on to Vernal, Utah. I stayed in touch with Louisa, and with Judi because she had taken Kevin with her on a trip to Alton.

When I left Vernal I headed north on US 191 and, for no particular reason, took the route on the east side of Flaming

Gorge Canyon. There's a pretty good climb up to the canyon and I hadn't gone too far before the rear tire went flat again.

This time, it happened on a two-lane blacktop, on a steep incline. I think the bike itself weighed about 500 plus pounds and I had added another 100, or so it seemed. I managed to pull the bike to the side of the road, on adrenalin, I guess. No one driving up or down the hill, offered to stop and help, until two guys riding BMW bikes stopped to ask what kind of help I needed. They were riding from Quebec to Mexico. They tried to fix it with an instant tube patch, but it wouldn't hold air.

We resolved that their best help would be to locate the Honda dealership in Vernal before it closed, and to send a tow truck. I could see what little money I had disappearing and it was only the second day of the trip.

The three of us got the bike to the shoulder of the road near the cliff overlooking the valley. The wind came up and dark clouds were blowing towards me. My attitude was going down faster than the temperature. I built a lean-to just before the rain started. It hadn't rained long before the flat bed truck arrived from the Honda store. They had made it in time. The rain stopped just as we were rolling the bike onto the truck. The young guy driving it dropped me off at the campground in town and told me he'd pick me up in the morning when my bike was ready. My attitude was improving as quickly as it had gone south.

My new Canadian friends were at the campgrounds and offered me a beer when they saw me heading their way. I felt like I should have been offering *them* something. I didn't have anything, but I was very grateful for their help, *and* their beer. I didn't have any trouble sleeping that night.

The next morning, as promised, I was greeted by the young man from the Honda store and carried to the shop to get my bike. I was told that whoever put the tube in, at Steamboat Springs, had pinched it, causing the second flat. I took the bad tube with me, planning to take it back when I eventually got back to Steamboat. I wasn't charged for the pick up of my bike or the labor…only for the tube.

I was off again, and continued across the dam road and the east side of Flaming Gorge Canyon, stopping to eat a big, late breakfast, knowing that I could cut expenses by eating only one big meal a day. I had a cooler and snacks with me on the bike. Shortly after I ate and was on the road again, I saw dark clouds and lightning off to the southwest and moving in my direction. I rode fast, and luckily I was on a pretty deserted and straight two-lane road by that time. I was in a race with the storm and it was gaining ground on me.

I made it to a truck stop where US 191 intersects with I-80, between Rock Springs and Green River, Wyoming. I took little comfort over being back in Wyoming. I covered the bike and headed inside just as the heavens opened and the downpour began. I made the coffee and pie last for more than an hour. Sitting there I looked at the map and questioned my decision to take the east side of the canyon and not the west. It seemed that I didn't have a shortage of things to second-guess myself about at that time.

I thought about cutting the trip short and going up to Jackson. I called Mary Meade and asked whether her guest cabin was available. She apologized, saying, 'no,' there was a family event coming up that weekend. So I was back to *Plan A*.

After a while I rode west toward Green River and found a campsite where I could pitch my tent for the night. Oh what a night it was…I had the only tent in the area. There were several "5th Wheels" and RV's. We had an incredible storm. I had staked the tent through the motorcycle and that's probably why it, and I, didn't blow away. There was lightning, heavy rain and incredible wind.

The next morning a few people from the RV's talked to me, saying they were amazed that my tent stayed up. So was I. I watched as they each pulled out and I was there alone. I waited until the sun was up high and dried my tent and some of my gear before heading back to the highway.

Going up the east side of the canyon also meant that I would be connecting with I-80 into Salt Lake City. I hadn't ridden on Interstate highways before and the force of the big trucks passing at 70 mph, and more, made for a wild ride.

Riding into Salt Lake City on I-80 is a beautiful sight. The city itself is pretty. I had been there several times for The Hahn Company visiting malls in Ogden and in Murray. I went into the city and south on State Street, recalling Fashion Place Mall was located in that area and my map indicated that I could get up into the hills near there.

My goal that day, in addition to avoiding anything that looked like a storm, was to get to the Big Cottonwood Canyon campsites and spend a couple of days relaxing. I found the US Forest Ranger Station and directions to the campground easily enough. I paid $4 for a site and was glad to have ridden that far with no flat tires and no rain or wind.

I found a restaurant and a pay phone about 6 miles from the campsite. I left a message for Louisa that I was okay and where I was going to be camping for a couple of days.

The next morning freezing rain and lightning awakened me. The elevation there was over 7000 feet, so any precipitation was going to be freezing rain or snow, even in August. The sun came out later and I was able to dry things out again.

Later in the morning I rode back up to the restaurant, ate a big breakfast and made phone calls. I called Judi, in Alton, to see how Kevin was doing. One of the things I had second-guessed myself about was the direction I was riding. I could have ridden through southern Kansas and up through the Ozarks of Missouri and into Alton. Of course that wouldn't have accomplished my goal of visiting with Dave Morgan in Sacramento or my efforts to find some direction with my life. I know it was Kevin's health issues that were tugging at me.

Next I called my old friend Brian Cole. I hadn't spoken with him often, but he was a aware of our separation. I told him about my travels and trials along the road. He laughed, saying it was a lot like "Then Came Bronson," a short-lived TV series from twenty years ago. Michael Parks played a drifter who rode his bike through California, facing challenges at every stop. I told Brian that I thought Parks had a better script than I did.

I called Fashion Place Mall, asking if they knew whether Doug O'Brien was still in Utah. They said he was living at Sandy and gave me his number. I couldn't reach him that day and didn't try again.

After visiting a Laundromat, I headed back to the canyon. I took some pictures and rode around the mountain roads for a while, then returned to the campsite.

There was only one other campsite occupied near mine. It had a truck with a pop-up camping tent on it. I hadn't seen anybody outside of it. A Ranger came by and honked the horn on his jeep enough so that I came out of the tent, where I had been napping, and two guys came out of the camper truck. One looked sort of slight of build, like me, but taller and the other looked and dressed like the Marlboro Man.

As they got closer to the Ranger and me, he started to tell us about a baby moose in the area, and that it meant the mother was nearby...that she would be dangerous and we should be alert to their presence. One of the guys spoke, saying...in an effeminate way...that I could stay in their tent if I wanted to. I didn't. The Marlboro Man look-alike echoed the invitation in a similar effeminate voice, with a surprisingly high pitch. I don't consider myself homo-phobic, and this was way ahead of the "Brokeback Mountain" movie, but I chose to pass on the offer. The scene was a little too surreal, and I decided to leave in the morning.

I was up early enough the next morning, but it took a while for the sun to dry the heavy dew off of the tent and I packed up closer to midday. I thought about calling Louisa again, but to her office phone. I was missing her and had no contact other than her voice on the answering machine at home. She was getting on with her life, just as I was, and I don't think she would have anticipated my calling her unless I had an emergency.

About noon I head down the mountain and back toward I-15 and the I-215 loop that took me back to I-80, west toward Nevada and California. Off to the southwest I could see a sky as black as a starless night. About 10 minutes on I-80 outside of Salt Lake City, the winds came up. I had a Cardinals' ball cap hooked on to a bungee cord and my backpack. I heard a noise and turned with a glance to see it flying toward the Great Salt Lake. I thought *I* might be next. I was leaning the bike into the wind and riding at an angle that I might have used to turn a corner at that speed. I was really holding on for dear life.

I rode like that for another 40 or 50 minutes and pulled into a truck stop at a place called Dell, Utah. I think the truck stop and the gas station made up Dell.

When I parked the bike, I had to be very careful dismounting, knowing that the wind could put it on its side faster than I could have caught it. I found a place that was sheltered from the wind's force and it stayed upright.

There were only three other customers inside, each at the counter. A young couple who belonged with a U-Haul truck and a car in its tow, sat together, and one guy who belonged with a big rig that was part of the shelter from the wind for my bike and gear. We all sat at the counter watching dirt and debris blow by our vehicles.

Over my pie and coffee I contemplated my next move. I asked the others if they'd come from the west and they had. I asked how far I could expect to fight that wind. The trucker spoke before either the man or woman sitting together, saying, "All the way to Reno…almost 500 hundred miles." Incredible! I could only manage, "Really?" He nodded, saying, "It's suicidal for you to be out there on that bike. You won't make it."

There was no hesitation in his comment, not maybe or perhaps. Nothing. I exhaled and focused on the pie, mumbling my thanks.

The couple left first, pulling on to I-80 eastbound toward Salt Lake City.

The trucker was leaving as I finished my coffee. He just patted me on the shoulder.

I followed him out and got on the bike, heading back toward Salt Lake City, more on autopilot than with any particular sense of direction. I felt defeated, *not* suicidal.

The winds were blowing from my right now. Again, I had to hold on with all my might. I heard myself saying, "God, just please get me home safely. Get me back to Louisa and the kids safely. God, I will make this work." That prayer became a mantra as I headed into the rush hour traffic of Salt Lake City.

I rode east on I-80, and then south on US 40 to get off of the interstate highway. I stopped at a gas station, with a convenience store, near the exit for Park City. After gassing up, I went inside for another cup of coffee. The clerk asked where I'd ridden from. Giving him the short version, I just said, "Dell." He looked as though he'd never heard of it. He said, "Well you just missed one of the biggest storms Salt Lake City has ever had. A lot of folks don't have power." I said that I hadn't missed all of it. I had stopped to put on the rain gear. Everything on my pack was soaked, too.

After looking at the big map posted on a wall, I decided to head south on US 40. He suggested that I might want to stay overnight at Heber City. "I don't know of any campgrounds down there, but you should be able to get a motel room." I thanked him and was on my way.

When I reached Heber City I got a room at a motel that had a Mexican restaurant next door. I needed a hot shower, a cold beer and some Mexican food. I hadn't eaten a full meal that day. I'd had only one meal each of the days I had been on the road.

I wanted a ground level room only because I didn't want to carry everything up the steps to the second level. It didn't work out that way. After getting everything up to my room, I opened my sleeping bag and draped it over the railing outside. I showered and headed to the restaurant.

I ate in the bar area, with no one else around. The dining room area was pretty busy. I ordered enchiladas and a beer and went to a phone to call Louisa. Again, I got the answering machine and just told her that I was okay and might be in Heber City, Utah for a couple of days. I hadn't thought about that before then. It just came out that way.

The cook and waiter was a guy name Juan. He looked to be a dozen years older than me, or more. I think he was a first generation Mexican. His English was better than my Spanish. For the dining room, he had the help of a young woman, who as I learned, was his daughter. Juan was pretty busy and I was dead ass tired, so we didn't make a lot of effort to talk to each other. The food was great and Juan told me where I could buy a six-pack of beer, pointing to a liquor store down the street.

I called Judi, who had returned to Denver, to ask how Kevin was doing. He was fine and she had a good visit with Chris, in Alton. He was working at a Jack-In-The-Box fast food restaurant. She asked about my trip. Just peachy, I told her. It was hardly the first or worst lie I'd told her.

I found the beer and went to my room, watched some baseball. It was when the Braves were going from 'worst to first.' I slept well and woke early. I headed back to the restaurant wanting to eat good before I got back on the road.

It wasn't even 7 AM yet and Juan was there. I asked if he stayed overnight. "Yes, I sleep in the back," he said. There was no one else around. I gave him my order and he gave it to his daughter who was cooking that morning.

Giving it my best "Then Came Bronson," I asked if he needed any help. I thought I'd stay there for a while. I needed the money and he seemed easy going enough. No, he didn't need any help. He and his daughter handled the restaurant. His wife and another daughter cleaned the motel rooms. Too bad, I thought. Michael Parks would have gotten the job.

I was on the road around 8:30 and headed back to Steamboat Springs, via US 40. A part of the scenery along that route is absolutely beautiful. I rode through Strawberry Plains, and then it got pretty stark, even the names said it…Starvation State Park. No wonder there are Native American Reservations between Heber City and Vernal, Utah. That's the kind of land the government would have put them on.

I rode straight through, making only the stop in Vernal for gas and a lemonade drink. I got into Steamboat Springs earlier than I expected, so I went to the restaurant where Deanna was waiting tables. I just sat out on the deck and she appeared through the doorway. She was shocked to see me back so soon. She was almost finished with work, so I waited and followed her to her house.

She wanted to treat me to dinner, so we walked back into town. Along the way I told her of my adventure, and of my prayer turned mantra when I headed back. I wasn't just talking with her as a friend, who'd been in a band I had worked with. I talked to her as a friend who had completed her Masters in Psychology.

I told Deanna that I knew I wanted to be with Louisa. I just didn't want to get back into the old issues that had dragged me down. She said," You need to find out who *you* are and what *you* want. She'll either accept that or not." That just *spoke* to me. It made so much sense. Of course, *who* I am and *what* I want were anything but clear to me.

Walking back to her house after dinner, she said, "I hope it works out for you and Louisa. I really do. But if it doesn't, you're welcome to come back here. I have contacts with the radio stations here." That really surprised me. There had never been anything romantic or intimate between Deanna and me. I told myself it was my friend offering to help. That night we drove somewhere southwest of Steamboat so she could rehearse with some other musicians for an upcoming gig. They were going to open for B.B. King.

Back at her place, much later, she went to bed and I slept on the couch, which was good, except for the cats that wanted to sleep with me. I left before dawn, heading to Denver. Boy, it was cold. It was the last day of August and still it was very cold riding through Rabbit Ears Pass. I stopped in Kremmling for gas and coffee and could barely walk when I got off the bike. My body was so tense from being so cold. Later, in Silverthorne, I shed about two layers of clothing.

CHAPTER 6
Where've you been?

I got back into Denver before noon. I dropped my gear off at the house...our house, leaving it all on the back patio. Then I went downtown to find Louisa. I knew it was about her lunch hour. I was walking up the sidewalk near the entrance to the AMOCO Building when I saw her friend Margaret Dunckhorst, who looked very surprised to see me. She said, "She's coming this way, about a block back." I thanked her and looked for Louisa. I saw her just as she looked up, seeing me.

When she walked up to me, she said, "I'm surprised to see you here. What's up?" I said, "I want to be with you, to put things together the right way, if you'll have me." She smiled, and said that's what she wanted too.

Before you think that's the end of this story, what I think of as a story of uncommon love, rather than a love story...read on.

I went back to our house on South Gilpin Street and Louisa went back to work. By the time she got home that afternoon, I'd cleaned up and put my things away. Later we went out to dinner, and then to the Taste of Colorado street festival downtown.

The featured act that night was country singer Kathy Mattea. For her finale, she sang her hit song, "Where've You Been?". (19) It seemed that we were back on track.

We spent much of the next day calling people to let them know that I was back, and that we were together.

Two days later, on Labor Day, we got a surprise call from my brother Bob. He and I caught up with each other, and then he asked to speak to Louisa. She listened, and then she said, "Bob, you don't have to do this." He spoke, and she responded by saying, "Yes. I appreciate that. Thank you. Talk to you soon. Do you want to talk with Perry again? Bye."

When she handed the phone back to me, I saw tears in her eyes. I listened as Bob told me that he apologized for the way he had treated her and talked about her. He went on to say that he'd entered AA, and a part of his therapy was to set things right. I told him how much I appreciated that, knowing how difficult it must have been. He said that he had to do it, wanted to do it, and that it hadn't been difficult.

I saw Chris Harrison that night. He was glad that I was back home. I saw Kelly and Kevin that weekend too. Kelly was always supportive of what I wanted to do or did. She wanted me to be happy, as I know each of the kids did.

We decided to take a road trip. How's that for a test of fire? We drove to Alton first, and then to Virginia to see Louisa's family, and the friends who knew that we had been separated. Mom had been supportive, and wouldn't have interfered if she had disagreed with my decisions. And we had a chance to visit with Chris, too.

He was living with friends, in a house that had been owned by a woman I knew as Fanny. It was at the end of the alley, adjacent to Grandpa & Grandma Fleming's house.

We camped overnight after driving as far as Bluefield, West Virginia. Then we drove to Richmond and visited Louisa's friend Charlotte, and then we made a stop to have dinner with our friends Michael and Kathy Lehmkuhler at Midlothian. We pulled into Newport News after midnight.

I was anxious to see, Louisa's parents, Paul and Carol, too. They had never treated me any differently while Louisa and I had been apart. I had talked with them during our separation, after I learned that Paul had fallen in the middle of the night and broken his neck. He was still wearing the "halo" when we arrived that night. During that trip Paul told me that I was the kind of person he would want for a friend, even if I hadn't been his son-in-law. We'd been friends before. However, I believe that comment brought us closer to the deep friendship we enjoy today.

We made the rounds, going on a picnic with the Dudley family at Mariner's Museum Park. They took us to a Japanese restaurant and hosted a get together before we headed home. It was during the visit at their home, that Richard asked what I planned to do when we got back to Denver. I didn't have a clue and that 's what I told him. He's been a successful homebuilder for years, and suggested that I would do well selling real estate. I had never considered it, but it sounded good and I told him that I liked the idea of helping people find their "home," and I'd check into it in Denver.

CHAPTER 7
The puzzle starts to come together

We stopped in Alton on the way back, as we have on every road trip to and from Virginia. Then we headed back to Denver, camping overnight briefly. That is to say we arrived late near Lawrence, Kansas, slept fast and left early. We were anxious to get back home. Louisa was due at AMOCO on Monday and I had to find work. Not long after that Chris Coons' Alton experiment ended he returned to Denver.

I called Maree McRae, who sold real estate in addition to playing music. I talked with her about my chances in real estate. She thought it was a good idea for me. I also called Mary Beth Reed, the agent who had sold us our house in 1983. She encouraged me to get into real estate too. She said the market was picking up after having bottomed out in the 1980's. Okay, I thought, real estate it is. But I'd have to figure out how and when after I found something to produce some income as soon as possible.

I went to work for Blue Cross-Blue Shield, as a temporary employee, working in Human Resources. I spent most of my time sifting through résumés using the guidelines they gave me. The people there were great, treating me like a full time employee. I worked there through the end of the year.

As the holidays drew near, I had less work to do. I found myself sketching a drawing that I later drew, using the mouse, on a very elementary graphics program we received on our first computer the following year. In 1994, I painted it on the front window of our house. I've included it in this book. I call it "Remember the Homeless in Your Christmas Prayers."

When my brother Bob went to Alton to spend Thanksgiving with Mom, he dropped a bombshell on her. To her surprise, he apologized to her for being so angry with her since he was a kid. She had no idea he had held any anger toward her. He said that he had been angry that she had let brothers Pat and Mike live with me in Virginia when they were in high school. He'd made a judgment that she hadn't tried hard enough to raise them without dad. Of course he had come to realize that she had done the best she knew how, and she had done what she thought was best for each of us. She was widowed little more than three months before her 36th birthday, and left with four sons, ages 15, 11, 4 and 2. That anger was at the heart of Bob's conflicts with Louisa, and most of the women he'd known. It was only exacerbated when his wife left him and Shelli, when Shelli was around 2 years old.

Kelly had moved into her own apartment for the first time. She found a basement apartment about a mile and a half from us, west of the Denver Country Club.

That was really working out well for her. When her car was in the shop, which became a frequent event, I carried her to and from work on my motorcycle. We got a late night call from her, screaming that somebody was looking in her window. I told her to call 911 and I'd be right there. The Volvo became a blue streak. When I arrived he, or whomever, had gone and the Police arrived right after I did. She gave them a description that fit a man who'd been tabbed the Washington Park Rapists by the media. He was later arrested and convicted. Sadly, there were other women who had not been as fortunate as Kelly.

CHAPTER 8
1992-Buckle Up for a wild ride!

How do I begin to tell you about my 50th year on the planet?

Okay, I'll start here. In January I started classes at the Colorado Real Estate Institute. I was granted my sales license on January 24, 1992 and joined Washington Park Realty, Ltd. Louisa and I were getting along great, and things were looking much better for our future together.

Dale and Linda Southworth are the owners and brokers of Washington Park Realty. When I applied there in 1992, Dale wanted to hire me and Linda didn't. Nothing personal, she said, just that she was due…and due very soon…with their second child. She didn't want to take on another agent at that point. They had two other agents then. She changed her mind, and I joined them. She, Dale and I became good friends in the months that followed.

A couple of weeks later our friend Natalie Hook asked me to sell her house in northwest Denver, near Regis University. That experience became surreal, and actually led to writing the book, <u>Surreal Estate</u>, in 2005.

On President's Day, I was sitting in the office at Washington Park Realty, and I met my next client, Kristine. She introduced herself and told me that she wanted to sell her house that was on Beeler Street near Colfax and 14th Street. I told her that I would talk with Dale Southworth, and enlist his help because I was new to the business.

When I talked with Dale about her, and the house, he said that she had been in about a year earlier and that he hadn't seen the house as very marketable because of the closing of Buckley Air Base, a National Guard facility and the number of 'HUD houses' in the neighborhood. By all rights, it should have been Dale's transaction. However, he told me to take it and he would help me with it.

Near the end of February Chris Harrison moved out. He was going to school at the Denver Diesel & Automotive College, and working as a mechanic for the Airporter Shuttle Service. He did leave behind Ginger, who had become his dog, since joining us in 1984. So there we were, 8 years and 8 months into our marriage…(do I deduct 8 months for the separation?) and no kids at home.

It had come down to the two of us, Gato and Ginger. Spice, the Beagle mutt Louisa had when we met, had died in 1987, her cat Gato had died in 1996, and Cinnamon, the dog we inherited with the house in 1983 had disappeared in 1984. Now I'm hearing Bill Withers' "Just The two of us,"*…"we can make it if we try…" (12)

After the scare at her apartment, Kelly had moved back to her mother's home for a short stay. She soon thereafter moved in with a girl friend, Kerri. It wasn't long before she moved again, and took an apartment with her boyfriend, Jeremy Nix. He seemed like a nice enough guy. However, he hadn't stayed with any job for very long, and after I got to know him I thought he was immature and lazy.

In early March we went back to Snowmass for the CLS meetings hosted by Chuck and Jean Strehli. We thought that we were ready to get busy with that business as well. Keith hadn't done anything with the business, but I hadn't done anything to help with it either.

"YOU USED TO LIVE IN MY HOUSE."

During that week, we spent a lot of time learning to cross country ski. Our mentor was Dr. Stuart Menn, a sleep disorder specialist from California. We had met him during our brief visit to the event 4 years earlier. We stayed with him, and several other people, in a house that he had rented, rather than at the Wildwood Inn. It was a good week for us and I felt that we were really on track for our personal and financial recovery.

Shortly after our return to Denver, Kevin was hospitalized again. He had a bronchial infection. He also had a complication in the form of the "trap door" in his esophagus having grown open. They could not correct it with surgery. They gave him an anti-biotic for the infection, but said there was nothing else they could do for him.

While Kevin was in the hospital we got a call from Bob and Betty McKann, our upline Diamonds in the Amway business. I'd never met them, but had previously talked with them on the phone. Louisa had known them most of her life, because her parents and the McKann's were best friends. They were on their way back to their home near Houston, having been to Alaska to visit a granddaughter. They wanted to stop over for a couple of days. I thought the timing was difficult, but we did say yes and picked them up at the airport. On the way home, they waited while Louisa and I visited Kevin.

Bob and Betty are two of the finest and most interesting people I've ever known. The timing of their visit was perfect. With the stress I was feeling over Kevin's failing health, I don't know anyone, or any two people whose demeanor and attitude would have been better for me to experience. They had built an extremely successful business, through Amway, during the years that Betty was an RN and raising their five children and while Bob was the Quality Control Supervisor for the Apollo splashdowns for NASA. Bob had been able to retire early, just as Paul had done. The fact that they were so close to Paul and Carol was a plus for me too.

April 6, 1992: Duke defeats Michigan 71-51 for the NCAA Men's Basketball National Championship. Of course it was a landmark day for Duke University, *and* a landmark day for me.

I walked about 5 blocks to a National Championship party that my friend Bill Michaels was hosting. I drank only two beers that night, which was unusual in itself, since there was a big supply available.

On the way back home, I threw up. The next morning, when I went out to run, I felt terrible. I wasn't fighting a hang over per se, but feeling ill and sluggish. I decided then and there that I was through with drinking any alcohol.

Of course, there were many people who doubted that I could or would stick with it. Strangely, I was not one of them. I had been drinking, most of my life, except for a brief period when my former wife, Judi and I were involved in a strict Baptist church, in Williamsburg in 1968.

For whatever reason, my make up provided me with the strength to walk away from cigarettes cold turkey on January 5, 1965. Now I was putting years of binge drinking behind me, exercising that same determination. As Judi had supported me when I quit smoking, Louisa was excited about supporting me as I became sober. By the grace of God, and with their help, I never looked back at either habit.

There were two other major factors that helped me stay away from alcohol in those first few weeks and months. I knew Kevin was dying and I didn't want alcohol to become my crutch for dealing with that. Louisa and I were working to make our relationship nurturing and I knew that I could not drink and be the kind of person I wanted to be, and felt that I needed to be, when I drank. There was no shortage of evidence on that point.

That was one step in my transformation. Another was on the horizon.

While we were separated in 1991, Louisa had joined 10:30 Catholic Community. Her friend Celeste Rossmiller had invited her to visit. Louisa then had invited our friend Rick Garcia to attend there. Rick had since gone through a divorce with Sylvia.

In April I started going to 10:30 Catholic Community with Louisa. I was reminded of how some people thought that Susan Shelton and I would be a couple after she and Brian had split, and Judi and I had split. A number of people at "10:30" saw Louisa and Rick as a couple. Their relationship was much like mine with Susan Shelton.

I was baptized in 1960, at a fundamental Baptist Church, while I was dating Linda Gillahan. Earlier, I mentioned the strict Baptist church that Judi and I had attended in Williamsburg. She had been a member of a Baptist church most of her life, and we had been married in a Baptist church in Alton. We left the Williamsburg church when we first separated in 1969, and found that the people we had been attending with didn't want to have anything to do with us while we were separated.

It was after we met John Harwood, that we began attending the Williamsburg United Methodist Church, and later Grace United Methodist Church in Newport News.

Soon after moving to Denver, I took the kids to the Washington Park Methodist Church. Chris was non-communicative about his experience. Kelly was not. She said there were too many old people and that she didn't want to go there. I hadn't been attending any church after her mother and I divorced, so it was easy enough for me to say, "okay." I didn't go to any church after that. Louisa had been going, with Chris and David, to Christ the King Catholic Church during that time.

There I was, newly sober, new to real estate sales, working on renewing our marriage relationship, watching my oldest son approach his death, and attending a Catholic church for the first time.

And, oh by the way, the 10:30 Catholic Community was affectionately called a "renegade" church. It's a lay led community that wasn't embraced by the Catholic Archdiocese of Denver. Of course, I didn't have a clue about what the latter meant. I enjoyed the people and had no trouble adjusting to the Catholic rituals. They appeared to have more in common with the Methodist rituals, than differences. I had been baptized so I thought it was fine for me to take communion with everybody else. Later I learn that that wasn't true of other Catholic churches. What I felt from the beginning was that it was a spirit-filled community. I called the good Reverend Harwood, in North Carolina. I told him that I was attending a Catholic church. He said, "Ah, those Catholics won't hurt you none."

Earlier I spoke to the values that Louisa had grown up with. I know that I was created from the love my parents shared. They instilled values too, such as taking responsibility for my actions, being compassionate, the value of hard work and knowing right from wrong. In 1992 I began to get my values in alignment with what I'd been taught by them.

My Dad died when I was young. My Mother has never known how far I strayed from the path they'd given me…until now. She has the strength to face it. She's faced more difficult news.

Kevin had been through a couple of hospital stays, and was sent home for "at home hospice," in May. The end of his life, about which we'd been prepared…or so we thought, was unfolding before our eyes. His digestive system was shutting down. It was a combination of his inability to swallow and keep anything down. Scoliosis was restricting his digestive track.

Louisa had talked Chris Harrison into taking Ginger to his house, agreeing to provide the food for her and his friend Jake's dog. So, we had become real empty nesters…except for Gato. Of course, cats don't really need to have you around much if they can come and go on their own. If she had learned to feed herself, she'd never have missed us.

We had become more active with our Amway business, and were meeting weekly with a group in Arvada. We named our business LP & Associates. We were contracted with Amway as distributors and business partners, not as employees. I had my first real estate closing, with the buyer I had met on Presidents' Day. We received an offer on the last day of the 90-day listing agreement, and she was already under contract with her next home. Financially, things were looking up. I was also dealing with new clients that were oblivious to anything except what *they*…more accurately, what the wife wanted.

The dynamics of going from the uplifting and supportive meetings with other Amway distributors, and the challenges of that real estate transaction, then to see Kevin, were incredible. Dale and Linda Southworth were of immeasurable help with the real estate, as well as being personally supportive.

Kevin "graduated" from school. I still have his lapel pin of the mortarboard that says '92.' That also meant that he would need full time care in the future. It was something we had all known would happen somewhere down the road. It had always been 'out there,' in the future. The future has a way of becoming 'now', often much too quickly.

Maybe for the first time, Judi got to see what the kind of person Louisa is.

Understandably, Judi was having a lot of trouble dealing with watching Kevin die. And there was little more that we could do but watch. Louisa and I would bathe Kevin, and she would clean his teeth. It was something to see. Although he was growing weaker, Kevin's disposition never changed. His smile and albeit weak laughter spoke volumes about how much he had brought, and was still bringing to our lives.

Chris Coons was on probation with the Lakewood Police Department. He had been arrested on a bench warrant, and I had arranged his bail. He had been charged with a curfew violation, and got into trouble because he had talked back to a Police officer who was breaking up a party. Chris' sharp tongue is a genetic disorder. As I said earlier, that apple didn't fall far from the tree. He wasn't a gangster, but for us, the timing was almost criminal.

In early June Chris Coons, along with ten or twelve other kids, were taken to the Arkansas Valley Correctional Facility, near Ordway, Colorado as a part of a program like Scared Straight. He was not yet 18 and it was an opportunity to clean up his act before all the rules changed. In the context of the legal system, they change dramatically at 18.

By giving up alcohol I hoped to influence Chris to do so. It didn't happen. He was in denial about its effect on him. We wondered whether we would lose Chris before we lost Kevin.

After his trip to the Arkansas Valley State Prison, Chris came to me about going with him on the next trip. He was struggling with asking me to go. He said that his mother refused to go. That was easy to understand. She was at the end of her rope with him, and was emotionally drained from watching Kevin's life slipping away.

Chris' real problem with asking me was that the trip would take place on June 18th, on our 9th wedding anniversary.

"YOU USED TO LIVE IN MY HOUSE."

He and Louisa had never gotten along. However, everyone in the family was more sensitive at that time, and becoming closer. I believe it bothered Chris more than it bothered Louisa or me that the trip would fall on our anniversary.

I agreed to go, and we picked up another youth, with his mother, and in the '81 Volvo we headed to Southeast Colorado in a caravan. We'd been having some problems with the fuel injectors on that car, but it appeared to be the only option.

The experience of something like going into a maximum-security prison for several hours is, I'm happy to say, a unique, one-time experience in my life. We met face to face with men who were serving life sentences for murder, and others serving 25 years for manslaughter and other crimes. Many, perhaps most of them were alcoholics and/or drug users. One of them looked Chris in the eye and called him an alcoholic. We didn't know how right he was. Each of them told him that he didn't want to be there. *To many he would be fresh meat.*

I recall talking with a young man, from northern Colorado, who said that he had a wife and two children at home. He was serving multiple years for manslaughter, having killed someone while driving drunk. It was one of several DUI offenses that he'd had. I had never had a DUI, through the grace of God. I had driven drunk, alone, with friends…and with my kids in the car. You've probably heard it said, and I said it then… "There, but for the grace of God, go I." I was so shaken.

On the way back to Denver, the car started to sputter and died around Fountain, Colorado. I walked to a phone to call Louisa. Chris was cursing himself. It was a hot June day, and on the plains of southern Colorado, under pressure, it was hotter.

Louisa and I were supposed to go to dinner before a business meeting, and that looked unlikely at that point.

After the car cooled down, it started and ran again…before quitting again. Our trip back to Denver took twice the time that it had going to Ordway.

I dropped off the mother and her son first, and then Chris and I had time for a quick shower. We did make it to dinner. It just wasn't where or for as much time as we had planned. We ate on the way to the meeting. I had arranged to surprise Louisa with an anniversary cake following the meeting. Our friends Bert and Katy Langeberg had picked it up and taken it to the Williams' home before we got there. It was a great surprise to her and the day was recovered. She and I were both glad that I'd gone with Chris, and I think it marked the beginning of the change in their relationship. It also marked the beginning of the changes in his behavior.

Louisa and I returned to Wyoming from time to time and added a few people, from Cheyenne, to LP & Associates. I felt like my life was going a million different directions.

July came and it made all of us nervous. Kevin's death was imminent and Chris and Kelly have July birthdays. I recalled that a friend in Virginia had died on the birthday of one of his daughters. I prayed that Chris and Kelly wouldn't have to live with that kind of memory.

We were all staying pretty close to home, and spending more and more time with Kevin. Judi's other daughter Jessica had made a trip back to Alton to see her grandmother, and was rushed back to Denver by Judi's brother Bob. I have a warm memory of a social worker talking with Jessica, who was little more than 5 years old at the time. The social worker had referred to me as her dad. Jessica replied, "Oh, he's not my dad. He's my friend." It's an age-old reality that people pull together during difficult times, and it was true for us, more so than it had ever been.

"YOU USED TO LIVE IN MY HOUSE."

On July 2nd, Louisa and I were at a business meeting in Arvada. When it concluded, I called to check on Kevin. Judi thought he had slipped into a coma. We rushed to her home in Lakewood. If he had, he'd come back out of it and greeted us with his beautiful smile.

A couple of days later Judi, with much apprehension, took Jessica to a 4th of July fireworks event. She just needed a break. Louisa and I stayed with Kevin that evening.

Louisa and I took Chris to White Fence Farm, for a belated birthday lunch on July 5th. It was a good time, but there was more of an air of relief, than celebration.

On Monday, July 6, 1992, Kevin began to slip in and out of comas. His IV had been removed 10 days earlier because the fluids were filling his lungs. We were in awe of his strength, going that long with no fluids. We had taken turns wetting his mouth and tongue with a wet washcloth and a Popsicle-like sucker that somebody had recommended.

His imminent death was becoming a reality. You've likely read about people dying with family at their bedside. So it was that we gathered around Kevin. Chris had been out front, leaning on his old Chevy, telling Kevin it was time to go. It tore his heart out to talk to him about letting go.

My right hand lay over his heart. We felt his last breath and heartbeat. We had all been crying, but then the floodgates really opened. Somebody called the police, and coroner. Judi called the funeral director she had asked to pick him up. I joined Chris Coons on the front lawn. He looked at the sky and said, "If there's a heaven, I want to go there to be with Kevin." I said, "Oh, there is a heaven, and he's there, free from his chains of CP."

Much later, around 2 AM, after the police and the coroner and the ambulance had left, Louisa and I headed home. She was in the Volvo and I was on the Honda. It was rare that I rode without a helmet, but I did on that 7-mile ride that early morning. The ride home was slow and quiet.

A few hours later, I awoke and went for a 5-mile run, talking to Kevin along the way.

Judi had arranged for a memorial service at her church, Trinity United Methodist Church, downtown. She, Louisa and I met with the minister, Susan, who would be conducting the service. I told her that I was making a tape of the music that Kevin enjoyed, and others that spoke to us about him. I called upon my friend Don Folguerus to help me put the music together for the tape.

The memorial service for Kevin was a celebration of his life. Several of us spoke about him, and what he meant to us. His brother Chris called him the strongest person he'd ever met. I don't recall much of what I said, except that I didn't say good-bye, I said "Happy Trails, Kevin. Happy trails to you, until we meet again." (13) I'm always anxious to tell people that he gave us much more than he ever required of us. He was my quick fix for a crummy disposition. Kevin loved to "sing along" to music by Dan Fogelberg, Crosby, Stills & Nash, and others. He'd kick up his heels and get his whole body into it enthusiastically.

After the service we had all gathered at our home for food and sharing of stories about Kevin. We didn't have the internment of his ashes for several more days. The latter caused a strain for Judi and Kelly. Kelly had initially been very much opposed to having Kevin's body cremated. At that point she wanted to get on with it, wanting some sort of closure. We were waiting for Louisa's parents to arrive from Virginia. Judi and Kelly didn't know how much they had connected with Kevin, in part to having their own son, Bruce, who had Cerebral Palsy as well.

We completed the internment after Paul and Carol arrived, with only the family in attendance. Kevin died a few months before my fiftieth birthday. When we placed his ashes and set up his memorial, it marked the first time I really felt old.

Our lives went back to some sort of normalcy, as do all lives after such an experience. Kelly's birthday celebration, on July 16th, was low key, as Chris' had been two weeks earlier. Louisa and I took Kelly and Jeremy to an Olive Garden restaurant for her birthday.

After that I looked at my life and wondered again, 'what next?'

In the days and weeks that followed I felt drawn to church. It was as though Kevin was there or something. I felt his presence every time I was there. My eyes teared up easily.

In some fashion, without actually planning it, I had been working on those promises I made to God, ten months earlier, when I begged him to get me off of I-80 and back home to Louisa and the kids.

Louisa noticed that I was kind of moping around. She asked about my running and I told her that I'd been kind of dragging myself around the park, without much energy. She related it to losing Kevin and suggested that I see one of the counselors that Hospice of Metro Denver had made available to us. I did that, in a private session a few times and then in group sessions, and it was helpful. Everything that Hospice of Metro Denver did or offered was helpful. I recall the initial interview. I was asked about the impact Kevin had on me. I said, and I believe it now, "Kevin made me a better human being."

Louisa also suggested that I explore the Read Aloud program that the Denver Public Library offered. I joined that too. I visited schools, or childcare centers that were a part of the Head Start program, reading children's books aloud to the kids. I think I did that almost weekly for about the next ten years before I took a break.

In August I got a call from my long time friend, Ronnie Meyer. We'd met when we were 13 and had been friends since. Ronnie, and his wife Linda, were at Sturgis, and he asked if it was to soon (after Kevin's death) for me to have company. I replied, "Not if the company is you."

They rode from Sturgis to Denver to visit us before riding back to Alton. It was the first time Louisa had met them, although she'd talked to Ronnie briefly years earlier and knew that he and I talked each time we passed through Alton. At Louisa's suggestion, I called my ex-wife, Judi, and invited her to come by the see them. Ronnie had been my best man when she and I were married.

In October Louisa and I took a ten-day tent camping trip through the Canyon lands of Utah, the Four Corners area where the states of Utah, Arizona, New Mexico and Colorado meet. We started outside of Moab, as millions do each year. We'd never been there, and as Keith Riker would say, it's "where God lives." It's a remarkable place, with a spiritually akin to that which we'd experienced at Chaco Canyon. We went to Monument Valley, where they must have filmed John Wayne and Randolph Scott movies. We camped along the Colorado River during the first few days, and the San Juan River on one of the last nights. We saw Devil's Kitchen, Utah and the cliff dwellings of Mesa Verde, Colorado.

The last night of camping was outside of Durango, Colorado. We awoke to the sound of gunfire. It was hunting season and we left in a hurry. The only orange I had with me was Broncos orange. I don't recall any other ten days in a row in my life that I had ever felt that good about.

1992 was nearing its end. My life had changed dramatically in that one year.

Before 1992 was ushered out the Colorado Rockies became a reality, holding their first "draft" party at Currigan Hall. I had committed to two season tickets, as a part of a group that Bill Michaels had put together, so I was invited to the big Draft Day party. For the trivia buffs, the answer is David Nied.

One of the people I ran into there was Dave, Chris Coons' probation officer. He asked how Chris was doing and I proudly said that he had really turned around. He'd paid his fines and completed his community service. Chris was working at a machine shop in west Denver. Dave grinned, and said, "Have him call me. I want to take him to lunch. He's the *only one* in that group that went to 'Arkansas Valley', that has *not* been in trouble again." Can you imagine how good that made me feel?

CHAPTER 9
How'd you like that ride?

My two season tickets commitments amounted to $28 for each of the 81 home games. That was $2,268. Other than our house, we hadn't spent that much money on any one purchase in our 9 plus years of marriage. Neither one of the cars we'd bought in Colorado had cost that much. Louisa was not excited about my having made that financial commitment, but accepted it as a part of my childhood dream. She also knew that the tickets could be used as a way to meet with real estate clients and prospects or partners in our Amway business.

The real estate market had gone white hot at that point. I had every reason to believe that I could handle that kind of financial commitment, and more.

We went back to Snowmass for the Strehli-hosted meetings in March because our business was growing. That's where we met Tom and Janet Kaye, from San Diego, who would become integral parts of our lives. Perhaps you too have had an experience where you meet someone, or in this case, a couple, and you know immediately that there is a strong bond. It just feels good to be with them. We enjoyed all of the people we met at those meetings.

We had invited one of those people, Tana Lucas, to stay overnight at our home, rather than spend the night in a motel before her flight home the next day. She had a ticket for a flight back to Cincinnati the next day. On the way back to Denver we stopped at the Easter Seals Camp to visit Kevin's memorial.

Louisa had developed an allergic reaction to coffee. I recall moving the coffeemaker from the kitchen during Tana's visit because of Louisa's reactions to it. I had been opening a window or two and turning on the fan above the kitchen stove to help circulate air so that the aroma wouldn't affect her as much. I had stopped drinking coffee in the car when she was with me, not even using a travel mug with a top on it. Hey, I'm a New Age sensitive guy.

I didn't understand it at all. I had been drinking coffee long before I met Louisa, and during the entire time that we'd known each other. It started bothering her after we moved to Colorado.

As her allergic reactions progressed, they showed up in a couple of ways. One was to block her motor skills. Here's an example: Louisa is a mortgage broker, and I'm a real estate broker. So, we were meeting with a mutual client, at a coffee shop…a well-known and small coffee shop, with lots of heavily roasted coffee. Louisa could not function, mentally or verbally. She had to excuse herself, go outside to run the numbers and return. The three of us ended up sitting outside. There are coffee shops that are larger and have good air circulation, and she's okay there.

Her allergic reaction can also give her a migraine headache. While the temporary stalling of motor skills might have been funny, no one laughs at a migraine. I did some research and found that caffeine has been known to either cure or cause migraine headaches. In Louisa's case, we're talking about the smell (to her), or aroma (to me).

There was a period of time when she talked about coffee with so much negative energy that it caused big…*huge*

"YOU USED TO LIVE IN MY HOUSE."

arguments between us. I was and am always quick to point out how I have compromised where and when I drink my coffee. On more than one occasion I have raised the question, and my voice, about whether I would have to live alone to enjoy a peaceful cup of coffee. I just couldn't believe that the subject of coffee could carry so much negative energy for anyone.

I even used pretzel logic about the subject. To wit: "I don't drink alcohol anymore! I don't run around! You'd think that I have a right to at least one f—-ing vice!"

For several years I have used a coffee cache, set up in the laundry room, in the basement, with an air filter running, doors closed and heat passages blocks, etc. My office is in the basement, and she's in the bedroom, two levels up. So it works for both of us. In the summer I enjoy having the coffeemaker out on the back patio for my early morning coffee. I just have to make sure that the windows, on the east side of the bedroom are closed. I also tell people that we're a mixed marriage: I'm a coffee achiever and she's coffee allergic.

Comedians have made fun of couples arguing over how the toothpaste tube is squeezed, or where it goes in the medicine cabinet. Been there, done that…let's add how the silverware is distributed.

When we fought it didn't take much to set us off. The only worthy issues were probably around step parenting and the days when I drank (and drove). Our love has always been passionate. The highs have been very high and the lows have often been very low. We haven't always had heated disagreements. I will tell you about some emotional freezing in the pages to come.

I gave up the motorcycle in '93. After Kevin died, my own mortality became something more than a given. I didn't feel safe on the bike, with the number of big trucks that seemed to be swarming over the Denver streets. The bike sat at the end of our driveway, with a For Sale sign, until it was sold. Louisa had the privilege of handling the transaction. David had taken me to a Father's Day concert at the Auraria Campus, featuring the Allman Brothers, Arlo Guthrie and others. While we were at the concert, Louisa sold the bike for $50 more than I had paid in 1990.

CHAPTER 10
When the mother-in-law speaks...

Louisa's parents asked us to go to the Amway convention, in Michigan in the summer of 1993. We didn't want to take the '81 Volvo, so we rented a Subaru wagon for the trip. Before we were to leave, Judi asked if we would be okay with giving Jessica a ride to Alton, to her grandmother's house. We had no problem with it, because we enjoyed Jessica, and we'd be going through Alton, to visit with my mother, on the way to Michigan.

It was really funny, because Jessica, who was six years old at the time, was a chatterbox. Somewhere in Kansas Louisa pretended that she was asleep so that Jessica might stop talking. It didn't work. She stopped talking...in mid-sentence when *she* fell asleep.

After delivering Jessica to my former mother-in-law, we went to my mother's place. We stayed there overnight, knowing that we'd return in a few days and stay a little longer. It was on the return trip that I learned about yet another bit of the synchronicity of our lives.

At the convention we connected with Paul and Carol, Bob and Betty McKann, and Chuck and Jean Strehli, our complete line of "up lines." We roomed with Richard and Ellen, Louisa's brother-in-law and sister. That was interesting, for me, because I really hadn't spent much time with them over the course of the 12 years that Louisa and I had been together.

It was during one of the lunch breaks that Carol's influence became more significant. We had been to a Reba McIntire concert, after visiting the product expos. Richard and Ellen went back to the exhibition hall. Carol told Paul and Louisa to get something for our lunch and we'd meet at a designated place.

She and I had just sat down when she said to me, "I love you too much to see you continue with your self-deprecating humor. You're a much better person than you think you are, or say you are." I was floored! It wasn't that she was so frank, that was how she was, but that she cared enough to say what she did, in the way that she did.

She then gave me a book, <u>What to Say When You Talk to Yourself</u>, by Shad Helmstetter, PhD. I have to admit that I 'didn't get it' the first time I read it. However, after the second reading a year later, 'I got it.' I saw a way to be more like the person I wanted to be. We enjoyed the convention and made plans to attend in 1994 too.

I laugh to myself when I think back to an exchange that Carol and I had when she and Paul visited us almost a year before that event, just after Kevin died. Louisa and I have a long standing agreement that she cooks and I clean. She had cooked a meal for the four of us during their visit and I was cleaning up. Carol, who seemed to be in two or three rooms simultaneously, darting around as she did, came to me, asking, "What can I do to help?" I replied, "Get the hell out of my kitchen." I knew she was being helpful, but her pace was almost frenetic. She took it the right way, laughed and joined Louisa and Paul in the living room, telling them she'd been banned from the kitchen. I really enjoyed my relationship with her. She appreciated that I could be as frank as she could be.

"YOU USED TO LIVE IN MY HOUSE."

After the convention, Louisa and I drove back to my mother's house in Alton. She and Louisa had become close, and she told Louisa things about herself, or me, that I had never heard her share with anyone. My mother is the quintessential private person. For better or worse, I have a healthy share of those genes.

I knew that I had a sister who had been born and died on the same day. She lived long enough to be named Brenda Sue. I knew, or had been told, that my mother had blamed herself for losing her only daughter, for having worked so far into her pregnancy. She worked, standing for hours, at factory that made ammunition. That is essentially what I knew, and of course, that Brenda Sue was born between my brothers, Bob and Pat. What I didn't know, or maybe I didn't recall because I had been so young at the time, was that her birthday was August 16, 1951. Louisa was born August 17, 1951.

I think that may have been when I threw my hands in the air and said, "Okay, God. I get it. We're supposed to be together and you were planning it long before we met. Sign me up" No doubt, He had already signed me up.

So it would seem that we were on the road to living happily ever after, or at least to 'growing old together.' Yet, deep inside I had a nagging feeling that I was living an old Peggy Lee song, "Is *that* all there is?" I was never quite happy. I saw some things as better, and enjoyed myself along the way, but I felt that I didn't know real happiness. When we fought, I was so angry that we hadn't found "happily ever after." I would say, and often scream that we shouldn't be going through the same things time after time.

As I've come to learn, even more recently from Dr. John DeMartini, in his book, <u>The Breakthrough Experience</u>, there is reason to be grateful for everything that happens, even that which causes pain. There was a positive that came from Kevin's death. There was a great deal more that came from his life, but a very important change occurred after he died.

It has become so easy for me to tell others that I care about them, in fact that I love them. That feeling stirred when I experienced Chuck and Jean Strehli and the others that I had met, at the SkiGlo meetings in 1988. The ways that they spoke to and of each other with such respect and affection was unique to me at that point.

I don't have memories of hearing "I love you," around the house when I was a kid, or my grandparents' homes, either. I don't recall having said it to my former wife very often, and it certainly wasn't a part of our daily vocabulary. I don't recall saying it to Louisa often enough, or to my kids, my brothers or my mother, with any frequency until after Kevin died. Somewhere along the line, after his death, we all began to express our love to each other in virtually every conversation, or as we part company, in person, on the phone and even on Instant Messenger. I like that about my life. I really believe that Kevin gave that to me. **Kevin gave us so much more than he ever required of us.**

I relate to Garth Brooks' hit song…"So tell that someone that you love, Just what you're thinking of, If tomorrow never comes…" **(15)**

CHAPTER 11
1993 Can it get any crazier?

Louisa and I were planning to go to a business function in Austin in late September. There were a lot of people working with her at AMOCO who were going to Texas too. They were being transferred to Houston. Others had been sent to Oklahoma City and still other had been sent home. She had been a full time employee for about 8 years, so we thought that she might be moved home, too.

Before we left for that trip, a friend called me and asked me to sell his house. It was located in a popular neighborhood where houses were selling quickly, and often being scraped, or raised, so that a new house could be built on the lot. I was about to learn some tough lessons that would serve me well in my real estate career.

I was going to visit the house that I was to market, and asked Dale Southworth to go with me. I knew that it needed some minor repairs and wanted Dale's input. He's been a contractor and would know better than I what to have done before putting the house on the market.

We noted ten items, that were all minor, and I presented it to my friend. He wanted what I thought would be an achievable price if he had those ten items taken care of. Once he had a few of them corrected, I put the house on the market. That was a mistake on my part. The other items weren't corrected after that.

Not long after that I listed another house nearby that was owned by one of his relatives. Shortly after I put it on the market I held an Open House. I now know that most houses don't actually sell to people who see it during an Open House. Most agents hold Open Houses for two reasons, because the sellers expect and/or want them to, and to meet buyers. More often, it's the latter.

I sent cards to follow up with each person who had registered as a guest during the Open House. A few days later I received a call from the mother of one of those people, saying that she was impressed with my follow up and wanted to have me help her find a house for her daughter. It was the daughter who had come through during the Open House. I remembered her once I heard her name because she was a very pretty young woman.

So, I had met a new buyer, and still had two houses on the market in the same neighborhood. The next Sunday, I held an Open House at our friend's house. We had a lot of people look at it that day, and over the next few weeks, but no offers. My friend was becoming anxious about it because he wanted to use the proceeds for an advanced degree. One morning, while we were meeting at a coffee shop, he raised his voice at me, exclaiming, "Just bring me a damn offer!" You've read enough to know that didn't sit well with me. I offered that he hadn't kept his end of the agreement by not completing the recommended repairs. I wasn't having any trouble getting people into the property. They simply weren't going for it at the price we were asking, given the condition it was in. The other neighborhood property that I was working on was getting prospects through it too and most of the feedback I got was that it was too small.

Meanwhile, I was meeting with the mother and daughter/buyers. Mom was actually buying the house for her daughter. Mom was an attorney who had also been a real estate broker in another state at one time.

When we found a couple of properties that the daughter showed an interest in, I offered some advice on the houses and the pricing. They had signed a Buyer Agency agreement with me. Then the mother said, "I don't care what you think." 'Well, okay then,' I thought. They made the offer they thought was right, or that the Mom did, and it was accepted. A few days later, during the inspection, I was sitting on the front porch and 'Mom' sat down beside me. She asked, "Do you think I've made the right choice for my daughter?" I wanted to say 'why ask me?' Instead I said, "Only time will tell." She said nothing more to me, except regarding procedural matters through the closing.

Sometimes, in real estate, you work with people that you want to work with again, and ask for referrals from them. Sometimes you don't. I filed that one in the latter category.

We hosted our first AMOCO Intern, Bill Dinklage, that summer too. We enjoyed his company and friendship.

We did work in the trip to Austin, and invited one of our friends, Ken Crouse, who had become a down line in our business, to go with us. He agreed, and rather than our Volvo or his car, we rented a car for the trip. We planned to drive straight through each way.

I had been driving the first leg of the journey and turned it over to Ken just outside of Raton, New Mexico. We were no longer on I-25, but had gone on US 64 southeast towards Texas. It's a pretty straight road and Ken was driving very fast. I thought I saw the speedometer reach 85 mph and started to say something to him, to ask him to slow down. The speed limit was 55 mph. Just then a New Mexico State Trooper pulled us over. The trooper was of the kinder and gentler demeanor…right out of Gary Cooper movies. He, very slowly and pleasantly, talked to Ken about his speed and wrote him a rather expensive ticket for it.

Once in Austin, we stayed at the home of our friend, Mary Beth Thompson. I had hired MB to be the marketing director for Pueblo Mall in 1983. She didn't stay at Pueblo Mall for very long, but we'd been friends since. She had moved to Austin a few months before our visit.

MB had a one-bedroom condo and we were sorting out the sleeping arrangements when I told Ken, "I know we'll find you up against the refrigerator." He had brought his magnetic mattress. MB wanted to let Louisa and me use her bedroom. She would sleep on the sofa. My brother Bob was driving up to Austin to see us too. He and Mary Beth had met when he lived in Denver, and she was happy to have him join us. He slept on the floor too. Bob was having some back problems and said the floor actually felt good.

The second night of the meetings, Bob went to the banquet with us. Mary Beth passed on it. Bob was enjoying our friends whom he'd met through dinner. We heard Brian and Marg Hays talk, and when they finished Bob turned to me and asked me to show him how the business worked. We went out to the lobby area and I "drew the circles" for him. He said, "So, this is what you've been trying to tell me all these years?" I told him that it was, and he asked how he could get started. He had met Bob and Betty McKann, and I connected them so that they could make plans to get together once they were all back in Houston.

The next morning, I walked Bob out to his truck as he was leaving to go home. He was complaining about his back hurting so much and promised to get it checked when he got back to Houston.

The trip home should have been uneventful. However, with Ken driving again, somewhere in southern Colorado and somewhere in the middle of the night, I awoke to find him reading while he was driving. I had a reading lamp with an adjustable chord that could be worn around the neck to read at night in bed not while driving a car.

I exclaimed, "Ken, what in the hell are you doing? Trying to get us all killed?" He just laughed and handed it to me. He's a great guy and he's also another good friend who is no fun to ride with…unless I'm the driver.

My brother Bob and I had been calling each other more frequently after he returned to Houston. He had registered as one of our down lines, and we also talked more because of his frequent visits to the doctors. The doctors had found a couple of fractured vertebrae and were treating them.

Not long after we returned from Texas, Kelly and Jeremy came to us, to tell us that they planned to be married. Kelly said that her mother was not in favor of it, that she didn't care for Jeremy or think that he was good enough for her.

I told Jeremy not to take Judi's opinion personally…that she wouldn't think he was good enough for Kelly if he had been Phi Beta Kappa and quarterback on the school football team. Kelly was her daughter and it was that simple. When I thought about my track record, I didn't feel qualified to pronounce their decision right or wrong. I just told them that I had learned that communication was a lot more important to a relationship, than sex. I've heard it said, and I agree, that a marriage can't survive on sex alone, or without it. I think the relationship has *no* chance without communication between the partners. It later turned out that Judi was more right than wrong about Jeremy.

Jeremy had joined the Marines and was stationed at Camp Pendleton. Kelly flew to San Diego not long after that, and they were married there. When she returned, she told us that she was going to move to San Diego while Jeremy was stationed there. I asked her to talk with me if there was anything that she felt she needed to clear the air about before she moved away. My little girl was about to move away from me for the first time, and for the foreseeable future.

We took a ride, but only to the park a block away. She talked about one concern that she had with Jeremy. They fought, often over little things. I knew something about how that worked. I asked her if he had ever become physical with his anger and she said, "No. I do." She said that she was more likely to fight physically than he was.

She also opened up something she'd been repressing for years, that she was angry with me about my Amway business. Specifically she was angry because I spent so much time and money on it, and felt that I hadn't given her the same effort. She said every time she got in my car, I was listening to an Amway tape. She could have been right, I don't know. I *do* know that I spent much more time on *any* job, or business, than with any of my kids. Just having told me how she felt seemed to relieve her of her anger about it.

Jeremy came home for Christmas, and his parents hosted a party for the newlyweds. They stayed with us, and made plans for their trip to California. Louisa and I volunteered to drive the rental truck, with their furniture, to San Diego. We could stay with our new friends, Tom and Janet Kaye, help Kelly and Jeremy find an apartment, and then rent a car to drive back to Denver.

A couple of weeks before we left for California, I met with my friend regarding his property that we still hadn't sold. I told him that we had, in the 90 days on the market, had over a hundred people go through it, and we hadn't had a real offer. I had a verbal nibble, but it didn't get as far as a written offer.

"YOU USED TO LIVE IN MY HOUSE."

I asked him to take it off the market during the holidays, and said that, if he completed the repairs by February, I would market it again. I also told him that if he didn't want to do anything else to it, and wanted to list it with another agent, that I would be fine with that decision, and that it would not affect our friendship. I even recommended the agent he might use. I wasn't smart enough at the time, to call the agent first, with a referral. He did use that agent and the started marketing the property in February. It sold for about $20,000 less a few months later.

We were ready to leave for California when Bob called to say that the doctors had told him that the vertebrae weren't healing and they would need to do more tests.

I showed Kelly and Jeremy the southern route to San Diego. It was the last week of December and I knew that, while it was a longer route, there were basically only a few places where they might run into snow, Monument Pass just south of Denver, and Raton Pass and Albuquerque, in New Mexico. That's the route we would take with the truck. They were going to leave a day after us.

We napped at a Rest Area in northern Arizona after driving that far the first day and much of the night. I called my Aunt Met, in Phoenix, from the Rest Area, and we stopped for a brief visit with her and my uncle Earl. Then it was on to San Diego, and Tom and Janet's house

The next day we met their daughter Elizabeth and went to the pier shopping area for lunch. Kelly and Jeremy were to arrive that afternoon. They were going to drive straight through from Denver. By nightfall they still hadn't arrived.

Tom invited me to go to the Holiday Bowl football game with him and another friend. While we were at the game, Kelly called to say that she and Jeremy would be in around midnight, had some delays and would explain when they got there. Tom, Louisa and I had gone to bed for the night before they arrived. Janet wanted to stay up and greet them when they arrived. Kelly had the directions, but had never met Tom or Janet.

They arrived a little after midnight and were surprised that Janet had stayed up until they got there. After brief introductions she showed them to the room they'd be using. The next day we were off to unload the truck and to find an apartment. But of course that wouldn't happen until Janet had served breakfast for all of us. I think Tom was off to work at daybreak in those days.

Kelly and Jeremy had not taken the southern route. They looked at a map and saw that the route was shorter, going through the mountains, over Wolf Creek Pass. I thought, 'Therein lies the problem.' They had gotten into snow and more difficulties than I care to relate. They battled the elements, car trouble, and each other before stopping for the night, and continuing on to San Diego the next day.

We accomplished both of our missions with the apartment and the truck, the former being in Oceanside, closer to Camp Pendleton. It was a rush job to get the truck unloaded and returned in the allotted time. We went back to San Diego, and Janet played host again the next day. At one point, Kelly said, "Are you sure you just met these people in March of *this* year?" We had become close friends in a short period of time. A lot of that had to do with our natural chemistry. Another part of it I attributed to the kind of people we'd come to know with Amway businesses of their own. There was an air of trust in that environment. Kelly was getting another perspective of Amway.

Kelly and Jeremy bid adieu to us during the day on New Year's Eve day. Louisa and I planned to spend New Year's Eve with Tom and Janet, and then we'd drive back to Denver the next morning.

Janet recalled that I had been connected with First Night, Colorado and suggested that we might want to go to First Night San Diego that night. I did a double take when I saw Steven Clark there. He'd been a reporter at Channel 4 in Denver. I don't recall where we'd met in Denver, but to my surprise, he remembered me.

As usual, we had a great time with Tom and Janet. Watching our wives, Tom and I talked about how the two women were like twin daughters of different mothers.

Louisa and I left early the next morning. We had good weather and were making good time heading home. That changed when she woke me up at 'No Name, Colorado,' as the snow began to fall. She asked me to take over the driving. The snow increased in volume and by the time we were at Vail Pass, it was a blizzard. The rental car we were driving, a Ford Taurus, handled well in the snow and we arrived home safely January 2nd. Kevin would have been 23 the next day.

Louisa often rode her bike to work, even during the winter. She took a spill on some gravel riding to work one day, falling on her tailbone. That, coupled with the hours sitting in front of a computer at work, she developed a herniated disc in her lower back. She got to the point that she had to stand during meetings at work, sometimes lying on the floor in her office or during a meeting. She hurt too much to drive. She also worked from home, using the computer while lying on her massage table. She had the table because she had been practicing touch therapy energy work Jin Shin Jyutsu, for six or seven years.

CHAPTER 12
Surrounded by pain…and lifted by support

February 5, 1994: Bob called to say that the doctors had found the cause of his fractured vertebrae. He hadn't talked with anyone, not even his daughter, Shelli. He had **cancer**. The words stopped. There was only crying on each end of the phone line. He went on to say that by the time they discovered it, the cancer had spread to a number of organs, and that he would start chemotherapy the next week. I just felt *empty*. I kept saying to myself, "Too soon. Too soon."

When I was ushered out of The Hahn Company, I was told that I would have to move my 401k. They had lied about it. I had finished there at the end of February 1987. I was to become fully vested on my eighth year anniversary of April 9, 1987. I believed that's why I was told to move the 401k. I didn't move it and I watched it grow with their investment firm over the years. Now, in 1994, I was instructed to move it by the end of the year. It was about a week or so after Bob's call that we went to a financial investment seminar and met Leslie Myers. While Louisa and I both felt a connection with her, we didn't meet with her immediately. Our plate seemed pretty full.

I was working with another new client at that time… another parent buying a place for a daughter. However, it was a decidedly different experience. The father certainly knew what he and his daughter wanted, but he was open to suggestions. He actually relied on my input. How refreshing. He and his wife lived in northern Colorado and their daughter, who was in school, wanted a condo in the Capitol Hill area. It made sense to them, and to me, to buy a condo for her rather than to pay rent for an apartment for her.

Before Louisa and I left for the SkiGlo meetings in March they had a contract on a condo that was going to work perfectly, with the closing scheduled for the end of March. Yes, Louisa was going to a conference at a ski resort, drop-foot and all. The drop-foot resulted from the herniated disc.

At Snowmass we roomed with several other people, in a large house that Dr. Stuart Menn had rented. We shared the large walkout basement room with Tom and Janet Kaye. They had flown into Denver to go up to Snowmass with us. Rooming with them became an important arrangement. Louisa's doctor had shown me how and where to insert the needles for her acupuncture treatments. He even used a marker to draw circles, not *the circles*, rather to show where the needles were to be placed. I asked him if I could do it from across the room, and he suggested that I might enjoy that more than Louisa. I wasn't sure why that would be a problem.

Nurse Janet liked to assist in the treatments, and it became something akin to the Comedy Hour. Then Janet became a great counselor for me when Bob, or his daughter Shelli would call. He was having a really bad time, and Shelli was having a terrible time with watching her dad suffer…knowing he was dying. I was torn between being where I was, and wanting to be with Bob and Shelli. She'd never had anyone but Bob.

I may not have gotten the full value of the business meetings that year. However, I was learning something that would be of greater value to me for years to come. The more time I spent with nurturing and caring people, the better person I seemed to be. It's been said and written about before… 'we are the company we keep…books we read'…etc.

"YOU USED TO LIVE IN MY HOUSE."

The father and daughter/buyers were using an out of state lender for their mortgage. He had used them before and it seemed like the right decision to him, although I didn't feel good about it.

It turned out badly at the closing. The mortgage company was located on the east coast, which meant dealing with the time difference as well as inconsistent communication, during the processing of the loan.

The closing was scheduled for Thursday, March 31st. Louisa, my brother Mike, Chris Coons and I were to leave for Houston immediately after the closing, in Mike's van.

The closing dragged on. Every time we thought the clients had signed the last document, something else was requested… from New Jersey. We were running out of time because the end of the workday, the end of the month. Rescheduling the closing would have sent it into the next month and increased the costs for the buyers. When it looked as though the closing would be postponed until Monday, I said, "Fine. I'm going to Texas. If it closes, send the check to Washington Park Realty." My clients knew why I was going to Texas and understood how I felt. The closer wasn't so positive about it. I left anyway.

With Mike and I taking turns driving, we drove straight through from Denver to Houston. I would rather have someone throw acupuncture needles at *me*, from across the room, than to do that again. However, reversing the route, we did it again 8 days later. Louisa wanted to drive, too. She did it for short periods, but had trouble sitting in the driver's seat. She spent as much time as possible lying on the van sofa or the floor. When we stopped for gas, etc, one of us would call Bob. We didn't know if we would get there before he died. Bob asked me about our route. I said, "You know, I was born in Wichita Falls, but I've never seen it. I think we might go through there." He said,

"It's a longer route that way, and you haven't missed anything." So we didn't go through Wichita Falls on that trip.

You can prepare yourself for something and still have it seem overwhelming. I had talked with Bob almost daily for two months. I knew he had cancer, and I've seen photos of people who had cancer at advanced stages. However, I know that Bob saw the reaction in our eyes when we saw him. He was a dark ghost of his former self. I hurt and I was consumed with grief and anger. I was angry with him for all of the years of his heavy drinking and equally heavy smoking. But I loved him, too. The hurt and anger were racing neck and neck throughout my being.

He was living with his girlfriend, Elaine, and her son Greg and daughter Paula. Bob and Elaine had met at a July 4th party and their relationship had since developed to an incredible bond. I thought it was strange that he had not mentioned her when we had seen him in Austin, in September. Our friend Mary Beth was **very** surprised to learn that he had a girlfriend back then. *That* caught me by surprise, too. I was left to wonder what that meant.

Elaine and Bob had fallen in love before he knew he was sick. Of course, the cancer was there, just not identified. The backaches had been around for several months before he went to the doctor. Elaine didn't have to stay with Bob, much less take him into her home, her life with her kids. Yet she did. She's an incredible, loving, human being.

Mike stayed with them, but Louisa, Chris and I were going across town to stay with our friends Bob and Betty McKann, in Seabrook. Bob and Elaine were still smoking, and Mike was a smoker so that worked for him. It didn't work for us, even though Chris was smoking at the time. He wouldn't be smoking at the McKann home. We left Mike's van with him, and took Bob's truck to Seaford. He was unable to drive it himself.

After we settled in, at Bob and Betty's place, I called Mom. Of course, she asked how Bob looked. I said, "You've seen people with cancer, even your brother, Gene. *But this is your son*, and it's going to be very difficult for you to see him." She would be flying to Houston a couple of days later. She asked me to write down two Bible verses, and told me to ask him if he had accepted Christ as his Savior. If he said no, I was to read the verses to him.

The next day we went back to Elaine's house. I asked for some private time with Bob and he and I sat in the back yard. I delivered Mom's message. He responded, "Of course I've accepted Jesus. I couldn't get through this without Him." That evening I conveyed that to Mom. She said, "That's all I need to know." From the moment she arrived, until we said goodbye the following Saturday, she never wavered. Everybody had been concerned about her and how she would handle it. Everybody but her, that is.

I was in awe of Louisa. I knew that she was in pain too. She never complained about it. On Easter Sunday, we went to church with Bob and Betty. That week went to a business meeting with them, and even out to dinner with a couple of Louisa's former AMOCO co-workers, and to a party for a friend of theirs who'd just become a U.S. citizen. I made time to do so many other things because it hurt so badly to see Bob in the condition he was in.

One day I took him into the city, to the M.D. Anderson Cancer Center for his check up. On the way home, I said I wanted to clear with him. Was there anything at all that he and I needed to clear up. He looked at me and said, "I don't have anything, and you don't or you'd have told me. I love you, big brother."

On Saturday, April 9th, Bob and Elaine were married in a beautiful park in Houston. I still have the video that Bob McKann shot. I've never been able to watch more than a few minutes of it.

Bob and Shelli had stayed with his friends, Bennett and Mildred Fain, when the moved back to Texas in 1988. After the wedding the Fain's threw one Texas size party for Bob and Elaine.

I think it was my brother Mike that had tracked down our distant brother, Pat. He was in Alabama, and was going to fly in for the wedding. True to form, he missed his plane and the wedding, and almost missed us too.

I made a decision that doesn't quite rank with those that I'll always regret, but I have second-guessed myself about it. Like so many other decisions, there's no way to undo it.

Mike and Louisa had to be at work on Monday. I didn't have a job to go to, but I did have a real estate business to tend to. So, we planned to leave in the evening of the party. I was determined that we were going to go, even though we'd miss Pat. Wasn't it him who missed us? We did meet him at the airport, long enough to say hello and then head back to Denver. Chris asked me, "Are you sure you want to do this? It's probably the last time you'll all be together." I knew that. Still, I said yes, because of my frustration with Pat. We left. Okay, it does rank up there with the regrets. I still can't change it. God, I hate that "C" word.

CHAPTER 13
Can we have some good news for a change?

Near the end of April, Kelly called to tell us that she and Jeremy were expecting a baby. We were going to be grandparents! She had been going to school at a community college near their home, and life was good for her. She sounded really excited.

Louisa and I had a goal of going camping each month, even if only for one night, that summer. On the Friday before Mother's Day we were about ready to leave for one of those trips, when Kelly called. Louisa thanked her for the Step Mother's Day card. It was a surprise for Louisa, and I think it was the first time Kelly had expressed her love for her. When I started talking with Kelly, Louisa could see that it wasn't good news. I sat on the kitchen floor and listened to her tell me about how Jeremy didn't understand how little money they had. If he knew there was money in the checking account he thought he had the right to take money from the ATM. They had checks bounced and he blamed her for trying to control him. The news about her pregnancy had been a momentary glimpse of happiness.

Kelly had been with Jeremy for two years. She knew him, and his lack of responsibility. She, like most of us, thought the Marines would change all that. Jeremy came from a long line of Marines, after all.

What I should have known then and firmly believe now, is that no one can change us. We don't change others, either. We can change ourselves and only ourselves.

After talking with Kelly, Louisa and I left for the camping trip. We felt that we *needed* it.

The next week, Leslie Myers, the financial planner we'd met in February, called and we talked about meeting at the end of May. I think that, in addition to dealing with everything in front of me, I was also not in a hurry to comply with the Hahn mandate.

CHAPTER 14
The mother of all camping adventures

The camping trip was another adventure. One of the agents at Washington Park Realty, Terri Colburn, offered the use of an old mining cabin, near Breckenridge, that she and her husband, Cy, owned. She said that it was rough and they'd run people off the property from time to time, and that the Nordic Center had taken over much of the land around it.

We left later than we had hoped and got to Breckenridge at dusk. It was a dark and stormy night...oh yeah, and it got stormier. We parked near the Nordic Center and walked around, looking for the cabin, following the directions Terri had given me. As the rains came, I got frustrated and angry, insisting that we either go back to Denver or sleep in the car, and find the cabin in the daylight. As I was fuming, Louisa continued to follow different trails in search of the cabin.

We found a building that looked like an older building that had a newer addition built on to it. There was an open door that led through a kitchen and into what was obviously a big dining hall. It seemed that Terri was right, that their property *had* been taken over.

I knew that we had found the place where *I* was going to sleep. I told Louisa that she could roam the woods in the rain all night if she wanted to, but my sleeping bag was going to be on one of those *picnic tables* in that dining hall. Surprisingly she agreed, and joined me. So there we were, sleeping on wooden picnic tables, somewhat smaller than a single bed. Some camping trip! At least we weren't out in the storm. There was a lot of rain, wind and lightning all around us.

In the morning the skies had cleared and we ventured out. I set up the Coleman stove for...you guessed it, coffee. Not long after that a couple of people came by and we explained our presence. When asked how we got into the dining hall we showed them the unlocked door. We talked with them about the mining cabin, and I think they were suppressing laughter they pointed in a northeast direction and said it was near the beaver pond. Louisa showed them the map we'd been given. We couldn't find the beaver pond, or obviously the cabin, in the dark the night before.

It didn't take too long to find the pond, or the cabin, in the daylight. I looked at it and thought we'd be better off nesting in the dining hall.

Rustic Mining Cabin: Maybe 12' X 10', with a bunk bed and a loft. There were old, nasty mattresses and remnants of food that animals or rodents had opened...flour and sugar, a stove and a kitchen table of sorts. Locals, or transients, had probably used it for booze and dope parties.

Louisa found a broom and we started cleaning up the place. It was no mean feat. By noon it was almost habitable enough to be condemned. I went outside to relax, with a book, while she went to the pond to do some fishing. It looked like everything would work out and I was feeling better about the trip, all the while thinking about Kelly's dilemma, and her pregnancy.

As is usually the case in these parts, the warmth of the sun is followed quickly by the cool of the evening. It's more apt to be the cold of night, in May, in the high country. We ate just before dark and decided to settle in for the night. My goal was to be out early and get the hell out of that cabin as soon as possible.

When darkness was complete, the show began. We weren't alone. I'd given some thought to the possibility of bears or deer, and had secured the door in as much as it was possible. It sounded like it was rush hour for the bats and rats.

Louisa lit a candle, thinking that would make, at least the bats, go back into hiding. While that might have helped, it didn't help that she had put it in paper drinking cup with wood chips to hold it upright. I was sleeping lightly and was awakened by the fire caused by the candles in the paper cups... sitting on the table that was covered by some cheap shelf paper. I jumped up, and she followed. We got the fire put out before the cabin caught fire. It would have taken only a few minutes to burn it down.

Louisa went back into her sleeping bag, pulling it up over her head. I did the same. I felt like I was fighting bats and rats all night. I was too busy praying for dawn to come, to get any sleep. She later said she slept well, thinking that I would be protecting her.

I was up and out of there at the crack of dawn. Louisa took her time to join me. We walked a number of trails, exploring the area, and it was around noon when we drove back to Denver. It took a while before I could locate the humor in that episode.

We spent two nights of the Memorial Day weekend camping. It was something that brought us closer together, even when bats and rats didn't surround us. Or perhaps, that we weren't aware of them. We actually returned to that cabin later that summer for a less eventful night and Louisa fished in the Beaver pond the next day…while I slept.

Leslie Myers and I talked again, and set an appointment for the 1st of June. It was time for me to move my 401k.

CHAPTER 15
Sometimes I wonder why God trusts me so much

Tuesday, May 31st, Louisa got a call from her father, Paul. Her mother had been in an auto accident while attending her 50-year reunion at Sweetbriar College in Lynchburg. Paul said that Carol had been kept overnight for observation, and that he was going to drive to Lynchburg to pick her up.

After Louisa talked with Paul, she called the hospital that Paul had named. It was obviously the wrong name and hospital. It was a veterinary hospital. Louisa made several calls before she located the right hospital, and learned that Carol was in ICU.

Carol hadn't had just an auto accident that required overnight observation. Paul was on his 4 hours plus journey and had no idea about what Louisa was learning. She'd been badly injured, when her car was hit broadside by two other vehicles. She suffered multiple injuries and the most threatening was a Subdural Hematoma. The impact had caused her beaded seat cushion to be thrown against her head, apparently causing that injury. *We* had given her that seat cushion.

We weren't all that Internet savvy in early 1994. Somehow, we managed to located flights to Dulles Airport near Washington, D.C. We could rent a car and then drive to Lynchburg.

Louisa was talking with nurses and doctors about Carol's injuries. They wanted to operate to relieve Carol's brain from the pressure caused by the Subdural Hematoma. There was a catch; only Paul was authorized to approve the surgery. He was, by then blazing a trail in his Buick, somewhere between Newport News and Lynchburg. There was no way to reach him. Louisa called her sister Ellen, relating that the doctor said they would prep their Mother for surgery and not begin it until Paul arrived. Now, in 2006, I find it hard to believe that doctors would accept her word, or that hospitals would allow it. *In today's world*, we might have lost Carol then and there.

We then called our friend Rose, who lived near D.C. and was also a friend of Paul and Carol. She said that she would pick us up at Dulles and take us to Lynchburg. There was a twist to that, too. Her car was in disrepair, so she borrowed the car of a friend…who, at the time, was in Mexico.

We were all converging on Lynchburg, Louisa and me, Rose, and of course Paul. Paul, expecting to pick up Carol and take her home, would learn when he arrived at the hospital, after his drive of more than four hours that she was ready to go into surgery. Paul was devastated because she didn't recognize him when he first saw her. I think that scared him more than it hurt him. They'd been together for close to 50 years at that point. After the surgery and still under the influence of anesthesia, she *did* recognize Paul.

An amazing week, revealing the best of human nature, was about to unfold.

When we arrived at Dulles, Rosie was there to pick us up and we were off to Lynchburg, with almost four hours of highway ahead of us.

By the time we arrived, Paul had gotten a room at a nearby hotel. We were ushered to the ICU where he was with Carol.

"YOU USED TO LIVE IN MY HOUSE."

We all ended up with rooms at the hotel that night. The next morning when we returned to the hospital, Carol was awake.

We had been scheduled to go back to the Amway convention in less than two weeks. Of course, we knew that it wasn't going to happen. Carol looked at me and said, "We're not going to the convention, are we?" I replied, "Not this year." She said, "That's horrible." I said, "No. Starving kids in Africa…that's horrible, missing the convention is not." She was gracious Southern lady. She would apologize if you told her you weren't feeling well. But I'm getting ahead of myself.

Richard and Ellen arrived and we all took turns visiting with Carol. Paul knew that he had to go back to Newport News for changes of clothing and toiletries. Of course, she wasn't out of the woods, and he wasn't going to leave until the doctors gave him the green light, that she'd be okay.

Carol's head trauma may have been the worst of her injuries, but her ribs and legs were badly bruised. There were a number of complications. It wasn't until she was in rehab several months later that it was discovered that her left leg was broken.

About midday a woman who had been president of the alumni association of Sweetbriar College contacted Paul. She and her husband invited all of us to their home for dinner. Pressing business required Richard to go back to the Virginia peninsula that day.

That evening five of us went to their home of Burt and Ann Reams for dinner. They insisted that we move out of the hotel and stay in their home. They were about to go to Virginia Beach for the birthday of one of their grandchildren. They were going to turn over their home to five people they'd just met. They said they'd be gone a week. We wondered whether they had extended their stay at Virginia Beach, in part so that we could have their home.

The next day Paul went home to retrieve the items he needed for a stay of undetermined length.

Something flashed into my mind. I had an appointment scheduled with Leslie Myers, sixteen hundred miles away. I called and told her where we were and that I'd reschedule when we got back to Denver.

Rosie asked me to drive her friend's car and I took her, Louisa and Ellen to the hospital. We later drove to the auto shop where Carol's car had been taken. What we saw was another car that was so extensively damaged that it was hard to believe that anyone had lived through the accident. It had been hit broadside by two cars. That's when we learned that the seat cushion beads that hit Carol in the head were those we'd given her.

Ellen and Rosie are both world-class talkers. I couldn't get back to the hospital soon enough. I pulled up as close to the entrance as I could, saying that I'd park the car and then come in. Of course, Ellen and Rosie thought I was just being the gentleman that I can be. Louisa knew my ulterior motive. She got out last and smiled when I said, "Thank you for being you." My ears and my mind needed a break. I took my time walking back to the entrance and the ICU.

We returned to Denver June 4th, after staying at Rosie's condo the night before. The next afternoon I received the call from Houston…Bob had just died. One of my first thoughts was that he was born in '47, had lived slightly more than 47 years. Add them and you get the year of his death, 1994. Another of life's uncanny twists of fate.

The next day, after mass, we were visiting with some friends in the social hall, when one of them said, "You two have had a lot on your plate. I don't know how you do it." I knew that it wasn't about us. We were all right. It was our loved ones who were suffering a lot more than us. I believe in the saying that 'God never gives us anything we can't handle.' However, sometimes I wonder why he trusts me so much.

We didn't go back to Texas. Bob had said that he didn't want us to do that. We had been there while he was still alive, and that's what he wanted.

Not long after that one of the members of "10:30", as we called it, hosted a potluck at a place he'd purchased near Evergreen. What stands out for me, about that day, was a comment a woman named Marie Morrison, made to me. We had known Marie during the food co-op days and hadn't seen her in several years. As we were renewing our acquaintance, she said, "You don't seem angry like you used to." I was more than a little surprised by her comment. I couldn't recall any incidences of anger outbursts around the food co-op. Obviously, she could. Apparently dealing with Kevin's death, and Bob's, and then Carol's close call, had taken some of the steam out of me.

CHAPTER 16
We are family…Hatfields and McCoys…that is

I was working a lot of temp work that summer. I'd been gone so much that I hadn't given much time to my real estate business. You've heard how cyclical the real estate business can be. I found at least two common threads with it and our Amway business. When I worked the businesses they worked. When I connected with people in a way that showed them that I cared about them, it worked. Maybe it's the same in most businesses. I'm not talking about jobs, per se. People buy houses year round, and people buy consumer goods year round. The only thing that makes either cyclical or go "up and down," is the person attending, or not attending to it. Of that, I am convinced. I submit that marriage, and relationships by any name, fit that description too.

I hadn't had a real estate transaction since the closing before we drove to Texas in April. Yes, that transaction *did* close after we left for Texas that day.

I was working in the mailroom at a US West office when I got the call from Louisa, telling me that Pat, Elaine, Shelli, Greg and Paula would be arriving at our place the next day. It would be their first stop on a road trip from Texas through Colorado, Illinois and Alabama. It was a farewell tour for Bob as they carried his ashes with them.

I recall that it was so hot the day they arrived that I was hosing down our house, to cool off the bricks. Shelli had a friend with her, a pretty young woman named Karen. Most of us went to a Rockies game that evening. Afterwards I talked with Shelli. She was having a lot of problems with the fact that Pat and Elaine had become a couple. I told her that it was probably not uncommon for two people to connect when they'd been through so much emotionally, as Pat and Elaine had done while nursing Bob until his death. Shelli felt that they'd been intimate in Bob's presence while he was still alive. I couldn't buy that argument and chalked it up to the stress she was under.

I talked with Pat and Elaine about their situation because I love them, and I knew that Shelli probably wouldn't be the only person who would make judgment on their situation. They knew that and accepted it.

They left a few days later, to see Mom, in Alton and then to Talladega, Alabama, to scatter some of Bob's ashes near where he had watched Davy Allison run his NASCAR races. They would ultimately place more ashes in one of Bob's favorite fishing holes in Texas. They were spreading them according to Bob's wishes.

Shelli, and Elaine and Pat were at odds the entire trip. If one of them wasn't calling me, the other was. They were supposed to be traveling in tandem, but angry words had them losing track of each other on the road. I just pleaded with them, saying, "For God's sake, I hope you don't end up on the Geraldo show!"

My next, and only other real estate transactions, came about in September when our friends, and neighbors, Jim and Kim Azevedo, and Kim's mother Cheryl decided to sell the duplex at the end of our block. Jim and Kim were moving back to Las Vegas, and Cheryl wanted to buy a place in Virginia Village. I sold the duplex and then helped Cheryl find her next home. I knew it was time for a change.

CHAPTER 17
There's good news too

On September 8th, our first grandson, Brendan Todd Nix, was born. Kelly said that she had gotten emotional and added Kevin's middle name, Todd, as Brendan's middle name. As exciting as that was, there was more to the story. Our friend Janet Kaye, played surrogate mom, visiting Kelly the day Brendan was born.

Another aspect to it was that Jeremy refused to depart with his unit, on their float. I was in the Army, and not the Marines. However, I was shocked when he wasn't thrown in the brig. Back in May, I had told Kelly that she needed to confide in the chaplain assigned to Jeremy's unit. The non-commissioned officers and commissioned officers alike, listen to the chaplain regardless of which branch it is. Through the relationship she had developed with the chaplain, arrangements were made to transfer Jeremy to another unit. My brother Mike is a former Marine. He could not believe they had done that. Missing departure of a float was a major mistake when he served in the Marines.

Pat and Elaine, along with Greg and Paula, moved to Denver about the same time. They rented a house about 2 miles south of us.

I was working a temp job at Met Life at the time, and my friend Ray Anderson had taken me to lunch to talk with me about joining him at a Century 21 office. I knew that I wanted to make the move. I needed a fresh start. However, I decided to stay at Washington Park Realty through the sale of Cheryl's duplex, and the purchase of her next home. Dale and Linda had been good friends and very supportive of everything that I was balancing, not only that year, but since I'd known them.

The sale of the duplex, and finding a place for Cheryl happened pretty quickly. After the closings, I told Linda, then Dale, about moving my license. Linda said she wasn't surprised by the move. She was more surprised that I hadn't left real estate.

I also decided, at Ray's suggestion, to upgrade my license to that of an Employing Broker. He thought that his new office, for which he was the managing broker, might add an office in Washington Park, and that he would want me to manage it.

When Brendan was seven weeks old, Kelly decided to come home for the duration of Jeremy's float. I arranged to have her stay the first night with my aunt Met, in Phoenix, and called a couple in Albuquerque, Daniel and Jennifer, whom we'd met at a Strehli-hosted function in Austin, asking if Kelly could have their number in the event she had car or weather trouble on her trip. Jennifer said to tell her to plan to stay overnight there and not drive from Phoenix to Denver. Kelly had never met them, and we'd met them twice. Kelly was getting another adjustment to her perspective of Amway.

Nine months after meeting Leslie Myers, I actually sat face to face in her office. I had brought all of the information on my 401k, which had grown to about $27,000 by that time. She showed me several options about how and why I should roll it over and diversify my investments. The connection, or comfort level, that Louisa and I had felt in February was still there. There was an immediate bonding, a sense of trust. A part of that are her natural demeanor and a part of her education.

"YOU USED TO LIVE IN MY HOUSE."

After gathering information from her, I took it home to Louisa, who is much more astute with finances than I am, and it made sense to her. So that's how we began our relationship with Leslie. Now, more than a dozen years later the relationship is even stronger.

We have two friends, Brian and Steve, who are passionate about the stock market, and manipulating their investments. I say, "What am *I* going to tell her to do? *She's* the one with the CFP, CLU and MBA on her business card."

As though I was going to audition for a job as a juggler, I signed up for a broker's license correspondence course, complete with video testing. That coincided with a visit by my mother, our repainting the guest room before her arrival, and my decision to work part time at the post office through Christmas. The latter was important because I wasn't actively working real estate during the license transition.

We started working with a different group of Amway distributors, that month too. Our friend Harry Maurer had made a connection with a woman name named Marianna Johnson, on our behalf. She was a Diamond, with a group called International Connection (IC) that met regularly at a hotel only a few miles from our home. With Chuck and Jean Strehli's blessing, we attended the IC December meeting, and heard another Diamond, Glenn Graff, speak to the group. I had a feeling that I'd met him, or heard his name before. I became convinced that we could get our business off the ground with the support of this new affiliation.

Mom's visit was great for us, except that she was here during a **very** cold spell. She went to First Night, Colorado with us. I ran in the FNC midnight run while Mom and Louisa took in some of the indoor entertainment.

The correspondence course was a disaster. The videos frequently didn't match the printed course plan or exam questions. The job at the post office wasn't any better. I had the idea that I could work the midnight shift, then nap and study. HA HA HA HA! Well, it didn't work out that way.

And somehow, I got caught in the cross hairs of a supervisor with an attitude. She was offended that I called her 'ma'am' when I addressed her. Three weeks into the job I was fired, along with three others on the same shift. I had been counting on the money, of course. However, I still felt a sense of relief.

The result of those struggles showed up as two efforts to pass the license exam.

I just knew that 1995 would be better.

CHAPTER 18
Movin' on…

Louisa *wanted* to be laid off by AMOCO Production, in '94 when lay offs were happening with increased frequency. Really. In fact, she was asking for it. She even asked to be transferred to a department that was going to be closed down.

My real estate business got a jumpstart from "Uncle Bill." Bill is a loveable curmudgeon, who could pass for Jack Benny on the phone. His neighbors had dubbed him "Uncle Bill." He called me, referring me to a woman who had inherited a small house across the alley from his home, about a mile north of our home. I called her and met with her. That referral would ultimately lead to three transactions with her, and a terrific compliment during the sale of that small house. She said that I was the only person she trusted outside of her family, plus Bill of course. She insisted that I call her by her first name, Corrine. That trust would later be tested.

So, with my new office and two transactions at the start of the year, I was feeling pretty good about our financial outlook. We did add a couple of people to our Amway business, too. Still, there was this shadow that I hadn't shaken. I wasn't satisfied, or even happy. I recalled that Louisa thought that I'd never let myself be happy. Her mother suggested that I use St. John's Wort, for what I became convinced, was depression. Maybe Louisa was right. Maybe I could never really be happy.

Carol had spent a month at the hospital in Lynchburg, and Paul had worked there as a volunteer to be close to her. He stayed with the Reams family during that time. When she was released, she didn't go home, but rather to a rehab clinic. She was finally sent home and required the use of a walker. Clearly, her health had not returned, and her recovery seemed to be happening at a very slow pace. When I talked with her she seemed mentally alert. Physically, and to some degree mentally, she was not the same person, as she had been before the accident. If you could read *their* story, you'd see a love story that movie producers dream of.

When it came time to pay for my Rockies' season tickets, it would be the last time I would do so. The prices jumped. They would be playing at the new Coors Field, with "replacement players." The players' strike had cancelled the '94 World Series. I wrote, in the memo of my check: "Ransom for Season Tickets." I told Bill Michaels that I would withdraw from the season tickets group.

We went to the Strehli's SkiGlo meetings again in 1995. While we were gone, two things were taking place at home. A friend was spraying the knockdown plaster on our kitchen walls as we began to dress up the house more. Shortly after our return, my brother Pat came to see me to tell me that he, Elaine and the kids were moving back to Texas. I knew that the Colorado winter would be difficult for him. Cold weather had always been tough on him since he broke his neck, while living with me Judi and me, in Williamsburg.

At the end of mass, on the following Sunday, someone announced that a temporary home was needed for a refugee couple from the Ukraine. Louisa and I just looked at each other and said we'd do it. The couple, Rost and Vicky Ditkosvky, had stayed a night or two with another couple from the church.

"YOU USED TO LIVE IN MY HOUSE."

However, their home didn't have the space for Rost and Vicky to stay longer. We were, after all, living in a house that had housed as many as 10 at one time or another.

Our new houseguests arrived at our home the next day. When we welcomed them, I anxiously showed them to our guest room, with a private bath. They looked confused. I laughed when I learned that they had thought that I was telling them to stay in there. Rost knew almost no English at that time. Vicky had been a guide at a museum in the Ukraine, and had advanced degrees. She spoke some English. Louisa was pretty efficient at communicating with them. When I tried, Vicky would say, "Perry. Please slow down."

They were with us for about ten days before they found an apartment about a mile northwest of us. Louisa stopped by there most days, on her way home from work, to help them with their mail, and such. Rost was learning English, from TV shows. Now, *that's* a scary thought. Not long after that, they moved to Salem, Oregon because Rost had difficulty with the altitude here. I guess the Portland area is, in many ways, similar to their home in the Ukraine, and there is a large Russian and Ukraine population there.

Rost was in Denver recently, and he took us to lunch. He has become very American, and is prospering as a capitalist. We really enjoyed Rost and Vicky, who (at this writing) have two sons now.

CHAPTER 19
Spats and Am-a-spats, or growing pains

David was living with the family of one of his friends, and working at a movie theatre. He gave us free passes as often as he could. To give you and idea of how I could say something that I thought was in jest, but would hurt Louisa and instigate an argument, I'll share this next story. We were leaving the theatre one night, and every thing seemed to be okay between Louisa and me. She sneezed, and I said, "I think you're allergic to life." That set off a pretty good argument about feelings and compassion. It also, as other arguments had, carried over to the next day when we were presenting the Amway business plan to a prospective couple. That didn't go well.

She had asked what time I wanted to leave. We left later than the time I had given her. We didn't arrive terribly late, only 5 or 6 minutes, but I am a nut about being punctual. I get all tied up in knots inside, when I'm running late. I shouted at her, in the car, "You don't have the right to make me late for an appointment that I set. Make yourself late on your own damn appointments if you want to, but not on mine!" There was a term that Amway distributors used, "AM-A-SPATS." It might sound funny, but for us, they were not fun.

We hosted AMOCO interns again that summer. Our guests were a young man from Georgia, and a couple who were newlyweds. I agreed to host a couple only if they both worked during the day. They agreed to it, but she didn't do it and everyday I learned some things about her that caused me to trust her less and regret having agreed to have them stay with us. They did leave early, having the opportunity to housesit for someone and a place to themselves. It was best for all of us that it happened that way. I'd be surprised if they're still married today. Then again, there are those who are surprised that we are.

A significant change took place just before we left to go to Austin for CLS meetings. Louisa quit her job at AMOCO Production. September 1, 1995 became her *personal* Independence Day. She had lobbied for months to switch jobs with someone who was about to be laid off, but didn't want to lose their job. I saw that situation in the Army. One guy couldn't wait to get out and another, who wanted desperately to stay, was being discharged for some quirky reason. Louisa wanted to leave, and of course, getting laid off would have given her a severance package. The powers-that-be said it couldn't be arranged, so she quit. I wondered if they had thought that she was bluffing. How could it be possible? You couldn't be around her for eleven years, and think for a minute that she was bluffing.

Pat, Elaine and the kids drove up to see us. It had been only two years earlier that Bob came from Houston to Austin to be with us. They were running late and we had an all too brief visit on the last day we were there…just before we headed back to Denver.

We registered two of Louisa's co-workers into our business. One of them, who registered in late 1994, dropped out of the business, and left AMOCO to focus on healing her breast cancer. We liked Julie quite a lot and missed seeing her. We had no idea, at the time, just how big of a role she would play in our own healing.

"YOU USED TO LIVE IN MY HOUSE."

The other, Cindy, joined us in the spring of 1995, and within a week took a road trip with us to meetings at a DFW Airport hotel outside Dallas. We had purchased another Volvo and we really enjoyed the road trips in it.

My real estate business was growing. It was as though the business looked entirely new to me. Century 21 provided great training. Dale and Linda Southworth had been helpful to me of course, but the Century 21 system greatly expanded my knowledge and enhanced my abilities. I met a couple who had moved to America from China ten years earlier, and by helping them buy their first home here, it turned into two referrals to their friends and family members who were also from China. I enjoyed them tremendously, and they welcomed Louisa each time we were together with them. They even took us to lunch during the celebration of the Chinese New Year.

That fall I met another couple, just before leaving that office. I had been showing them houses from mid-September well into December. Most of the time the husband and wife had to look at the houses separately, although both were with me at the same time. They had two small girls, and one would stay in their van with the girls while the other looked at the house, then trade places. (I had changed offices the first of December, and they stayed with me.)

That went on until a Saturday in December when the husband had to work and the wife hired a babysitter for the girls. On that day, on the first house we visited, she said…as she crossed the threshold…"This is it! I have to call Frank and have him come to see it, now." She did and he did, and I delivered that contract on Christmas Eve.

CHAPTER 20
New clouds on the horizon

Kelly and Brendan had gone back to Oceanside when Jeremy's float concluded. There were more phone calls about money problems, largely created by his misuse of it. She was going to school at a nearby community college, and in addition to taking care of Brendan, was caring for other kids in the neighborhood while their parents worked.

A red flag went up as Kelly and Jeremy were set to drive home for Christmas. Jeremy was ready to leave, but the parents hadn't picked all of the other kids up. He got angry and left without her and Brendan. Yes, he actually drove to Denver without them. Kelly and Brendan flew home. I thought that she was being stretched to the limit, raising two kids; one was a toddler and the other a Marine.

The day after Christmas, while I was at the Century 21 office I'd just joined, Louisa called me, asking, "Is there anything that you have to do, that you couldn't do by phone and fax?" I said, "No. Why do you ask?" She suggested that we pack that day and leave for Alton and Newport News. We left a couple of hours later.

I might have mentioned before, that we would drive straight through to Alton, and stay with my mother a day or two, and go straight through to Newport News. My Mother's house was about 30 miles from being exactly half way between Denver and Newport News. On the return trip we'd usually stay in Alton a day or two longer.

We spent two nights with Mom on that trip, took her to dinner the second day, and I connected with an old friend, Bill Piepert, who'd been a Realtor. He gave me his fax number in case I needed it for the transaction I'd left behind in Denver. I called our friends Ronnie and Linda Meyer, telling them we'd visit them on the return trip. We headed out for Virginia before dawn the next day, arriving in Newport News late that night, as in almost the next day technically.

While we were there, Louisa called, got a call from, or had run into Steve Wilson, the guy who had rejected her in 1981. She asked how I felt about her going to see him. I was okay with it, feeling that I had finally come believe that she'd rather be with me. I hadn't really felt that completely, until after our separation in 1991. Carol praised me for my trust in Louisa. I went to bed just before she came home. She told me how much it meant to her that I had trusted her and how happy she was to be with me.

I didn't have an old girlfriend that I wanted to see, and even fewer who might want to see me. I had burned some bridges.

We hadn't seen Carol since we left the hospital in Lynchburg, about 18 months earlier. She was not making great progress. It was amazing how Paul cared for her. He had to lift her at times, prepare meals and more. I don't know how many meals he'd prepared during their marriage, before Carol's accident, but I'm guessing it would be in the single digits.

A big snow delayed the start of our trip. Louisa and Paul had set out for church, only to return. They couldn't get out of the parking lot of the condos where Paul and Carol lived.

I did have a good visit with my old friend Paul Phillips. He'd gone through a rough time with his divorce, and said he hadn't handled things well. He was really proud of his kids, and spoke glowingly of them.

We left for Alton during snowfall and drove in it until we got past Charlottesville, then we didn't encounter any the rest of the way.

We spent another two nights with Mom before heading back to Denver. While we were there my uncle Gary called to tell me that our childhood friend, John Dorman, had died. He'd been living in New Mexico. In my mind John had led a pretty troubled life. I hoped that he had found happiness in the Land of Enchantment.

Along the way we discussed Louisa's Mother's health and how Paul was carrying such a load…not literally, Carol was a small woman. Louisa talked about flying out to Virginia at times to help him.

CHAPTER 21
New Year, New Beginnings

We hit the ground running after we returned from the trip. I had a closing scheduled for the end of the month, and new real estate prospects. We also had several new prospects for our Amway business. As I'm relating this to you, it occurs to me that I'm using the term "Amway business," which we rarely called it. We used the terms home-based or networking business. We didn't hide the affiliation with Amway. It was a business that was grossly misunderstood that we wanted an opportunity to show *what* it was, and *how* it worked, rather than have someone assume that we wanted him or her to sell soap for us. We were aware that people laughed at the business. By and large they hadn't met the people we'd met, so we have no trouble with our belief. Amway certainly didn't need me to defend it.

My January closing was delayed until the 5th of February, and we left on the 9th for CLS meetings in Dallas.

Our friend and cross-country skiing mentor, Dr. Stuart Menn, was the featured speaker. During the meetings I was approached by one of the SkiGlo conference leaders. She said, "Louisa tells me that you're not coming to SkiGlo next month." I said, "That's right. I haven't hit the goal I set for this year, and I'm tired of going back at the same level each year." Well, I/we hadn't done *that*. We had enjoyed some growth. She continued, saying, "That's bulls——-. We love you and we want you there. Figure it out."

Well, I didn't go. However, I took her comments to heart, with appreciation that she cared enough to talk with me about it. I could have said that I wasn't going because my real estate business was really growing. It was, but that wasn't the reason that I didn't go.

I didn't go because I had been called for Jury duty. I drove Louisa to Snowmass and went back to Denver. The jury duty call didn't get beyond the courtroom questions by the attorneys. So I went back to Snowmass on Friday, to attend the banquet and drive home with Louisa on Saturday. She was angry with me because I had taken the Volvo back to the dealership for maintenance without discussing it with her. That set off an argument that lasted somewhere past Glenwood Springs. I went into a funk. I thought things were going pretty well, and then again, I thought I just couldn't win.

It seemed that all of a sudden, I was among the top producers in my new office. The leads seemed to be coming at me from every direction. We were finally playing catch up with our finances.

Sometimes I think that I am a weird-behavior magnet. I've had some pretty unusual experiences over the years. None were harder to understand that what transpired between our friend Deanna Webb and us that year.

Deanna married the bass player in the band she sang with at Steamboat. We had met Chris and really enjoyed him. One of the agents in our real estate office was a pianist, and knew Chris. He called him the best bass player in Colorado. They stopped for a visit on a road trip to Florida. Deanna knew that Louisa is a map collector, and she asked to borrow some maps of highways between here and Florida. No problem.

It was sometime later that summer when we wondered why she hadn't returned the maps, in person or via the mail. I called to ask and was blasted for 'thinking that she had meant to steal them.' Since then we have heard from her only once. Shortly after my call, we received a letter telling us how much stress she had on her and that we weren't being understanding and that she'd get our maps back to us. Well, she didn't. So, Louisa is out of luck with maps of those states, because I don't ever plan to drive to Steamboat Springs to get them.

Louisa made other attempts to contact Deanna, as a friend, not abut the maps. I think it hurt her enough that she decided to wash her hands of the situation. That was very hard for her to do.

In May we were headed back to Texas for CLS' event called Hoe-Down. It was more like a family reunion event.

Recalling the trip with Ken in 1993, he'd been ticketed for speeding. In 1995, with Cindy driving, on the trip to Dallas, she was ticketed. This trip it was Louisa's turn. She was furious. I don't think I had ever seen her that mad at anyone but me. I didn't think she'd been speeding either. It was more of a surprise that she didn't get in more trouble as she argued with the trooper about it. She even followed up with letters protesting it…to no avail. I wasn't laughing because getting the ticket itself wasn't funny, and because I knew better.

Over the years I've said that I've never had a speeding ticket. That's not true. Shortly after Kevin was born in 1971, and after he'd been transferred to Riverside Hospital, I was pulled over and ticketed. I'd just gotten off work at WBCI radio, and was making my way through the 'S curves' around Eastern State Hospital when the lights appeared in my rear view mirror. I had seen the trooper when I passed him a mile before that. As we came out of the 'S curves,' he pulled me over near James Blair High School.

I was cited for going 35 in a 25 mph zone. I pleaded my case, complete with my destination. Don't they always ask, "Where are you going in such a hurry?" The next day I called a lawyer I knew. His advice was to always plead 'not guilty.' When I appeared in court, *that* lawyer was the judge. I pleaded not guilty, of course. He asked me what happened, and I told him about having seen the trooper at least a mile before the lights came on, and about being pre-occupied with my new son who was in ICU. The judge asked the trooper if what I said was true. He confirmed that it was. Then the judge said, "Case dismissed." Sure glad I cleared that up. I have not been pulled over for speeding since. And that's the (real) truth.

CHAPTER 22
True Empty Nesters

After Chris Harrison was bribed to take (his dog) Ginger, we were left with Gato, and the fish. I had inherited Kevin's fish tank and an assortment of fish. It was in the spring of 1996 that Gato's health began to fail. She wasn't as spry as she'd been in previous years. Another thing that I should tell you about her is that she and I didn't really enjoy each other for several years.

There was at least one occasion when Gato awakened me by walking across my head. When I pulled the covers with a jerk, she jumped off the bed. Other times I would throw a house slipper in the vicinity of where she was resting and watch her dart across the room.

After Kevin died, she must have sensed my hurt. Her disposition around me changed and likely mine around her as well. Whenever I sat down to read or watch TV, she would curl up in my lap or close at my side. I didn't know then, or even until much later, that she would have a lasting affect on me.

In May, after the trip to Dallas, Louisa flew to Oregon to spend some time with Rost and Vicky. I took her to Colorado Springs to catch her flight.

We'd been to a presentation on land sales at South Park... yes, it *is* real...When I went back to pick her up six days later, we'd stay in 'the Springs overnight and then tour the land the next day. We had put a refundable deposit on a site. It was the first time we had been financially optimistic in years. The land was being sold in 5 acres parcels, and the lot we had reserved was really barren. We opted out and were given a full refund of our deposit. It was while we were there…the evening before the land tour that Chris Harrison went by the house and found Gato. She appeared to have died that day.

There we were, almost thirteen years of marriage later… after the five kids, two dogs and a cat, it came down to the two of us, and a half dozen fish. I'll say this for fish, they don't shed, and you never have to let them out of the house and back in.

A light went on in June. We were at a home meeting, SNT's as we called them…Sunday Night Training. Marianna Johnson was visiting with us, and was accompanied by a woman we'd met previously but hadn't seen in a while. That night I felt an attraction to her that I hadn't felt or recognized in the same way before. I felt that it was mutual. At some point I was asked to share what the business had meant to me. I talked about what it had meant to our marriage. Even though there were times when we disagreed, even had AM-A-SPATS, I felt that we were closer because we were learning to work together and how we complemented each other. Afterwards I felt a shift in how I felt around the woman I mentioned, and felt her body language to me was different. Maybe it was just my imagination. I've had great adventures in my mind.

I thought about it a lot afterwards, and realized that I had unknowingly honed a defense mechanism that went into action without my calling upon it. I would edify Louisa, and/or our relationship when I was in the presence of someone with whom I felt a mutual attraction.

CHAPTER 23
Coming or going?

My client Corrine had moved into the house I had helped her find, and she asked me to put her duplex on the market. A few months earlier, she had agreed to rent both sides to my son, Chris Coons, and his friends.

When I put it on the market, I was assured that they would cooperate with our efforts to sell it. Instead, it became the quintessential renters-live-here story. Most Realtors can spot a rental property when they stop in front of it. This one really jumped out at you. It was ugly. I would go by and find unlocked doors, beer cans and bottles, a roach or two, and I don't mean the crawling kind, and even a passed out body or two. Chris was one of the culprits.

It wasn't working and they'd been late with payments often enough that I knew that the only reason they were allowed to stay is that my son was a tenant. Corrine asked what she should do. I said, "If it was my place, I have them evicted." She replied, "You know, one of them is your son." Of course, I was all too aware of that. I reaffirmed that I'd have them evicted. So, she did.

I helped Chris move…none too soon. She had to hire a cleaning company to get the place back to the poor condition it had been in before the guys moved in. Then she had it painted, and in the late fall of 1996 we got it sold.

1996 was also the year that Chris Harrison met Brandy Maldonado. Her brother Dan was one of Chris' roommates. She was quite bit younger than him, but it was the most serious we'd seen Chris be with any girl.

Our anniversary date, June 18th, has been a business magnet. A part of it could be something that I learned from Linda Southworth, too. She'd say that if business was slow, you should plan a trip. Once you've locked in the reservations, the clients will find you. In '96 we were planning to go to Durango for our anniversary. A couple I had already had two transactions with called and said they were ready to sell and find another house. Could I meet with them? I told them about our plans to go camping for our anniversary. They were happy to wait until we returned. That went well.

Almost immediately I got *another* call. This time from a couple that had been referred to me by someone I had worked with while I was with The Hahn Company years earlier. The question? Could I meet with them and show them a few houses that evening? They were moving to Colorado and would be here until Sunday on this trip. Louisa said we could have a late anniversary dinner. We cancelled our camping trip.

I didn't complain about either call. One couple I had worked with and really enjoyed being with. The other couple, even at the outset defined every agent's dream client. They had a limited amount of time to look at houses, knew they wanted to be close to her work location. They found the house they wanted and had time to complete the loan application for the mortgage. The loan officer said, "You should clone that couple," referring to their credit history and qualifications to borrow for a mortgage.

"YOU USED TO LIVE IN MY HOUSE."

The next month the Dudley's came to Colorado for a vacation. Richard and Ellen brought Elizabeth, Joshua and Anna with them. John didn't make the trip, choosing to stay home and to stay off of his broken leg.

We had spent several days rooming with Richard and Ellen at the Amway convention in 1993. Other than that, I had spent little time with them since Louisa and I had known each other. I like the family, and they were easy houseguests. They had a rental car and took time to travel the state. We did play tour guides long enough to introduced them to Lower Downtown and also the Bucksnort Saloon.

It was a hectic time for me, with a lot of real estate activity. When I had to meet an appraiser at one of the houses I had on the market, Richard wanted to go with me. It was only a few blocks away, so we walked to it. Richard had difficulty grasping the prices of houses in our neighborhood, as we walked and talked about what one or another house had sold for. His frame of reference was the type of homes he built in Virginia that were new and bigger, with more amenities, and yet sold for not much more than those in our neighborhood. The house was in good shape, and under contract for full price. I had helped the sellers find the house three years earlier. That couple was the first of two who had called on our anniversary in June.

The house was a typical Washington Park bungalow with a lot of stained wood, and an updated kitchen. While the appraiser was in a different part of the house, Richard asked, "Where's that coffee shop you told me about?" I told him that it was three blocks east. He said, "I'll meet you there. I'd better leave before I say the wrong thing in front of the appraiser." He couldn't see the value for the price.

It was the only year that Louisa was not gainfully employed. She was of course, working with me as we grew LP

& Associates, but she'd been away from AMOCO Production for a little more than a year and had spent most of it just enjoying not being employed. I called it "The Year of Making Soy Milk."

She had been a big help with our real estate office campaign for Easter Seals. We were gearing up for the annual rally weekend and Louisa had sold a lot of tickets, which gave people admission to the various activities of the rally. Century 21 and Amway were both major contributors to Easter Seals, and of course we had our connection with them through Kevin and the Easter Seals Handi-Camp.

I was finding some relief from juggling my business appointments by sanding our kitchen cabinets, and cleaning the copper plated handles. I knew it hadn't been done in the thirteen years we'd live in the house, if ever.

We saw the Amway business model changing before our eyes. There was more emphasis on building organizations through showing people how to shop for themselves, more than being distributors or sales people for the Amway products. We were now in the Network Marketing business. Some of the top achievers were affiliating with each other, as never before, and developing umbrella organizations. In 1996, our parent group, CLS International, aligned with International Connection (IC). We had been meeting with an IC group in Denver, for almost two years, so we were more familiar with IC than many of the CLS associates. The official integration of CLS to IC would take place at the annual meetings, to be held in Little Rock, Arkansas.

About a week before the trip to Little Rock we were sitting in the living room discussing something and our back door burst open. A young girl, appearing to be in her middle teens, ran into the living room. She was screaming, "I need to call my Mom! Please, call my Mom!" Louisa took her hand and suddenly, two cops ran in through the back door, too. Then one appeared at the front door. One of the cops asked, "Do you know this girl?" We said, no, that she had just run in. Louisa said that the girl just wanted to cal her mother, couldn't she do that? She was still holding the girl's hand. One of the cops said, "No ma'am. She's going with us. We've been chasing her from the park." Louisa continued, saying the girl should be able to call her mother. By that time, the cops had taken over and led the girl out. One of the other cops stayed behind and told us that the girl had stolen a purse in the park, and then jumped in somebody's car and wrecked it. She had run into our neighbor's house, through it, out the back door and over the fence between our yards. The cops had told her no, and then they warned her that she was interfering with an arrest as she had continued to debate with them. In today's world, I would immediately think that the girl was on methamphetamine or some other drug. She might have been for all I know.

After they all left, I unleashed a verbal blast that became a hot argument for the rest of the evening. We still drove to Little Rock, even though we weren't on the same page about our business. Well, we just weren't on the same page about life.

Louisa said that she thought I wasn't any happier with more real estate business than I had been when it was slower for me. At that stage of my real estate career, I was still taking personally, a lot of the challenges that are part and parcel to it. I'd had some transactions that were really very easy, and some that had me tied in knots inside. As you might guess, I *did* take her comment personally.

We got into a fight about it just before the annual family picnic for my real estate office. Having settled it to the point that we could go out in public, we got to the picnic about half way through it. That was a scenario would repeat itself.

By the time we left for Little Rock, we were back to a peaceful co-existence. Each of us knew that we'd be picked up by the excitement of the conference and the people we'd be with there.

The conference was just what we needed, where we needed to be. There was always an air of positive energy at the conferences, and this one had excitement and an almost electrical energy about it. There were thousands of people, including dozens whom we knew or had met previously. It was there that we heard Olympic Gold Medallist Dan Jansen, and the "self-talk" author, Dr. Shad Helmstetter.

I seemed to hang on every word from each of them. It was Dan Jansen who summed our relationship, saying, **"When you think you have tried everything, just remember…you haven't."**

By the time we left we were sharing goals and dreams, as we had never done before.

CHAPTER 24
New beginnings, again

Shortly after the Arkansas trip, Louisa called her friend Celeste, asking about data processing jobs that she got from time to time. Celeste must have passed along Louisa's name to her friend Judith who was about to move away. Judith was looking for someone to help with a project for Walter Page. Louisa had never heard of Walter or his project when she received a call from him. He used Judith's name and Louisa began to put the pieces together.

Walter had some sort of grievance with his landlord, and his insurance company. Louisa took over transcribing his almost hieroglyphic notes. They seemed to work well together and Louisa's role evolved into managing his business, from her home office.

For the most part, my thoughts were about adding income. I had a very good year in real estate in 1996. However, she hadn't worked. While I couldn't argue with the fact that she deserved a break, I couldn't help but wonder what our lives would be like if we were on the same page for one whole year.

Chris Coons moved back in with us that summer too. He went to work for Caterpillar, and it was easier for him to get to work from here, than from the west side of town. Then he changed jobs and worked for a commercial copying/printing company in the Denver Tech Center. Kelly and David had boomeranged for a time too, making Chris Harrison the only one of the kids who hadn't.

One of the things that added to my stress came in the form of a young couple I was working with. We had found a house they wanted, and they offered a contract that was accepted. Then it seemed that they were overcome by what we call 'Buyer's Remorse.' They were second-guessing themselves and the sellers, and me. My clients were expecting their first child, so I factored that into it as well.

I approached them, and asked if they wanted to be released from the contract, suggesting that they might be experiencing Buyer's Remorse. They insisted that it wasn't the case. They were making their first home purchase as well as having their first baby, so yes, there was some concern and fear. They repeated that they wanted the house. I suggested that they relax and let the process work, because they were making each other and every one connected with the transaction, crazy. I added that she certainly didn't need any additional stress during her pregnancy.

The sellers' agent and I were careful not to let the angst spill over into our business relationship. We found a mutual ground of respect and desire to do the best we could for our clients.

It got to the point that, by the time we got to the closing near the end of October, the sellers didn't want to be at the closing table with my buyers. The sellers had agreed to close in escrow and would return for their money after the buyers had completed their part of the closing.

Jeremy was about to be discharged by the Marines. He and Kelly had endured some rough times during their first four years of marriage. He had survived a number of events of his own making, and also a tour in Somalia. Recently he'd been driving armored personnel carriers. I was optimistic for him because there was a lot of road construction in and around Denver. I thought he would easily qualify to drive an earthmover of some size and earn a hefty hourly wage. He just didn't want to. He and I had had conversations whenever they would visit, and when he came home for his grandfather's funeral. I knew that he had a lot of talent as an artist. I could relate to that, as I do too. He seemed to lack the confidence that he could do that, or much of anything well.

When they arrived in Denver, they moved into a house a few miles east of us, in Virginia Village, and probably at a bargain price. Jeremy's uncle was their landlord. Not long after, they separated and Kelly and Brendan moved in with her mother. They later reconciled, and Jeremy moved in with them at Judi's house. Still, there were many differences between them, most of which were based on Kelly's sense of being responsible, and Jeremy's lack thereof.

In October Jeremy and I visited over a cup of coffee… my bonding effort. I wanted to get to know him. I wanted to be there for him, and help him work through his personal challenges, hopeful that he would be a better husband for Kelly and father for Brendan.

While Kelly and Jeremy were on their marital roller coaster ride, Chris Harrison and Brandy Maldonado became engaged.

As the year was drawing to a close, two events of significance took place. We wouldn't see the effects until later, in 1997 and in 1998.

Maybe Louisa was right. Maybe I could never be happy. I knew that I was talking a lot more about how hectic my year had been, rather than how productive. People around us believed in me, and in us. I wasn't getting it.

On Thursday, December 12th, I reviewed my 1997 plan with Mike Turnquist, one of the owners and managers of the Century 21Professionals office. While I had felt comfortable with, and appreciated by both Susan and Carlin Joslyn, the other owners, I just never felt that Mike and I were connecting. He told me to revise my plan and that I ought to aim higher and take on more responsibilities as a top producer and leader. I was there to sell houses, not to mentor other agents. I was feeling enough stress getting as much done as I had. I was not enjoying it.

I enjoyed our network marketing business. It wasn't growing as fast as I wanted, but I did get a rush when I was meeting with other people about it. I saw a greater profit potential and a lot less liability with it, than with real estate.

The day after my meeting with Mike, we went to the office's annual holiday party. I received an award for having produced the highest amount of loans placed through our in-house lender. Almost a year later, I would learn the significance of that award.

A few days later, we drove to Vail to have dinner with Chuck and Jean Strehli. In addition to our respect and admiration for their leadership and business success, we really enjoyed their company as friends. It was well worth it to us, to drive to Vail for dinner with them and then drive home. However, I did something that evening that made absolutely no sense. And I wouldn't realize it for several months.

Over the first weekend of 1997 we went to a CLS/IC Dream Night in Dallas. The conference started on Friday evening and lasted through Sunday afternoon. On Saturday morning we rushed out to Carrollton to see friends, Pat and Babu Iyer, and their daughter Monica. We had stayed with them on two previous trips to Dallas. We had not communicated well with them, and they were expecting us to visit longer than we had allowed time for. We hurried back to the morning session after about an hour visit.

"YOU USED TO LIVE IN MY HOUSE."

While the conference was uplifting, and filled with information that we could use to build our business, it was something that I missed that said a lot about me. During the Saturday afternoon session, I went to our room to watch the Broncos in a play-off game against Jacksonville. Louisa didn't want me to miss the session, but I was focused on doing what I wanted to do.

It wasn't bad enough that the Broncos blew the game, but more importantly, I had missed something I had never heard at any other conference. Louisa was hurt that I had chosen the game over the conference, especially because I had missed it when she was on stage describing her dream. She said that she had told more than a thousand people in the ballroom, about her dream of taking our family on a vacation cruise. I had never heard about it. Because I had opted out of that session, I still hadn't heard about it. I really felt selfish. I felt ashamed that I hadn't been there for her. That was a low point for me. I just wasn't plugged into the rest of the conference and the drive home was pretty silent.

Chris Coons decided to move to New Orleans in February, and continue to work for his current employer. The company wasn't transferring him, but told him that an opening was available. It was obvious that the move coincided with Mardi Gras. After he applied for work with the same company he was told that he would have to cut his hair, which he declined to do. He wasn't ready to give up the long hair that he had been wearing in a ponytail while working.

Near the end of the week he called me and asked whether I thought that his Uncle Pat and Aunt Elaine would let him stay with them in Houston. I replied that of course they would. He said, "Great. Because I have just enough money left to take a bus to Houston."

Chris stayed with Pat and Elaine, Greg and Paula for another month or so before moving into his own apartment. He's remarked, several times since, how much gratitude he feels for their having welcomed him into their home. The same printing company hired him, without having to cut his hair. He worked a late night shift, and he said that he spent most of his time at work making copies of legal documents.

A couple of months later he went to work for Pappas Seafood Restaurant. The move signaled a number of changes for Chris. And still more for others.

In March, while Chris was living in Houston, David had 'gone country'. He had made a leap from heavy metal music to country, country bars, and even bull riding. I recall that he brought home a video of one of his bull rides. I was not at all sure that we wanted to see it. Well, we did watch it and were happy to see that he was at least wearing a flak jacket.

David had been engaged to a young woman named Melanie. They had lived together for a while that year before they broke off their engagement. We liked her, but agreed with his decision to end the relationship, and his reason for doing so.

Louisa went back to Virginia for several days, in March, to help Paul with Carol, more to give him a respite. During one of our phone conversations Paul remarked that Louisa was quite a taskmaster. I said, "I know. Why do you think I sent her out there for a week?"

I had taken her to Colorado Springs for her flight to Virginia, because the fares were cheaper from that point of origination. She had a long trip, having been caught in delays and cancellations because of winter storms. She went first to Minneapolis-St. Paul, and after having her flight cancelled, dragged her luggage from one end of that airport to the other…and back…was able to get a flight to Raleigh-Durham, through the middle of the night, connecting to Norfolk. She had done all of that complete with a full tilt migraine. It took a long time for her to arrive at her destination, and it took a couple of days longer for her baggage to arrive.

CHAPTER 25
Cat-Scratch Fever?

After leaving the Colorado Springs airport, I stopped by the home of one of our newer business associates to drop off some training materials. I wasn't there very long. That night I came down with a cold and sore throat. The next morning I felt even worse. I thought back to where I'd been and what I could have done to come into contact with anyone who was sick. I couldn't place it.

I was working a temp job at the DTC. The work and the pay were ok. However, I was feeling bad and mired in a funk. I was depressed about being sick, about the lack of real estate business, and in fact having to resort to temp work again. At one point, in the privacy of a restroom stall, I prayed, "Dear God. If this is how my life is going to be, please take it." Once again he wasn't ready for that.

I had told them a lie about coming in at noon on Wednesday, so that I could make the office sales meeting and tour of newly listed properties. We went into a property that reeked of cat odor. I had gone in, and right down into the basement, made a quick 180° turn and hurried out. The stench had taken my breath away. The smell reminded me of the house I'd been in when I had dropped off the materials to our new business associate a couple of days earlier…although this time is was *much, much* worse. The other house I had been in had several cats. This property was vacant and still had a much stronger smell.

The cold became more like bronchitis and the flu. I went back to the office and picked up several things before heading home. I couldn't sleep in bed, opting to sleep almost upright in an easy chair.

For days I wondered about the cat odors, and how it could affect me so severely when I hadn't had any apparent reactions to Gato when she was alive. She had died a little more than ten months earlier. We later coined my allergic reaction as The Ghost of Gato, saying, 'You will not have another cat!' She and I had become close, so I guess she had staked her claim.

Kelly and Brendan stopped by briefly one evening that week. I really enjoyed him, and thought that we had a special connection. Of course, he humbled me from time to time. When they came in, I said hello, and he went right by me, asking, "Where's Mema?" I said, "Brendan, you could say hello." It didn't faze him. He said, "Hello, Papaw. Where's Mema?" Seeing how sick I was, they didn't stay.

When I picked up Louisa at airport she was shocked to see how sick I was. She knew, of course that I had the flu, or a cold. She hadn't known just how sick I had been and still was. I spent the month of March 1997 in some phase of that illness.

Three months into 1997, I still had no real estate activity going. That was right on the heels of my most productive year. I'd lost a month because of the illness…a month of inactivity in both businesses.

Walter Page was planning to move his family to Texas, and asked Louisa to run the Denver business for him, from her office here. He and I talked about my listing their home for sale, but he chose another agent to do it.

CHAPTER 26
Count (on) the change.

Chris Coons was the only one of our kids who became a smoker. David had toyed with it for a while, collecting coupons for a pool cue stick. Louisa agreed to buy it if he'd stop smoking. That worked. Kelly may have toyed with it, as I had as a kid. I don't think Chris Harrison ever tried it.

When Father's Day rolled around each year, I would tell Chris Coons that all I wanted was to hear him say that he had quit smoking. He had been with us when we traveled to Houston in 1994, and saw Bob dying of cancer. Even after that, he still smoked, as did my brothers Mike and Pat.

It had been a few months after that 1994 trip that Louisa and I took Chris Coons and David to dinner to celebrate their having completed their GED programs. They had each dropped out of high school, which is a misnomer. That's like dropping out of a basement window; as little as they were in high school. At dinner that evening, Chris was talking about a friend who had just lost a relative to cancer. I said, "And after what you've seen, you still smoke. Can you begin to feel how Custer felt seeing all those Indians?"

Well, on Father's Day, in 1997, I got *that* call from Chris. **He had quit smoking**. He also said that he was sober for the first time in 8 years. The call came only weeks before his 23rd birthday.

The weeks and months passed, and still no real estate activity.

I was struggling for answers. I'd gone from being one of the top producers in the office to having produced zero, zilch and nada, in the first six months of 1997.

We were attending an IC conference at the Keystone Resort over the July 4th weekend. I was searching for something, anything that would give me a clue about what had gone wrong. Something the speaker on stage said, clicked with me.

I went back to my day planner when we got back home. A simple entry, about our dinner with Chuck and Jean Strehli in December, opened the floodgates. I thought about our conversation that evening. I had whined to them about how hard I had worked to produce the business I had that year, and how much real estate I would have to sell to produce the kind of income I could expect, with the same activity, in our network marketing business.

I had read "What To Say When You Talk To Yourself," by Dr. Shad Helmstetter, *twice*. I had read at least five of his books and had seen him in person at least three times. I had read countless other books on attitude and positive thinking, before I spent that evening telling them…and *of course, myself*, how difficult my business was. Pardon me folks, but that's what I call mental masturbation.

I had set the table with my attitude and my words, and I had been eating from that table for almost 7 months. I had literally talked myself out of business.

By that time, I knew that I was finished at Century 21 Professionals, and possibly with real estate. Call it delayed burnout.

In mid-August, I got a call from one of the temporary employment agencies that I had worked for a couple of times. I hadn't done any work for them in over two years. They had an opportunity that sounded interesting, in large part to the state I was in at that moment.

"YOU USED TO LIVE IN MY HOUSE."

I agreed to interview with the Colorado Water Conservation Board, (CWCB), for a temporary position, assisting in the writing of contracts. The job commitment would be for 90 days and it would pay $16 per hour. Both looked pretty good at the time. Bill Stanton, the department supervisor and three of his staff member, with whom I would be working, if hired, conducted the interview.

I met with Susan Joslyn about taking a leave of absence. What I really asked was to leave my license active with the office, but to be excused from the office policies regarding sales meetings and sales tours. If any business developed, that my new work would allow the time to do, I would do it through that office. I think it was a difficult choice for Susan, for fear of setting a precedent, and showing favoritism. Based on my activity the previous year, and our friendship, she approved it.

Bill Stanton was one of the easiest people to work for, that I'd ever experienced. However, there were some incredible office politics being played out between others in the department. Bill was aware of it and coached me on how to stay clear of it. The latitude he gave me was a key element of my working there. I had been working with our friends Bill and Laura Michaels to help them find a new home. Only a few days after I started at the CWCB, I found what I thought was the right place for them.

After calling Laura, I set the appointment to show them the house. I had ridden my bike to work that day, so I took off early and rode from downtown to the Hilltop neighborhood where I met Bill and Laura to show them the house.

They agreed that it was the right place for them. Well, Laura was convinced. Bill was apprehensive because Hilltop is an exclusive neighborhood, and at the time he had trouble visualizing himself there. They asked me to write the offer. It was September and I had my first transaction for 1997 under way.

On the day that the Michaels' offer was accepted, Bob and Betty McKann arrived for a visit, to help us with our business. So, I was then juggling the network marketing business, a real estate transaction and my temp job at the CWCB. We had scheduled new business associates and prospects for Bob and Betty to meet with us.

Their first day in Denver Louisa dropped me off at the CWCB office. When I left work that afternoon, I waited for almost 30 minutes for her to pick me up. I'd gone back into the office to call her twice. I walked home. Just after I arrived, they arrived. When Louisa saw me, she realized that she had forgotten to pick me up. I was so angry that it took all the decorum that I could muster, to control myself in front of Bob and Betty. It wasn't the first time that someone had forgotten to pick me up. Louisa had done it two years earlier, and when I was a kid, my mother had once forgotten to pick me up from dance lessons. In both of those cases, they made it worse by making light of it. Obviously, I hadn't gotten over it.

The three of them had met with a couple that we had been helping with their business. We'd actually done too much, 'feeding them instead of teaching them to fish.' They told Bob and Betty that it was our fault that they hadn't seen more growth. Louisa said, "It's probably best that you weren't with us."

A few days later I went to a presentation on changes in policies regarding our real estate Errors & Omissions Insurance, hosted by the Colorado Real Estate Commission. I had made inquiries about the process and costs to set up a home office and have my license placed there.

Louisa and I did the math. In the six years that I'd been selling real estate, she and I had generated 85% of my business from our contacts; sphere of influence. Regardless of what the office had set as my 'split,' I was keeping about 65% of my gross closed commission. We didn't like what we saw in those answers. At that time, I was paying the corporate side of Century 21 8% from the gross closed commission, *before* the office split. At the time, the Century 21 market share was about half that amount.

Bringing my license home was one consideration. Doing something other than selling real estate was another. We understood that building our network marketing business meant delayed gratification.

I got permission to take off two days, from the CWCB, the first week in October. We left for Fort Worth, for what CLS/IC called Free Enterprise Days (FED), on October 2nd.

We planned to visit with my niece, Shelli, and her husband A.G., who lived in Fort Worth. I also wanted to meet his parents, who lived about 20 miles west of Fort Worth. We had planned to do the latter, when we first arrived. We were in a caravan of three vehicles and one of them had tire trouble, which delayed our arrival. We had to cancel the plans to meet A.G.'s parents.

We did contact Shelli and A.G. Shelli had met Bob and Betty at my brother Bob's wedding. Much had happened since then, but they all remembered having met each other.

We visited over dinner and looked forward to seeing them again on our next trip to Texas. I had always felt close to Shelli, and had a sense of responsibility for her after Bob died.

When we returned from Fort Worth, Kelly called to tell us that she was pregnant and the baby was due in March. I must tell you that I was not excited about the prospect of her and Jeremy having another child. I could only hope for a healthy baby and one whose parents would both be there.

I also had the closing for Bill and Laura's purchase a few days after returning from the Texas trip. Bill looked at the commission check that was written to Century 21 Professionals, when he asked, "Why in the world are you giving up so much of this to them? We would have come to you anyway…no matter what company you were with." Bill knew what part of the check I'd end up with. I said, "Well, this is the last one they'll get. That party is over." It was the first time that I verbalized my change of office. It had cost me about $3,000 to handle that transaction through that office.

Susan Joslyn had approved my leave of absence, hoping that I'd return to her office on a full time basis. It was situational in the sense that I had been excused from a lot of office activities, still ran the Michaels' transaction through that office, and took time to coordinate the office's activities for the annual Easter Seals fund raiser.

Other than avoiding the infighting of the department, I was enjoying the work at the CWCB, and excited about how our network marketing business was growing. It had evolved into LP Enterprises, and I felt that Louisa and I were making progress in our relationship. I attributed that to the growth in our business and the fact that I was happier being more productive.

We'd missed Chris Coons' birthday with our trip to Keystone in July, and we were in Texas for FED on Chris Harrison's birthday. David had moved into an apartment in Aurora. Kelly and Jeremy were living in an apartment complex in Golden. We felt that we did a pretty good job of communicating with the kids, and being available to help them.

We had kept Brendan fairly often, and felt that we had a good connection with him, too. Judi was worried whether Kelly and Jeremy would make it over the long haul. She said she was afraid that Kelly would be left with the two children to take care of by herself. I told her that I hoped they would stay together and both be there for the kids. However, when I thought of all that Kelly had already dealt with, I responded that I didn't think that being left alone to take care of two kids (as opposed to three, including Jeremy) was the worst that could happen to her.

Brendan's third birthday was one cause for celebration that month. Seeing your kids grow up fast is one experience. As any grandparent knows, seeing your grandkids do it is quite another. Brendan didn't go through the "Terrible 2's." He was very well behaved.

CHAPTER 28
You…err, we bought what?

In September we went to a timeshare presentation. That wasn't unusual. We'd learned how to play that game. We had gone to several others. We'd be polite and listen to the offers, all the while knowing that we would not be buying. Louisa's parents had owned several at one point and used them as incentives for the people in business with them. As a matter of fact, they had wanted to give us one of the two or three remaining, when we had visited with them nine months earlier. It was located at the Outer Banks of North Carolina, on a golf course. We couldn't see ourselves using it. It was too far away and we don't golf.

We did use it…as leverage during that presentation. I was feeling better about myself because I was working at the CWCB, and our business was growing.

During the timeshare presentation, I saw that Louisa was interested. She's a great question person, and she was asking specifics. The sales person was crossing the line of being rude. You may have had that experience with timeshares, but this person was really giving me a rough time. She thought that I, since I too sold real estate, should not have been there, knowing all the while that we would not purchase. I immediately thought of all the free consulting I'd done over the past six years.

Louisa reminded her that we were invited, and asked if there was anyone else we could talk with. The agent gladly got up and went to another room. I said to Louisa, "Are you serious about this?" She said, "It's in Colorado. We could use it without going across the country, and the kids could use it. So, yes, I am."

A guy named Larry replaced the previous agent. He introduced himself as the owner. Louisa said something to him about the other agent. He apologized for her and said that she had a migraine. He had sent her home.

Louisa went on to discuss the sales pitch with Larry. I watched. He then asked me for my thoughts. I told him about her father and mother having one on the market in North Carolina. Why would I want to spend $7500 for one in Colorado when we could have one, for free, in North Carolina? He asked how much Paul wanted for it. When I said that I didn't know, he offered the use of their phone and said, "Call him."

Well, I did call him. I told Paul what we were doing and why I called. I came back to the table and said, "$5000." So, Larry said, "Looks like I have to match that. It's yours for $5000 if you buy right now." He left so that we could discuss it. I was still not sold on the idea. We decided to do it and when he came back to the table...with the contract, and a guy named John, to help us. We said that we were taking his offer. We completed the contract, and then asked for time to find our own financing. Their financing was in the double digits. We left a $500 deposit.

On the way home, we discussed the fact that the 1991 Volvo was paid for, and that we could probably get a personal loan with it as collateral. We did line that up, and Larry gave us a discount of 10% for paying cash.

Chris and Brandy's engagement ended. She realized that she was too young to get married, and needed some room to grow. Chris was devastated. When he would talk with me about watching the Nuggets, who were terrible at the time, I said, "You must get a life." The Nuggets' record that season, 11 wins and 71 losses. I don't know how watching them could have boosted anyone's spirits.

December: David told us that he was joining the Navy, and his departure was eminent. He received a signing bonus and the promise of medical school after boot camp. He wanted to be a corpsman.

Chris Coons was enrolled at a community college in Houston. There were other positives to come out of 1997. At that point, none pleased us more than to see the two younger guys make the strides that they were making.

BOOK FIVE

CHAPTER 1
Things out of synch, and socket.

Broncos beat Steelers…cheering leads to separated shoulder. How about that for a tabloid headline? Actually all I did was raise both hands in the air… perhaps too enthusiastically. Just as the right shoulder separated, the phone rang. It was Bob McKann. His call had nothing to do with the game, just checking in to say hello. I explained that I just separated my shoulder and would be happy to call him back later.

In the past, when I had separated my shoulder, I had gone to a hospital, received a dose of a knock out drug and they'd put it back in place. We were really surprised that it happened. It hadn't happened in a long time, and I usually can feel it when the shoulder is loose or feels strained. Louisa mentioned the East West Clinic that we'd noticed when exiting I-25 at Arapahoe Road. She called. They were closed until Monday morning. I decided to wait. I walked through the house, and up and down stairs, working to increase my blood flow, hoping that I could get enough relief to put the shoulder back in myself. It wasn't going to be that easy.

We were scheduled to take our friend Richard Petty (really), to DIA (Denver International Airport) on Monday morning. His wife, Judy, had flown to California ahead of him after her mother died. Louisa called Richard to tell him what had happened and that we planned to visit the clinic as early as possible and then take him to DIA.

I slept a little, while sitting up in bed. When I moaned about the pain, Louisa would say, "Breathe. Damn it, breathe.!" She wasn't sleeping either. She was propping my arm up all night long.

She got us into the clinic shortly after they opened. I met Dr. Herr, who said, "This will be a $100 lesson on how to do this yourself if there is a next time." The $100 was the charge for the office visit. He told me to lie down on the table, on my chest, and hang my arms over the side. The right side was hanging there with relative ease. I had been lying there, at a forty-five degree angle for ten minutes. Then I felt him put a handle in my right hand, and when I gripped it the weight pulled and the muscles moved, bringing my shoulder back into place. I looked down and it was a toolbox that I had held. I knew we could do that if or when my shoulder separated again. We do have toolboxes and Louisa has a massage table.

We took Richard to DIA and stopped for breakfast on the way home. He insisted on treating us to that. I reached across the table for the coffee and my shoulder came loose. I took the full pitcher of water and with my right hand held it below the table. It didn't work. My shoulder did come back in with a little maneuvering, and it has stayed in through the years. (See the image of me knocking on my woodenhead for luck.)

We knew that we'd be going to the Great Lakes Training Center, near Chicago, for David's boot camp graduation, and on January 25th, we knew what his graduation gift would be. Of course, he told us what he wanted, and he said, "That's all I really want." The Broncos beat the Packers in the Super Bowl XXXI, 31-24! He wanted a Broncos' Super Bowl Champions ball cap.

The other major event on the horizon was the birth of our second grandson. Kelly was having trouble with her pregnancy, and we were concerned for her and the baby. There were of course the immediate concerns for them and how they would survive the delivery. It seemed to push back, temporarily, a concern for their long-term future.

We'd pretty much run the tires off of our 1991 Volvo, with the trips to Texas, and one to Virginia. In February, we decided that it was better to rent a car to drive to David's graduation, than to buy new tires and then put 2,000 miles on them immediately. The car we rented was billed as medium sized, but after driving Volvos it felt small and I felt that I had to be focused on driving it every moment behind the wheel.

We stayed in Seward, Nebraska on the way to Illinois, with a couple whose house I had sold in 1996. Pat, the husband, had worked with my brother Mike, and had been transferred to Lincoln. Pat wasn't home, but Ellen went out of her way to make us feel comfortable the few hours we were there.

Over the years we've had a number of arguments that amounted to 'knit picking.' We got into one of them on that trip, somewhere in Iowa. By the time we reached Cary, IL we were barely civil to each other. We were going to stay in Cary, with friends, Bruce and Doris, whom we'd met at SkiGlo. They would be staying at our place a few weeks later. It was a short drive to the Navy base for the ceremonies.

Somehow we put aside our badgering of each other long enough to enjoy David's graduation. He had won a stripe during boot camp, and graduated with distinction. When we greeted him after the ceremonies, he said, "I finally finished something." Everything that we had hoped the Marines could find in Jeremy, the Navy was bringing out in David.

We went to David's graduation luncheon and basked in the praises being heaped upon him by those who had guided him through boot camp. We toured Chicago before returning him to his unit that night.

We drove back into Chicago to join Bruce and Doris, and the Maurer's, and went to an IC business meeting.

While we were gone I picked up a message from one of my 1995 clients. It was another referral. I had been working with the wife's sister already. On that transaction we had discovered that the seller had falsified an important item on the Seller Disclosure. My client opted out of the contract. At that point, I didn't know whether she was still in the market for a house. I was excited that the family was still referring me to others.

We had lunch with David the next day before heading back home. We went south to stop in Alton for a brief visit with Mom, leaving the next day for Denver. I couldn't get out of that car soon enough. I've heard that brand referred to as old folks' cars. I think driving them might age people. They probably were young folks when they bought them.

We had about two weeks at home before heading to SkiGlo. We did put new tires on our car before that trip. Before going to Vail, to meet Chuck and Jean for dinner, back in 1996, I had bought a set of chains for that car. We would need them during the week while we were Snowmass in 1998.

When we returned to Denver, I met with the new prospective clients, as well as my client who had opted out of her contract. She and her husband weren't ready to look at that time, but indicated that they would be in the market later. They were appreciative of my efforts and took Louisa and me to lunch at a terrific Asian restaurant during a Chinese New Year celebration. They were among the three Chinese immigrant families that I had the pleasure of working with.

I had another client that came through someone in our network marketing business. She was in another line of sponsorship, but we'd met through the IC meetings. She asked me to meet with her mother, to help her sell her house. I did, and I came to regret it. In those days, particularly in the early days of running my own office, I wasn't postured to turn down business. Nine years later, I would not be her agent. That's one of the few points that she and I would ever agree on.

CHAPTER 2
Enter, Smiley Riley

Our second grandson, Riley Patrick Nix, was born on March 18, 1998, while we were at Snowmass. Kelly's complications were such that medical staff saw their window of opportunity to do the C-Section, at that time. His Irish name was chosen because he was expected to join us on St. Patrick's Day.

On the 21st, while coming home from Snowmass, along with Bruce and Doris, we detoured to the Grand Mesa, for our first look at the timeshare we purchased. We were happy with what we saw. The small ski resort was bustling and we were able to see the unit we'd purchased.

We didn't get to see Riley until later that day. He was still in the hospital, in ICU. He was small, but strong. Looking at him today, it's hard to imagine that scene.

We were at the hospital pretty often. Louisa had been practicing the energy touch therapy, JinShin Jyutsu, for several years. She spent a considerable amount of time holding Riley's tiny little fingers.

Louisa was wrapping up her work with Page One, closing the "Denver office." She began to explore her options. She recalled the award that I had won, while with Century 21 Professionals, for bringing the highest dollar volume of loans to the in-house lender. She decided to become a loan originator.

After talking with several companies, she joined a small

firm in Cherry Creek. She was now *my* in-house lender. She learned the business, and quickly. I was concerned about some things that I had heard about one of the people in her office and discussed it with her. She's a person of integrity and I knew that she would do the right thing, personally and professionally. I was concerned that others might judge her by the company she kept..

It all worked out and it was great experience for her. The owners of that company decided to close the office, and less than a year later Louisa was with a second company.

In June, we went to Powderhorn for our first stay there. We had camped at several places around Colorado, but we hadn't spent time on the Grand Mesa. It's just beautiful.

We met a couple from Destin, Florida and a family from Austin, Texas. We spent some time hiking with Jim and Joyce, the couple from Florida. One day, while hiking, Louisa spotted a coyote about a hundred yards away. She started calling to it and Joyce screamed for her to stop. She had to make several efforts before Louisa realized that she was serious. Joyce's concern was that coyotes are known to travel in packs. The coyote looked in our direction, but went its own way. We saw some cat tracks and some bear tracks, but no other animals. I'm always cautious…Louisa would say that I'm afraid…about bears. I told them, "I don't eat health foods and take supplements to be some gourmet snack for a bear."

The couple from Austin, Oscar and Ann, and their families were in the unit above ours. We had the two of them down to our place for coffee and tea. While visiting with them, we learned that they too, were in business with Amway. We became friends and have gotten to know them, even while they relocated from Austin, to Copenhagen, to Boulder.

We were there on our 15th anniversary and decided to go bike riding and then find a place get our anniversary dinner. We took the bikes to the Burlington Trail near Grand Junction, and after a while drove along the Dolores River in search of some quaint restaurant for dinner. We found it…in Telluride, about 130 miles down the road. As we were getting close to Telluride we saw tents and campers galore…a mini Woodstock, given the way the people were dressed. Maybe that's an oxymoron. Louisa asked, "When is the Telluride Bluegrass Festival?" I replied, "June, I think." It was the 18th of June.

Closer to Telluride we stopped. We were told that no more traffic was allowed in Telluride at that time. Louisa pleaded with the traffic control person, telling her about our drive for an anniversary dinner. They gave us a two-hour pass, to get into town, eat and leave. We not only found a place to enjoy, Sofia's Mexican restaurant, which we enjoyed very much, we found a place to park only a couple of blocks away.

I laughed about how out of touch with the music business I had become. Bruce Hornsby was appearing at the festival the next day. Years earlier, while living in Williamsburg, Virginia, I had known his parents. I called his Mother, Lois, when we returned to Denver to tell her how we had just missed him. We had no shot of getting into the festival at that late date.

It had been a long drive home that night, complete with a deer in the headlights. Fortunately, because of the dense fog, I was driving at about 15 mph when we saw it in front of us. He stared at us and then slowly moved off the road. I wonder if the deer have an expression for how *we* look when we see them in front of us on the road.

On the return trip, we drove straight from our condo at Powderhorn to Aurora, rather than home. I had to meet a couple, and the house inspector who would go through their new home for them. Louisa had put together their loan, too. I'd found an inspector who would do the job on a Saturday.

That day I realized that I was as busy, with my own real estate office, as I had been during my previous best year, 1996, with a "big brand name" office. I was balancing five clients in various stages of active transactions, and lining up classes for my license renewal.

Louisa was new to her work as a mortgage broker, but had at least two of my clients committed to her. She was working on loan applications for the others too, even though she knew they were still talking with other lenders.

It looked good for us financially, seeing how we could work together. I really thought we had turned a corner in every aspect of our relationship.

The summer was flying by. We were growing our business...now referred to as Distribution Technology, heading back the hills, to Keystone for the IC Summer Seminar in a few weeks.

CHAPTER 3
Caught up in the net-working

There was mounting tension and a number of power plays going on within the local IC Denver group. It encompassed several different lines of sponsorship. For the most part we all got along well, understanding that we could help each other through group participation. We had brought outside speakers and had an appearance of synergy.

One person had been named as the area leader, having had larger business years earlier. He was rebuilding and wasn't really any further along than several of us within this blended group.

It was a lesson in the differences between designated leadership and moral leadership. I found it interesting that, not long after that period, IC would come up with a tape, as a part of our monthly series, using that theme.

We were heading back to Keystone for the annual IC summer seminar. A couple of our downline were going with us. We had been adding people to our group and had a lot of momentum. Somehow we missed connecting with that couple, at the Park 'n Ride where we had planned to meet them. They'd gone ahead and we arrived late. When we arrived, we were ushered aside and told that we'd be featured on stage, along with a select group of distributors that had experienced a surge in growth. I think it intimidated Louisa to be on stage at that time. Just as we were being lead to the stage she whispered,

"Just don't let us become like Larry." I understood what she meant. However, it was ill timed and I felt that I hadn't been allowed to enjoy the moment. I was thinking about her comment and what I felt was her fear of success.

For my part, I was reminded of my work with Ed Reid. I could spend time with Larry, over coffee, and we even ran together once at Keystone. However, when it came to "the business," we were very much at odds.

Louisa and I had two closings coming up together at the end of July...that she would miss. She flew to Virginia to help with Carol, after Paul had eye surgery.

The second of those closings had the air of a three-ring circus...and not in a good way. The tone was set when the sellers wouldn't sit in the same conference room. The closer had to go from one room to another to have the (former) spouse sign documents. We represented the buyers and the wife didn't make things any easier. She was essentially saying that Louisa had lied to her about their loan. I knew that I could reach Louisa by phone and offered to do so. I had already called her once. I said, "Let's put her on the speaker phone and you can tell her that she mislead or lied to you." The wife backed down. She knew that she had been told the truth. The issue was about money being escrowed for insurance. Even though it's commonplace she didn't want to do it. She said, "I know everybody has to do it. I just don't like it." I said, "You don't have to like it. It doesn't help, or change it, by saying that you were lied to about it." It was as though the negative energy we'd felt during our initial visit to that house, had worked its way into the transaction. I don't recall that I'd ever talked to a client like that. Her husband sat quietly during the exchange.

CHAPTER 4
As a matter of record

As a matter of record, I did ask our kids if there was anything that they specifically wanted me to leave out of this story. I don't recall asking Louisa the same question. After Kelly said, "How about everything?" I said that wasn't an option, and she and the others said that they wouldn't ask me to leave out anything.

Having said that, I have to share a funny story about bailing Chris Harrison out of jail in August 1998. Jail was one place that I had never pictured him.

It began in the middle of the night. We heard a loud banging on the front door. We couldn't tell who it was, from our upstairs bedroom, and when Louisa and I called out, asking who was there, there was no answer. The loud knocking continued.

I went to the basement to wake my brother Mike, who was living with us at the time. I grabbed a baseball bat and Mike grabbed an iron skillet and we went to the front door. As we were pulling the front curtains aside, Louisa came down and said, "It's 'Slime'…Stephen Forrester." She opened the door and he explained, in short breathless bursts, that Harrison had been put in jail. He told some bizarre story about their having stopped at a construction site to use a portable toilet. They'd been out and had the need. Unfortunately for them, they were in a rather exclusive neighborhood that was patrolled regularly. The Police computer showed a bench warrant for Chris Harrison, for not fulfilling community service as a result of a DUI a year earlier.

I went to the Arapahoe County facility and arranged bail for Chris. He insisted that he had completed the community service. However, he hadn't kept a record of it. So he got to do it again.

At the same time, I was covering for Washington Park Realty, while Dale and Linda visited their families in Illinois and Michigan, and for Lisa Kaiser, another solo broker I had worked with at C21 Professionals. She was with relatives in Alabama.

Chris Coons had been admitted to the University of Texas, which was an incredible feat. He was initially accepted as an out of state student, although he'd been in Texas for about a year and a half. When he appealed the decision, they asked him to write a paper stating his position. He said that he knew he was in when they gave him that assignment. It was his writing that had led him to move to Austin. An instructor at the community college in Houston had suggested that he should get into UT and develop what he felt was a natural writing talent. Chris won his appeal.

It seemed as though Kelly and Jeremy might make it. Kelly was entering her senior year at Metro State that fall. Jeremy was working as a Customer Service Manager for a Ford dealership.

I also spent a good bit of time helping Chris Harrison. His driver's license had been suspended, which was adding insult to injury. His prized Mustang had been totaled in an accident, and he didn't have his license with him. While he was dealing with that, he'd been subpoenaed to have a blood test to confirm that he was not the father of a baby by a former girlfriend. I drove him to the clinic for the blood draw, and also to court for the hearing. It was worth it, as the DNA proved to the legal system what he and the young woman knew, that the child was not his.

Even with all of the activity that we had going, I still felt a need to create more cash flow. I took a temp job with the Colorado DMV. They had a computer based billing issue. While I am neither a geek, nor an accountant, I was able to come up with a solution that helped them recover thousands of dollars. At the end of the three weeks that I'd been there, I was asked to apply for an IT position. I declined. I wasn't really qualified for it, academically. Also, I really didn't want to be a full time employee for any entity.

CHAPTER 5
I still haven't found the right fit...

That Fall Louisa attended a real estate seminar on my behalf, while I was participating in a home inspection with one of my clients. A real estate guru named Brian Buffini was pitching a way to do business by referral only. We liked the idea because we realized that we had provided most of the leads that became transactions since I'd started selling real estate in 1992. There had been a couple of walk-in and floor time call-in clients, but still, we had generated most of the business through people we knew.

She asked me to check my day planner for a specific date in January. When I told her that it was open she said, "Good. I'll be going to Virginia to help with mother while my dad has his eye surgery. You can attend the Buffini retreat." I was open to it, but laughed, and asked her if she was signing me up so that she'd know where I was when she was gone. She said, "I wouldn't pay $300 to know that, and I just paid $300 for you to go." I knew that she had to be very impressed with the guy to commit to $300 or any thing close to that.

With everything in our lives appearing to be on track, we got a real surprise from David. He was transferring from the medical school at Great Lakes to Camp Pendleton, where Jeremy had been stationed a few years earlier. David would be a corpsman assigned to the 1st Marines. His surprise wasn't about the Navy, though. He told us he was going to be married. We had no idea that he had been in a relationship. He said that he'd known her for quite a while and that they'd been 'just friends' initially.

David arranged for us to meet her and her family. She was living with her parents, had two sons by two different men and was 24 years old. I'm thinking, 'David! What **are** you thinking?'

The young woman, her mother and her sister were friendly enough and the kids were really cute. The older one, whom I think was three years old, was clinging to his mom, or David and had nothing to do with the rest of us. Her father was in his bedroom watching TV. He didn't come out to meet us. I decided to go meet him. No big deal. We shook hands, he returned to the TV show and I left the room. It felt surreal. From the outset I had doubts about David's new family.

The next day it was back to my own world. I had a walk-through with my clients, and new friends, Chris and Sandra Johnson. We had met in May, and looked at several homes before they decided to go with a new build in Highlands Ranch. Their closing was scheduled for the end of October.

CHAPTER 6
Should I stay or should I go?

Louisa and I had been planning a free back-to-school concert for kids since July. We asked our friend Bonnie Phipps to schedule her band...The Elastic Band...to perform for it. Bonnie has a great reputation for entertaining kids.

Initially we planned to host the concert in Washington Park at the end of August. However, the park permit wouldn't be available until the third week in September, when I had planned to visit my mother for her birthday. I had scheduled that trip long before we started planning the concert. I had enough experience with special events to know that several factors have to come together to make it happen, not the least of which is the weather. I had a permit, and the required liability insurance, based on a projected audience of 100 people. The weather was perfect and the turn out was much higher than we had projected. It was probably three times higher. There were no incidents and everyone had a good time. It was good PR for my business and for Louisa's, with Financial Mortgage Services.

I hadn't met my goal of being with Mom for her 76th birthday, and I was having trouble dealing with that. Once again, I had put business ahead of family. I rationalized that, at least this time it was for *my* business, and not some big corporation.

Kelly had brought Brendan and Riley to the concert, and they stayed over with us through the next day. I stayed in

Denver another day, to watch the Broncos beat the Raiders. I don't recall my rationalization for that.

I left for Alton the following Monday and spent a week with Mom. Originally, I had planned to stop near Kansas City. Our friend, Mary Sellars, had arranged for me to stay with her sister and brother-in-law, whom we'd met through the Amway business. I had trouble following the directions to their home, and decided to drive straight through to Alton. I did stop and leave a message for them. It turned out that Jim was away on business and Sharon was at work when I called. She had forgotten that I was coming by. It worked out ok. I didn't have any trouble driving straight through. It wouldn't be the last time that I had that experience.

I had a good time visiting with mom. I wasn't stopping on my way to somewhere else. I was there for her and we both enjoyed that. Still, I heard my internal alarm go off after three days there. When I returned to Denver on Friday. I didn't drive straight through. I stopped in Kansas to visit our friend Tom Schrag. On Saturday, I had a fleeting thought about driving through Fort Riley as I passed by. When I call my old Army buddy, Tom Jindra, he usually asks whether I've gone back to visit our old stomping grounds. Maybe someday, I'll be ready to do that.

CHAPTER 7
Win some. Lose some

That fall I was enjoying another winning season for the Broncos. I was balancing watching the games and showing houses to our new friends Albert and Marcellina Otii. All in all things seemed to be going well for us.

Our friends David and Julia Scoggins came to visit that fall too. Julia had been here before, but it was David's first visit. So far, it's been his only visit. The weather was unusually dismal. There were low hanging clouds and we had light rain through most of their visit. David still jokes that he doesn't believe we have any mountains here. He didn't see them during their entire visit. Actually, he did…by driving up into the foothills. It was good for us to be with them. They're a couple that married young and had stayed together since. I have learned a lot from their relationship.

The day after the Scoggins left, we were off to Texas for another IC Free Enterprise Day weekend.

During the month of September Louisa had gone to a presentation at Mi Casa, a business center for women. She met Betsy Kester there, and Betsy told her about a program called the Denver International Program (DIP). She invited us to hear more about it at a social gathering. As I understand it DIP was founded on the Denver University campus more than 20 years ago. The organization facilitates an exchange program, typically for professionals and middle management employees, as opposed to a student exchange. The visitors would be working with a local entity in their current career field. About every five weeks they move to a different host family, and most are here for a three-month stay.

They're always looking for families who are open to hosting someone through the program. It was in the middle of September that we agreed to host someone that fall. We would host a young woman from Germany, Karin Ebel, a psychologist, already staying with another host and working at a clinic. At the same time, another young woman from Germany was staying with a host family on the west side of Washington Park across from us.

Karin joined us the last week of September. She was easy for us to be with. She was willing to find things in the kitchen on her own, ate the foods we eat and didn't smoke. She and Louisa talked with each other a lot. That increased my reading…taking refuge in the basement.

A couple of weeks later Karin joined us for a brunch with Chris and Brandy, on Chris' 27th birthday. Karin's birthday was a week later.

Karin stayed in our house while we went to Fort Worth for the Free Enterprise Day Conference. Louisa also let her use the older Volvo, against my better judgment. The car ran okay, but had a list of nuances that one should know to drive it. Karin was okay with it and appreciated the freedom that having a car to use would afford her. It turned out well enough. She'd mastered the list and the car, even taking it into the foothills for a mountain drive.

During that FED we heard Julie Pyburn for the first time. Most people would call her a motivational speaker, and she does motivate. I came away feeling that her approach was not only emotional, but she laid out a plan for how to bring out the best in us. She'd been a teacher, and I can see how she could be a positive force for high school age kids. One thing in particular spoke to me...that our character is defined as our actions when nobody is watching.

IC also introduced a new website that allowed us to show prospects, and those already registered in our business, how to maximize the business as Distribution Technology. I really felt that I had grown, and that we had grown as a couple, as a result of that weekend experience.

I hadn't come any closer to accepting David's fiancée or her family, as a part of my life. I thought I had an open mind, and then after only a few minutes with (any of) them, I was tied up in knots inside. On one occasion I took the older boy to the park. He was fine until I said we had to leave. When I picked him up he started screaming that I was beating him. Of course everyone looked. Fortunately they could see that I was only holding him. All the while his arms and legs were flailing about. I wondered how Julie Pyburn would influence me in that struggle. Was I being judgmental? Absolutely.

I had seen David grow so much since he joined the Navy, that what I was seeing happen in his personal life, made no sense to me at all.

David's plans to get married were firmed up, and we hosted his fiancée's family at our house for a dinner, making every effort to get to know them. For me, it was a real struggle. I felt absolutely no connection with them. Still, I wanted to be there for David, so I made contact with Roy Johnson, a guy that I'd met through my friend Bill Michaels. Roy's wife worked for one of the downtown hotels and arranged for us to get the honeymoon suite for David and his bride, at a nominal cost. I thought I was doing what I could to help in spite of my own misgivings about their marriage.

I was making another judgment...about our business, and

it didn't sit well with Louisa. I looked at the list of people we had sponsored, and those we had been prospecting, and came away with the feeling that we were sponsoring below our ambition level. I know who I am, and where I come from. I don't believe that I was being condescending or arrogant. What I saw was, by and large, a group of people whose lives we thought we could improve, and I thought that *that* was arrogant. What I learned about the business, when looking at those who had created the type of success that I aspired to achieve, was that they were *used* to succeeding. The real leaders expected to succeed, and I didn't see that in our "group," or prospects. I struggled with admitting that because I really liked a number of them, on a personal level.

I told Louisa that I thought she had a Mother Teresa complex. Now *that* was not well received. She was already unhappy with me on a personal level and my comment didn't serve to improve that situation.

Of course, there was somewhat of a balance in all of that. Somewhere along the line, I had run into a woman whom I had known in the early 80's. We met her husband, and we talked with them about our business, and the distribution technology model. They invited us to dinner, and we responded to their interest, promising to provide more information via email, video and audiotapes, etc. Shortly after doing so, I received a terse message that I could pick up the Amway materials. I was more than a little surprised at her tone, because I had told them the source of the products that are available through the distribution system, when we had dinner with them. Oh well. My mantra was one that I had learned well..."Some will... some won't...so what."

Louisa felt, and rightly so, that I was not giving David and his fiancée much of a chance, and that I hadn't accepted her or her family. She was right on all counts. I had been seeing our relationship growing in many positive ways, and I saw a storm cloud gathering over this situation.

On Monday, December 21, 1998, David and Herschell were married. And the Broncos lost to Miami that night. The day didn't have a chance. It was a civil ceremony…the wedding not the game…attended by Louisa and me, the bride and groom, the bride's sister and Chris Harrison. Chris had been pining over not having Brandy, but he did bring a young woman with him to the ceremony. Wow! I think an accurate term would be *hot*. He said that they were just friends, and that she knew David from school, too. It didn't matter who she was, or what she looked like, Chris was (still) in love with Brandy. It's just that her presence made the matter of the wedding ceremony easier for me to take.

A couple of days after Christmas the bride's family hosted a reception for her and David. It was such a big occasion that her dad actually joined us for a while. They had the Broncos' game on so I made it through the afternoon without much interaction with them. Although I had arranged for their stay in the honeymoon suite, David was aware of my feelings about what was going on, and I was almost officially on the outs with him and Louisa.

Not long after Christmas, David was on to Camp Pendleton, without his bride. She wanted to stay home with her family. A few days later Louisa flew to Virginia to help with Carol's care and to give Paul a break.

When I talk about Louisa's flying to Virginia to help with Carol, I don't mean to imply that her sister Ellen wasn't helping. She was. She also had her own family to care for, and the four kids were still all at home.

My focus was staying plugged in to the IC meetings, and

the Broncos play-off games. This was also one of the rare times when the coffee issue had a humorous side. Forget the stories about how the mice play when the cat's away. When I returned from dropping off Louisa at DIA, the first thing I did was move the coffee maker up to the kitchen. We laughed about what a wild and crazy guy I had become. Louisa returned a week later and the coffee maker was once again sentenced to the basement.

The Broncos made it through the play-offs this time, beating the Jets in the AFC Championship game at Mile High Stadium. They were headed to their second straight Super Bowl appearance. They were going to play Atlanta, coached by the former Broncos' head coach, Dan Reeves. Chris Coons had shown more faith in the Broncos' title run than most people I knew. He had purchased a ticket several weeks earlier and was flying home to be here for the Super Bowl game. He said he'd missed the celebration when the Broncos beat the Packers the previous year and he didn't want to miss it again.

The Broncos blew out Atlanta in Super Bowl XXXIII on January 31st. Chris stayed long enough to enjoy the parade and celebration honoring the Broncos, and then flew back to Austin.

People who know me well know that I bleed Cardinals **red**, as in St. Louis Cardinals. Why then aren't they mentioned on every other page? I was caught up in their three World Series appearances in '82, '85 & '87. Louisa has frequently said that she didn't know I was a sports fan until we moved to Denver. Obviously she didn't see me watching the only World Series they won in the 80's…in '82, while we were engaged, and just before I ran the Marine Corps Marathon in D.C. Of course they were robbed in KC in '85 and outplayed by the Twins in '87. *And* they only make play-off appearances in the even numbered decade…at least since the days of Dizzy Dean,

"YOU USED TO LIVE IN MY HOUSE."

Pepper Martin and The Gas House Gang of the 30's. I came along in '42 and it's been the even numbered decades since. They did win 3 out of 4 World Series appearances by the time I was 5.

What Louisa has noticed is that I am a huge Broncos' fan. I actually became a Broncos' fan before we moved to Denver. It started when they picked up Charley Johnson in '72. I'd been a fan of his when he played for the football Cardinals in the 60's.

Not long ago I learned that he is *Dr.* Charley Johnson, professor and academic department head of the chemical engineering department at New Mexico State University. I know you're glad that I shared all of that with you.

CHAPTER 8
The end of the century

The year had started off with a lot of excitement, and then settled in to more changes for our family. Some were more dramatic than others.

On February 10th, our niece Shelli, and her husband A.G., had their baby, Robert Arthur Stockstill. Robert's names came from his two grandfathers. God, how I wish Bob Coons could have been here for that occasion.

Louisa and I were making a concerted effort to get out and meet more people, with the intention of building our business. We knew that more changes were coming up in 1999. We were told to get ready for an entirely new business model.

We went to financial seminars in the evening. You know the kind. A financial planner invites you to a dinner and a presentation. We went with a focus on meeting people that might become prospects for our business. With the same goal in mind we were also attending free classes offered by Microsoft. Had I known what was coming down the pike for our business, I would have put all of my attention into the latter group.

In February I happened across an interesting newspaper ad. It was particularly interesting to me, because it offered a free pass to a movie. I saw an opportunity to take Louisa out, and help patch up our latest argument.

I picked up the pass for two people, for the preview of a new film, "Office Space." I didn't know anymore about it than the ad on the ticket revealed. When Louisa came home, I ushered her out and told her we were going to pick up sandwiches and go to a movie. She didn't know what was going on. What movie? Where? How much would it cost? The only cost was for our sandwiches. The movie was funny and she liked the fact that I had just taken it upon myself to get the ticket and for us to go. We eased back into post-argument life, and set out to find out more about the free movies being offered.

Now, 7 years later, we've probably gone to hundreds of free movies, sometimes seeing two back to back at different theatres. We have met some interesting people and made friends with people over the years of standing in line waiting to be admitted. At times we saw it as a prospecting tool for our business. However, it never materialized as such.

Our business model was changing to E-commerce. We would be partners with Quixtar.com, an internet-based "sister company," to Amway. We learned that, on September 1, 1999, everything that we had purchased through catalogs, then through phone and computer ordering, from Amway, would be available through a new Internet site. We purchased business card size CD Rom's to use to introduce the E-commerce business model to prospects.

At the same time we learned of a new product line called Magna Bloc. They offered a line of therapeutic magnetic products developed by Dr. Robert Holcomb, at Vanderbilt University. We were so impressed with the effectiveness of the products that we purchased them for ourselves and sold several applications to others. We had a goal of reaching the 25% bonus bracket that spring, and saw the Magna Bloc line as a big boost. We didn't reach that goal, but drove our business to a higher level than we had enjoyed at any time previously.

CHAPTER 9
The incredible spring of '99.

David hadn't convinced his new wife to move to San Diego. He had filed for a spouse allotment to be set up for her and the boys. It dragged on and she accused him of not filing for it. I called upon a USMC Lt. Colonel who was a member of the local IC group, to find a way to help her with it. We were told that she could get an ID card locally and would be entitled to use the commissary and facilities at Buckley. She refused to drive to Buckley get the ID.

We opted not to go to the meetings at Snowmass in March. We had a lot of momentum, sponsoring new distributors, soon to be called Independent Business Owners (IBO's) in the Quixtar system, and selling even more Magna Bloc products.

We were in Denver in time for Riley's 1st Birthday party, and the family tradition of letting him dive into the chocolate cake. I thought back to my reservations about Kelly being pregnant with him, and saw how everything was working out for her and Jeremy and the boys. A week later two worlds turned upside down.

David became Dave somewhere during his first year or so with the Navy. I don't recall when we picked up on it. In late March he called to say that he had received a letter from Herschell telling him that she didn't love him and wanted a divorce. Initially she had promised to join him in California after he returned from his first float. That's a six-month deployment with temporary duty at various locations in the Pacific Rim. He'd gotten his 'Dear John' letter from her on the second stop of the float, in Singapore. We talked with Dave and made every effort to comfort him. Regarding the financial aspect of it, canceling an allotment to a spouse, once it has been issued, is much more difficult than starting one. It wouldn't be cancelled until the divorce was final and the papers had been registered with the Navy, several months later.

Within hours Kelly called to say that Jeremy had walked out on her and the boys. She had believed that they were happier than they'd ever been. She said that she'd learned that he had been having an affair with someone at his workplace. When his girlfriend was fired, he walked out with her. He left his family and his job at the same time. **It was one week after Riley's 1ˢᵗ birthday.**

At the time Kelly was delivering newspapers in the morning and going to school full time. She was about to start her week of finals at Metro State with graduation hanging in the balance.

We called Chris Harrison and Chris Coons to tell them what was going on. Chris Harrison had started dating Brandy again, saying initially that they were just going to be friends, then it became much more serious, quickly. When I called Chris Coons and told him about what was going on for Kelly and David, he said, "You and Louisa are okay, aren't you?" I was happy to reply that we were more than okay. We were doing better than ever.

Kelly's sister Jessica stayed with her so that Kelly could continue with the paper route each morning. We each pitched in to help her with the boys, and there were times when Kelly would call and not be able to talk, just cry. I drove over to her apartment to take the boys to the playground and give her time to herself, or just to be there for her. Kelly had a lot support from family and friends, and we were all looking forward to her graduation from Metro State.

I had been serving as a Lector at 10:30 Catholic Community, and was rehearsing with the choir for the Easter Mass in April. At the same time, Louisa and I were immersed in what was becoming a major controversy. One of the parishioners had died in a plane crash on Christmas Eve, and her estate was donating a rental property to the church.

The controversy centered on whether the property should be sold at fair market value, as one group within the church suggested, or whether we should help the tenants purchase the property. They had been good tenants, and had enjoyed a good relationship with the now deceased owner. Louisa and I lined up in favor of the latter. She took it upon herself to help the tenants get their finances in order so that she could get a suitable mortgage loan for them. It was a long process, and the community was divided over the issue.

Both businesses were growing and I had a new listing coming up in Washington Park. On April 20th I began my day having coffee with my friend Bill Michaels, and then I started walking through the east side of Washington Park with fliers promoting my new listing. I was also scheduled for a Read Aloud session that afternoon.

As I was walking south on High Street, there seemed to be the same news blaring from several houses as I passed. A duplex being remodeled had a large boom box blasting the news. The workers were standing at the front door of one of the units, listening. I stopped.

Students were being gunned down at a high school in Littleton, some 10 miles southwest of us. It would be summed up in one word forever: **COLUMBINE**.

It was as though we were all experiencing life in suspended animation. The tragedy of the Columbine massacre was everywhere and anywhere we turned. Every media outlet was covering it. Friends and family from across the country, called to see how close it was to us and of course, everyone locally talking about it. A quiet, suburban community was changed forever.

Business stopped immediately. The weather turned foul. Nature's mood mirrored that of our community and beyond.

Washington Park had been one of the hottest neighborhoods in what had been a hot Denver market for almost 8 years. No one looked at my new listing until May 1st. I talked with other Realtors who were seeing the same affect on their business. Our plight paled dramatically compared to how the lives of those directly affected had changed.

We had been focused on the pain and confusion that had taken over Kelly and David's lives, and still pushing our businesses forward. All of that was suspended for weeks.

CHAPTER 10
Asking the right questions

Louisa and I went out to dinner one evening, to an Indian food restaurant on what was then called Restaurant Row, on Seventeenth Avenue. There was only one other customer in the restaurant. A young man sitting at a table nearby, talking continuously on his cell phone, while eating. That was uncommon in 1999 and would probably not be allowed in many restaurants today. It didn't bother us, and Louisa took advantage of hearing his half of the conversation to talk with him when he ended the call. It wasn't as though she was eavesdropping, it was that one couldn't help but hear what he was saying.

We were always on the lookout for prospective associates for our E-commerce business, and also real estate and mortgage clients. Louisa is **much** better about talking to strangers than I am. She excused herself for interrupting, explaining that she couldn't help but hear what he had been saying on the phone. He had been lining up a DJ gig in Boulder. Louisa told him that I had been a DJ...common ground, you know. He introduced himself as Nick Noyes, and Louisa introduced us. I told him that I had been a radio DJ in what seemed like another life. It had been years ago.

We talked with Nick extensively and a few days later visited him and his roommate, Aaron, to talk with them about buying a house together. They were quick to explain that they were college classmates and friends, not "partners." Louisa did some background work with them and it turned out that they put their plans on hold. They were each qualifying for their pilot's license, and continuing their advanced degree work.

A few weeks later we sent birthday greetings to David. He celebrated his 25th birthday somewhere in the United Arab Emirates. Of course he emailed about the unforgiving heat, and how they tried to sleep by day and work by night when the temperature was only around 100 degrees. He said the UAE soldiers were even worse than the heat. Here was the new and improved David, talking about *their* lack of discipline.

I had talked with Kelly about a graduation present. It was a cause for real celebration. I was the first in our family to graduate from high school. I had spent over four years going to college night school classes, earning enough credits to be a qualified junior. However, I didn't finish with a degree. Kelly would be the first in my family to graduate from college.

When I couldn't get a straight answer from Kelly, regarding a graduation present, we came across a cell phone offer that prompted us to buy the phone and cover start up fees. She would have a nominal monthly charge. I also took a photo of her, taken when she was 12 years old, wearing big frame glasses…quite nerdy looking, and had it screened onto an oversized t-shirt. I had the phrase, "Have You Seen Her Lately?" added to it.

We gave Kelly the phone before the graduation ceremony. She thought it was a great gift and that she would use it only to check on the kids while she was at work. Of course, she had yet to find a full time job.

We all gathered at the Blue Bonnet Mexican Restaurant, a Denver favorite, for a graduation dinner and party. Her best friend, Michelle, had reserved a room for us. She had a direct connection. Her father was one of the managers. At the party we learned that Kelly had been using the phone to check the Colorado Avalanche score during the graduation exercise. So much for limited use of the phone. I also surprised her with the t-shirt, saying that I had it made, intending it to be her only gift when she had not been helpful with gift ideas. Kelly got a kick out of the t-shirt. We all challenged her to put it on, which she did. Brendan ended up wearing the t-shirt during the party.

We had most of the family together for Kelly's graduation party. While David was thousands of miles away, Chris Coons came home for it. While he was home he, Kelly and Chris Harrison got together for an AV's game.

It didn't take Kelly long to land a job, as a counselor for the Planned Parenthood Clinic at Rose Medical Center. Given the controversial history of those clinics, I was less enthusiastic than I had hoped to be.

Chris Coons and I went to a Rockies game. I think the latter was one for the record books. Cincinnati just bombed the Rockies…24 to 12. Two days later, he rode the bus back to Texas, which probably made that game seem shorter.

CHAPTER 11
Life and death changes

As the family went back to work and school, I had a day that took me from an emotional high to an exhausting new low. That morning I had written a contract for a client who had cancelled a contract a year earlier because of unresolved inspection issues. They had reappeared and we had found the right house for them this time around.

That night, I ate some canned enchiladas sauce and contracted food poisoning. I had never experienced food poisoning before. If I had ever "wanted to die" from a virus or hang over experience, it couldn't have compared with that 12 hour period. I had stopped eating "red meat" in 1975, due to digestive problems. The list grew to include beef, pork, duck and lamb. I always have some HCL with Pepsin handy, in case I eat any of those items unknowingly. I don't want to imagine that night of food poisoning without the HCL with Pepsin.

June 4, 1999: Louisa's sister Ellen called to say that their mother had died. We called Dave in California and he made arrangements to fly to Virginia. Louisa, Chris Harrison and I left for Virginia, in the '91 Volvo, that evening. We drove straight through to Mom's house. Well, almost. We had a brief stop near Columbia, MO. I had changed the spark plugs a week earlier and one of them blew out on the highway. We limped into a shopping center just off I-70 to buy spark plugs. Then it was on to Mom's house. We stayed the night and left early the next morning for Newport News. We had planned to go to Virginia in July for Louisa's 30-year high school reunion. Those plans were now in question.

It had been a little more than five years since Carol's auto accident in Lynchburg. She never fully recovered, and in recent years her health had steadily declined. We knew it was a double-edged sword for Paul, who loved her so much and who had been so drained from caring for her. Regardless of the timetable, it's always heart breaking to lose someone you love. Paul had celebrated his 79th birthday in April and Carol would have been 77 in August. They'd been together since their college days at THE UNIVERSITY (of Virginia). They'd had children together and had lost children together. They were each an only child and so much of their lives had been spent with just each other, although they'd had Ellen, Louisa and Bruce along the way.

We went to church with Paul, at Mt. Carmel, on Sunday. I always enjoy visiting there. On that day, I felt the mass was particularly spirit-filled. I felt that our church, 10:30 Catholic Community, had lost the spirit of Jesus, primarily through all of the bickering over the property that had been left to the church. I told Paul about my experience at Mt. Carmel, saying that I had sensed the kind of spirit that I want for our church in Denver. I knew then that I wanted to move on to a different church.

I remember the day of Carol's funeral being so incredibly hot…103 degrees. All of the men were wearing suit coats. We were told that we should remove them at the internment. She would have wanted us to do that. Dave wore his Marines Alphas and insisted on keeping his jacket on.

After the reception we gathered at Paul's condo and Louisa said that she'd stay for a week or so. Chris and I would drive back together. That was an interesting trip, and it was the first time he and I had spent any real time alone together. Chris had never driven anything like a Volvo with a Turbo, and he really enjoyed taking it up the mountains in southwestern Virginia and West Virginia. I thought I'd have to pry him loose from the steering wheel.

We stopped at Mom's house again, and we spent a day showing him around Alton before heading back to Denver the next afternoon.

Our next-door neighbor, Louise Graber died on June 6th, while we were in Virginia. I made it back to Denver in time for her funeral service.

The timing was almost too much. My brother Bob had died on June 5th, 5 years earlier. For some reason, dates and places stay logged in my memory. It's usually more helpful than not. However, June had taken on a new look, with deaths of family and friends on the 4th, 5th and 6th…and my dad's death on the 14th. There are two dates in June that shed some positive light on the month. June 18th, our wedding anniversary date is one, and the 19th, which was the date of my discharge from the Army is the other. I didn't have any trouble with the Army. I had a pretty easy 3 years. I had learned a lot about life, and about myself. To say that I was ready to leave Fort Riley, Kansas is an understatement.

CHAPTER 12
Can we have some fun here?

I had a listing appointment near Louisa's office on the morning of our anniversary, so we decided to make our celebratory meal a long lunch. While we were eating, Chris Harrison called and offered us two tickets to the Rockies and Marlins' game, courtesy of his employer, Goodyear. We had no other plans and it was a beautiful day, so we accepted. Going to a ballgame on our *anniversary* would not normally be something Louisa would look forward to doing. We knew the seats would be pretty good, and she was looking forward to it as much as I.

During the 3rd inning, I excused myself to go to the Men's Room. On the way I asked one of the ushers about getting our anniversary announced on the big reader board. She said that it had to be arranged three weeks in advance. I returned to my seat. During the 7th Inning Stretch, a Guest Host came down the aisle and called out to everyone in our section: "Do we have a Perry and Louisa Coons here?" Louisa jumped up and raised her hand, thinking there was some kind of emergency. He then said to everyone. "Let's all sing happy anniversary to them. They're here to celebrate their 16th wedding anniversary." Everyone cheered and then they all sang to us. He then gave us a certificate commemorating the event. Louisa is almost impossible to embarrass, so I was really enjoying the moment. She asked if I thought Chris did it and before I could say anything in reply, she called him. He hadn't done it. So then she thought it was his boss who had given us the tickets. No one else knew where we would be sitting.

Everything was cool. Todd Helton topped it off by hitting a walk-off home run to win the game. As we passed by the usher I had initially approached about the reader board, she asked, "Was that okay?" Louisa gave me a look of surprise, knowing that I'd put one over on her, and then poured the remaining water from her bottle over my head. She laughed, and said, "You said you were going to the restroom." I confirmed that I had. I was no less wet for telling the truth.

A few days later, Kelly and Chris took me to a Rockies game for Father's Day. They spared no expense, either. We sat in the Rockpile and were washed with sunshine all afternoon. We laughed about that at the game and had a good time. They even bought my lunch, from Subway.

CHAPTER 13
The heat is on

We added more people to our business that month, including my friend Ray Anderson. It was the ease with which we could now order products and have them shipped direct to us that made the difference to Ray.

The IC Summer Seminar was approaching and Bob and Betty McKann had insisted on hosting Paul for the event.

We picked up Paul, and Bob and Betty, at DIA, on July 1st. It was a scorching, 'must have the car air-conditioning on' day. We had them all in the car around 2 PM. I was anxious to get to Keystone because the event started around 6 PM.

However, we stopped by to introduce our upline to a new associate whose office was just off I-70. We'd met him at a business-to-business expo a couple of weeks earlier. He didn't have much time to visit, which was okay with me. It was so hot that the car AC was barely handling it with all five of us in the car, and the window open while Bob talked to him. We were on the road pretty quickly, and I noticed the engine temperature was climbing as we neared the Evergreen exit.

I stopped at a gas station-convenience store and checked the antifreeze. I added some water and we were on the road again. The over heating continued and got much worse going up the hills past Idaho Springs. It was getting late and it was becoming obvious that we wouldn't be on time for the opening event.

The car over heated again just before the long climb to the Eisenhower Tunnel. It was dark by the time the car had cooled down enough to put the ice-cold spring water in the radiator. We waited for the engine to cool. Cold water could have cracked a hot engine block. I had called for a tow truck that never arrived. We were finally able to put enough water in the radiator to start up the hill. Of course the engine heat was rising fast and as we came out of the tunnel, I put the car in neutral and on that 8-mile Long, 6% grade, "hill" down to Silverthorne, I even turned off the engine and coasted in neutral I was scared to death and I didn't tell anyone in the car what I was doing. We got to our hotel around 9 PM. The next morning I took the car to a garage less than a block away.

Bob rented a car for the next couple of days, while the thermostat and water pump were being replaced in my car. Thermostats are usually very inexpensive, as auto parts go, and easy to change. Had I know that was the problem I could have changed it in Denver, in much less time than all of the stops had taken. The water pump might not have broken if the thermostat hadn't become stuck, causing the overheating.

It was a nightmare that I had to get beyond so that I could absorb the information about Quixtar that I knew would be forthcoming.

The seminar was very productive. Chris and Sandra Johnson came up for part of it. They had lunch with us, Paul and Bob and Betty and then we all went out with Chuck and Jean for a while before getting ready for the evening program. Chris agreed that they'd stay for the evening presentation. That was no mean task, as he does not like to be in a vehicle in the mountains.

We left the seminar early on July 4th to take Bob and Betty to DIA. We made that trip without any automobile incidents. Paul left for Virginia a week later.

"YOU USED TO LIVE IN MY HOUSE."

Kelly had filed for divorce. While we were at Keystone, she was in Las Vegas with her friend Robin's brother, on a hiking trip. The grandsons were with Jeremy. I told Kelly, "Don't move those boys to Las Vegas." She said that she and Robin's brother were "just friends" and that she had no intention of moving to Las Vegas.

A couple of weeks later we received a call from Woody Phaisawang. Louisa had worked with Woody at AMOCO. I had met him and knew that Louisa had a high regard for him. He and his wife, Siri, wanted me to help her find an investment property. That didn't work out as she had hoped. However, it was good that we reconnected.

A number of things came out of that call. First, we began to develop a friendship that has grown stronger since. We really enjoy Woody and Siri and their daughters. Secondly, Siri introduced me to Thai cooking…not just Thai food. She is an incredible cook, and I've eaten some pretty good Thai food since she first cooked for me. I haven't found any that compares with hers. Another thing that happened was the result of that meeting and a few other events that came together at the right time.

On the first evening we looked at a house in Lakewood, across the street from one I had sold in 1998. That was the occasion when an ex-wife wouldn't sit in the same room for the closing, and one of my buyers had become confrontational. I hadn't seen them since then. They saw my car and came over to say hello. Afterwards, Louisa, Siri, Woody and I went to the Phaisawang's home in Aurora for dessert. We were impressed by the addition Woody had made to their home, virtually doubling the size of it. The craftsmanship was superb. On the way home we talked about the deck we had always wanted to build above our front porch, opening the bedroom to it. We knew then, that we wanted Woody to build it when the time was right.

A week later we were to go dinner at their home, with Siri promising to fix a special Thai dinner for us. Unfortunately Louisa had a migraine headache that evening. She insisted that I should go without her, so I did. Siri's meal had sweat pouring out of every pore in my body. Yet, I loved it and continued to eat it. They sent some home with me, for Louisa.

CHAPTER 14
When does change become upheaval?

I had become estranged from some of the members of our church community. In my mind, greed had reared its ugly head. That's another judgment on my part. What wasn't left to judgment was the way Louisa was treated in the community's open meetings. She was treated rudely for her efforts, and treated so in front of those attending. None of us involved in the transaction, charged, or accepted any financial compensation for our work. Before the transaction closed, we had begun "church shopping."

In early August, Louisa approached a couple that had stopped to pick up a flyer at a house for sale a few blocks from our home. She simply asked if they were looking for a home in the neighborhood, and whether they had a Realtor. They answers were yes and no, respectively. She gave them our cards and a couple of days later they called me to set an appointment for an interview. They already had their home Under Contract. They'd been selling it themselves, saying 'never again.' I liked them already.

I sometimes get caught up in stories about the strange things that I've experienced in my years of selling real estate. Hence the book I wrote in 2005, <u>Surreal Estate</u>. However, this couple, Bill and Phyllis, deserve a mention because they are two of the nicest, most pleasant people I've ever dealt with in any business transaction. Fortunately for me, they stayed with me when their first contract was pulled out from under them.

After we started looking at homes, they became Louisa's clients, too. We found a place just before we were ready to head back to Virginia for Louisa's high school reunion. We were Under Contract and had gone through the inspection. My clients were also out of town, visiting family in California.

On the first night, after the reunion dinner, we returned to Paul's condo. I had a message from the agent for the sellers of a property we had Under Contract. She said that the seller wanted to cancel the contract because he had a better offer come in. Like almost all real estate transactions, there is a domino effect involved. The sale of Bill and Phyllis' place had yet to close, and the agent for their buyer was out of town on a hiking trip where there was no cell phone service. All parties knew all of that before we left. The seller had said that he was okay with it, and that he'd wait until the agent returned to be assured that the buyer was good to close on Bill and Phyllis' house. Now, the seller was using that loose end to get out of his contract with Bill and Phyllis. The seller's agent claimed that she was helpless and had to follow the seller's instructions. I was livid. She accused me of yelling at her and she was right. I know that I said that I would never do business with her again.

It took a while to relay the information to Bill and Phyllis, because they were in California while we were in Virginia and a 3 hour time difference, as well as almost 3000 miles. I caught up with them, and shared the news. They took the high road. Their Earnest Money was being returned and they said only that the seller had shown his true character. And I thought, 'or lack thereof.'

While we were in Virginia we added one new couple to our business and two brothers to Chris and Sandra's group. We were on a roll as we headed toward September 1st and the Quixtar launch.

"YOU USED TO LIVE IN MY HOUSE."

We drove to Alton on the 16th. Then we spent the next day, Louisa's birthday, driving across Kansas. Do we know how to have a good time, or what?

The next Sunday we went church shopping again. We visited St. Elizabeth's, on the Auraria Campus, downtown. We discovered that we knew the priest who was celebrating mass and several people in the congregation. The next week we visited St. Dominic's Catholic Church on the west side of town. I think it felt a little too traditional and formal for us. The following week we went to St. Ignatius Loyola. Louisa recalled that Celeste had told her about it a few years earlier. I recalled that I had dropped off one of Albert and Marcellina Otii's daughters at the Loyola school during the inspection of the home they bought in 1998.

On our way home, we looked at each other, and almost simultaneously, "I hope that felt as good for you as it did for me." We both agreed that we'd found our new church home. I know that I had felt the spirit of Christ that I was seeking.

Loyola is a Jesuit community, and I was somewhat familiar with the Jesuits from Regis University. While 10:30 Catholic Community was a lay-led parish, the Jesuit priests from Regis would often celebrate mass there. Loyola's make up is unique in my church experience. It is a diverse community, racially, culturally and by observation, in it's social-economic make up as well. There is an air of warmth and openness that I hadn't experienced in any other church.

That diversity was reflected in three couples we became fast friends with. We'd known Albert and Marcellina Otii before we discovered St. Ignatius Loyola. We met Sal and Chris Molina in a potluck buffet line shortly after we started attending Masses at Loyola. Not longer after that we met Bill and Mary Thompson. The latter two couples would later become real estate clients, too.

We also learned that Bill and Mary are also Quixtar IBO's. Shortly after we began attending Loyola, Louisa spotted a necklace Mary was wearing, as one she had seen in the Quixtar catalog. She commented on it and Mary said that she could show her where to get it. Louisa told her that she knew where to get it. I later called Mary to ask her the proper name for it and ordered it for Louisa for Christmas.

The next week we linked...the new term for sponsoring... two more people into our business. By September 1st, we had added, err...linked 10 new IBO's as business associates.

On September 3rd I submitted the third, full price offer on behalf of Bill and Phyllis. They were great through it all. I should have cloned them. The sellers were out of the country. I didn't know whether to laugh or cry. It all worked out and they're still in that house today...Bill and Phyllis, that is.

CHAPTER 15
Just say 'no,' then again, 'yes.'

About a week or so after the launch of Quixtar, I actually turned down someone who wanted to register as an IBO. He was a Realtor I'd met a year earlier, and he wanted to register without telling his wife. He said he'd started a number of business ventures, and she would be upset if he started another. We were sitting outside a coffee shop when he asked me to call in his registration, offering to write a check for it. I just said no. I thought it would be wrong to deceive his wife, and that it wouldn't take long for her learn about it. If he ordered products, or if he linked others, she would have to know...sooner or later. I told him to talk with her about it, and if she was open to more information, we'd go from there. He didn't want to do that, so we didn't get him registered.

When I told Betty McKann that I'd turned down someone, she asked, "Are you crazy?" I didn't debate the possibility, but when I told her the whole story, she agreed with my decision.

While in Fort Worth, we also had an opportunity to visit with Shelli and A.G., and to meet Robert. My heart ached for my brother Bob.

The featured speaker at the conference was noted author and lecturer John C. Maxwell. Just before the conference I had read his book, <u>The Leader Within</u>. I didn't understand at the time, the groundwork that was being laid for my development. It would take a few years and an experience that was more than a lecture, to help me see it.

We decided to stop overnight in Dumas, Texas on the way back to Denver. The next morning I went to a local fast food restaurant for coffee. As I pulled into their parking lot the car died. It wouldn't restart. I got my coffee and walked back to the motel. Louisa and I began to make calls and found a garage that would take a look at it. Several hours later we were headed home with a new timing belt. It was expensive, but could have been more so. I was fortunate that the belt broke when it did rather than while we were cruising at 60 mph or better.

1999 wasn't over and we had already added 14 new frontline IBO's and 8 downline. Louisa and I were in synch and excited about our future together. The initial glitches with Quixtar had been worked out and the site was becoming everything we heard that it would be. Initially more people were logging in than the servers would accommodate. Some stayed, some became frustrated or even angry. It didn't take long for it to shake out. There were thousands of pages of products and services available. There are even more today.

In October we hosted our second houseguest through the DIP. We had enjoyed having Karin Ebel with us, and were still in touch periodically via email. Our new houseguest was from Ghana, Africa. At the time Louisa and I had some knowledge about Africa through the African immigrant families we knew at St. Ignatius Loyola. Albert and Marcellina had migrated years earlier, from Kenya and Uganda, and there were families from Nigeria and Sudan as well. During and after hosting Anthony Donkor, from Ghana, we became much more knowledgeable and closer to the African community.

Anthony Donkor arrived and we began a friendship that is still very special to each of us, more than 6 years later. Anthony understood that Louisa's father was coming for a visit and had agreed to go to another host family while Paul was here, and then return to our home.

He worked as a Field Manager for Habitat for Humanity, in Ghana, and was working for their office in Denver during his stay.

We visited Marcellina and her class at the Montessori school, where she had gathered paper, pencils and other essentials for the school that Anthony and his wife Jarvis had established.

Anthony and Jarvis had seen pre-school age children in and near their hometown of Weija, who had been left to fend for themselves during the day while their parents would often walk for miles, to the capitol of Accra, to find work.

They had taken the children in, and their 2-room home became smaller. They used one of the rooms as a classroom. Their dream was to build a school building. We were given the opportunity and inspiration to help them achieve that dream. You can explore more about their school, Hope International, by visiting their website, http://www.hopeinternationalschool.org.

In November I asked if I could join the choir at Loyola. Maria Rose, the director, welcomed me enthusiastically. I had watched them and listened to them intently since we started attending mass there in August. It was a giant step for me, given that I had been singing publicly again only recently. The fact that I was doing it at all was largely due to the encouragement from Rubyetta Cain who directed the ad hoc choirs for the non-denominational services during the CLS events. She had been a music and chorus teacher. Rubyetta and her husband, Bob, were Emerald Direct Distributors in the CLS International organization. As I recall, they'd been childhood friends of the Strehli's.

Rubyetta heard something in my singing and encouraged me to step out and take solo parts. I had never had that kind of encouragement before. I had sung with a few groups 'way back when,' before blowing out my voice in 1980. It was like one of David Letterman's "Stupid Human Tricks." A group of us had gone to a softball game to watch Dave Morgan, and to cheer him on…on his 30th birthday. I drank too much and yelled too loud, too often. I couldn't speak above a whisper for weeks. Whereas I had once been able to mirror Frankie Valli's falsetto, that range disappeared for years.

Another person who welcomed me to the Loyola choir was Oather Moore. He was the only man in the choir before I joined him. He said other men had come and gone, and in fact he had come and gone, and come back. It was a challenge for me to sing beside him. He has this wonderful, rich baritone voice that I heard much more clearly than my own tenor, and at that point tentative, voice.

As we prepared for Christmas, I found that my voice still wasn't strong enough to sing during practices and masses over several consecutive days and nights. I began to sing more at home and in the car to strengthen it.

In late November I made an appointment with Fr. Tom Jost, the Loyola Pastor. I felt the need for some counseling. I had so many things going well in my life that I just didn't understand the nagging feeling that I was missing something. I was back to thinking about the song, "Is That All There Is?" Even back then, before I really got to know and appreciate Fr. Tom, as I do today, I really enjoyed his homilies. When he preaches, he paints verbal pictures for me. I understand so much more about Jesus, the Bible and the Catholic Church because of his eloquent homilies. Still, after meeting with him, I felt that he wasn't going to be right for me as a counselor. Since I didn't know what it was that I wanted, I didn't know who could lead me to it.

"YOU USED TO LIVE IN MY HOUSE."

That fall Kelly was riding the bus to work, with a stops, to and from, at the Auraria Higher Education Center Day Care Center. I have this vivid memory of her waiting for the bus with Brendan and Riley…and Riley on oxygen for a period of time. He had a pretty rough winter, as did his Mom.

I think we met Brandy's dad, mom and stepfather for the first time that Thanksgiving. Chris and she were living in her townhouse in Thornton. I'd met her brother Dan, when Chris had lived on Glencoe. Chris and Brandy hosted the family that Thanksgiving. Shirley was easy to like immediately and so much more outgoing than Brandy. I was thinking that Brandy must be more like her dad. When I met him, I saw the similarity. John's very likeable too, but in a quiet, laid-back way. I didn't know Brandy well, but I appreciated how happy Chris was with her in his life. After seeing what Kelly and David had gone through, it was really special to see Chris and Brandy enjoy and respect each other. Mark, Brandy's stepfather seemed distant, almost aloof. It took me longer to warm to him. Maybe I saw too much of myself in him

True to their word, Chris and Brandy were married in Las Vegas on December 20th.

Paul joined us for Christmas, arriving early in the week, and Dave came home on Christmas Eve. To our happy surprise, he joined us for Mass.

A few days after Christmas, Dave and I were sitting in the living room, and he said, "You seem so much more laid-back now." I laughed and replied, "Guess who doesn't live here anymore." He took that in the right way and we had a good laugh. David seemed to be happy and at peace with himself. He was anxious to share the stories about his six-month tour.

We hosted Christmas dinner and then we all went to the

holiday lights show at the Denver Botanical Gardens. It was fun…but it was also incredibly cold that night.

Before Paul left for Virginia, he joined Ray Anderson and me during one of our many coffee meetings. Ray and I had been meeting for coffee, almost monthly, since we met in real estate school in 1992.

Paul also met Leslie Myers over coffee. Louisa joined us because we could take the coffee into the adjoining Barnes & Nobles store and the aroma of it cooking at Starbucks didn't bother her.

We gathered in an area that had a sofa and chair, and bookcases on three sides. I had this feeling that someone was listening to us. I saw someone walk by slowly and then again, as though she was circling the area where we were sitting. I saw her the second time, and because she looked very different from when I knew her in the 80's, it took a while for me to recognize her. I think she must have seen the recognition my face. She didn't come by again. It was Carol Woelber. I'd long since forgiven her for not being the friend I thought she was, when I needed one. I would have been happy to talk with her if she had stopped to say hello.

Paul flew back to Virginia before New Year's Eve.

BOOK SIX

CHAPTER 1
The new millennium

That New Year's was the year of Y2K. Paul, like almost everyone I knew, didn't want to be in transit, or away from home as the big ball dropped, or the calendar page was turned.

Kelly, Dave and I ran the Y2K 5k in Washington Park. My friend Bill Michaels was the event coordinator, and he reserved the bib number 2000 for me, 1999 for Kelly and 2001 for Dave. We had a lot of fun with it. Louisa joined us with Brendan and Riley, and we walked over to South High School afterwards for the spaghetti dinner, but didn't stay because of the big crowd.

Kelly and the grandsons went home for New Year's Eve. Dave went out. Later that night Louisa and I went to a low-key New Year's Eve party on the northwest side of metro-Denver. The drive home was sort of eerie because there were so few vehicles on the road.

New Year's Day was on a Saturday and it was one of those rare occasions when I just vegged, and watched college football bowl games all day and into the night.

I started the New Year and millennium considering a change of name for my real estate business. I had set it up, at the end of 1997 simply as Perry Coons, Broker. I now had the itch to change it to a DBA, but couldn't come up with a suitable name, so I didn't.

Dave left for Camp Pendleton later in the week. He was assigned to the 1st Marines Division as a corpsman.

I recall that we drove to Louisville that night, to have dinner with Ann and Oscar, the couple we'd met at Powderhorn in 1998. We enjoyed their company, and regrettably the distance has made our visits to infrequent.

Ronnie Meyer told me during their visit last summer, that a 40-year reunion was being planned for July of '00. He said that Larry Donahue was one of the people coordinating it, so I called Larry to ask how I could help from Denver. He welcomed the help, particularly using the Internet. His wife Kathy was the one who put together their email messages.

The momentum we had enjoyed since the launch of Quixtar didn't carry over into the new year. I began to see our E-com business group slipping away. We coordinated a home meeting for Chris and Sandra, at their place. None of the people we had invited showed up. No active IBO's. No prospects.

Louisa and I began to second-guess each other again. One of the new IBO's had moved back to Michigan and wasn't communicating with us. Another quit after she became irate that she couldn't find a refrigerator for her sister, at a big discount. She later moved to Hawaii with her sister. Maybe she'd still be living here, if only she'd have found that refrigerator on sale.

We even began to bicker over things such as a newsletter that I wanted to send to our group. Louisa had started one years earlier and dropped it. I had been writing a weekly email on health and nutrition for a couple of years. I had been getting a lot of compliments about it and I thought that was bothering her.

We had the grandsons fairly often, to give Kelly a break and because we always had a great time with them. At one point Kelly said, "I don't know what I'd do without *your* lifestyle."

"YOU USED TO LIVE IN MY HOUSE."

Bill Michaels and I began to talk about going back to Cheyenne for a visit in July. It was the tenth anniversary of the statehood festival. I'd lost touch with most of the people I had known there. A few had joined us in the Amway business in the early 90's and had later dropped out.

In February the family hosted a reception for Chris and Brandy. It was the first time we had celebrated their marriage. Several of their friends were there too, and none more surprising than Jake Seay. I remembered Jake as a kid who was usually acting like a jerk. He'd matured and his entire demeanor was different. He had a pretty young wife, Kelly, at his side. I think Jake was aware of how he'd acted as a kid and he was enjoying how people saw him differently.

Louisa saw Jake and Kelly as prospects for our business. I knew that Chris would not be in favor of his mother calling Jake about it. Chris is very private, and I think he assumes everyone else is equally so. I don't know many people who are. It's like the former kettle calling the pot black. I was, for most of my life, as private as Chris. Thanks to Louisa, I gave up that illusion years ago. Sure enough, when Louisa asked Chris for Jake's phone number, he asked, "Why?" She told him and he said, 'oh, he wouldn't be interested in *that*.' Thousands of people have made that decision for others over the years, perhaps millions.

In February we finally closed the transaction that had put me at odds with some of the members of the 10:30 Catholic Community. We felt good that the tenants had qualified for the mortgage and would now own the house that had been their home for 12 years. I still saw it as a win-win situation for them and for the members of "10:30." The new homeowners were able to purchase the property below the current market value, and the church community received thousands due to the generosity of a former parishioner.

We hadn't had any local IC meetings for nearly 2 years. There had been so much bad blood flowing through the power struggles that the meetings sort of evaporated. As a group we hadn't seen growth, and I became frustrated with the regular attendees talking about how it used to be…"back when." It was as though they couldn't see what Quixtar had to offer. None of us were bringing new people to the meetings often enough.

Larry Carr called and asked if we would host a meeting of some of the people who'd been active in organizing and coordinating the meetings in the past. I was surprised because I didn't see that kind of sharing as his M.O. We did gather a group that represented about 6 different lines of sponsorship within IC. It appeared that we had a consensus to move forward when Larry said, "Good. I talked with Glen Graff and he'll be here in two weeks to hold a meeting for us." I shook my head. It was déjà vu all over again. (thanks, Yogi!)

He had set us up to put everything back into motion with him taking charge. I said, "No. I am not going to support that. I will not go back to where we were two years ago. Obviously, you're each welcome to do what you want to do. I am out." A couple of others made the same decision that night and others called to discuss it later before deciding that they wouldn't support re-establishing what we'd ended two years earlier.

We went to the Strehli's SkiGlo conference at Snowmass again. It was the 30th anniversary of the conference. We decided to look at potential rental properties for our group for the next year. We'd seen some erosion from the big build up around the launch of Quixtar, but still felt that we were on the right track to grow our organization.

Chuck Strehli had taken a bad spill while skiing downhill the day we arrived. He'd sustained a concussion and the doctor told him that skiing was off limits for that week. WOW! I couldn't imagine Chuck *not* skiing at this event or ever. At the reception Jean said, "I'm putting you in charge of keeping Chuck off the ski's. Take him snow shoeing with you…*please*."

The day of the outdoor picnic, Chuck, Tom Kaye and I had our snowshoes and after a bus ride up to the trailhead, we walked up to the cookout. Chuck was almost racing up the hill. In fact, he said, "Let's go to the Nastar site." That's where the skiers do competitive trips down through the slaloms. Chuck asked the guy in the booth if he and I could race down on our snowshoes! Thank goodness the guy said no. We were all over the place and he was something to keep up with. At some point, Tom decided not to. Tom was used to riding the boogie board on the surf at San Diego. Snowshoeing at Snowmass Mountain was not his thing. When we stopped for lunch, I told Jean that I had a new found, even higher regard for her.

That night we went to Aspen, along with our friends Tom and Madge, to hear Haden Gregg sing at the St. Regis Hotel. While we were there we met a guy from Little Rock, whose daughter lived in Denver, and only about 2 miles from our home. He asked about our Aspen visit and we told him that we were attending an annual business function. We exchanged cards, and he invited us to stop by while he was visiting his daughter in Denver the following week. We saw it as an opportunity to prospect her, and possibly him, for our business.

I had asked Jean to counsel with us, and she agreed. She started by saying that she thought I probably talked too much, and/or said too much to prospects. Her thoughts were based on the health and nutrition email that I had been sending out. Jean can be a tough taskmaster. She comes from the heart and I learned that you don't want to ask her something if you're not ready to hear a direct answer.

When we returned to Denver, I jumped back in to our business activity, and my real estate activity. I was also covering the business for Dale and Linda Southworth while they visited family out of state. They each had an active buyer, and I felt glad that I could help them. I wrote one offer for them, and showed a few places to the other buyer, who wanted to wait for Linda's return before offering a contract on what she had seen.

I was still searching for what I wanted to do while building our E-com group. I knew that I wasn't satisfied with real estate. I applied for one marketing position, and sent a feeler out on another. I really didn't want a "job." I just wanted something more fulfilling and I didn't know what that was going to be.

I made a long list of new prospects and also those I labeled as prospects to exhume. Some of them had nominally been in business with us before, and a couple had been a couple of times.

Going through that list and making myself call them, wore me down. I felt as though I was letting down everyone, including Louisa, the Strehli's and of course, myself. Everyone expressed a lot of confidence in us. Many called us leaders, and I just didn't get it. Louisa had gone to a couple of meetings without me, first because I was working with a real estate client and then because I was depressed and didn't want to go. She was taking the lead, such as working with our friend Madge on a Women's Day Out event. Once again, we weren't functioning as a team.

I could look at the reports about Quixtar, and know it wasn't "the business" that was at fault. We were told that Quixtar had generated $250 million in volume, in 8 months… that it had taken Wal-Mart 12 years to reach that level, and Amazon.com 3 years to do it.

CHAPTER 2
Winds of change

A few weeks after we returned from SkiGlo, we caught wind of a meeting to address a movement to have Washington Park recognized as an historic district. I'd learned of it a month or so earlier and had met with one of the founders of the movement. Their goal, as she expressed to me, was to establish a strict criteria to control the remodels of homes throughout Washington Park. She said that she and a former neighbor had gone to various hearings when homeowners presented their plans to remodel, seeking permits and often for variances from the established building codes our city plans. I told her that it sounded as though her group hadn't gotten what they wanted, so the historic designation was their next step. She didn't disagree with my analysis.

We were, and remain opposed to any such restrictive designation. We'd like to see more diversity in our neighborhood, not less. Louisa was in the 7th grade when Reston, VA was developed. Even as a 7th grader, she was so opposed to the concept of Planned Unit Development (PUD), that she wrote a paper on it. One of the more humorous aspects of that effort was that the two co-founders moved out of Washington Park. One had done so and was still at the forefront of the effort. The other moved later, and I was told that she and her husband built, or purchased, a house that was everything they had fought against in Washington Park.

One of the free movies that we saw that month was "Rules of Engagement," starring Tommy Lee Jones and Samuel L. Jackson. While we were waiting in line I struck up a conversation with a couple standing behind us. That's when we met Lane and Renate Edstrom. We talked until the start of the movie and afterwards. Louisa whispered, "Are we prospecting them, or are they prospecting us?" I was enjoying getting to know them and I did think we could work with them if they were interested in our business. It wasn't something I was prepared to venture into at our first meeting. We exchanged phone numbers and agreed to get together for another movie. I had too many experiences of wanting to talk about our business before I got to know the people I'd just met. There were times when I was glad that I'd waited, and times when I second guessed myself, or learned that they were already registered with Quixtar. It was a hot commodity.

In April we spent a weekend at the luxurious Broadmoor Resort in Colorado Springs, courtesy of White Crown Federal Credit Union (WCFCU). The Credit Union League held its annual meeting there and credit unions from across Colorado were represented. I was told they held it in Denver one year and no one came. Louisa had been elected to the Board of Directors for WCFCU, so it was a perk for the hours she volunteered to serve on the board. She attended sessions with the keynote speaker and various break out sessions to learn more about how the credit union could better serve its members. I felt that it was serving me very well. I attended the dinners with her, socialized during the vendors' exhibitions, etc.

I saw the opportunity to meet people who might be looking to create more cash flow or build financial freedom. Both were among our goals. I did meet a few couples and a single woman there with her parents, who were likely prospects. The single woman, who was also a college student in California, was interested and we agreed to visit by phone a week later.

We knew that Bob and Betty McKann would be in Williamsburg that weekend, and that Paul would be visiting with them. As it turned out they hadn't made the trip because Betty had been in an automobile accident. Rosie and Gary, a couple who were also in business with Paul, and the McKann's, were using their condo.

On Palm Sunday, while we were at brunch, at the Broadmoor, I received a call from Rosie. Paul had suffered a seizure and had been taken to the hospital. He had fallen and cut his head.

We talked with her further on our way back to Denver. Paul was kept overnight at Williamsburg General Hospital, and she and Gary would take him home the next day.

One of the first couples we connected with, at Loyola, Bill and Mary…I love it…I've called them William & Mary. Okay, it's not hilarious, but it's my kind of humor. Oh, the point…they also became real estate clients that spring. Mary would correctly say that its Bill's thing. He buys investment properties, and then he spends time making changes in them, sometimes doing too much and incurring physical injury. At least Mary knows where to find him. Bill, a math professor, with a checkered past not unlike my own, is also one of the wittiest and funniest people I have ever known. At one point, while looking for the second property he would buy as my client, he said he was going to buy a house a year until Mary let him buy a truck.

My 40-year high school reunion was approaching, and a number of us began exchanging emails. I called Ronnie Meyer to talk with him about the four of us getting together for the reunion. They'd been our place a couple of times since '92 and Louisa had grown to close to them also.

About a week before we went to Alton for the reunion, I was attending the Denver Board of Realtors marketing session, which was not something I did with any regularity. I guess I was supposed to be there that morning. Someone named Sherry made a pitch to replace herself as the executive director for a local non-profit, The Community Housing Resource Board (CHRB). I didn't know the agency, but she explained that their mission was to educate Realtors, and others, about Fair Housing. I thought it sounded interesting and certainly agreed with the need to educate Realtors, lenders and others about Fair Housing issues and practices. My experience had been that we were basically taught what *not* to say and do, to avoid claims of discrimination. I decided to apply for the position. It would be a paid, part time position, with a maximum of 25 hours per week. I thought it might be ***that something*** I had been looking for.

Before leaving for the reunion trip, I met with Sherry, and the chair of CHRB, also the co-owner-broker of Nostalgic Homes, Carol Ann Sinclair. I knew of the company and that it was well respected in the Denver real estate market. I gathered enough information, and was favorably impressed with Carol Ann, so that I decided I would take the position if they offered it to me. Later, I would realize that I hadn't asked enough questions. That is a shortcoming that I continue to strive to improve upon.

That was the first Spring and Summer that we faced a drought, and the forest fires of huge magnitude. There was a fire burning southwest of Denver, closer to Pine Junction and Bailey. We had felt closeness with the BuckSnort Saloon since 1985, and have friends who lived in the area. It was then that we got a surprise call from Mark Richey, the former lead singer for Sashay.

"YOU USED TO LIVE IN MY HOUSE."

Mark had heard that the BuckSnort was in danger of being burned down, or that it had been. He said that had talked with Keith Riker about a Sashay reunion to benefit the BuckSnort. I can see the area with web cams that are available on-line and told him that the fire hadn't reached that specific area yet.

We were busy catching up, and talking about music. Our son Dave had turned us on to Phil Vasser. Mark hadn't heard of him at that point. I told him, I thought I heard a lot of Bruce Hornsby influence in Vasser's music. Then he asked me to listen to a song he'd written. I listened and it sounded pretty good. He said he'd like to send me a CD with it and have me pitch it to people. I wasn't going to go down that road again… for no revenue. I mean…Mark is like family to me. But I have family I wouldn't loan money to. I told him that I'd do it if he listed me as one of the writers. I never received that CD, and I haven't heard form Mark since. Go figure.

I got a call from Carol Ann while we were driving to Alton, offering me the CHRB job. I accepted and agreed to meet with her after my trip. She asked me to drive to Breckenridge on the 22nd. She'd be participating in the summer meeting of the Colorado Association of Realtors.

CHAPTER 3
A door closes and another opens

When we got to Alton, we visited with Mom for a while and I called Ronnie Meyer. I was surprised to hear an answering machine greeting. I left a message, welcoming him to the 21st century and asked him to call me. He later got a computer, saying that I shamed him into it.

We met Ronnie and Linda before hand and ate dessert first. It was a good thing because that was the best food we'd get that evening. The first night activities were held in a small private room adjoining a smoky bar. Still, renewing friendships and acquaintances was enjoyable. There were light hors d'oeuvres…such as small weenies, etc. We were hopeful that the next night would be more promising.

We made the trip for my high school reunion. I had thoughts about who might, or might not be business prospects from my graduating class. After going to the first night activities I had penciled in only a couple of people. Most of my former classmates were either retired or looking forward to being retired. Few people talked in terms of the future in any other manner. In that sense, I'm really out of step with many people my age.

The second night event was dinner and dance. Is there a template for high school reunions? The dinner and dance was held at The Sportsman's Club. I had never been a member, but recall having gone there with my Dad, so it had been around for a while. It's a club for hunters and fishermen. I remember watching my Dad shooting clay pigeons. Anyway, the event was held in a large ballroom facility and the food was pretty basic, but tasty. I had no complaints about it. It was kind of eating at a big, really big, diner.

More importantly, as with any reunion…particularly after 40 years, re-connecting with friends was almost magical. I remembered most, Charlie and Marilyn Wall, Jim and Marilyn Wolfbrandt, Sam and Jo Bono, Arthur and Jo Greenwood and so many others.

There was one good-looking blonde who challenged me to remember her. It was embarrassing, but I didn't recognize her. She told me she was Sandra Rives. When I had taken Sandra to the Jr. Prom, she wasn't a blonde. I had to tell her that she had gotten prettier through the years. It's just the truth.

Sandra and I went to ballroom dancing classes when I was 13. She later emailed a photo of the two of us, dated 1955, from one of those dances.

Of course we spent a lot of time with Ronnie and Linda, and other guys who'd been in our hot rod club, The Carb' Kings.

Louisa and I don't go out to dance. We had enough of the smoky bars when she was hawking Sashay tapes. So, when we're at a function such as the reunion, she wants to dance…a lot. I don't know how we visited with so many people and danced so much, but we were really enjoying each other at the time.

Chris Coons, and his sister Jessica Kaid were in Alton when we were there for the reunion. Chris had finished up a road trip there, having been to Boston and then to Chicago with his buddies from Texas. They'd be riding back to Denver with us, so I told them we'd be stopping in Newton, KS overnight and then drive on to Denver the next day.

"YOU USED TO LIVE IN MY HOUSE."

We had spent Louisa's birthday, the year before, driving across Kansas, coming home from her 30-year high school reunion. It was somewhat fitting that we'd be in Kansas on our 17th wedding anniversary, after *my* high school reunion. After introducing Chris and Jessica to Tom and LuAnn Schrag, and visiting for a while, Louisa and I set out to find a place for our anniversary dinner.

We didn't drive as far as we had in 1998. We settled for an Applebee's. We were okay with that. We were happy to be together. The food was good. The service wasn't. I guess it should be expected, particularly in a small town that the wait staff is going to know one or two or more of the customers, personally. Our waiter did and he spent most of our time there visiting with his friends seated near us.

I knew that Chris was not likely to enjoy Tom's company. Let's just say that they are at opposition ends of the political and cultural spectrum. Tom's a redneck of the first order. He's also a Renaissance Man. He's been an opera singer, football player, as well as farmer and rancher. He also has a heart as big as all outdoors. We met him through the IC meetings. He was a widower at the time and we learned that he'd been a devoted husband to his late wife. He's achieved a good measure of success in the business world too.

Chris and I went out for coffee the next morning and he really didn't want to talk about his impression of Newton or our friends there. We always have plenty of things to catch up on when we settle in at any local coffee outlet.

I drove to Breckenridge a couple of days later to meet with Carol Ann Sinclair, and then back to Denver. We were hosting a family cookout. Sherry wasn't at the conference. She and I would have a transition meeting the next week.

When Sherry and I did get together, the first red flag went up. The atmosphere was pleasant enough. She and I were sitting in her backyard, with her husband, drinking coffee. However, she was on the phone a lot, and my recollection of the verbal transition was...'this box has this, and that box has those, and I don't recall what was in those boxes.' I wasn't too concerned because I had dealt with similar situations on a number of temp jobs. It wasn't uncommon that my first task was to sort out either paper files or computer-database files. And there were dozens of zip files that she emailed to me.

The next day I was on the job representing the CHRB at the Metro-Denver Fair Housing Task Force meeting. Imagine my surprise when one of the hosts appeared in the person of one who had been an antagonist, mostly for Louisa, during the sale of the house controversy at 10:30 Catholic Community. I thought the facility of that meeting was appropriately named, The Conflict Center.

CHAPTER 4
Step aside and watch your roller coaster life

I looked ahead to July, which would be eventful. July 1st marked the 17th anniversary of our having moved into our home. July 2nd was Chris Coons' 26th birthday. Then of course, Independence Day, the IC Summer Seminar at Breckenridge, Kelly's 28th birthday on the 16th, and a week at Powderhorn during the last week of the month. Of course, I was never far from the memory of Kevin's passing on July 6th. Had it been 8 years already?

Not to slight any of the preceding dates, but I was really looking forward to the week at Powderhorn. I was in the middle of my most productive year in real estate. I had just taken on the new position with CHRB, and although we had celebrated our 17th anniversary in June, we were struggling with each other over our E-com business.

We struggled a lot more over how to do it, and when who did what, than anything to do with Quixtar itself.

I was required to track and report the exact number of hours that I worked for the CHRB. On July 4th, I divided the hours into reviewing existing files and the forthcoming events and tasks that I'd been told to address. I needed to get a handle on it because we would be in Breckenridge the 6th through the 9th, and we had decided to camp at Lake Dillon, rather than use a hotel room for the IC seminar.

When I looked back at all of the conferences we attended, in Colorado, Michigan, Texas and Arkansas, I could count only 4 occasions that we'd had anyone in our group attend with us. I saw that as a huge stumbling block to growth. We had not duplicated ourselves, which is the essence of the business. If I included the weekly meetings that we had attended between 1992 and 1998, the news didn't get much better.

I didn't bring the best of attitudes to the IC Summer Seminar in 2000. I think that staying at a campsite instead of a hotel, where there is more opportunity to learn, and to network, was a reflection of that attitude. I was no longer in the water with both feet. One of the real disappointments that I dealt with was that none of our children was even the slightest bit *open* to look at our business. It's one thing to take in information and then make a judgment and another to be close-minded. I had been assured that that situation was more common than uncommon. Still, it was a burr in my saddle. There's a temptation to take it personally when you see it in more than one area.

That was not the only area where my attitude needed adjusting. I was embroiled in a contentious situation within the choir at Loyola and I had already begun second-guessing myself about taking on the work with CHRB.

With all of that swirling around me, it was amazing to me that my real estate business was going so well. I had to wonder how much of that blur was of my own doing.

I got a wake up call...an attitude adjustment from Executive Diamonds, Pat and Betty Kaufmann. Their presentation was titled, "How's Your Dash?"

It's such a simple concept, presented in a direct and eloquent manner by the Kaufmann's. "DASH" (Dreams, Adventure, Significance, Health) IC 2000, is that period of time, typically shown on a head stone or tombstone at a grave, between the dates of our birth and our death. We focus on those dates more often than on how we spent the time (the DASH) in between. I think you could have knocked me out of my chair with a feather.

I saw a bright spot on the horizon, distant, but there. I really wanted to get Louisa to give up the '81 Volvo that she was driving, and enjoyed so much. I thought that, with the multiple streams of income, I could make it happen…at least the financial where with all would be there, this year.

The day after we returned from Breckenridge, I showed Chris and Brandy a house that they would later make an offer to purchase…and live in for next 5 and a half years. Chris had actually spotted the house while he was road testing a car he'd worked on. He had moved from his job at Goodyear to an Elway Nissan dealership in Federal Heights. Now, we'd focus on selling Brandy's townhouse that they were living in.

I was spending about 2 hours a day going through the CHRB files and not feeling any better for the exercise.

I managed to work in a visit with an old high school classmate who hadn't attended the reunion, but who lived only about 10 miles south of us. We met over coffee. (What else is new, huh?) The years had taken some kind of toll on him. I was really surprised, but not by how he looked. I would have recognized him anywhere, even though I hadn't seen him in 40 years. However, his demeanor and attitude made my own look bright and cheery. He really wasn't interested in catching up beyond that visit, or the class reunion. He knew about the latter from a relative in our class who had attended the reunion. I told him that Ronnie and Linda would be visiting in a couple of weeks and he had no interest in getting together. I think the surprise was that he had been one of those guys who could always get a laugh when we were kids.

At the same time I had connected with one of my closest childhood friends, Charlie and linked him to Quixtar. Even that hit a snag. They claimed they had no record of it, even though we did it "mouse-to-mouse," with both of us on the site from our own computers simultaneously. I think Charlie got frustrated with it and decided to drop it. Too bad, because he has the kind of drive that I see in those who succeed with it. Like me, Charlie wasn't ready for retirement either.

I was developing a good relationship with the CHRB chair, Carol Ann. That was a good thing for me, because I came to realize that it was her baby. I was the executive director in name…as long as she agreed with what I did. I believed in the work, and the mission of the CHRB. I think real estate agents could be more aware and proactive about fair housing issues.

Louisa and I were due to leave for Powderhorn the last week of July. Years ago, Linda Southworth had told me that planning a trip will bring business to your door. And so it was, with Brandy's townhouse. The day we were to leave for Powderhorn we got an offer on it. Chris and Brandy accepted the offer and we left the next day.

You might think that leaving with that good news we would be headed for a great week together. Guess again.

We knew that the week at Powderhorn would be a working vacation week. We had each taken work with us before. I had a briefcase full of the CHRB files and my assignments from Carol Ann. I had another full of real estate transactions and would be making and receiving phone calls regarding the offer for Brandy's townhouse and the house that she and Chris would be buying. I had another bag for our Quixtar files and contacts that we would be reviewing. Louisa had her mortgage files and current transactions to take care of too.

When we're at Powderhorn I put the coffeemaker out on the deck that is at the opposite end of the unit. Well, the smell drifted in and Louisa got very angry about it. I became defensive and we both erupted. I stormed out and drove without thinking about a destination, finding myself in Cedaredge, about 40 miles away.

After driving around the area, I went back to our condo. It was July, but it was really cold inside that unit. And no, the air conditioning wasn't on. I think a good bit of the day had passed before we got tired of avoiding each other and we began to talk through it.

While we were at Powderhorn, Louisa booked a trip to Grand Rapids, Michigan. IC was holding the annual convention in Grand Rapids in September. I was surprised that she had done that. She hadn't shown much interest in it in recent months. Never the less, we made plans to travel with our friends, Tom and Madge, flying to Chicago and then driving to Grand Rapids.

The rest of the week was part working on the stacks we'd each brought with us, and part vegging out on whatever the cable channels had available. I still had two hours blocked out each day, for work the CHRB. I was reviewing the annual budget, and the grant that funded it.

I had never written a grant, so I made a note to talk with my friend Ben Levek when I got back to Denver. Ben had extensive experience in grant writing.

I learned that the person I'd be reporting to, at the Denver Community Development offices was leaving that position, and I'd meet with her replacement, Laurie, next week. I called Carol Ann, and Doralynn…the secretary…asking them to go to that meeting with me. Denver provided a grant, which made up most of the funding for the CHRB. I think Doralynn and I were the only people on payroll. For the most part, the city was underwriting the cost of classes and other venues to promote fair housing education.

I logged 36.5 hours of work during my fist month with CHRB. I was being paid $20 an hour, which I thought was a pretty good supplement to my income from real estate and our E-comm business.

Most of those 36 plus hours were spent reviewing files and making phone calls. I didn't see how it would have a negative impact on my other business pursuits. I would soon find out.

A lot of the work for the CHRB involved meeting, and often shmoozing, with people who held positions of authority with city or state agencies. That was sometimes interesting and good, and at other times it was not. I met a woman named Nancy, who worked for the state and found her to be a great source of helpful information. She was also one of the people the CHRB called on to teach some of the classes, and *that* was a dreadful experience. Then there was Donna, the director of a non-profit that the CHRB worked with. We had three appointments, over the course of my first six months. She didn't show up for any of them. Now, *that* will impact a schedule. Well, I did meet her in person in April 2001, at the Fair Housing Expo.

Now, watch the huge red flag as it is hoisted over the CHRB and the City & County of Denver. We, who would be Carol Ann, Doralynn and I, had a meeting with Hillary, who was leaving the position with the Community Development office, and Laurie, her successor. Two of us in that meeting were new to our positions. The other three should have had some experience with each other. They really didn't because *my* predecessor had "handled" everything herself, rather than to include others. So, three of them, based on their responsibilities should have known what only Hillary had known, and Laurie had just learned.

The CHRB had not filed a report with the city since May. The CHRB had not filed for reimbursement of expenses or payroll funding since February. I'm thinking, 'what in the hell am I doing with this outfit?'

I talked with Louisa that night and she wanted me to calm down about it. She pointed out that I would be paid for the hours I would spend playing catch up for the CHRB. I was more caught up with, 'why didn't the chair and the secretary know?' I was two months into a one-year contract, and of course, the pay was adding to our income. I had my sights set on getting Louisa out of the '81 Volvo and the additional income would help me convince her that we could handle it.

There were some positives other than the money. I enjoyed working with Doralynn, and Laurie with whom I developed a good friendship.

We flew to Chicago on August 31st. I was ready to 'get out of Dodge.' I *didn't* take any CHRB work with me.

The IC conference was good. The highlight was the surprise appearance by Rich DeVos. Rich is a gifted speaker and author. He has contributed so much to the personal growth of millions of individuals that it far outweighs any financial impact he may have had on their lives. He had undergone heart replacement in 1997 and he loved talking about his new heart. I happened to run into him, literally, just before he spoke. He was leaving the men's room as I was entering.

The other highlight was running into, not literally, Lee Trevino and Gary Player in the coffee shop the morning we were leaving. They'd been playing in a golf tournament in Grand Rapids over the weekend.

Whatever positive impact we might have hoped the IC Annual Convention would have, on our business growth, didn't come to fruition. Actually, it was about that time that Louisa decided that she wouldn't work the business with me anymore. She felt that it was putting our marriage in jeopardy. I didn't buy it. I do think it served to exacerbate the issues that we had to deal with. I didn't see the business as the cause of any of them.

We'd heard many times, and had known of a few instances where working together in the network marketing business... and probably in many others...will either bring a couple closer or be the demise of their relationship. I wasn't ready to give up on either.

We were back in Denver on September 3rd and I was back to my juggling act. I had an offer on our friends' home in Lakewood, and of course, the CHRB. I saw my work revolving around my schedule for the CHRB and it wasn't what I had in mind when I signed on in July.

Brendan's 6th birthday was coming up too. Jeremy wasn't involved in his life, or Riley's. Their male role models became Chris Harrison and me primarily. My brother Mike was more in touch with them, than their "biological father." Not surprisingly Kelly had another name for him.

We saw Brendan briefly after school on his birthday and then we were off to Breckenridge for a credit union conference. Louisa was serving on the board of the White Crown Federal Credit Union. This was another perk that I enjoyed because of her service.

You may have heard it said about one athlete or another, that 'he was quietly having a great year.' That's how my real estate business felt. I was focused on the squeaky wheels, the time the CHRB responsibilities were taking, and whether I could, or would, build the E-comm business alone. Meanwhile, my real estate income was the best it had been since I established my own office.

Almost without noticing, our income was growing to new heights. Louisa was working with my clients and also clients for several other agents. Once they learned of her integrity, they had few, if any misgivings about her being married to a Realtor. She would never bring someone else's clients to my business. Of course, when a buyer already had their own lender, I had to make sure that their lender understood that I respected their business too. Neither of us would jeopardize our integrity over a transaction. Simply said, you won't make a living off of one transaction. However, you do have to live with how you handle the transaction.

We had met Cynthia Morris at a cooking class at Wild Oats market. In addition to teaching that class, she had started a business of her own, offering personal coaching. I think the term was Life Coach. She offered an introductory session by phone. I did talk with her because I am open to exploring things I don't understand. I didn't take on her services and I think it came down to my own struggles with being accountable to anyone other than me. I was almost 58 years old and when I looked at that aspect of my life, I could see that the only time I was open to being accountable to anyone other than myself was during my three years in the Army. It wasn't much of an option there, but there were guys who fought it. One of the real challenges for me to be happily married was that issue.

Deep inside I wanted to be a husband and partner that Louisa could feel both respect and passion for. She often talked about a Clint Black song, "Love She Can't Live Without." I'm insecure enough to think that she was hearing it in personal terms. I wondered whether she stayed with me because she didn't know how to leave. She bought the CD, "D'lectrified," and we still listen to it as much or more than other CD's we've purchased since. I'd hear that song...and even to this day...draw inspiration to give her of the kind of love she can't live without. I love singing along with that CD, and that one song still sends chills through me. I think that one of the challenges for long term relationships is the danger of becoming too comfortable with each other. Of course, I'm speaking for myself.

CHAPTER 5
Breaking through...

That fall Kelly met Pete Blood through an Internet dating service. She had met a couple of other guys that way, and had dated one, Aaron, for a while. Pete, as we quickly came to know and appreciate, was different. Pete has staying power.

We were enjoying the best financial year of our marriage. We had a joint closing scheduled at the end of the month, and a lot of momentum.

We were working with people from Loyola, Habitat for Humanity, DIP and others to raise money for Anthony's school, Hope International.

My father-n-law was soon to arrive for a visit, the Broncos were winning, the Cardinals were headed to the NLCS after sweeping Atlanta in the play-offs and Chris Coons would be coming home for a visit in a few weeks.

In the fall of 2000 our lives appeared to be headed for happily ever after.

Still, there had to be clouds looming on the horizon, somewhere. One, my challenges with the CHRB, was no longer a surprise. A second was harder to understand, originating from within the Loyola choir. The other was coming from so far away that I was about to be blindsided by it.

At the end of October I had coffee with the CHRB treasurer, who also served as the legal advisor. I shared with him my misgivings about the CHRB. He said that he understood and that he probably would leave the CHRB at the end of his term.

I was intent on replacing the '81 Volvo. We discussed the possibility of giving it to a charity and taking the tax write-off. Louisa liked that part of the idea. However, she wasn't sold on giving up the car or spending money on a newer one. We hadn't had car payments for some time.

One Saturday morning in November I pulled the trigger. We had always been on the same page when it came to making a major purchase. I didn't want to wait any longer, so I said, "I'm going out to find a new car. Do you want to come with me?" Of course she did and we discussed what I had in mind. We knew that we wanted another Volvo. I told her that I had seen an ad, for a small, independent dealership, while I was buying parts for the '81 recently. So we set out to find Rocky Mountain Eurosports. We didn't find it at the address I had copied down, so I called the number on the ad and was told that they'd moved. The person who answered the phone gave me the new address.

We went on to meet Jeffrey Frazier and a different car buying experience. We looked at what I'll call a very vanilla Volvo. It would be perfect for somebody like the euphemistic Plain Jane. I had called Chris Harrison, and asked whether he could join us and check the car. Fortunately, he did. We each drove it and it seemed to be a good car, priced fairly. Chris said, "Mom, I think you'll be bored to death in this car, and get very tired of the standard transmission in the traffic we have here." His words were like manna from Heaven for me. She was disappointed and tired from it all, so she went home and Chris and I continued.

We ended up with another car that Chris endorsed. As it turned out she loved it then and still does.

The experience was different for us in that we worked through wide differences of opinion about replacing her car when she didn't agree that it was necessary to do so. We also worked through our opinions on what that car would look like, and more importantly making car payments again.

I saw the experience as a positive step for our relationship. It was win-win.

When we picked up the car, she drove it home and by the time she got here, she wanted to celebrate the event by going out to dinner. It was also getting too late to take time to prepare something. Somehow we set off the alarm on the car and had to scurry to find the book and instructions about turning it off.

The next day I took our new car.... actually a '96 Volvo 850 Turbo...to DIA to pick up Chris Coons. Before leaving I noticed that the dates on the temporary tag had been written with the month that ended a week earlier. We made it back to the dealership without being stopped by the Police and my paranoia was laid to rest.

Much of my work for the CHRB was centering on writing the grant for the funding for 2001. I felt inept, and that I wasn't getting much help. I was advised to basically cut and paste from the current budget that had been written by my predecessor. I knew that I couldn't take that advice, and I knew that Laurie would never accept it when she read it on behalf of the city.

We celebrated my 58th birthday a day early, watching the Broncos come from behind...very far behind...to beat the San Diego Chargers. Our friend Margaret Dunckhorst had given us the tickets as a birthday gift. For three quarters I wished we had stayed home and watched it on TV. It was one of the coldest days I experienced since moving to Denver.

Of course, the Broncos were even colder...falling behind by 3 touchdowns. Then, suddenly Gus Ferrotte almost single-handedly orchestrated the comeback in the second half, and Denver won 38-37. Margaret's seats were in the legendary South Stands and it was a great place to be during that comeback.

Thousands of people had left the stadium and had to be amazed when they heard or heard about the final score. I had come pretty close to being among those thousands.

It was special that Margaret gave up her seats (cold as they were). It was also the last season that the Broncos' would play at Mile High Stadium. Thanks for the memories.

A couple of days later I had coffee with Bill Michaels to celebrate his birthday. We each had become accustomed to, and enjoyed the change to a cup of coffee and visiting for an hour or so.

Louisa and I had agreed to donate the '81 Volvo to the Emily Griffith Opportunity School, through Big Brothers & Big Sisters of Denver. We assembled all of the maintenance records and the title, and they picked up the car on December 6th. It was an easy date to recall, as it took place on my brother Mike's 45th birthday.

It was near the end of the year and I was taking stock of the various events and changes I had experienced.

We certainly enjoyed financial growth in our real estate and mortgage businesses, while our business with Quixtar had slowed to a snail's pace. I was convinced that it wasn't about Quixtar. It was about us. It was the one area that we had found we were still struggling with each other and how to approach the business. Louisa had ceased to be actively involved in it and it was easy for me to put my focus on real estate.

We had been instrumental in helping Anthony take a significant amount of money back to Ghana for the school,

Hope International. Until that time, I had never been involved in anything that had felt that personally gratifying.

We went to visit Pete, Kelly and Brendan and Riley on a snowy Christmas Day. When we arrived, we were surprised to see Chris Harrison pull up behind us, and even more surprised to see David get out of his car. We had no idea that he was going to be home for Christmas. He went with us to visit others that day, and then the biggest surprise. He was staying at Herschell's parents' house, making an attempt at putting their relationship back together. They had been communicating frequently, and in fact he would be driving one of their cars back to Camp Pendleton. I hadn't really thought of her or her family because I believed that David had severed the relationship. Old feelings stirred all too quickly.

A week later we took him out to dinner one night, picking him up from their house and dropping him off there. He said she knew that she wasn't welcome to join us. I wanted to make the most of our visit with him, and he and I set a date to take the tour of Mile High Stadium before they tore it down.

CHAPTER 6
The coldest days…

It was January 2001, and most of my work was with the CHRB. I didn't have any real estate business at the time. David and I were going to go to Mile High Stadium for the tour sometime before he left for Camp Pendleton.

He was still staying at Herschell's parents' house and we picked him up once to watch Brendan and Riley.

Our IC leadership had become a part of a larger group affiliation, called e-Alliance, and we had been asked to take part in it by our upline. Our participation had been nominal for months.

We had made plans to get together socially with a couple that we had met in July, while attending the IC Summer Seminar. We met Michael and Karen with a group of people at the Breckenridge Jazz Festival. We enjoyed them, and also thought that they could be prospects to join us in our business. After rescheduling with them a couple of times, we agreed to go to dinner and movie with them at the Cinema Grill, which we'd talked about at Breckenridge.

The 26th was going to be a busy day. I had a Fair Housing Task Force (FHTF) meeting that would take most of the morning. Then Dave and I would have lunch and take the tour of Mile High Stadium. That night we were to meet Michael and Karen at the Cinema Grill.

Only one of those things happened. After the FHTF meeting, I went to pick up Dave.

He came out to the car with no coat and said that he wasn't going to go. He went on to say that until I, and the rest of the family, accepted Herschell; he wasn't going to talk to us. He wanted to tell me in person, so he had waited until then.

My feelings were a mixture of shock, disappointment and defiance. I went to lunch and took the tour of the stadium alone.

That day marked the start of a very difficult period in our lives…the coldest days.

What began as a discussion with Louisa about what had happened quickly changed to a full-scale argument before becoming a gulf in our relationship. I felt that I was being blamed for David's decision.

I wasn't the only one in the family who had negative feelings about Herschell. I believe my feelings were the strongest. I didn't feel responsible for David's decision and yet, I couldn't deny that my stand had put him in an awkward position.

We had been arguing, loudly, for what seemed like hours when I realized that it was time to leave for our evening with Michael and Karen. That wasn't going to happen. I had only two numbers for Michael and left messages at both his office and home. I never heard from him again.

I was being judged as the person who kept David from talking to anyone in the family. Louisa and I were at odds to the extent that we had open talks about who would get what if we divorced.

At the end of February our friend Sal Molina asked me to market his condo in Lakewood. He wanted to use the 1031 Tax Exchange program to roll the money over into another investment property.

Then I was called for Jury Duty. It was the fourth time that I had been called since we moved into our home in 1983.

I had been called during the Tivoli grand opening in 1985 and was granted a reprieve. It happened again while I was coordinating the Wyoming Centennial in 1990. In 1996 I was given another. This time around I made it as far as the jury interviews and was not selected to sit on the jury.

I was reconciled to serving on a jury. It seemed appropriate. I could have used the break from the CHRB responsibilities that I had come to regret accepting, and no longer wanted.

After being dismissed from the potential jury duty, I regrouped and met with Sal and his wife Chris that evening, about selling his investment property and their goals for the new property.

It was about that time that Kelly, Brendan and Riley moved in with Pete. We were amazed, and thrilled, at how well Pete adapted to the new family, and they to him. I heard that Pete, who is usually a man of few words, said to Kelly when he saw her unkempt apartment, "Promise me one thing." She said, "Okay…what?" He said, "That my house won't look like this." It doesn't. Another example of how people can change if the reason is strong enough.

I began to see the end of my relationship with the CHRB when my efforts to give it a presence at the annual Realtor Rally crashed and burned. The keynote speaker arrived late due to an early morning fog and some of the breakout sessions and collateral events would be cancelled, including ours. I was taken to task at the next board meeting.

On the following Saturday I got a call from the brother of Chris Harrison's best friend. I'd only met Jason once when Louisa and I had called Chris after that Broncos come from behind win against San Diego in November. He was at a bar with his friend Stephen and Stephen's brother, Jason. We stopped by the bar and spent a few minutes with them.

Jason's call that Saturday, three months later, was urgent. He'd just met the woman of his dreams and they wanted to find a house before they married. They stopped by our house and I talked with him and Michelle about selling her Townhome and helping them find a home together. Real Estate in 2001 was off to a good start.

The next day I met with our friend Bill Thompson at a property he wanted to buy, and at 6:30 that evening with a couple that Sal had referred to me.

I met with Michelle at her townhouse in Arvada. She's a lovely young woman and I could see why Jason wanted to move quickly to cement their relationship. I talked with her about her motivation to sell and heard some hesitancy in her response. She went on to say that she had some reservations because they'd only known each other a month. However, when I explained the potential binding contract, she said that it was what she wanted to do, so we moved forward. I hardly knew Jason, so I wasn't making any judgments about whether she should or shouldn't sell her place and buy one with him. I just wanted her to know that there is a point at which it is difficult and costly to be released from a contract. I wasn't about to counsel *anyone* on relationships at that time in my life.

It was during that period that I made a mistake with my real estate business that I would regret for some time. I agreed to market the home of our friend Bonnie. The real estate business had been very active throughout Denver for almost a decade and I didn't see the slow down coming. Bonnie insisted on waiting until she had the house and the yard just right, perhaps in May. In the interim I was helping her as a resource for the repairs and changes that she wanted to make.

March 1st Louisa and I went to a movie together. We weren't comfortable with each other and hadn't been since

"YOU USED TO LIVE IN MY HOUSE."

January. We had existed with each other and the gulf was widening rapidly.

By the end of the week were at such odds over David that I moved into the guest bedroom. We didn't have conversations. Our communication was a short comment or even a note that one of us had taken a call for the other.

It was the lowest point in our relationship since our separation in 1991. Even then we hadn't talked about dividing property or proceeds that would come from the sale of our house through a divorce. We did in 2001; just before the silent treatment we gave each other.

During the 2001 freeze out, as we came to call it, we were also working with 3 mutual clients. It was a very strained and uncomfortable time for both of us.

We hadn't done much with our E-comm business in a year, and Louisa was even less active than I. So imagine my surprise when she registered for the SkiGlo conference at Snowmass in March. I hadn't planned to go and I wasn't asked to go with her.

She gave me a note with the address of the house she'd be sharing with others, and the phone number for it. By the time she left there was hostility in her eyes each time our eyes met, which didn't often happen.

It was snowing hard the morning she left. I was going to Michelle's townhouse to put the sign up and the lockbox on the door. My car wouldn't start. I called Chris and he said that he could come by and look at it. He came before she left and could see the anger between us.

He said that he thought I had a blown head gasket and asked her to take me to get a rental car. She said, "Let him walk." Then she left. Chris gave me a ride and I came back home to get the sign and lock box. Half way to Michelle's place,

I decided to wait until Monday. I couldn't think of anything but Louisa driving to Snowmass in a snowstorm. It was the kind of storm she would also prefer that I drive when we were together. By most descriptions we weren't *together* that day.

Later Chris called me to say that she called him when she arrived at Snowmass. She'd had some problems with the wipers, but other than that her trip was okay. I was furious that she had driven in that storm and no less so, that she called *him* to tell him of her safe arrival, rather than to call me.

I did get Michelle's townhouse on the market that week, and three days later we had three above list price offers. We had some bumps in the road with that transaction. However, we closed the sale on Holy Thursday about four weeks later.

While Louisa was at Snowmass, I met with Leslie Myers for coffee and focused on my contract with the CHRB; specifically how I felt that I needed to end it. I talked about giving up the $20,000 or more of income it provided. She said, 'there was a day when you didn't *have* that much. You can get past that.' She's also a former nurse and she could see the toll it was taking on me.

Louisa returned from Snowmass on St. Patrick's Day, arriving first at Pete and Kelly's where we were having a birthday party for Riley. Kelly was aware that we had come separately and asked me about it a couple of days later. She also sensed that we weren't "together" that day.

Louisa and I both knew that we needed to talk and resolve to move forward, past David's decision to cut himself off from us. One of the reasons that I was so stung by his decision was that I had seen or heard about so much of that behavior in my dad's family. There were brothers and sisters, and in-laws who didn't talk with each other, or my grandparents. Some of them went to their graves with that.

I explained to Louisa that I felt the need to leave the CHRB. I agreed that I would work through a transition and not renew my contract. At Louisa's request, I would wait until the first of June, which was my contract date, to do so.

Louisa and I were happy to have our freeze out behind us. We enjoyed making up. While she had been at Snowmass I had an experience that had solidified my decision. I was meeting with Carol Ann at one of her offices one morning. I had an appointment with a client at 11:30 AM. She was frequently leaving our meeting to tend to her real estate office business and I could see that I would have to leave, short of covering everything with her, to make my appointment. I did and she was not pleased that I wasn't available to her to finish our meeting. I was also late for my appointment. I felt that I had to put my priority back on my own business.

CHAPTER 7
And then the great thaw

On April 1st, I dropped off some paperwork to one of my clients around 8 PM. Rachelle remarked that I had put in a long day. I laughed, saying, "Don't feel sorry for me. I'll be at the Rockies & Cardinals' season opener tomorrow and get home in time to watch the NCAA Championship." It was that kind of flexibility that had kept me in real estate through the lean years. Now I had that and a respectable income too.

In late April we went back to The Broadmoor Resort for the annual Credit Union League conference and enjoyed the weekend away from our normal routines and responsibilities. That event is a heck of a perk, and Louisa always learns something that helps her in her role as a member of the board of directors for our credit union.

We left The Broadmoor in blowing snow that Sunday and drove straight to the hotel where I had stayed for so long in 1983. It had become a Radisson Hotel. It was the same location and brought back memories of my six months there, and also our ten days there with the five kids, dog and cat.

I was going back there for a Loyola Choir Retreat. With the help of two facilitators we were attempting to iron out the differences between some of us. We almost got through it without any personal barbs, but not quite. I left agreeing to stay in the choir at least through the end of the year, to see what benefit might have come from the retreat. Oather had said, "Don't you leave me alone here again." He had seen other men come and go, and was often the only male in the choir.

Now, I know that won't be much of a mystery to anyone who has been involved in a church choir, or some other entity that supports the church activities. There are dynamics that play out because we are individuals with our own agenda, attributes and warts. It doesn't make any of us less Christian, or Catholic…and I'm confident that it applies to other religions as well. In our situation, I connected with how one other parishioner described our situation: "It's just some people with some old bad habits."

In the middle of May I told Carol Ann that I would not renew my contract with the CHRB in June. That didn't go well. I moved up the timetable because of some actions by one of the board members and my predecessor, that I believed were done to embarrass me.

I was happy when they told me who was going to replace me. I had met her and believed that she had a better make up for it, and probably more applicable experience. I was convinced that I had made the right decision for everyone concerned.

My real estate business jumped to a higher level almost as soon as I'd told Carol Ann that I wouldn't be renewing my contract with the CHRB. It was easy to see that I had only been draining my energy by doing something without having my heart in it.

In addition to serving the five clients I had at the time, Louisa and I put ourselves to another test. Working together with clients was going well. We then entered into another arena…manual labor. I've never been much of a fan of it myself, but we seized an opportunity to cleanup the south wall of the basement.

"YOU USED TO LIVE IN MY HOUSE."

We had uncovered another half-baked job that had been done by one of the previous owners of our house. The south wall was damp and crumbling. Fortunately it was not the foundation. Someone had plastered against the wall with no air space and moisture had set in. Louisa had added a sealing caulk at the exterior base of the house already, but the damage had been done. It's probably because Colorado is so arid that we didn't uncover mold.

At the same time, the church across the street from us was building new classrooms and had an industrial strength dumpster on the property. We sought out the construction foreman and had gotten approval to move our excavated plaster to that dumpster. We started that project in May and were happy to see it end in June, and happier that we'd done it together *without even one argument*. Or maybe I've had a memory lapse about it. If so, I'm okay with that. I like believing that we got through it okay.

There was one occasion when I went ballistic. However, it wasn't because of, or aimed at, Louisa. I'll share more on that in a moment. I wish you could have seen it.

At some point in May we decided to use the Powderhorn timeshare week that we had banked with RCI. We'd never traded a week before, so we were learning how the process works. We initially thought that we'd go to New England in the summer and stuff ourselves with seafood. However, nothing was available on such short notice. Then we looked, on-line, up the west coast from northern California through Vancouver, B.C.

We did find a place outside of Vancouver. We wanted to sleep on it and when we returned to make the reservations, it wasn't available.

Finally, we found that we cold go to Mazatlan and enjoy the ocean and fresh seafood. The room wouldn't be available until the end of June, but we were okay with that. We hoped to be able to see Anabella Gavica, who was our houseguest in 1986, and meet her family.

Near the end of May we received an invitation to a graduation party for the son of one of our previous clients. I had helped Joe and Kathy with three different purchases and taken their son Travis to a Nuggets game years earlier. As many Realtors could tell you, we sometimes hear, 'oh, we'll have to have you over for dinner,' from some clients. Joe and Kathy were among the few who actually did. I must add that a few did take us out to lunch or dinner…and 'William & Mary' went above and beyond most others to show their appreciation for our efforts.

Friday, June 8th, I was having coffee with Ray Anderson when I received a call from Louisa, asking when I'd be home. Ray and I can talk at length, so I told her that it'd be about an hour. She said, "Be ready for a surprise." I conveyed that to Ray and we both wondered just what she was up to.

When I got home, she said, "You'd better sit down for this one." I did and with no small amount of trepidation. She went over the amounts of money we'd been getting from the closings and where our checking and savings accounts stood at the time. Then she got to the punch line. She reminded me that we had talked about adding a deck above the front porch and open up our bedroom to it…someday.

She went on to explain that we could pay off the loan on the '96 Volvo, which we'd just purchased 8 months earlier, and then take a small second loan for part of the deck construction. The latter would of course be tax deductible, whereas the car was not. We'd still be paying a large sum out of pocket for the deck. The surprise in all of that was her exuberance, not just willingness, to spend that amount of money. Louisa is of

Scottish heritage and proud of it. Of course, it was *Louisa-nomics* that got us through the lean times after The Hahn Company fired me in 1987.

I was as surprised as she thought that I would be and I enthusiastically endorsed her plan.

We really wanted our friend Woody Phaisawang to build it, but Woody was committed to another project. It was also Brandy's birthday. We celebrated that the next day because I had plans to go to the Cardinals & Rockies game, with my brother Mike, that night.

During the next week we attended another timeshare presentation. Don't ask me why. The presenter was Larry Cornelius, from whom we'd purchased our Powderhorn timeshare. Millions of people have had bad experiences with timeshare presentation, including us. Millions have gone to them just for the gifts, including us. And, millions, including us, have purchased timeshare properties, or bought into the newer points system, or vacation-weeks system. There was something special and unique about seeing that the presenter is one you know and can trust. We still had no intention of buying another timeshare.

Larry was pitching timeshares on the Big Island, Hawaii. I had flashback to Mom's visit in 1994, when she was looking at one of our Amagram magazines. She was reading an article about an event in Hawaii, and spending a lot of time on each photo. She asked, "Do you think you'll ever go to Hawaii?" I related it to the event that the article was written about, and confidently said, "Yes, and you can go with us." She just laughed. Now, I was listening to Larry more than I might have been without that memory. He was lowering the price and Louisa and I talked about the opportunity to take my mother and her father to Hawaii. Paul had been to Hawaii a few times, with Amway and had taken Louisa with him in 1976.

When we decided to make the purchase, she called out across the room, "Damn you, Larry!" He'd made another offer that was too good to refuse. He laughed, knowing that we were ready to make the purchase. It must have been close to midnight when we signed the contract. A part of their offer that we didn't refuse was to make a down payment in cash, and accept their offer to pay the balance with interest free payments for one year.

During all of the euphoria I had a real estate listing going nowhere fast. It was the listing with our friend Bonnie. We decided to host a "Broker Open," with lunch and treats for other Realtors, thus exposing the house to those who hadn't found it on MLS.

Shortly after the food was laid out and the door was opened, our friend Ray arrived. When we closed up two hours later, he was still the only Realtor who had come by. I was bummed. Bonnie was growing increasingly frustrated with the situation, and with me. I didn't learn about the latter from her. She took it all to Louisa. Bonnie and I had words about *that*. I advised her that I thought with the delays of waiting until she had the house "just right" and the flowers had all bloomed, before putting it on the market, coincided with the market dropping off. I suggested that she use a different Realtor. She did and it sold much later for much less. I didn't much care for the way that I handled it or talked to her, and I think that it was Louisa's friendship with her that allowed her to put up with it.

That's about when I went ballistic at home too. Actually, it was across the street from our house. One afternoon, I looked outside to see a big earthmover taking down a tree across the street from our driveway. The fence along the church and school property had been taken down. They were opening up a driveway across from ours.

"YOU USED TO LIVE IN MY HOUSE."

I jumped in the '91 Volvo and pulled it out onto the street, blocking the earthmover. The driver jumped down from it, screaming at me. I screamed back that it was absurd to put a driveway in exactly across from one of only three driveways on the whole block.

Howard, the construction foreman who'd been so kind as to let us dump our old demolished plaster into their construction dumpster, arrived and he was (understandably) upset with me. He reminded me in pretty straight forward terms how he's helped us with our project. I was sorry to bring him into it. However, I was not willing to accept a driveway across from ours. Louisa stood in our yard in disbelief of what I was doing and saying. I said, "My car is on a public street and if you move it, I'll have your asses arrested!" Just think of all the protesting that I didn't do in the 60's. I was suddenly an activist.

Two days later it was resolved. I hadn't moved my car for two days. It was explained to me that the church/school had planned to put the exit at the south end of their lot, but the city had denied it and gave them the location across from our driveway. There are no houses facing the location the church/school had wanted to put the driveway in. There are no driveways there, only an alley access.

If the church/school wanted to change it, they would have to apply for a new permit and go through the whole process again. I'd like to say I couldn't believe it. However, I had seen the City of Denver planners in action before and it wasn't the first thing that they had ever done that made no sense to me.

I relented and moved my car. The city had given me notice to do so, also. Howard and I made up and we later took him to lunch to show our appreciation for what he'd done for us. By that time he was able to laugh at it all, especially my outrage.

The day before we were to leave for Mazatlan I got a call from Nick, the young man we'd met at the Indian restaurant two years before. "Hi, Perry, this is Nick Noyes. Do you remember me?" Of course I did. He said, "I'm ready to buy a condo." I asked if it could wait a week, since we were leaving for Mazatlan the next day. He said that it could and I promised to call him upon our return.

So, there we were…in Mazatlan…the last day of June. It wasn't their high tourist season and that was fine with us. We had lunch with Anabella's parents at their home, along with her brother Martin and his wife Paulina. The next night Martin and his cousin Anton took us out. We went horseback riding at a beautiful ranch an hour from the city, and most of the other time was spent at the beach, or in a restaurant, or napping. It was a great week.

When we travel, I don't make coffee in the hotel rooms. I find a coffee shop nearby and that's where I have my first cup of coffee each morning. Our room, a large two-room suite, was in the older part of the Hotel El Cid. Each morning I walked across the street to the beach restaurant, where the staff was just beginning to put things in order to open. I was given, and not charged for, the fresh coffee each day. I would take it to the beach and there on the shores of the Pacific Ocean, in a chaise lounge, have my first cup of coffee. I knew I could get used to that.

That was a long way from where we had been, with each other, just a few months earlier. Still, we both were smarting from David's boycott of the family. We had no idea whether he was still with Herschell, whether she had moved to California to be with him, or whether they might be married. We didn't know whether *he* was still in California.

"YOU USED TO LIVE IN MY HOUSE."

We celebrated the 4th of July in a foreign country. That was different. The El Cid rolled out a big 4th of July party and buffet. We didn't hang out with the other Americans. We could have done that at home. Everyone in and around Mazatlan made us Gringos feel welcome.

Shortly after we returned from Mazatlan I contacted Nick to begin the search for his condo. He also had a co-worker to refer to me, a young man from Iran who was about to be married.

By the end of July I had matched my best full year of production in real estate. I still had active clients, and prospective clients "in the pipeline."

CHAPTER 8
The future's so bright...

It seemed as though we had barely unpacked from the trip to Mexico and we were packing for a trip to Virginia. There had been enough time to find a condo for Nick, primarily because he knew what he wanted and was easy to work with.

We flew to Virginia on August 1st, for a group birthday party. Louisa and several of her classmates were celebrating the big 5-0 that year. We returned to Colorado on the 6th, along with Louisa's sister Ellen, and our niece, Anna. We just changed some bags and picked up food when we got home, then headed to Powderhorn for a week.

Ellen and Anna were the first, and so far the only family members to enjoy Powderhorn with us. It was interesting for me to see the sisters together, interacting, for a whole week. Ellen and Richard, along with Anna, Elizabeth and Joshua, had been here in '86. However, they were also out exploring Colorado a part of that time. This experience was different...just as the sisters are. I think their relationship paralleled mine with my brother Bob, in the sense that they weren't close as kids...and at times had been antagonistic toward each other. They had developed their friendship as adults, as Bob and I had.

After Ellen and Anna returned to Virginia we were ready to start the deck addition project. We wanted to hire an architect and sought out the one who had designed a remodel of another house near ours. Louisa contacted a couple of builders and through them, found Bill Baer, the architect we wanted to hire. Bill met with us and drew up the plans in less time, and for less money, than we had expected. We then set out to hire a builder.

Over the next month or so, we talked to a few builders, from companies large and small. We differed on the different contractors. I wanted to hire a more experienced contractor, and Louisa favored a younger guy we'd met through Howard, the construction foreman.

I don't want to make too much of our differences about hiring a contractor. We were in a pretty good place with each other. We'd had two good trips together, were moving forward with the addition of the deck and both of us were productive in our businesses. There was that lingering issue of being estranged from David. It was just beneath the surface, but still there. Either of us could have erupted, using the choosing of a contractor as fodder. However, it didn't come to that.

Louisa's birthday was coming up and I wanted to do something special for her. I scheduled multiple activities without her knowledge, which is no mean feat. It is so hard to surprise Louisa because she has to know something about everything that's going on. Okay, she's nosey.

We spent the first night at the Indian Springs Resort at Idaho Springs, about 45 minutes west of Denver. It was a night relaxing in the hot springs and dinner out. The next day we drove to Snowmass and looked for the Pine Creek Cookhouse at Ashcroft. While attending the SkiGlo conferences we'd had gone cross-country skiing into the beautiful valley and enjoyed lunch there, often sitting on the deck in the Winter sun..

We passed by the restaurant not recognizing it in the summer landscape. Louisa wanted to show me a hut where

"YOU USED TO LIVE IN MY HOUSE."

she and the other skiers had stopped for lunch a few months earlier, when she was at Snowmass without me. She said it was named "Kellogg" and was part of the 10th Mountain Division hut system.

We then explored an area where we had seen a huge tent, like those used at wedding parties, etc. It was outside, in the front of the 'Cookhouse. We enjoyed our lunch there and set off for Basalt to visit with Haden and Tori Gregg. We found them at a summer festival where Haden was performing, and later spent time with them at their home before driving back to Denver. Louisa felt great about everything we'd done to celebrate her 50th birthday.

Woody called to say that he was available if we had not already chosen a builder. We were ecstatic. We hired Woody and began the process of having the plans approved by the city. That involved our securing a homeowners permit for the construction. Woody was licensed in other municipalities, but he didn't want to deal with Denver. Louisa, who has the handyman genes in our family, passed the tests for the electrical homeowners permit and the general contracting permit. I *can* do some of those things, I choose not to for the most part.

One of my jobs prior to the addition of the deck, was to dig down at the support columns, for our front porch, to see how far down they went.

Louisa and I have a longstanding agreement that she cooks and I clean. For the most part I have maintained the yard and the cars, and I took over the laundry chores in 1987. I had more time on my hands than Louisa had. She also says that I want the wash done sooner than she does because I change clothes more often. I know that, with my running, it's not uncommon for me to have changed clothes a couple of times a day at times.

We had thought about going to the IC Annual Convention, in Nashville, in September. However, we were both at a place with our E-comm business that we chose not to go. I had contacted my longtime friend, Austin Roberts, who lives near Nashville to tell him that we might be there, and then again that we weren't going to be. That's when I learned that he and his wife were no longer together. I sent a note to her as well.

We agreed that we would rather take group growth and excitement to the convention, rather than to go there, get all pumped up and come back only to fizzle out, as we'd done so many times before. We didn't have that growth or excitement at the time. And we wanted to be with Mom for her birthday. There was an annual conflict of dates with the convention and her birthday.

Before setting out on another road trip, I decided that it was time to get a new pair of glasses. My ego had been winning that battle for too long. I'd worn reading glass for years, but hadn't given in to the reality that I needed glasses full time. I think I was about 9 years old when I stared carrying my first pair of glasses in my pocket.

Following a late session at the IC Summer Seminar a year earlier, I was pulled over by a State Trooper. Of course he asked if I'd been drinking, and of course, I hadn't been. He said that I'd missed the lane changes a couple of times, when they went from turn only to straight through. I thought that the lines were worn and I probably hadn't seen them clearly. So, my sight challenges weren't new or suddenly upon me.

I thought, 'I'm almost 59. It's about time that I accepted that part of who I am.' So, I scheduled an eye exam, hoping that I would have the new glasses for the road trip.

CHAPTER 9
"Where were you when the world stopped turnin'…"

We, like most people can tell you the exact spot. I had finished a 4-mile run and was walking the block to our house when I saw her on the front steps…calling out, "We've been attacked!" Of course the words made no sense. She repeated it and I ran to her. She was shaking, saying, "Hold me." When I held her she told me about what she had seen on the TV news.

It is so rare that Louisa would be watching TV on any given morning, and only slightly less so on any given evening. Actually, she received a call from someone, telling her about what had happened and urging her to turn on the TV.

As we watched the terrifying sights, we of course, thought of David. It was a military action against our country and Dave was serving in our military. Like virtually everyone else, we had a TV on in the guest bedroom next to Louisa's office, in the family room next to mine, and I pulled out an old TV that David had left with us, and put it in my office.

We made calls to the kids, and to our parents. Didn't we all reach out a little extra at the time?

Ten days later Louisa began to try to reach Dave. She had been struggling with how to reach him, thinking that he might have already been moved. The gulf of silence had to be crossed. She finally reached him and they talked at length.

Then I talked with him. It was as though there had never been a negative issue between us. After a while Dave talked about having ended his relationship with Herschell some months earlier. Dave said he had been writing a letter to us about it. He didn't want family influence in his decisions with Herschell. He just hadn't gotten to the point to discuss it with us. All was forgiven and all was well...a great light on the darkest of days.

It was during that week that I heard a longtime friend giving a news report for ABC News Radio on KOA in Denver. Steve Taylor was the name and I recognized his voice immediately. Steve and I had worked together at WBCI-FM in 1969. I had heard him in 1998, filing a report on the outcome of the Unabomber trial. I searched the internet to no avail. This time around I was more Internet savvy and after a couple of weeks we connected and began catching up. I'm happy that we've managed to stay in touch since.

During all of the national discussion of how many more people *could* have been injured or killed in the attacks on the World Trade Center, in New York City, I thought about a football game. Actually, I thought about the fact the Broncos had played host to the NY Giants the night before the attacks. I recalled that the game stared at 9 PM, Eastern Daylight Time. That meant that the number of New York area residents would have been up even later, the night before that they might have been otherwise.

I had just taken a listing that had been delayed since July. "9/11" had the same effect as "Columbine," only more dramatic. No one I know was thinking about business...except those who saw it evaporate before their eyes.

My new listing was the result of a divorce. It will always be the last divorce listing I have ever taken; filed away under

"YOU USED TO LIVE IN MY HOUSE."

"Lessons Learned." After the long delay and the market changing from a Sellers' Market to a Buyers' Market, my client said, "I'll need 24 hours notice for showings." I stopped taking notes, and told her how the market had shifted. She then said, "Well, if it's any sooner, my paraphernalia may be out." Of course, I didn't want to know about her paraphernalia. Her husband wasn't there at that point. He had moved out earlier. I covered it in more detail, in <u>Surreal Estate</u>. However, I'll add that she ran over my For Sale sign with the rental truck when she moved out.

We had plans to go to Alton for my mother's birthday, and after 9/11, Louisa had some reservations about the trip. She didn't want to be away from home and she didn't want to be home alone. She went with me.

We were going to drive, so it didn't have anything to do with being in a plane. It was the sense of insecurity that most of us had been feeling at the time.

I recall that Pete had been attending a business conference in Orlando when air traffic was halted, and Kelly was to have joined him there. She didn't go, and his trip was extended a couple of days as flights were rescheduled.

Louisa put her misgivings aside and we made the trip to Alton. We had an American flag in the back window of the car that was given to us by the VFW post that my dad had belonged to when he died. Maybe you recall those days when people were standing on bridges, waving the flag and we'd all honk as we passed by them.

I'm old enough to know my parent's and grand parents' generations' values. I think our country has slipped dramatically. I recently told a friend that the only time I feel old, is when I see how our country's values, in the world spotlight and privately, have slipped since I was a kid. Maybe I'm over simplifying, but

I believe we've become addicted to comfort and convenience. I'll yield to Tom Brokaw's claim that the WWII generation was the best generation. I see that as a direct correlation to this story and specifically why more couples don't work through the hard times, and too often not even through the minutia to find happiness together. It scares me know that I almost gave up on us. I almost did. However, Louisa didn't let me

We had seen Paul when we'd gone to Virginia for Louisa and her classmates' birthday party. So, we had discussed a trip to Hawaii with him, and he was ready to go at the drop of a hat. We planned to go in June 2002. We planned to talk with my mother about it during the September 2001 trip.

Mom was surprised when we told her that we'd bought a timeshare condo in Hawaii. We have the rights to it every other year, in the even numbered year. We had to persuade her that it was real and not just a dream. She said that she would go with us…but that she couldn't afford it. We told her that we planned to pay for her trip, and for Paul's.

None of her brothers or sisters believed that she would go. They each talked with her, lobbied on our behalf, for several months. I don't know whether that influenced her decision. Mom knows what she wants and what she will do.

We always take Mom out to dinner a couple of times while we're there, and of course, out to lunch or dinner on her birthday. She wanted to go to the Lodge at Pierre Marquette State Park for her birthday lunch. However, it was raining hard and she didn't want to be on the River Road during the wind and rain.

So, we looked at options. I told her that we ought to go to Fast Eddie's, a popular restaurant and bar. She thought I was kidding at first, and I must have caught her in a good moment, because she agreed to do it. I asked my uncle Gary to join us.

He'd eaten there many times, and particularly when he was a cop. We ran through huge puddles and a downpour, getting inside just before their big lunchtime rush.

Mom loved their big shrimp and we had a good time. Louisa took pictures of us, and a couple of Mom eating the shrimp. I told her I was going to put the photos on the Internet for all her church to see. I don't recall the exact words of her threat. However she was convincing. I didn't know at the time that I'd be writing this story.

We visited with a couple of my high school classmates, of course including my longtime buddy, Ronnie and his wife, Linda. They wanted to see the plans for our deck. After my three-days-in-Alton alarm went off, we drove back to Denver.

After our return it was right back to work. I met with Majid, the man from Iran that Nick Noyes had referred to us, to look at a couple of condos. He was very easy to talk with, and I asked him about his recent trip to Dallas, and whether he felt that he was being scrutinized with his Middle Eastern looks. He said that he knew that he was, and felt it. He also expected it and dealt with it ok. He was more concerned that he would have trouble getting his fiancée to the U.S. since the attacks. He wanted to deal with that before continuing the search for a condo.

If I had any misgivings about the deck project, it was beginning at the end of September. We enjoy Colorado's weather, but we also know that it can change in the blink of any eye. Snow isn't that uncommon is September, and even less so in October and November. Woody believed he'd have it completed by December.

He brought one person to help him, an affable guy named Tony. Louisa and I joined them. We still had access to the construction dumpster at the church/school across the street, which made the disposal of the old roofing, much less costly.

At the same time, we were hosting our third house guest through the DIP. Karaba Mwai, a young computer technician from Nairobi, Kenya. While Woody was working on the new deck, Louisa was also replacing a lot of the electrical service, pulling wire through walls and ceiling space. Karaba said to me, "In Kenya, this would be a man's job." I laughed and replied, "I'm not in Kenya and I really don't give a hoot if she wants to do it."

Replacing electrical wiring and opening the upstairs room exposed several short cuts that had been taken by the builders of that room. The electrical had never been grounded and the room wasn't squared, nor did the west facing wall rest on the support beams at the front of the house.

Louisa corrected the former, and Woody modified the design of the front of the room, with Bill Baer's approval, so that a gable was integrated into it and the room became 18" longer.

I had heard that couples often fought, with some becoming seriously estranged, during remodeling projects. Somehow we avoided that opportunity to be at odds. We often ran out to stores together, to purchase building supplies, in Louisa's 850 Volvo, which we called her truck because the back seats fold down, and also in Woody's old Suburban. The latter was a stretch for me, literally. I had to stretch my legs to reach the pedals.

One of the bright spots in my approach to real estate is the opportunity to get to know the people I'm dealing with. Well, it's usually a bright spot. It was in this case.

In the middle of all of the activities I was involved in, I found the time to run with Dan Pittaluga. We had met Dan and Martha at Loyola, and were drawn to them and their children. Initially it was the singing, both being very gifted singers. We helped them find and purchase a house late that summer, and Dan and I had talked about running together.

Being a fireman he had odd hours, but had some concurrent days off too.

We arranged to get together at Sloan Lake, on the west side of town, because it was close to equal distance from both our homes. It's a three mile loop around the lake and Dan, about 25 years younger than me, was putting me through a faster than usual pace. We also talked about their home purchase. He was grateful that I had nagged him about adding Martha to the title. My point was the unpredictability of his work, being a fireman, and that she should be on the title in the event that anything happened to him. Whoever it was that handled the Quit Claim Deed for him, at the title company, had given him a better explanation than I had, and he was very grateful.

We got together for a few more runs before his doctor convinced him to stop running because of problems with his knees.

All of those thoughts come jumping out at me as I think about Dan, Martha, Marcus and Christina Pittaluga. Dan died suddenly, in 2004, of a massive heart attack. To add that Dan died unexpectedly falls short of the shock and hurt that engulfed his family and all of us who enjoyed his remarkable presence.

I could see that my time with the Loyola choir was coming to an end. I hadn't seen much change in attitudes, or practices, since the retreat. There was a conflict over what the program would be on November 11th...Veteran's Day. Oather and I are both veterans, and particularly in light of the 9/11 attacks and subsequent sending of our troops to Afghanistan, we felt strongly that we should be honoring the veterans, and those currently serving in the armed forces. It wasn't only that we lost that battle, but how the topic of Veteran's Day was dismissed. I went to a different Catholic church on Veteran's Day and knew then, that while we would continue to participate the Loyola community, I wouldn't last past Christmas with the choir. I told only Louisa and Oather, that I would be leaving the choir.

Louisa and I like to attend church together. It's one of the things that we do that helps us through the tough times. When I was in the choir we often drove separately, and I sat with her only during the homily. I was looking forward to going with her, and being with her. However, it would be misleading to say that my decision to leave the choir was based on those reasons. I felt such a burden with all of the dynamics involved. I didn't feel that we were singing the God's praises, but rather we were performing. I wasn't there to perform. It doesn't mean that I was right, but for me it was real.

I've sung with the choir on a few occasions, and with a few 'pick-up' choirs for special occasions, including the funeral mass for Dan Pittaluga. I miss it but not enough to return to a steady diet of it. During the choir's summer break there are times when, after we arrive at church, Louisa will say, "Aren't you going to sing with Stacy?" or someone else, and I do. All through that period, and since, I've served as a lector too.

Woody was making a lot of progress on the deck. We took photos of the before, during and after phases of it. The "before" photos show the ugly box that Louisa called it when she saw it for the first time. The "during" photos show the demolition of the front porch roof. It's always scary to see any part of your home being demolished. Tony wasn't dependable, and Woody did much of the work himself, or with his wife, Siri, helping him. I recall the colder days, and even in light snow, when he would continue with some of the detail work. He wasn't just fulfilling a contract; he was demonstrating his friendship, dedication and of course, his character.

I had continued on with the Fair Housing Task Force for almost four months after my contract with the CHRB had ended. I chose to leave to give more attention to my business. I had served as co-chair for several months, and knew it was time to move on.

One of my new jobs was to sand the baseboards in the upper bedroom so they'd be ready for Louisa to paint when the construction was completed.

I was renewing two licenses at that time too. My driver's license would be renewed before my birthday, which was fast approaching. I was also taking classes that would give me the necessary credits to renew my real estate license. I had until December 31st to complete the latter, and found an accredited on-line course that was a great help.

On my birthday we went to Govinda's, a buffet at a Hare Krishna temple. We've been there several times, and a few on my birthdays. This year we went with our friends Bill and Mary Thompson, who are vegetarians. It's a very peaceful place and we enjoy the food.

A couple of days later I started the day with a mutual birthday celebration with Bill Michaels, over coffee. While our conversations are usually light hearted, and more about baseball than anything else, my thoughts about his impact on my life, are never far away.

About a week later Louisa and I were in Leslie Myers' office for the annual review of our investments. Louisa had moved her Amoco 401k to Leslie's office in 1995, a year after I had moved mine. We had enjoyed sound financial growth under her direction.

During this review, I was lamenting on the high cost of health insurance. We carried catastrophic health insurance with a high deductible, and a high monthly payment. We hadn't seen a doctor since 1995, other than during the 9News Health Fair that we'd gone to for physicals the past couple of years. Knowing that we make it a point to eat right, exercise and take a lot of food supplements, I was really tired of throwing away money on health insurance.

I was ready to drop the insurance. Leslie said, "If Michael did that, and then came up with *the big C* I would be very angry with him." I said, "I have already pissed off Louisa for a lot less money." Neither of them was amused. Can you believe it? They talked me out of dropping the health insurance.

True to his word, Woody completed the deck in December. And the "after" or finished deck photos confirm that we achieved what had been a dream for almost 18 years. We immediately talked about having a house blessing and open house in the summer.

We had worked through big projects together, with a lot of help, and without the harsh verbal exchanges that were so common early on in our relationship. Both Louisa and I were closing out a productive year with our mortgage and real estate businesses. I had to let go of two listings that I probably shouldn't have taken, and a third was limping along. Still, it was the highest income I had ever earned.

Even more importantly, David was coming home for Christmas. As you can imagine, after what we had all been through, for most of 2001, it would be a special homecoming.

Just before Christmas we took Brendan to see "Harry Potter." As happens too often we were late. We arrived just as the movie started, expecting to use our debit card and learning that we needed cash. We have friends who owned 2 stores in the mall and Louisa went to borrow cash from them.

She took Brendan with her and I waited and waited and waited. Finally, I went to one of their stores and then to the other. My mind was racing with all kinds of possibilities. I went back to the theatre and asked whether they'd gone in. I was told that they hadn't. After waiting another twenty minutes, Louisa emerged from the theatre. I went ballistic! The theatre manager had told someone to tell me that they'd gone in, etc. I was allowed to join them and he comped our tickets.

Brendan liked the movie and was oblivious to what happened with the ticketing. There was a lesson in that for me. Once again, I had focused on the wrong event.

During the week between Christmas and New Year's, I met with a couple, Peter and Meredith that I'd been referred to by the wife's, sister, Chelsea. I'd met Chelsea at the Fair Housing Task Force meetings months earlier.

Peter and Meredith wanted to move back to Colorado. They were living in New Jersey and commuting to Manhattan each day. They later brought up 9/11 and their story was that Peter been spared because he had missed his train. Meredith, not knowing that he had, spent hours frantically trying to reach him. Had he not missed his train, it's likely that she would not have seen him again.

We looked at a few properties around metro-Denver, spending more time getting them reacquainted with the area, than looking at houses. When we took a second day to look, their parents came along. One of their fathers had lived on our block, and the block south of us years earlier.

New Year's Eve was quiet and we moved into 2002 expecting another great year.

CHAPTER 10
Just when you thought it was safe to…

The year 2002 was full of surprises, some more welcome than others.

One surprise came about pretty early. That's when I found my real estate For Sale sign on the ground, having been run over by a truck. I wondered, 'is this an ominous sign, or just a broken real estate sign?' It was a little of both.

The real estate market had slowed significantly. Fortunately, Louisa still had refinance loans to work.

Like most people, but perhaps with a keener interest, we were watching the military action in Afghanistan. David was serving as a corpsman for the 1st Marines Division. In February he was accepted at the medical training facility at Fort Sam Houston, Texas. He was going to school to become a physical therapy technician.

We got a call from my sister-in-law Elaine, telling us that our nephew Greg was coming to Denver in March, with a friend whose sister was living here.

Most of our activities were centered on our family, spending more time with Brendan and Riley, and helping as much as we could while Kelly was pursuing her Master's Degree. As I watched Kelly during that period, I found myself telling others that she was my hero. At some point, I shared that with her. She faced so many trials, so early and with great dignity.

We were also making plans for our trip to Hawaii. My mother had been waffling on whether she would go with us. She asked if we were trying to fix her up with Paul. I made it clear that we were not. When I told her that I was about to order the tickets for her flight to Denver and the tickets for the four of us from Denver to Kailua-Kona, she reversed her position. She didn't want to be in a plane for the five hours from Los Angeles to Kailua-Kona. She wasn't going and that was that. She asked if I was angry with her. No, I wasn't angry, just very disappointed that she let her fears rule her life. I knew that she wanted to go to Hawaii. She just wouldn't let herself do it.

One of the surprises started with another unexpected phone call from Louisa. I was leaving the Denver Board of Realtors marketing session when she called. She asked what I had to do after the meeting. I told her that I had a couple of errands to run before heading back home. She urged me to come right away...though nothing was wrong.

When I got home, I came through the back door and was greeted by Chris Coons. I like those kinds of surprises. Chris had made the trip with a friend who had family in Morrison. We were able to get the family together for dinner the next night with Chris and Greg both there. I know other families can relate to how difficult it can be to coordinate a night out with short notice, and this challenge involved 12 people who could make it, and 2 who couldn't.

The next day my first real estate clients of 2002 appeared. Louisa had talked with them previously. They called her because they wanted to change Realtors. I said that I could meet with them. Then, if it turned out that I worked with them, I'd give a referral fee to the previous Realtor because Louisa had met them through that agent. The clients didn't understand that, but wanted to meet with me.

Chris, Kelly, their sister Jessica, Brendan and I had planned a trip to Kevin's memorial on the day the couple wanted me to meet with them. Our trips to the Easter Seals Camp almost always include a stop at Jenny's in Empire for fresh homemade pie. We took time to do that too, and then it was back to Denver and on to Northglenn to meet Marco and Claudia.

I made it to the appointment on time and we had looked at a couple of houses, when Marco said, "I can work with you." They went on to talk about the other Realtor, and what I heard wasn't unusual. They felt they'd been shown houses that weren't what they'd ask to see, and weren't where they wanted to live. It was more a matter of miscommunication than anything else. They felt that I was listening to them. After we get clients pre-qualified financially, and determine what they can afford to buy, or want to spend, then I don't care where they want to look. I tell them, "I will show you houses where you want to live. Where you live is up to you, not me. I'm not going to live with you." It usually works well for clients to work with Louisa and me, as a team. She and I can differ on some aspects of the transaction, and sometimes do. However, we communicate and work through any differences. I can tell you, as I've told every client we've worked with…Louisa is the most tenacious person alive. It's not always that much fun to live with, but it works great for her clients.

I met with Marco and Claudia several times, looking at several houses over the next 4 weeks. She'd like a house enough to make an offer on it, and he wouldn't. Then they reversed positions. They were easy to be with, and their son Michael was an easy kid to have along during the showings. I was concerned that they were missing some good houses, and about Claudia's pregnancy. She was due to deliver a baby the first of June and I knew that they wanted to be in a new home by then.

Their Realtor and mortgage broker team also had two trips on the horizon. We would be gone for a few days in May and a week in June.

CHAPTER 11
Meetings of the minds...and of the brothers

Near the end of April, after looking at a couple of houses, I told them that we would be flying to Texas at the end of the next week. I said, "I hope that you will talk with each other, while we're gone and come up with the type of house that you can agree on. Otherwise, you may have to buy two houses." Claudia said, "No. We will buy one house and we will be in it before this baby is born." I liked her attitude about it. However, the window of opportunity was closing, so I had my doubts.

Louisa and I were going to fly to Austin, pick up Chris Coons and drive to San Antonio for Dave's graduation from the medical school at Fort Sam Houston. Chris and Dave had missed seeing each other, by as little as 24 hours in some cases, and hadn't seen each other in about 5 years. It was probably also the only circumstances in which Chris would ever visit a military installation.

We were going to be with the same two boys who'd been promoted from Merrill Middle School to South High School because the faculty was tired of dealing with them. They'd dropped out of school, gotten their GED certificates, and now each was excelling in their chosen endeavors. Dave was graduating as a Physical Therapy Tech for the U.S. Navy and Chris was carrying better than a 3 point GPA at UT. They both made us feel very proud.

We had a lot of fun on that trip. We had no difficulty finding Chris' apartment, and he was ready to go when we got there. Remember that this was about eight months after "9/11", so getting into Fort Sam' was not as easy as it would have been a year earlier. There were armed guards posted at the entrance, and we had to have a Visitors Pass. That meant showing my driver's license and signing a bit of paperwork. Dave met us at the Guest House and we had a brief reunion.

The next day we went to David's graduation and reception, then we were off to tour San Antonio, and of course, The Alamo. When we returned to Fort Sam, Dave was ready to drive back to California, to Camp Pendleton.

Chris, Louisa and I headed back to Austin the next morning. Chris took care of some errands and we agreed to meet that afternoon at a coffee house near the University of Texas campus. That gave us time to catch up with our friends Jerry and Barbara, whom we'd met at the SkiGlo Conference at Snowmass a few years earlier, and to visit the CLS International offices.

Chris was anxious to show us the UT campus before he went to work. We would see him later, because we were going to dinner where he worked, Romeo's, with Jerry Cass and Barbara Haynie-Cass, and another friend, Belle Laning, who lived near Austin.

That evening we enjoyed the fellowship and the food at Romeo's, and we got to see the bat population of Austin. We had Romeo's hold our bill until we returned from seeing the bats. When we were reseated, Chris rolled out an incredible array of desserts, compliments of Romeo's. I made sure that he wasn't paying for it and he said he couldn't afford to, that the manager offered it. Chris was able to join us briefly, and we were then off to Jerry and Barbara's house for the night.

The next morning I encountered some of the changes that "9/11" forced. Everyone was aware of how much tighter the security screening had become, and I think most people were okay with it. However, a security screener gave me the option of drinking the full bottle of water I was carrying or dumping it, because it wasn't sealed. I drank it. Chug-a-lug, chug-a-lug.

Soon it was back to Denver and back to work. I found a house that I thought Marco and Claudia would like. It presented an opportunity and a challenge. The opportunity was that they could get it for less money that the initial price because a previous contract had fallen apart and the sellers were anxious to sell it. The challenge was getting the inspection and appraisal done, their loan approved and closing the transaction in a matter of less than three weeks.

It took a lot of cooperation by a lot of people, and the full participation of the moon and the stars to make that happen. My brother Mike handled the inspection and Louisa had their loan approved pending a qualifying appraisal.

Chris and Brandy agreed to go to Hawaii with us. Paul arrived in Denver a few days before our departure date of June 1st.

We closed the transaction for Marco and Claudia on May 30th, and had a full day to focus on our trip. We followed up with a call from Hawaii and learned that Claudia had the baby while Marco, their family and friends were cleaning and painting rooms in the house. They had it ready for her when she came "home" from the hospital. I thought back to what she had said the last time I was with them before going to Texas.

CHAPTER 12
The best-laid plans...

Our plan was to meet at Chris and Brandy's house and leave our car in their garage. Pete would pick up all of us there and take us to DIA in his van.

On the morning of our departure, Louisa came to me and said that Paul was unstable and probably pre-seizure. We'd learned the symptoms, even long-distance. She went for a walk with him and it didn't change things. When Paul is in that pre-seizure state he doesn't engage in conversations and his walk has an unstable gate. He's usually very sharp and full of energy, so it becomes very obvious when that's going on.

We all met at Chris and Brandy's house, and of course everyone was concerned for Paul. We felt that we could deal with the situation and continue on. Louisa guided him through the check-in at the airlines counter and through security. Once we boarded the plane, I was seated a few rows ahead of Paul and Louisa, beside Chris and Brandy. I was positioned so that I could meet Paul if he walked up the aisle and, if necessary, guide him to the restroom. When he is in the pre-seizure state, he sometimes becomes belligerent, so my job...with Chris' help if necessary was to get him to the restroom and *not* the cockpit door. While he didn't bolt toward the cockpit, he did have a seizure while sitting in his seat.

The flight was not a direct flight. We had a layover, at Los Angeles International (LAX).

During the layover we all went to the food court. Paul had seizures again. Louisa and I were able to convince others, including the security guards, that he would be okay. Thank God Chris is very strong. He held Paul at his arms and shoulders, keeping him from falling out of his chair. It was a long layover that seemed longer at the time.

The next leg of the flight was without incident. After we landed in Hawaii, he picked up his suitcase and started to walk away when Louisa stopped him. He had no clue where he was going. Then Louisa and Chris went to the car rental booths, while Brandy and I stayed with Paul. Paul was still in a semi-coherent state. He got up and picked up his suitcase again. I asked if he was tired of waiting and wanted to leave. He said replied, yes. I said that I was too, but that we had to wait for the cars. We got to Waikoloa Village an hour or so later and finally got to the condo. Louisa put Paul to bed. It had been a long day for all of us, but for Paul in particular.

When he woke up the next morning, he remembered only some of the events of the day before, or the trip. He seemed to recall everything after we reached the condo. We knew that he would be apologetic and we were eager to assure him that all was well. We were in paradise.

Paul went to the beach, and to Mass, with Louisa and me. The rest of the week was a lot of fun and Paul didn't have any seizures. He was his normal happy and sharp self once again.

Paul and I toured a coffee farm one day, while Louisa, Chris and Brandy went horseback riding. I introduced Paul to Frapuccinos. We were already great friends. However, I think that gave him a new appreciation for me.

June 8th: A day of highs and lows. We wrapped up our last day in Hawaii on Brandy's birthday. We were glad she was with us. We enjoy her and are very happy that she's a part of our family.

Our first week in Hawaii went by much too quickly, which I'm sure, is the norm. Our flight would be a red-eye through LAX to Denver. We celebrated Brandy's birthday over lunch at "Forrest Gump's," in Kailua.

We didn't have any glitches with security until they pulled Louisa aside for the spot-check. There's always a lot of private laughter…not at the security checkpoints…about how they select those for the impromptu last minute security check before board a flight. Humor is forbidden at the point. I was allowed to wait with her.

Louisa is a master packer. Her carry-on items were gasping for air…including a piece of cake. Of course, they couldn't find anything dangerous in her bag. However, a long delay ensued because the security checker couldn't repack it to close. Louisa made an effort to help her she was chastised in no uncertain terms, at least twice. Finally, a supervisor told the checker to let Louisa help so that the plane could depart. We were the last two to board the plane, with glaring eyes cast upon us.

There weren't any other delays in flight or at LAX. We returned home the afternoon of the 9th. The air was filled with the smoke of a huge forest fire, some 30 miles southwest of Denver, which came to be known as the Hayman Fire.

That evening, while catching up on email messages and the news…don't you love that part of a week away…I saw something that made me feel even more tired.

I keep up with the news in Alton and Hampton Roads on the newspapers' web sites. When I read the Daily Press obituaries, which comes with aging, I saw that Don Bentley had died on June 8th. Don had played many roles in my life, boss, antagonist, friend and mentor. He saw something in me that I hadn't been able to see. He introduced me to sales when I was working for him at WBCI-FM & WMBG-AM in

Williamsburg. It wasn't just that he wanted another salesman working with him. He wanted me to reach higher than I thought that I could. I just sat back in this chair and looked at the computer monitor thinking about all that he and I, and his family, had been through. I wrote a brief note and went off to share my thoughts and feelings with Louisa. She had met Don in 1991, when we visited his office in Williamsburg. I was glad to have her to share with that night.

Now, in the middle of June, I was getting anxious for my real estate business to come to life. I was thinking more and more about our dormant business with Quixtar. Did I want to make another run at it? I had never doubted the viability of the business model. However, I had grown some deep seeded doubts about our, or my, ability to be successful with it. I could see it as a logical answer to the inconsistencies of real estate. I knew it, but I didn't feel it. I didn't feel the energy, or the passion for it. Louisa wasn't interested in rocking our currently balanced boat, our relationship.

CHAPTER 13
Road trips!

I was still marking time with real estate, and no closer to working at building our E-commerce business, when Dave arrived in August. He was being transferred from Camp Pendleton to a Naval Hospital at Charleston, South Carolina.

Louisa suggested that I take a road trip with Dave, and fly back from Virginia. I hadn't gotten myself moving, so she was eager to help.

I enjoyed the trip with Dave. We had never had that kind of time together. I think that was about the time we began to adjust to calling him Dave. He'd made the name change and I think it suits him better. He's very easy going, and easy to be around. Dave had never had the pleasure of visiting my hometown, so we made the first stop at my mother's house in Alton.

After that brief visit we headed to Locust Grove, GA, just outside of Atlanta, to pick up a puppy he'd purchased over the Internet.

We were driving into Kentucky I suggested to Dave that he should stop to pick up a map for his mother. She collects them. I said that way we wouldn't be in her doghouse. I said, "I've been here before." He said, "Kentucky or her doghouse?" I said, "Yes." He stopped for the map.

When we picked up Kota, an Australian Cattle Dog who was about 4 or 5 months old, we stayed over at a nearby motel. Kota was already house trained. He was awake and anxiously awaiting an open door when we first stirred. After breakfast, it was on to Newport News.

I knew that my friend Austin Roberts had moved from Nashville to Virginia Beach. I borrowed Paul's car and visited him there. We had lunch and caught up with each other in person, for the first time in twenty years.

We had a good visit with Paul, and with the Louisa's sister Ellen's family, Dudley's. Then Dave and Kota left for Charleston, and I was set to leave for Denver at 0-dark-30 the next morning. There was no way I would ask anyone to drive me to Norfolk at 4 AM. I took a cab.

In early September Ronnie and Linda Meyer came to visit us again. Louisa was looking forward to seeing them as much as I. She called out to me when she heard their Harley in the driveway.

We took them to the BuckSnort Saloon again, and then one evening we rode the light rail downtown to The Cheesecake Factory. On the way, Linda and I discovered that our grandfathers had both worked on a similar train, called the Inter-Urban that ran from Alton to St. Louis, when we were kids.

Ronnie was in awe of The Cheesecake Factory and as soon as we got home, I was on the Internet searching for one near Alton. One was about to open at the St. Louis Galleria. We stayed up late, sitting on the deck until Louisa convinced us that we were being too loud. They headed back to Alton the next day.

Somewhere between the very enjoyable road trip, which had been Louisa's idea, and a forthcoming shorter road trip back to Alton for my mother's 80th birthday, storms clouds were gathering.

Someone at church, whom Louisa knew better than I, asked me to talk with her fiancé about selling his house. It was on the market and had been for quite a while. I told her that I couldn't initiate a call about it. However, I'd be happy to answer his call about it. Had I initiated a call, I would have been interfering with the existing listing, which is known as "going behind the sign" in our business. Take note of one of the aforementioned gathering clouds.

I have probably repressed the cause of the impending clouds. It would produce an ice storm in our relationship. Over the years we had gone from the extreme verbally violent arguments to freezing out each other.

There are road trips that are almost too much fun. Then there are those best described by The Grateful Dead's song, "Truckin'." As they so eloquently put it…"What a long strange trip it's been…"(19)

I'm not sure you'll believe this. I lived it. Otherwise, I might not believe that any two people would do what we did on that trip. This story is true, and this part is particularly hard to admit.

Whatever it was that had caused that gulf between us had brought on a freeze out, with a harsh edge to it. We were going to Alton for Mom's birthday. We had made plans to stop over near Kansas City to visit with Jim and Sharon Barnett each way.

During the few weeks that I'd been home from the road trip with Dave we became so at odds with each other that we weren't speaking. You may recall that we had some experience in that behavior. We'd spent three weeks like that in 2001. This was different. We were going to be in a car together for about 1800 miles. Louisa wouldn't have gone if it hadn't been Mom's 80th birthday. My brother Mike was going to meet us there and we were going to take Mom out for her birthday lunch along with her sisters, some of their spouses and a couple of her brothers. Have I mentioned that we weren't speaking? Yes, I see that I have.

Louisa huddled under a sheet in the passenger seat while I drove. She had her space and I had mine. We weren't speaking. I drove to Kansas City. She rode along. That's roughly 10 hours. We didn't speak.

When we arrived at the Barnett's house they greeted us warmly and we greeted them warmly. Sharon showed us to the bedroom we would be using.

We did manage to speak in short sentences, giving each other polite answers, and the appearance of being together. We wouldn't have fooled Kelly, but she wasn't there. We took Jim and Sharon to dinner, and while we were eating the other gathering storm cloud appeared. I took the call and explained that we were having dinner...in Kansas City, and that I'd follow up when we returned to Denver.

We left the next morning. I drove while Louisa retreated to her sheet. That part of the trip took about four and a half hours. We had a good visit with Mom, and the others who joined us for the big lunch celebration at the lodge at Pierre Marquette State Park. We were polite to each other.

We'd been in Alton long enough. My internal three-day alarm went off and once again we headed to Kansas City. I drove and Louisa huddled in her seat, and her sheet. We stayed over with Jim and Sharon again. They didn't have time to go out to dinner. They were getting ready for a family reunion and new carpet had been laid that day. Mary Sellars, Sharon's sister, arrived, so we visited with her to. We were polite to each other. The next day we returned to Denver. I drove and Louisa...well, you know by now.

I'm recalling a Roger Miller song that I'd played years earlier, "Husbands and Wives." (20) What a different trip it would have been, had we put our pride aside.

"YOU USED TO LIVE IN MY HOUSE."

It's still hard to believe that any two people, who love each other, could take such a trip and behave that way, and *especially in a car*. We did and I feel embarrassed to admit it. While it's difficult to share, we did grow from it…several months later, on a ranch in northern California.

CHAPTER 14
Sometimes a great mystery…or two…

After returning to Denver, I contacted the client who had called me while we were at dinner in Kansas City. We made an appointment and I started my research about the property. It had been on the market over a year and if I did agree to market the property, I would be the third or fourth Realtor to do so. I get bored easily. However, I think there are times when I would be better served if I could just embrace boredom.

As I drove up to the property the outgoing agent was removing her sign. She was so pleasant it gave me cause to second-guess myself. I met with the client, whom I'd seen but didn't know. We attended different masses at Loyola. I took the listing.

About nine days later we had an offer come in, then another and then another. I contacted the client to make an appointment to present three offers. We reviewed each offer, and submitted counter proposals for two of them. One was accepted and we were' Under Contract.' My client had waited over a year for that contract. It was September and I had my second transaction of the year underway. The closing was scheduled for the end of October. I was tip-toeing through some issues with my client, in part in respect to why I thought he was having difficulty letting go of the property and also because Louisa would be dealing with him and his fiancée later.

There wouldn't be any boredom around that weekend. Brendan and Riley were spending the weekend while Pete and Kelly went out of town. That was reason enough for Louisa and I to resolve whatever issues had caused the great gulf of '02. There are so many stories about what the grandsons have said that it should be captured in another book. Art Linkletter was right way back when and it's still true today…'kids say the darndest things.'

The boys know that we eat our meals together and that we say grace before each meal. On most occasions, Riley is ready to eat once the food is in front of him. I recall Brendan telling him, "Riley, wait till they say grace. They always do. They love God *a lot.*" To his credit, Riley often leads us in the prayers. On another occasion, while Riley was having toilet training challenges, we were getting them ready for school and Louisa asked Riley if he had to go to the bathroom. He said, "no!" Brendan then said, "Well, it's knockin' on the door."

When Pete and Kelly returned she was sporting an engagement ring and a funny story of how she almost missed it. Their wedding would be in July '03 and we were all ready to celebrate with them. The grandsons were excited. We were excited. Louisa and I felt the great between us gulf was but another strange memory.

We went out to dinner, using a coupon from one of the timeshare presentations. As I pulled into a parking space, I got a call from our friend Bill Thompson. He said that a friend had accepted an offer, from a neighbor, to purchase her house and after looking at it; she thought she might need an attorney. He asked whether I thought she might. I said, "If she thinks she might need an attorney, she does." I recommended an attorney, Carl Fritz, whom we knew from Loyola. I knew that he had practiced real estate in the past and still handled some real estate clients.

That offer fell apart and Bill put me in touch with the seller, Helen, to market her property. She had already moved out of state with the belief that her home had been sold.

I did take on the listing, based primarily on Helen, and her predicament. Because it had recently been appraised, I didn't anticipate the time it would take to sell the house.

At the end of October we were ready to close the sale of the house for my disgruntled client. I offered to take him and his fiancée to lunch after the closing. He declined. He also didn't speak to me at the closing. Now, I think that I'm pretty quick on the uptake. Call me arrogant if you will, but I don't usually have trouble figuring out why someone is upset with me. I couldn't figure out why I wasn't this guy's "new best friend." That was not my goal. However, after over a year and a few Realtors later, a simple acknowledgement would suffice.

A few weeks later another client popped on the radar. Better yet, repeat clients. A couple I'd helped find a house in 1996 now wanted to sell it and buy a bigger house. In our market that is spelled bi$$er house. Yes, I'll be happy to help you find a bi$$er house. Thank you.

They had looked, more in the mode of tire kicking than buying, in 1998. They made it clear that they were ready to purchase another home this time.

A mutual friend of my disgruntled, now former, client, told me that I was being called a liar by said former client. I called the latter, and said 'if you believe that I lied to you, which is to misrepresent what I say or do, then call me on it.' I've typically saved my lies for those I love or have loved. I've usually done *that*, when reacting like a typical male with his back against the wall. You know, 'I did not have coffee with that woman,' or something akin to that. Somewhere deep inside I thought the disgruntled former client was a good guy, but I didn't feel the kind of love that would cause me to lie to him. For me, it takes a special love to lie to somebody, one that translates to a fear of loss. How's that for pretzel logic?

So, I called him on it. It really was a simple misunderstanding. I had referred to the buyers' Realtor as he or him. My client had been at home when the agent showed the buyers the house. The agent was a woman. Well, I checked it out and found that, yes, she was a woman, but not an agent. She shouldn't have been showing the house for her husband. So we cleared that up. My former client apologized and thanked me for clearing it up. I learned more about the burdens he was carrying and we've actually grown to like each other. We're still not close enough for me to lie to him though.

We sometimes go to Jose Oshea's for dinner on my birthday. They send us a birthday coupon every year. Louisa said she'd pass on it this year. We weren't still at odds; we'd resolved everything about the weird road trip.

About that time my brother Mike called about us getting together somewhere to watch the Broncos game. They'd be playing at Seattle the Sunday before my birthday and Jose Oshea's would honor the coupon. I usually don't go anywhere to watch the Broncos' games. I like to watch the action and not get distracted by side conversations. Mike and I hadn't been out to watch a game since the days and nights when he, Bob and I would get together at some bar to watch them in the late 80's. I hadn't gone to bars, per se, since I quit drinking in 1992.

We went to Jose Oshea's and by half time I was ready to go home. The Broncos and Seahawks were playing in heavy rain and mud, and the Broncos were winning handily. I made a pitch for leaving and Mike reminded me that we rarely got together like that so why didn't I have more to eat and have another cup of coffee. I was okay with that because Mike and I

"YOU USED TO LIVE IN MY HOUSE."

have grown close, despite the age difference, and of course, he said the magic word…"coffee."

I had started with lemonade and switched to coffee. I whined enough that he gave up with a couple of minutes left in the game. On the way home he missed the exit from 6th Avenue to I-25. I pointed it out and he said that he'd been daydreaming and that he'd go to Speer Avenue. I said, "You can take Kalamuth to Alameda." He did.

When we got to my house he said that he needed to come in to 'use the facilities.' When we walked in we were greeted by dozens of people. Louisa had done it again. I learned that it was Kelly's idea, and that Louisa, she, Chris and Mike had pulled off the surprise party for my 60th birthday. It seemed like people kept coming out of our basement. I thought of the circus and all of the clowns getting out of a small car. It was a great surprise and I saw people whom I hadn't seen in a long time. Of course, there were the appropriate birthday presents, such as prunes and prune juice, etc. Kelly gave me a walking cane with a horn and a rear view mirror. Chris and Brandy gave me a gift that I still use daily, a New American Bible.

Louisa had surprised me on my 40th and 60th birthdays. I'll be on guard on the 80th.

I was looking forward to working with my repeat clients and it wasn't only for the bi$$er house. My experience with them in 1996 was brief and easy and they had since met Louisa, so I saw an opportunity to involve her as well. The 2002 experience would not closely resemble the 1996 experience.

Actually the finding the right house aspect of it was similar to 1996. They didn't really look at too many houses before they found what they wanted, and we received an offer on their existing house pretty quickly. I was about to get reinforcement for my belief that real estate is about so much more than houses.

Louisa wouldn't be handling their loan. They had already talked to a lender. Louisa's really okay with that. She respects other lenders and the client's right to work with whomever. I respect that also. Then I have to make the client's lender feel comfortable with me, and assure them that I will not try to switch the clients to my favorite loan officer. As she says, she's not going to make a living off of any one transaction.

As far as my clients are concerned, they're good people and they have a sweet daughter. You know something else is coming don't you.

We had their home Under Contract very quickly. I was offered an opportunity to share, extensively, in the cost of the items required to resolve the inspection issues on the sale of their home. I passed on that opportunity. I had already committed to covering other costs.

We found a bigger house and they wanted it for about $30,000 less than the list price, and they got it. They wanted it with a new furnace and they got it. They wanted it with a new roof, and got a generous seller contribution. There's the something else that was coming. I didn't see any "win-win" in their demands. I saw them as demands, not requests.

The house was vacant and had been on the market for about a year and a half. The sellers had built a new home. My clients were, of course, aware of that. I was working on their behalf as a Buyers' Agent, so I had researched everything I could legally pursue and had informed them accordingly.

We scheduled the closings for December 30, 2002. That's a Monday and scheduling a closing on a Monday is a no-no. What was I thinking? There were issues with the loan for the buyer of my clients' home and the loan hadn't been submitted in a timely manner.

On December 30th, we would close on the sale of my clients' home with the title company I recommended and then with the seller's title company on the property they would purchase.

My closer called me to say that to tell me that the lender's underwriter had not finalized the buyer's loan and it wouldn't close on the 30th. So there we were, my buyers, the sellers and their agent and their closer.

You might think that the sellers agreed to close because they weren't going to let a live buyer get away. There's probably a great deal of truth in that. I also believe they are the kind of people who *do* believe in win-win. Maybe it's some of both. They did agree to the closing of the sale of their property with everything held in escrow, contingent upon the buyer's property closing within 24 hours. The sellers were people I would like to have known better. Of course, there's no protocol for that relationship when you're on opposite sides of the table.

We scheduled, what should have been the first closing, for the next morning…on New Year's Eve. I went home to dinner.

My going home to dinner, and all of that stuff about the closing, is not insignificant to my story about Louisa and me.

I was no closer to knowing what I wanted to do with my future than I had been six months earlier. At dinner, after telling Louisa what I've just shared with you, and the parts that I won't share publicly. I told her, "I want 2003 to be my last year in real estate."

She asked what I wanted to do instead of real estate and I didn't have a clue. Even though I was about to realize a lot of money for the transaction that would, ('please, Dear God') close the next day, I felt like I'd had enough.

We did make it through the closing the next day, and on the way home I called my longtime friend RayAnderson to share the tale of two closings.

As strange as 2002 had been, I could not have imagined all that would happen in 2003.

BOOK SEVEN

CHAPTER ONE
Reinventing one's self...or reverse engineering?

I had told Louisa that I didn't know what I wanted to do. I really felt that working our E-com business would be more interesting if even one of the people in our group wanted to do that too.

I called Linda Combellick, one of our E-com associates to thank her for some advice she had given me a few months earlier, regarding my singing a solo at church. She has a beautiful soprano voice and teaches others how to best use theirs. We agreed to meet and catch up over coffee. We each talked around the subject of being active with Quixtar and settled on meeting again to see whether we could pool our energies to create a positive force.

That weekend I called my friend John Harwood, the minister who officiated our wedding. I like that better than saying he married us. Whatever. I told John about how I was drifting. I wasn't happy with my work, my wife or me...my life. My grandsons were still a joy to me. I loved my wife and family and I was looking forward to Kelly and Pete's wedding. Still, Peggy Lee was singing that song again.

I told John, "I am praying for direction." He replied, *"Then you'd better pay attention. If you're really praying for it, you'll get it."*

I met with Linda again...our associate whom I'd met with about our E-com business. She had a long list of people to contact and it was enough to convince me that I too, could develop a prospect list and get busy. I was convinced that I could, and knew that I should. Still, there was no real stirring inside to do it.

I had worked with Linda when she initially joined us and my concern was that she didn't see the big picture, in that she was focused on a few of the products that she was using. The other was her propensity to say too much, rather than listening to what the prospect might want. However, we did agree to move forward together. I wanted a running mate, and I like her personally. She really cares about people and wants to help them.

Louisa had been looking for some signs of life in me. I think she saw a glimmer of hope when I decided to work with Linda.

Louisa suggested that we accept an offer of free accommodations that had come from a timeshare company. So, we planned a trip that would include a couple of nights in Anaheim, giving us an opportunity to tour the Nutrilite farms and packaging facilities. We also had a couple of nights lodging at the Rio in Las Vegas. We scheduled the trip for March.

Shortly after that we received a voice mail message from our friend Julie Smallin, regarding a personal growth seminar that she'd taken. Louisa had worked with Julie at Amoco and she had been a business associate when we were Amway distributors. In the mid-90's Julie left Amoco and had not renewed her membership as a distributor, almost simultaneously, to focus on recovering from cancer. We had seen her in passing a couple of years later, but hadn't heard from her or visited with her in about 7 years.

I was curious about the personal growth company and the seminars. Louisa said she'd heard enough on the message to know what it was about and wasn't interested in the seminars. However, she was excited about the opportunity to see Julie.

That was definitely a role reversal. Louisa has a high degree of curiosity about almost everything, and my curiosity is not as vast as hers.

I have often told people that I had been pretty invisible in those days. I didn't like being with myself, or my wife, and I was not excited about my life. Louisa has added that I was cold and that our marriage was strained, again. Perhaps for different reasons, we were both looking forward to the trip to California.

We went to Julie's house separately because Louisa was calling clients, and again I was the more curious one. I knew that I needed and wanted something. I could only hope that I was going to find it soon.

Most Realtors would call Julie's house *cozy*. That translates to small. It was full of people when I arrived. I knew only Julie, but I recognized the presenter. I couldn't place his name or where I'd met him. I'm good with names and faces, so I was pretty puzzled. People talked about "the basic." "When did you take the basic?" I thought of my Basic Training in the Army, and looking around at those in the room, I ruled out *that* basic.

Louisa arrived just as the presenter was about to start and recognized him right away. She said something like, 'before you start, I want to say hello to Bill. We haven't seen him in years.' Then I knew. We'd met Bill when we were attending the Amway home meetings at the home of Alan and Pat Williams in 1992 and 1993.

Bill, along with Julie, of course, brought instant credibility to whatever he was going to talk about.

Bill followed a prescribed format and talked about a company named PSI Seminars, and their "Basic" seminar. He pronounced the company name as though PSI was spelled sigh. He's a civil engineer by profession and was making the presentation as a volunteer because of his experience with the program his was describing. Half way through the presentation I knew that I was going to sign up for "the Basic."

After Bill finished, Louisa asked about my thoughts and I told her that I was going to do it. She agreed that she would too. The next "Basic" was scheduled for early March, when we would be on our road trip, so we agreed to attend the April session. On the way home, I thought about John Harwood's comment, "...pay attention..." Was this my answered prayer? I wouldn't know for at least another 8 weeks, if then.

Our attention went back to our upcoming road trip, which gratefully would be very different from the trip to Alton in September. Louisa had clients to work with also. I didn't.

I did spend more time meeting with Linda and giving her suggestions as to how to share the E-comm business with her prospects. With rare exception she wasn't involving me in those meetings. IC had developed a training system that enjoyed a good track record. She wasn't following it, and I wasn't keeping her on track. I was really doing her a disservice by not giving her a course correction.

In an effort to help her, I invited her to go with me as I was going to follow up with a prospect. I had met a personable young woman when I purchased a new cell phone. When I offered information about our E-comm business she said she wanted to know more, so I had left an audiotape with her. Now, two days later, I was going to meet with her about it, away from the store where she worked. Linda was eager to go with me.

I asked the young prospect a lot of questions. She told me about her major in school, her short and long term goals, and about her family. When she said that she wanted to focus on school at this time, and that we could stay in touch. I agreed to do that.

Walking back to my car Linda said, "You didn't mention Quixtar one time." I said, "It wasn't about Quixtar. I wanted to know about her. That's where we start. The business opportunity is too big for most people to digest in one meeting. I wanted to know if she has goals and whether Quixtar could be a vehicle to help her reach them." Linda said, "I almost interrupted a couple of times, to talk about Quixtar. I didn't because she's your prospect." I just said, "Good decision."

We left Friday evening, March 7th for our trip to California. We stayed the first night, in Pueblo, with our daughter-in-law's father, John. We experienced something short of panic when we discovered that I/we hadn't loaded Louisa's hormonal drinks or our food supplements for the trip. I offered to drive back home to get them and Louisa wouldn't hear of it. When John left for work the next morning…at 4 o'clock, we left for Phoenix. That was one of those rare occasions when I drank coffee in the car. Driving at 4 AM? You betcha. Louisa yielded to my need, opening the sunroof and burying herself in a sleeping bag.

Pueblo to Phoenix is only about an 11-hour drive. After driving straight through to Alton, which is 14 plus hours, that trip seemed easy. We were back to our normal road trip routine, enjoying each other's company and switching drivers every three hours.

We stayed with my aunt Met, one of my dad's sisters, and visited with my cousin Mike and his wife. After an evening on the back patio and a bucket of chicken, we all went to breakfast at a nearby restaurant the next morning. Then Louisa and I were off to San Diego, where we stayed with our friends Tom and Janet Kaye. We enjoyed a meal of fresh fish, that Tom had just caught, and then a sunset at the beach. The next morning, it was back to the beach for breakfast with them and then on to Anaheim.

We went to the Nutrilite facilities shortly after we checked into our room. The manufacturing and packing facilities are Buena Park, which is a short drive from where we were staying.

I had also contacted Dave Morgan about having dinner with him and Carolyn. They drove from Ventura to Redondo Beach to have dinner with us. When I thanked Dave for doing that, he laughed, and said that 'everything is 45 minutes away around here.' I know that Dave was happy to see us together after all these years. Even though he was in our wedding; he had doubts about whether we could stay married. He'd been privy to the volatile relationship we had during the early years.

Our second day there would be a long one, with a pleasant surprise included. We were up early and drove east to Riverside County to the Nutrilite farms. All of the exploration of the Nutrilite facilities was a part of my rebuilding my confidence and enthusiasm for being more active with our E-comm business.

After the tour of the farms, we drove to Temecula, where we would have dinner with other friends, Vince and Arlene Poulos that evening. They were driving up from Fallbrook. Vince was exploring too. He was looking for something to do beyond his very successful electronics business. Louisa has known him since high school, and I had met him and Arlene in 1982 when they were visiting Virginia.

We were also going to use the computers at the Temecula library to check our email messages. Driving into the parking

"YOU USED TO LIVE IN MY HOUSE."

lot, I got a pleasant surprise. I saw a sign reserving a space for Dan Crowe. Dan is a very good children's entertainer whom we'd met in 1989 through our friend Bonnie Phipps. Our grandsons loved his concert video we'd had since then.

Once inside the library we asked about the sign for Dan. We were told that he would be performing for kids that afternoon. After checking email and having lunch, we returned to visit with Dan. He told us that he'd be performing for kids at the school, in north Denver, where Bonnie was teaching, a few weeks later and invited us to bring our grandsons.

After dinner with Vince and Arlene we faced an hour-long drive back to Anaheim. We'd been on the road to the Nutrilite farms before 7 AM. We were back in our room at midnight and would leave for Las Vegas in what seemed like a few hours later.

Bob McKann once told me that he thought I knew people everywhere. While I have burned some bridges along the way, I still enjoy many friendships throughout the country. In Las Vegas, we planned to catch up with friends, who were also former neighbors, and clients.

Louisa had taken $50 of mad money with her to Las Vegas. She had never really been there, save a gas stop on our trip from San Diego to Denver in January 1994. I had been there in the early 80's as the Regional Marketing Director for The Hahn Company, when Fashion Show Mall was in my region. I had never had the urge to gamble money. I've taken many chances, but that's a different topic.

Louisa didn't know that the casinos are a part of the hotel lobby and that the machines are virtually everywhere in Las Vegas. When we checked into the Rio she was aghast at the cigarette smoke throughout the casino. She decided that we would be in the lobby area to and from the buffets only and that she'd take the back stairs to and from our room. I chose to go with her. Our room was incredible. It was a large room with a view of Las Vegas.

Louisa and I were enjoying being with each other. For my part, I hadn't changed anything substantial, except to be away from real estate and that I was looking forward going to "The Basic" a few weeks after the trip.

I had heard that Bob Sorensen was managing a property, in Las Vegas, for Trizec/Hahn. I pursued that info and had called him about meeting with him, too. I had known Bob since 1975. I had worked with and for him, traveled with him while I was a Regional Marketing Director for Hahn. He'd been involved in my transfer from Virginia to Colorado, awarding us the 'trip to anywhere in the world' for the success of the opening of the Tivoli. He had also signed off on my dismissal.

You could say that we had a well-rounded relationship. I like Bob and I was long past the fact that I had been fired. I did still have strong feelings about *how* it had happened, but not the eventual results. I believe that the firing might have saved my life. It very likely saved my marriage, and it taught me a valuable lesson about independence. Now, I feel grateful. Remember that I had actually told Louisa…"Sometimes I wish they'd just all go away, or even fire me."

I was drinking far too much during those years. It was the norm. Of course, I could have chosen to abstain. I didn't. I think that, in that environment, I was self-destructive. I also came away with a conviction that no one employer would ever again control my income. When I was fired, we had the 5 kids with us and we lost more than 70% of our income. I would never again put myself, or my family in that position.

Louisa and I had breakfast with Bob and there was no ill-at-ease feeling. We were longtime friends catching up with each other. We promised to stay in touch. We haven't.

"YOU USED TO LIVE IN MY HOUSE."

Our former neighbor, Kim and her daughter Heather showed us around Las Vegas. It reminded me of Martin and Anton showing us around Mazatlan two years earlier. We were hanging with the locals, and Las Vegas was as foreign to us as Mazatlan had been.

We knew that the CLS SkiGlo Conference would be taking place the week of our road trip. We had made reservations for the annual Friday night banquet, telling only Chuck and Jean Strehli. It was great to visit with everyone we knew and to meet some of the new participants. We were able to share information that we'd picked up from Nutrilite, which is annually one of the top brands in the Quixtar sales volume.

We stayed with Stuart and Charmaigne Menn, and met their new son Seth. We left Saturday for the final leg of our journey. As we drove into Denver on March 15th the temperature was a balmy 75 degrees.

We joined Riley's birthday celebration the next day. His birthday was coming up Tuesday, which was a school day.

We love the Colorado weather. However, we know that it can change dramatically and quickly. Such was the case that March. We saw our weather go from temperatures in the mid 70's on Saturday and Sunday, to blowing snow on Tuesday. Oh boy, did the snow blow! Many measurements topped 36" in the city and more in the foothills.

We had gone to the store out of need on Sunday. Before a long trip we get the refrigerator and cupboards down to almost nothing. Then we stock up a day or so after we return. It's a good thing that we did that in March 2003, because nothing was open for a couple of days. In our neighborhood, most of the bungalows were built in the 1920's. Ours was built in 1922. Several collapsed under the heavy snow. We were fortunate beyond description. Our metal storage shed collapsed under the heavy snow, not our house.

Everyone began to emerge by Wednesday and we walked the neighborhood taking pictures.

As we began contacting clients and associates we learned that it would take another week or more before business activities were back to normal. Well, I didn't have any real estate going at the time. I was calling on people for our E-comm business and being available to Linda for hers.

CHAPTER 2
Discovering layer upon layer

April 16, 2003 we reported to the registration table for the PSI Seminars Basic seminar. It was taking place at the hotel that had been the Stapleton Plaza Hotel when I first came to Denver in 1983, where I had 'pseudo-lived' for six months, and where we stayed that June, with the five kids, a dog and a cat, for ten days, and where the church choir retreat had taken place.

The place was packed. There were over 100 people registered for the PSI Basic that weekend. The format is for sessions on Thursday and Friday evening, and then all day Saturday and Sunday.

The PSI Basic was the first experiential seminar I'd ever attended. It wasn't a lecture seminar. We did have a facilitator, Tim O'Kelly, from California. I began to see myself in a different light as early as Friday evening.

You won't find details about the PSI Basic on these pages. At the outset we made an agreement to share with people our energy and attitude, and not the details of the seminar. The point in the confidentiality is simple. It's only right that each individual has his or her own experience with the seminar. To those who say, 'we'll I'm not going to attend it, so tell me,' I ask why they would want to know.

I will tell you one aspect of it that I think is beneficial for everyone, and was very beneficial for me. Those who attend with someone with whom they have a relationship, are required to sit at least four seats apart from each other. That is designed to allow each of us having our own experience. Had we not done that, Louisa and I might have been elbowing each other all weekend, with "did you get that?" "They're talking about you." or, "you need that."

On Sunday, as we broke for lunch, Louisa came up to me and asked whether I planned to go to the next level, a 7-day seminar called The Life Success Course, or PSI-7. I already knew that I wanted to get everything this company has to offer. However, I said, "Well, yes. But we've got Kelly's wedding coming up, etc." She said, "Well, I'm going." So, I said. "I'll go too." I had been the curious one in February.

The Life Success Course takes place on a ranch in northern California. We were the first in the class to sign up and scheduled our "PSI-7" as it's also called, for the next month. We also registered for the Men's and Women's Leadership Seminars, the next advance courses that would follow PSI-7.

I was excited because I had discovered and rediscovered things about myself that I knew would help me become a better person. Still, I would have to apply them. I liked the idea of adding another layer, or perhaps peeling back another layer a few weeks later.

Back in the real world, I still had no clients. Many other Realtors had seen their business drop off sharply in 2003. I did have an out of state referral that provided my only real estate income in the first four months of 2003.

Louisa had joined a business-networking group at the end of April. I recall the morning that she called me about membership for me. She said," The Realtor just left this group, so get your butt over here." She called back to say that I didn't have to come right then. She had completed an application for me, complete with payment, and that I could fax it to someone after signing it. I went to their Visitors' Day the next week and became a member of Business Network Int'l, (BNI).

A week later we were headed to California. It was easy for us to make arrangements to be gone. We had to book and pay for our airfare to San Francisco and a room the night of our arrival. PSI provided charter buses to take us to the ranch early the next morning. We also booked a room for two nights after the weeklong seminar, to enjoy San Francisco. Louisa hadn't been to San Francisco before, and I had been there only briefly on a business trip in 1986. She reminded me that I had promised her a trip to San Francisco, when I called home during that trip.

When we arrived at our gate at DIA on May 16th we ran into Juan Panzardi, who'd been in our PSI Basic class. He hadn't booked a room, and we knew that ours had two beds, so we offered him one of them.

After arriving at San Francisco International Airport, and a long wait for the hotel shuttle, we registered and put our bags in our room. We then asked for a public transportation schedule. We wanted to go into the city. The three of us went to dinner at Gaylord's and walked around Pier 39 afterwards.

Juan was calling home and getting no answers from his wife. At one point her turned to me and said something that became the inspiration for this book. I'll share that with you in a while.

There is a scene that almost defies description that takes place when 80 or 90 people gather in anticipation of the bus ride to PSI World's High Valley Ranch, home of PSI Seminars advanced courses. The level of energy is so high that there's a constant buzz akin to standing under giant power lines, even at 6:45 AM.

I won't tell you about the specifics of the PSI-7, The Life Success Course for the same reason that I didn't tell you more about the PSI Basic. I also believe it would be very challenging to relate to you, my day-to-day experiences.

I recall looking out at the ranch as our bus passed through the main gate, I looked across the landscape, taking in the beauty. There were horses and cattle. I thought about how I'd heard "the ranch" in revered terms, and wondered what was in store for us.

Without the experiences of PSI-7, the work Louisa and I have done, and continue to do with tools that we discovered, exhumed or picked up along the PSI journey, that it is unlikely that she and I would be together today.

We have enjoyed more positive growth in our relationship since April 2003, than in the almost 20 years together before.

Louisa told me, after the week at the ranch, that she could see changes in me, even before I expressed my thoughts about them. I had no pre-conceived notions about what PSI-7 would be like.

What could I have experienced that would help me with the direction I had been seeking? I know that each of us has a different story to tell about PSI-7. I know that I confronted some old demons. I saw what I *could* be like, what I *could* do and accomplish when I really opened up.

I met some great people, several who've become close friends. My PSI-7 'Buddy" Courtney Krenz and his wife, Debbie, my second daughter Tanya Avedovech, my 'girlfriend,' Jennifer Payne and of course, Rob Rohe top that list. Another, a woman from Denver whom I hadn't known before PSI-7, made a comment to me that has very special meaning to me. Tamara Bianchi, said, "I like you because I can trust you." There are dozens of others that played a big part in my, very positive, PSI-7 experience.

CHAPTER 3
Of those to whom much is given….

The following Saturday the charter bus returned us to the San Francisco airport and we caught a shuttle back to our motel. That evening we walked to a neighborhood Chinese seafood restaurant for dinner. Louisa asked what she could do to support me. I said, "Hold me accountable." Be careful what you ask for.

The next day we took public transportation into the city. We ate lunch in Chinatown and then caught another bus to see the Golden Gate Bridge, Pier 39 and across town to the ocean side of the city. After a dinner at Pier 39 we headed back and readied ourselves for an early flight and the return to reality.

Independent of each other we had set 90 days goals during the PSI Basic in April. We each had set a goal of redecorating the living and dining rooms. Louisa had offered to host the rehearsal dinner for Pete and Kelly's wedding. That would be July 25th, and we wanted to complete the redecorating before that.

We began sanding and stripping paint about midway through June. Louisa had picked out the paint colors and the wallpaper, and we gave ourselves about four weeks for the completion of the project.

Chris Coons came home for the summer. He wanted to be home for his sister's wedding and decided to come for a longer visit. Dave also came home. He had shoulder surgery just before his trip and arranged to have his rehab time coincide with the wedding.

On Monday, June 23rd, Chris, Louisa and I were prepping the rooms. We'd covered furniture and had begun stripping paint. We took break and Louisa and I were going to the Mayan Theatre to see "Whale Rider." Then I got a call from Ronnie and Linda Meyer's daughter, Tina Davis. They'd been in an accident on their motorcycle on Saturday. Ronnie had been killed instantly and Linda was in a coma. ***Oh, my God!***

I whaled. I could hardly breathe, as I tried to explain to Louisa and Chris what the call was about. When they visited us in September, Ronnie and I had been talking about when we met. Denny Harrison had introduced us when we were 13. I had been best man for Ronnie when he and Linda married. He'd been my best man when I had married Judi three years earlier. I used to kid him that I did a better job for him than he did for me.

Louisa convinced me to go to the movie. I knew she was right. Whale Rider is such a great movie that it helped me to get caught up in it.

I sat out on the deck most of the night. The next morning I looked around at the work we had begun, knowing that I would be going to Alton and leaving it behind for several days.

I went to my computer and read the email that Ronnie had sent the morning of the 21st. We had been exchanging email messages virtually every Saturday morning for almost three years, since I had 'shamed him into getting a computer.'

Here's what he said.…**"Perry&Louisa: What a great morning, good to be alive and well, hope you all are the same…Try to get all our work done early today then relax later. Seems like always plenty to do, and I guess that's good, went to my Dr. last week everything looks pretty good and that's always the best news."**

Louisa didn't want me to go right away, in part because I was so shaken and also because we didn't know whether Linda was going to survive. We had already decided that I would go alone. It hurt Louisa to stay behind. She really cared for them. Chris wanted to go with me, but had just taken a job, which he needed to pay rent in Austin. Louisa asked me to wait at least until Wednesday. It all seemed to be too much to process.

Linda died on Wednesday. I was ready to get on the road. I had driven it straight through before. Still, Louisa was convinced that I was not emotionally ready for the long 14-hour drive. I left on Friday.

On Saturday, after spending some time with mom, I visited Ronnie and Linda's friends and riding buddies, Dennis and Beverly Day. It was easy to see their connection with Ronnie and Linda. A little while with Dennis and I felt that I'd known him for years.

I also spent time sitting on Mom's front porch by myself. I read my Bible and The Beatitudes, one in particular jumped out at me.

There was a memorial on Sunday and the funeral would be on Monday. I had told Louisa that I had some things to say at the funeral, if allowed. She talked with Kelly about it, and Kelly said, "Dad will be okay. He's got a lot of faith. Remember that he said a eulogy at his son's memorial service." It was true. I would be okay. Talking about Ronnie and Linda would help me. And I felt buoyed by what Kelly had said.

I saw several of my high school friends at the memorial service including my cousin Ron Nelson. My old friend Charlie Wall had cut short a business trip to be there. I believe he drove in from Phoenix. I also talked with Ronnie's sisters, Chris and Darla and with Terry and Tina, Ronnie and Linda's son and daughter.

CHAPTER 4
Something good will come of this…it must

Before the funeral on Monday, I asked Ronnie's sisters Chris and Darla, and their son and daughter, Terry and Tina, if I could speak about Ronnie and Linda. They said that I could and were each happy that I would do it. I then told the minister that I was going to speak. He asked if I knew what I was doing, whether I was speaking from the heart. I knew what he meant. Of course, I was speaking from the heart. However, he wanted to know whether I had notes and a plan about what I would say. He had been in the same situation often enough to know that people could break down or ramble on. I told him that I'd be okay.

When it came time for me to speak I said a prayer, which I shared with the 100 plus people in the chapel. I've always attributed this prayer to Dorsey Deaton, a Triple Diamond with Quixtar and an ordained minister. "Lord, fill my mouth with meaningful stuff, then give me a nudge when I've said enough." Dorsey, I hope that's accurate. I know it works.

I looked out into the chapel and had a thought that could have side tracked me, or even stopped me. It's the chapel where we had my dad's funeral in 1958 and I hadn't been in it since. I could see where I had sat at dad's funeral, and I recalled that my friend Ronnie Meyer was sitting next to me.

It was helpful to have notes. However, it was a time when the words came out on their own, as though I didn't choose them. I said, "Something good will come of this. It must." I was to speak of two people whom I had known most of my life. Two people, pure of heart. As I alluded to earlier, I am confident that they have seen the face of God.

I told those in the chapel a little about my friendship with Ronnie and Linda, of forty some years, and how we teased him when he was falling in love with her. He was smitten. Then I told them one story that spoke what kind of friend he had been.

While I was in the Army and stationed at Ft. Riley, Kansas, I had been home for Christmas leave. Ronnie took me to Union Station in St. Louis to catch a train back to Kansas. It was snowing pretty hard, and I had made us late by oversleeping. I missed the train. I had until midnight to report or I would likely lose my job as driver for the Battalion Commander.

Ronnie said, "Screw it. I'll call in sick and drive you back." He drove me back to Fort Riley in his Porsche…with no heat and no defrosters. We made it before midnight and that was before Interstate highways. Ronnie stayed two days before driving back to Alton. I thought about that again when I passed Fort Riley driving back to Denver on I-70 the day after the funeral.

I got back to Denver on July 1st, the day before Chris Coons' 29th birthday.

I thought about the fact that we had moved into the house on July 1, 1983. Now, twenty years later, we were getting rid of some of the awful colors we'd inherited and lived with for so long.

Chris was working on his birthday, so I called the restaurant manager and told him that my baby boy was celebrating his birthday that day. They did their best to embarrass him, and celebrated with him all day and well into the night.

I went to an E-com business luncheon. A friend from church joined me, and then joined us in our business. In the midst of all that was happening, our E-comm business had taken off.

A few days after I returned from Alton, Louisa and I were walking in the park and I was sharing with her my experience of talking about Ronnie and Linda at the funeral. I hadn't thought of it as a eulogy until it was reported as that in the Alton newspaper.

I told her that I had realized that I have a gift for speaking that gave people something to think about afterwards. I felt compelled to do something to utilize that gift. I was already serving as a lector at Loyola. I was thinking in terms of reaching more people.

We talked about my desire to write and be published. Perhaps that would give me a forum to speak to more people. At PSI-7 I had more clearly defined what I believe is my purpose in life: *To impact lives in positive and healthy ways*. I began to consider several ways that I could live my purpose. Another seed had been planted for what would become this book.

A week before her wedding date, Kelly came by the house. She looked around at the furniture that was covered and the paint stripper, etc and said, "Why did you have to do this *now*? It looked just fine!" We told her that we had, independently come up with the redecorating as a goal and that it would be finished by her wedding rehearsal dinner." Granted, it didn't look as though it would be and we knew that we would have to have a lot of help to get it completed on time.

Chris had been helping us when he wasn't working. After Dave arrived, he helped to the extent that he could with his arm in a sling and we put my father-in-law, Paul, to work shortly after his plane touched down. Our neighbor Karen

Stoumbaugh pitched in and our friends Lane and Renate Edstrom even put up wallpaper in the dining room. I don't do wallpaper...in any room...under any circumstances. So, I was particularly grateful for their help.

It was quite a sight to see us scurrying around to get things in place for the reception, and get to the rehearsal on time. I think that Paul, Chris and I were the last to leave the house. Kelly was amazed when she and Pete arrived. The place looked good. The i's that weren't dotted and t's that weren't crossed were not noticeable, with one exception. Pete stood in front of the living room fireplace, looking at the windows above the mantle. He said, *"Those* are really clean." We hadn't put those windows back in because they hadn't been painted yet.

I told Kelly, at the dinner, that I didn't know if she could be any happier than we were, that she was marrying Pete. Of course, I expect that she was and is. We love the guy. He's great with her and I believe that he's more of a father to Brendan and Riley than Jeremy has ever been.

Pete and Kelly took their honeymoon two weeks later. They went on an Alaskan cruise. Our gift to them was that I would stay at their home, with Brendan and Riley through the week or ten days that they were gone. With Louisa's help, I played "Mr. Mom," getting them off to their summer activities, going about my workday and picking them up, etc. It was fun to have that experience with them. The grandparent thing is even better than advertised.

CHAPTER 5
Sometimes a gentle nudge, or perhaps a body slam

Louisa spent the second weekend in September as a volunteer staff member for the PSI Basic.

We had two trips on our agenda for September. We hadn't done anything special for our anniversary and we had never stayed at a bed & breakfast, so we scheduled a weekend at a B & B in Estes Park for the third weekend in September. The other trip would be to Nashville, for the annual IC Convention on the last weekend of the month.

September is also a big month for birthdays in our family. Brendan's birthday is the 8th, and so is my Aunt Frances'. Pete's falls on the 13th and my Mother's is on the 18th.

It had been almost a year since Louisa and I had made that trip to Alton for Mom's birthday when we weren't speaking to each other. I felt like I'd been on an emotional roller coaster all year. I had virtually no real estate business. Our PSI journey had begun. Our E-com business was growing rapidly. There were the deaths of two close friends and then Pete and Kelly's wedding. What next? I couldn't have imagined it.

We checked into the B & B and visited with the owners and other guests. It was a very pleasant atmosphere. We hadn't really been to Estes Park as tourists. We enjoyed seeing the Elk and the historic Stanley Hotel, and the shops.

On Saturday, we enjoyed the B & B breakfast with other guests. Then we were off to see the sites. We seemed to have trouble finding a place to eat lunch. We looked at one menu and then another and another. We settled on sandwiches from a small kitchen at the front of a bar. I watched the cook put together my fish sandwich. I rarely eat fried foods, but by the time we decided on that location, I was ready for about any food. I had some misgivings about the place and the cook. Nonetheless we took our food to a bench on the street and ate lunch.

Just before sunset we went to see the Elk population in the Rocky Mountain National Forest. That's a sight to behold. And yet, I was distracted by feeling of discomfort that I thought might be the onset of a cold or virus.

It was dark when we got back to Estes Park and we began to search for a place to have dinner. I hadn't been feeling well for about an hour and I felt that I could have done without dinner. It was probably as late as 8 or 8:30 PM when we sat down at an Italian restaurant. I excused myself before the meal came. I went to the restroom, more because I was feeling a lot of discomfort and pressure in my abdomen than the typical restroom visit.

When the meal came, I couldn't eat. The food looked good. I just felt bad. I was up and down throughout the night. I was convinced that I was coming down with the flu, but I didn't have any nausea.

Sunday morning I felt worse. I willed myself to go to breakfast, thinking that it might help to eat. The food was very good the previous morning and I liked the fact that the kitchen was open and clean. I started with a cup of coffee. I took a sip and took it to the kitchen sink. I told Louisa that I needed to go back to bed. It's a notable occasion when I don't have that first cup of coffee.

I woke up several hours later, still feeling very ill. The B & B owners had let me sleep beyond the checkout time and offered some food. I declined. I asked Louisa to drive home. As bad as I felt, I was sure that it wasn't food poisoning. I'd experienced that before and it involved extreme nausea.

I called my Mother just before we left for Denver. That's when I learned that my Uncle Leonard, one of her brothers, had died. He'd been in a nursing home for some time.

The next two days were like torture. I had appointments to show our E-comm business to prospects and it seemed that I was battling to control my bladder. I was in a lot of pain every time I relieved it. On Wednesday Louisa took me to see Dr. Dave Dahlhauser, our chiropractor, who practices a holistic health approach for natural healing. Dr. Dave, whom we'd met in our BNI chapter, said that I had something going on with my kidneys, and that it could be mold. He recommended a product that would probably help detoxify my body…my words, not his. Louisa said, "get well. We've paid for the trip to Nashville." That trip was two days away.

That night I awoke in a pool of sweat. I put beach towels over my sheet and woke up again later with them as wet as the sheet had been. I felt better than I had in almost a week. I was drinking a lot of cranberry concentrate and water and had agreed to abstain from coffee. Really.

A year earlier we talked about taking excitement to the conference rather than finding it there. Since returning from PSI-7, I had added ten new business associates. Our associate, Linda, had added four.

I felt okay in Nashville. We played tourist and went to the convention sessions. I wasn't full of energy and I didn't run while we were there. I hadn't run since our first morning in Estes Park. That's almost as rare as a day without coffee. I had agreed not to drink coffee until after my kidneys had cleared up. I hadn't had any since that last sip at the B & B.

Our business associate, Linda had gone to the conference too, although she didn't attend every session. She had a friend who lived nearby and spent time with her, too. I might have second guessed her on that, but I thought…'we're adults here and she's paying her own way.' It was also in that setting that I discovered why she had struggled so much with her business. We had an opportunity for impromptu role-playing with Gil Stewart, a friend from Colorado Springs. Gil and his wife Debbie are successful IBO's. As Gil and I wrapped up the role-play, he said to Linda, "It works every time." She replied, "Well, it doesn't work for me!"

I know enough to know that building that type of business depends on helping others achieve their goals, first. Zig Ziglar has said it millions of times, "You help enough people get what they want and you'll have what you want." It won't work for us if our focus is making it work for ourselves first.

The week following the Nashville trip, I was running again. I didn't feel ill, just sluggish.

That Saturday we visited with some prospects for our E-comm business, whom we'd helped get into their home a few years earlier, and later went on to a friend's birthday party before going home. I told Louisa that I had to leave the party because I started feeling ill again and was having lower back pain. I'd been in and out of their restroom as much as I'd socialized. Over the next few days the pain and restroom visits increased dramatically. At times I had been incoherent and off balance. On Thursday we were back at Dr. Dave's office.

Dr. Dave was very concerned that whatever was attacking my kidneys hadn't cleared up. He told Louisa that she should get me to the hospital if it continued. She wanted to contact one other natural healing practitioner who'd been recommended by Dr. Dave, and was unable to get me in to see her on Friday. Dr. Dave called Friday night, urging Louisa to get me to the hospital. Louisa had been holding onto her hope that the issue could be resolved without a hospital visit. We hadn't used our "catastrophic" health insurance and really didn't know how to go about it.

CHAPTER SIX
When you least expect it…

I had been an outpatient several times, for shoulder separations. However, I had stayed overnight in a hospital on only 3 occasions after I was born. I had been hospitalized when I had Pneumonia when I was 5, an auto accident in 1969 and another in 1980. Those were my only overnight stays in hospitals. I had been taking good care of myself for years.

In all the years I had known Louisa she hadn't been in a hospital…as a patient. She had some basal cell removed just before we left the Kaiser coverage in 1995, and she does have a benign cyst on an ovary. She's very in tune with her body and is committed to healing ailments naturally. Of course, she had hoped that I might be healed that way too.

On Saturday morning we called Kelly, who managed the pre-natal clinic at Rose Medical Center, and she said, "If you have to go to the hospital, go to 'Rose.' The food is great.' Reason enough for me. We had been considering Rose, and also Porter Hospital, which is closer to our home.

With that bit of information Louisa rushed me to the Emergency Room at Rose Medical Center. That was October 11, 2003. Much of what I know about that day was told to me. I was delirious. I was bloated *and* dehydrated. I know I had x-rays and ultrasound and that I was in a room quicker than I might have expected.

I do recall a few things clearly. Louisa said, "If I lose you, I'm going to replace you with a dog. I'm not going to train another man." I asked her to make it a Chocolate Lab. I told her that if I ever lost her, I was going to replace her with a condo next to Coors Field.

Kelly was allowed to sit in on the doctors' meeting the next morning because she was a management level employee, as well as my daughter. She didn't say much at the time. However, she later said that she was afraid she was going to lose me.

Chuck Strehli called from Austin to say that I was the last person he ever expected to call in a hospital. I replied, "me too."

Sometime in the next 24 hours, I would hear that I had total kidney failure, due to E.coli in my blood. That's when it hit home that I was very, very sick.

Louisa called Father Tom Jost, our Pastor at St. Ignatius Loyola Catholic Church. He brought with him good wishes and prayers from our parish...and a sacrament for healing. Through our family and friends from Loyola, CLS/IC, PSI and others, we knew there were prayers given for me in many places throughout the world. I promise you that I could *feel* that energy.

I didn't have a primary care physician at the time. I hadn't been to a doctor since August 1995 when I had a full physical before Louisa left AMOCO and our Kaiser Permanente coverage. We had been going to the '9 Health Fair', which is a great service, and were up to date on the basic aspects of our health.

We put a lot of energy and money into maintaining our health. I now know that I had become arrogant about it. I don't think I took my good health for granted, but I expect to be healthy, because of everything I do to maintain it. Still, I was as vulnerable as anyone and I had to admit that.

The doctor who was assigned to me was Dr. Robert Contiguglia. I guessed that he was about the same age as I. I liked him immediately. His bedside manner is 'old school.'

Dr. C, as most people call him, sat with me and listened. We had conversations, actual dialogue. I learned about his passion for soccer very quickly. He was President of the U.S Soccer Association, and the U.S. representative to FIFA, the governing body for world soccer. He is a teacher, and there were always a team of physicians around him and attending to me.

He explained that they had found E.coli in my blood and what they would use to get rid of it. His theory about how it got there, and mine, differed. With all due respect and much affection for Dr. C…I still think it was that greasy and unkempt restaurant and cook in Estes Park that was the source of lunch that day and of my demise.

There were terms thrown at us, such as White Blood Cells count, Creatinine, Sodium levels, and others. The Sodium level was of particular concern to Louisa. We were told that it was too low and if it was raised to fast, it could cause permanent brain damage.

I had a big private room and Louisa set up shop there. She had her laptop and her files and she worked from there each day. Louisa arrived before 8 AM and left close to midnight, and not before using her Jin Shin Jyutsu touch therapy to help my body heal. She wasn't ready to get that dog.

One doctor gave me a word association test. He said something like, "repeat what I say: car…dog…tree." I replied, "Volvo…Lab…Maple." Louisa said, "He's improving." I wasn't trying to be funny and I hadn't passed the test.

I can best describe the care I received as the best anyone could hope for. The nurses and doctors manipulated my fluids so that I became hydrated and was able to walk the halls my second full day in the hospital. Kelly had been right about the food at Rose. Even on the renal restrictive diet, it was good.

Chris Harrison came by Monday evening and walked with Louisa and me. We were able to go outside and to the end of the block and back.

My brother Mike came by, and Chris Johnson who brought a book that I want to recommend, <u>Hugs for Coffee Lovers</u>, by Jeanette Littleton. I liked that book so much that I gave a copy to another coffee lover, my mother, for Christmas. Another couple from church, Cosmas and Emmanuella Agwu came by…unfortunately at a time when I wasn't having visitors.

I was making progress, but Dr. C and the other doctors weren't happy with my numbers, specifically my Creatinine level. He was going to a FIFA conference somewhere in Eastern Europe and left another physician with instructions about where my numbers needed to be…to either have dialysis or be released. That's a pretty wide range. Dr. C said, "If they're not where I want them by Wednesday, you'll have to go through dialysis. Everyone else will tell you to bring a book. Don't bother, you'll be too sick to read."

Evidently the Creatinine level had dropped then leveled off. He said that I was improving and faster than he had expected. He gave some credit to the good physical condition I'd been in before contracting the E.coli. He also said, "If you want a second opinion, you're still ugly."

Before Dr. C left, he talked with me about getting more electrolytes in my body. He said that I could have a Coke, or a sports drink. Louisa was quick to tell him that we don't drink sodas. I said, "I drink Root Beer." She grimaced. Dr. C said, "Have a Root Beer." My brother Mike brought a 6-pack of Root Beer that afternoon.

I was making progress. However, my kidneys still weren't functioning. The numbers were good enough for me to be released on Friday, and I didn't have to go through dialysis.

"YOU USED TO LIVE IN MY HOUSE."

I was given a prescription for the antibiotic that I had been getting through the I.V. The doctor who signed off on my release said that my kidneys would probably start working within 24 hours.

CHAPTER 7
One step forward, and…

Louisa drove me home on a beautiful, sunny day. It was October 17th. As she was putting things away, I sat on the front porch swing. Karen Stoumbaugh, our neighbor to the South joined me on the swing.

I became very thirsty and was frustrated with all of my bodily functions not being in good working order yet. Louisa was busy and didn't see me get the juice out of the refrigerator. I drank the wrong thing at the wrong time and caused a setback for myself. She came out to the porch where Karen and I were, and saw the prune juice. She exclaimed, "You can't drink that!" She scared the hell out of me. I had no idea what was wrong. She took the glass out of my hand and said, angrily, "Didn't you even read the list of what you can have and what you can't have?" I hadn't. The red flag I hadn't seen was potassium.

I went to bed, feeling terrible, not only for what I had done and hadn't done, but in physical discomfort. I was already weak and I felt much worse than I had when we left the hospital. I think, for a brief moment, she was ready for that dog.

Louisa was scheduled to leave for the PSI Women's Leadership Seminar (WLS) in two weeks. That meant that she would be flying back to California and be at the ranch for 9 days, away for about 12 days. She had expressed concern to Dr. C, about being away. He told her that I should be able to care for myself by then. So, any setback was of more concern.

My kidneys started working again the second night I was back home. That, of course was great news. However, I was still very weak. I weighed 112 pounds. That's 20 pounds less than I usually weigh, give or take a big meal.

I had told friends that I wasn't ready for any visitors. I was just too weak to sustain any conversations. My friend Bill Michaels had a hard time with that. Other friends, Linda Combellick and her daughter, Jacqueline, brought a meal for me. They'd prepared so much that I invited them and Louisa to join me.

A week after leaving the hospital, I had an appointment with Dr. C. Louisa went with me, wanting to hear something definitive about my condition and whether she should go to California, leaving me alone. Our next-door neighbor, Karen, is always there for us and eager to help if I needed her, as were her parents, Ed and Vera, and other friends.

Dr. C told me that I was progressing; that he didn't think the prune juice caused a setback. He also said that I could resume a normal diet...even coffee and that I no longer needed the antibiotic. He also told Louisa that she should go to California and not worry about me. The latter part was essential to me. I wanted her to go to the WLS and be able to have her own experience without worrying about how I was doing.

She left for WLS two days later. I drove her, and another woman to DIA. I also drove myself to another appointment with Dr. C just before her return. Our friends Courtney and Debbie Krenz, whom we'd met at PSI-7 came by one evening while she was gone, bringing dinner to me.

I told my Mother that I felt like a newborn baby. All I did that week was eat, poop and sleep.

When I picked Louisa up at DIA, she was shocked. She expected to see me looking much different; much better. She said that I looked like a 90 year old man.

"YOU USED TO LIVE IN MY HOUSE."

She went with me to my visit with Dr. C that week. That's when he lowered the boom. He knew that I had been used to running, having already said that my conditioning contributed to my recovery. He said that he wanted me to go back to running, and that he thought I had been babying myself. Louisa almost cheered. She had been concerned that I planned to put off any running until January. Dr. C said, 'just run. If you run a block and are tired, stop. Run a mile…whatever you feel is okay. You know that your body will tell you.'

I had been scheduled to go to the Men's Leadership Seminar (MLS) a day after Louisa returned from the WLS. Of course, I didn't have the stamina and Dr. C wrote a letter to PSI saying that I wasn't cleared to travel anywhere. I was given the options of going in March or July 2004 and chose the latter.

My 61st birthday didn't have the same flair as the surprise party a year earlier. However, it certainly had real meaning. I didn't know how sick I had been until I started recovering. I had spent six and a half days in the hospital and a lot of it putting my life into perspective. I told people that I thought the Lord had pulled me aside to make me take stock and get my attention. The experience was a true blessing.

Not only had I lost my close friends Ronnie and Linda Meyer that summer, there were five other men from our high school class who died between June and September. I knew each of them well. Ronnie's was the only one that was due to an accident; the others were through various illnesses. There may have been female classmates who'd died too. It was harder to know that because so many women, in my generation, changed their last names, assuming their husbands names when they married.

CHAPTER EIGHT
Recovery

Enter 2004. I had gotten back into disciplined exercise. We were planning to go to the SkiGlo conference at Snowmass in March, so I wanted to be in shape for it.

While I was so focused on my physical recovery, our E-com business was slipping away. I hadn't done anything with it since September, so many of those who registered in 2003 hadn't done anything either and didn't renew their membership.

My real estate business looked brighter. I still had Helen's house on the market and one of the members of our BNI chapter gave me the opportunity to market his home. Paul Campbell and his wife Peggy had built a new home and were ready to move into it. I was asked to sell their patio home.

Louisa had taken a lot of time away from her mortgage business to help me with my recovery. She was essentially rebuilding it too. She had grown a lot from her WLS experience and I saw a more confident woman in virtually all aspects of her daily behavior.

The big snowstorm in March 2003 had collapsed the old metal storage shed that had been on the property when we bought the house almost 20 years earlier. While Chris Coons was home that summer, he and I had taken most of it apart. I hauled it to the metal recycling facility in Pete's truck. The concrete pad was there, as well as two sides of the old structure along the corner of the fence. Louisa decided to build a wooden shed that spring.

The first weekend in March I volunteered to staff the PSI Basic. Up until that point I had been happy with every experience that I had with PSI Seminars. There had been exercises that challenged me in a number of ways; I felt that the results were worth it. I could see our marriage becoming stronger with each passing day.

I hadn't anticipated the challenges that I would meet as a volunteer. The entire staff was made up of volunteers. I had met the Chief of Staff, Vicki Edgar when Louisa staffed with her in September. She challenged me to participate in the PSI 90-day program called Pacesetters Leadership Dynamics (PLD). I was pretty well dug in, in my resistance to "play PLD." Like everyone else who goes through the Basic, and PSI-7, I had heard many things about PLD, and not all good. That wasn't the cause for my resistance about it. I was reluctant to commit to a program that was 90-days long.

When I got home after the first night of the PSI Basic, I told Louisa, "Vicki's pushing me to play PLD. I'm not taking the bait."

The second night, when I returned home, I said, "I signed up for PLD." She laughed and said, "Okay, you can pay for it." The initial cost was less than either the PSI Basic or PSI-7.

The other challenge was the facilitator. While I had connected with the facilitator for our Basic, in April 2003, I made no connection with the facilitator when I staffed the Basic in March 2004. It was more than having not connected with him, and I knew it. My feelings were so strong that I thought, 'if he had been the facilitator for our Basic, I might not have stayed for the four days.' What a shame that would have been...based on results. I did meet that facilitator again, and came away with a better feeling about him and his work.

CHAPTER NINE
They call it "The best game in town."

The day after the Basic classes ended I went to the PSI Denver office to look at the PLD schedule. I would be on PLD Team 29. Without saying too much, I will say that I had scheduling problems with some of the requirements.

We had booked our timeshare condo, at Waikoloa Village, Hawaii and it conflicted with one of the weekends where attendance was required for the entire team. I looked at the Team 30 schedule and I had a conflict with that also. Well, I was really upset. Pete, Kelly, Brendan and Riley were going to Hawaii with us. Pete and Kelly were employees and had scheduled their vacations for the week we had reserved. I called Louisa and she suggested that I call Kelly to see whether they could reschedule their vacations, and that we could call Paniolo Greens at Waikoloa Village about rescheduling our week if they could. I fumed more.

I called Kelly about it. When I got home, I called Paniolo Greens and learned that we could reschedule, for a nominal fee of $25. They next day Kelly called to say that, not only could she and Pete change their vacations dates, it worked better for them too. With the dates changed, Brendan could go to a camp that he would have otherwise missed.

So, I was a member of the PSI Denver PLD Team 29. Then I learned that the Team 29 informational meeting would take place while we were at the SkiGlo conference in Snowmass. By that time, I was eager to play PLD. I decided to drive back from Snowmass, attend the meeting and return the next morning.

We went to the SkiGlo conference in March and I really thought I had experienced a major breakthrough. Louisa was back on board. She and I agreed that we could work together and build the business to levels higher than we had ever achieved. We set our goal and were committed to reaching it by September. We both believed that was something that we could achieve, and my reward would be the Volvo C70 convertible that I'd been talking about buying for a long time.

Before we left for Snowmass, Louisa called our friend Haden Gregg. He told us where he would be playing, and said, "Be sure to come early. We'll have a surprise guest." WOW! What a treat that was. His surprise guest was Vince Gil. I was told that Vince and his wife, Amy Grant were skiing Snowmass Mountain that week. Amy didn't appear with him when he sat in with Haden and his band.

Another thing happened that week that wasn't related to our E-comm business and yet it would signal another paradigm shift.

Father Tom left a message that I had been nominated for Pastoral Council. I returned his call as a courtesy and to confirm what he already knew. I hadn't been confirmed as a Catholic and wasn't eligible to serve on Pastoral Council. It started my wheels turning, or rather returning to something that I had begun to think about as I drove home from Ronnie and Linda's funeral almost nine months earlier.

I had been attending Catholic churches for more than twelve years. I had been serving as a lector at St. Ignatius Loyola, as I had at the 10:30 Catholic Community. I had sung in choirs at both churches. However, I had not converted to Catholicism.

"YOU USED TO LIVE IN MY HOUSE."

When I discussed the call and my thoughts with Louisa, it came out in this manner. I had been a practicing Catholic and yet I felt as though I wasn't committed…participating in areas that were comfortable for me. I told Louisa that I would enroll in the RCIA* program and seek confirmation.

* The Right of Catholic Initiation for Adults.

The RCIA program is a series of weekly classes than I would attend between August and confirmation at the next Easter Vigil.

I asked my friend Bill Thompson to act as my RCIA sponsor. After all we had a good friendship, attended the same church, had each been Methodists. Even our ex-wives had the same first name.

Once we were back in Denver we began contacting new prospects. I was aiming at a fresh start and didn't want to try an E-comm version of CPR with our associates who had done little or nothing in the past.

It was also time to play PLD, the 90-day program that I had enrolled in with PSI Seminars. I was excited about using that program to achieve the goals we had set at Snowmass.

As with the PSI Basic and the Life Success Course (PSI-7), I won't go into details about playing PLD. Whether by design, or by its evolution, it serves as close-up of one's life. As I said, I wanted to use the goal setting aspect of PLD to serve the business growth that Louisa and I sought. It didn't work out that way. Some people "play big," in PLD and some don't. I struggled. It was a veritable roller coaster ride for me. My primary goal became reaching its commencement exercise.

Louisa wasn't playing PLD with me. Rather, she wasn't on the team. She was supportive, and of course she experienced my mood swings. When people asked whether she was playing, I said, "No. She's in the side car."

At the same time we were also hosting another houseguest through the Denver International Program.

Juan Cedillo is a remarkable young man from Guatemala. I believe he was 27 at the time. Though they'd met and married in Guatemala, his wife Cecelia was back in her home country of Belgium with their son, Xhun, and Juan was furthering his education.

Even before Juan saw and enrolled in the PSI Basic* we had begun to develop a friendship, very much like ours with Anthony Donkor, whom we also met through DIP.

I added the * above because Juan was sponsored into the PSI Basic by my teammates on PLD Team 29.

Juan said that the PSI Basic changed his life, his words, not mine. I am more likely to say that my life has changed in many positive ways since taking the PSI Basic. Juan didn't ask me to speak for him.

We met Cecilia and Xhun, via a webcam over Internet and look forward to meeting them in person. Juan returned to Guatemala after his DIP sponsored stay here, and completed his studies. He then moved to Belgium to be with Cecilia and Xhun. Our lives are blessed through his friendship. I believe, and I believe that Louisa will agree, that Juan will have a dramatic impact on our world.

I was disappointed in having my SkiGlo goals swept away. I was more disappointed in myself. I would say to myself, 'you've been through tougher things than this.' Yet, I wasn't using my potential and I wasn't living my purpose.

Full of anticipation, I was eager for "First Weekend" of PLD. Louisa said I looked as excited as a kid going off to school for the first time. The first day set the tone for the roller coaster ride I took for the next 90 days.

There were meetings once a week. During one of those meetings in April, I was listening to one of the players, Mike,

"YOU USED TO LIVE IN MY HOUSE."

who was calling in from his home in New Mexico. I began to think about the fact that I would be calling in from Hawaii in June. My coach came to me after the meeting, asking "Where were you tonight?" I knew what he was talking about and told him what I'd been thinking about. He said, "Think about what you might have missed tonight, while thinking about something that will occur in June." It hit home. I was often caught up in 'the next thing,' rather than being present in the present. I'd seen it happen before, resulting in missing instructions and not being able to complete a task or problem completely. It had happened at home, work and play.

Our run at the level of achievement that we had set as a goal in March was in disarray in April and dismantled by May.

CHAPTER TEN
Another day in paradise

The PLD commencement exercise, known as ACK Night (for Acknowledgement), was set for June 26th, a week after our last day of vacation in Hawaii.

On June 12th we flew from Denver to the Kailua-Kona Airport. We didn't have to go through LAX on that trip. We left my car at Pete and Kelly's and took her van to an airport parking lot. We were excited about going to Hawaii with them, and yes, especially with our grandsons. Neither Brendan, nor Riley had seen the ocean and they had been excited about going to Hawaii for several months.

I recall that the topic of using the Hawaii timeshare with them started as a joke in 2002. When we confirmed that Chris and Brandy would be going with us, I called Kelly to talk with her about when she, Pete and the boys could use it. Pete answered and I told him that Chris and Brandy were going with us. I said, "You and Kelly are welcome to use it in 2004." He said they might use it for their honeymoon. Kelly said it was the first time she'd heard him talk in terms of marriage. I said, "Good. Then we can go along to take care of the boys."

After getting settled into the condo we all went grocery shopping. The next morning Louisa and I went to mass at the church where we'd gone with Paul two years earlier. The priest's homily was about people who got married on the beach, and it wasn't in support of them. We looked at each other and smiled, because we had been married on the beach and recalled that the Catholic Bishop in the diocese where Louisa had been a member, in Virginia, wouldn't allow a Catholic ceremony there.

We were six days away from our 21st anniversary. We were happy with each other, even though we'd seen another run at our E-comm business fall short, and I hadn't played PLD up to my expectations. Our relationship had changed dramatically in the past couple of years…for the better.

Pete and Kelly really gave Brendan and Riley a great vacation and dozens of memories to take back to the mainland and share with their friends. They did all the touristy things, including the glass bottom boat rides, hang-gliding and snorkeling. We snorkeled with them and enjoyed being at the beach with them. The boys stayed home with us one night so Pete and Kelly could have a date night and enjoy a Luau. On Wednesday we drove around to the Southeastern side of the island to see Volcano National Park.

When Louisa, Paul and I had been there two years earlier, it had been a chilly and rainy day. There were areas where we hadn't been allowed to go because of volcanic eruptions and fires. This year we were allowed full access and actually got to walk across the lava fields created by the 2002 eruptions. It's still very warm underfoot, and safe when caution is exercised. We have some great photos of red-hot lava as close as 8 feet, and also from 50 yards away as it fell into the ocean. It was a great experience for each of us, and of course, something very special for Brendan and Riley, who were 9 and a half and 6 respectively.

On the trip back to our condo, I became very ill. I was so sick that I couldn't focus and drove only a few miles before asking Louisa to drive. The boys were riding back with us so that Pete and Kelly could have the evening for themselves.

"YOU USED TO LIVE IN MY HOUSE."

I went to bed as soon as we got home. I had a fever and chills, and no idea what had caused it. The next morning I didn't want to get out of bed. Louisa took Brendan and Riley to the beach, and Pete and Kelly went out to see the sights. I slept all day. I finally got up that evening and felt pretty good, but weak. I think I might have been okay had I gone out that day. However, I was focused on feeling good on Friday, our 21st wedding anniversary. I knew that evening that I'd made the right decision.

Louisa and I spent our anniversary day going to three different beaches and relating it to having been married on the beach. To get to the first beach, which looked like something out of a movie set, we had to walk through some pretty large brush. When we came to the beach opening, Louisa looked down and saw a piece of lava rock shaped like a heart. Happy Anniversary! We took pictures at each beach and asked others to take pictures of us together. That evening we went out for dinner at the King Kamehameha's Kona Beach Restaurant. We could have gone to a more romantic restaurant to be sure. However, we wanted seafood and we wanted to eat where the locals eat. It was a seafood buffet that rivaled the famous seafood buffet at the Rio in Las Vegas…*and* the locals were eating there. To us, that is a very good sign.

We enjoyed our anniversary day and night, and talked about how much more nurturing our relationship had become during the past two years. We had become each other's best friend.

The next day we were up early, packing for the flight home, and yet not ready to leave our home away from home. We all went to the beach, allowing time for our swim suits to dry sufficiently to be packed and then we were off to a big meal before the red-eye flight to Denver.

We went to lunch at the same restaurant where Louisa, Paul and I had eaten our first lunch in Kona, in 2002. The food and service are good and it's not terribly far from the airport. Pete was anxious. In the scene that unfolded we saw a side of Pete that we hadn't seen before. However, Kelly had. Contrary to his typical laid-back disposition, he was becoming impatient, checking his watch every few minutes and encouraging the boys to settle down and eat. I think he might have inhaled his food. When we left the restaurant and headed back to the car, he was on what we referred to in the Army, as a force march. He would look back to see that we were still behind him, but he was focused on reaching the car.

Once we'd gotten to the airport, returned the cars and gone through security, we had time to sit and wait. Pete was still anxious. We were sitting across from him and Kelly. She offered to get drinks for us and he looked at his watch. I said, in jest, "he's afraid that you might miss the plane." Kelly looked at Pete and then at me, and said, "No. He's afraid that *he* might miss his plane. He'll be okay if I do." She said it's the only time that she sees him like that. He took the kidding in good spirit, albeit solemnly.

Louisa didn't go through the last minute security screening and we were off in due course. We had an all night, uneventful, flight and arrived back in Denver the next morning. It was Sunday and I was 7 days away from ACK Night. I was also a little more than a week away from closing the sale of Helen's house that I had been working to sell for over a year. We sold it for considerably less than the original appraisal in 2003.

Three weeks after my PLD ACK Night I was off to California for the PSI Men's Leadership Seminar. I left Denver on Kelly's birthday, July 16th, and would return on the 26th, the date of the first wedding anniversary for her and Pete.

CHAPTER ELEVEN
Leadership

I had heard many stories about the PSI Men's Leadership Seminar (MLS). I knew that a part of the activities would be outdoors, and probably strenuous. I had recovered pretty well from the bout with kidney failure and felt healthy again. I wanted to be stronger. Starting in April, I had increased my running miles, and also how I went about them. I was back in training mode.

There were two primary aspects to my training. I was running 5 to 7 miles every other day, with my backpack full of filled water bottles. I started with 4 bottles and increased to 8 as I increased the miles. I also added hill running.

Those who know Denver know that Ruby Hill, in Southwest Denver along the Platt River, is a popular hill for sledding in the winter. It's about 3.5 miles from our home. I ran that route, up Ruby Hill and back, with the backpack full of the filled water bottles at least twice a week until we went to Hawaii in June. I also ran a 10-mile route, without the backpack, once a week. I had a favorite route that I had run as Coors Field was being built, which included the Cherry Creek Bike Path.

By July 16th, I felt that I was in shape for anything that MLS might have in store for me. Nine months after being hospitalized with acute renal failure, I felt that I was probably in better shape, at 61+, than I had been when I ran my last marathon 19 years earlier.

On the trip to MLS I was traveling with Richard Grunewald. We had met him and his wife, Joey, at a Christmas party in 2003. I love those two people. They've been together since high school and they are great relationship role models. To put that into perspective, Richard is only a few months younger than me. They and I had both been on PLD Team 29. I think that Richard and I had similar PLD experiences as well.

When we reached San Francisco and registered at our motel, we ran into several other guys going to MLS. The next morning we met more, as we checked in for the charter bus ride to the ranch.

There would be 93 men at our MLS. There were men of virtually every culture, professional background, religion, and persuasion. There were men from Japan, and Canada, and one, a professor from Hawaii, who was originally from Great Britain.

I think that it was on the second day of MLS that I began to get my lessons from PLD. Several lights went on and I began to see why I had played PLD the way that I had and what I had learned from that experience. It was then that 'I got it.'

Because of the challenges that I dealt with at PSI-7, and the tools that I learned from that seminar, Louisa and I have enjoyed a nurturing relationship. I was discovering even more about myself at MLS, in many ways.

I had to acknowledge that I had not given my all, and had not fully participated in relationships with family or friends in a dozen years. I realized too, that it wasn't coincidental that Kevin had died 12 years earlier. I thought about how my perspective of my life had changed during the hospital stay in October. It was being tweaked again.

I didn't call Louisa until the next to the last day of my MLS. I called her and simply said, "I'm bringing home the

"YOU USED TO LIVE IN MY HOUSE."

man you married." Louisa had once upon a time called me *dynamic*. She had referred to me in many different ways since, and not all were flattering, and none of them included the word dynamic. Of course, I had been, or acted out, many of the names and descriptions she had used over the years. Only a couple of months earlier, she had said that I was 'all talk.'

It's no secret that MLS includes a formal commencement exercise, complete with formal attire. The exercise itself is unlike anything approaching graduation that I had ever experienced. I saw myself in a different light that night too.

I awoke early the final morning of MLS. Around 4 AM I finally gave up lying awake in my bed. When I wake up I want to get up and get on with the day. That morning I got up made coffee (of course), and sat outside in my under shorts and a t-shirt. There were about four of the men from Japan up at that hour too. We talked for a few minutes. They made every effort, all week long, to communicate in English. They were excited and a few of them took off in the golf carts to see a special memorial on the ranch.

By 5 AM I had showered, shaved and was dressing. As we gathered for the final meeting and send-off brunch, everyone began to kid me about what I was wearing. "Didn't sleep last night, Mr. Coons?" was among the comments. I had put my tux back on for the trip home.

At the final meeting, Rob and Dan, two of the facilitators asked me to stand and say why I was wearing the tux again… or still. I told them that I was doing it for my wife. I had become too predictable and wanted to bring home the guy that had once upon a time acted on his feelings more than he contemplated the results…or something like that.

One of them, I think it was Rob, said, "Be aware of those around you and take in the looks they give you today. Let us know how that goes." I hadn't thought about how different it might be to see someone traveling in a tux. Later I would realize that wasn't the only thing that I hadn't thought about when I decided to wear the tux.

We had our brunch, said our farewells to those who boarded a different bus and headed back to San Francisco. There was a large contingent from Colorado, which is not unusual for any PSI event at the Ranch. Several of us walked through the ticketing and common areas of the airport together. We all were aware of people pointing as us because of some of the items we had with us and at me in my tux. It was very interesting. We had another meal together before we parted company and headed for our gates.

I hadn't anticipated what would happen when I went through security in the tux. I set off alarms and was asked to step aside for the search. While the security guard was asking me to remove my cuff links, metal buttons, bow tie, and cummerbund…he already had my shoes of course…my 'LS Brothers, Richard Grunewald and Carl King were on the other side of the security area, egging him on. One of them said, "Watch out Perry, he's putting on a rubber glove."

The security guard dismissed me and I joined them and others as we headed to the gate.

Our plane touched down near midnight. Louisa, Joey Grunewald and Sue Payne had been waiting for me, Richard and Jeff Land in the 45 minute waiting area about 5 minutes away. Sue picked up Jeff at a different level and Richard and I waited for Joey and Louisa to pick up us.

Louisa had been poised to take a photo as soon as she stopped the car. Unknowingly, she had the camera set on 'preview' and became flustered, trying to figure out why it wasn't taking the picture when she pressed the button. She started asking about the tux and so on. I told her that I'd explain on the way home. She took a photo of Richard and Joey and they took one of us.

When I backed into the driveway, I didn't see my car. I asked about it and she mumbled something that I didn't understand. Louisa said, "I'll open the garage for you." When the garage door went up I saw my car in the garage. The surprise was that a car would fit in the garage. It had been full of lumber and other things since we had the deck built almost three years earlier. She had cleaned it out while I was away. She had wanted me to think that my car had been stolen. I couldn't see that she was having a hard time maintaining a straight face. It was a great homecoming.

Louisa had been looking forward to this day since November 1, 2003, when she returned home from WLS. While there are different exercises between the WLS and MLS, we remain committed to letting each other, and others who haven't gone to either, have their own experience. Louisa had waited eight months to share her experience with me and she was anxious to hear details about mine. Obviously, she knew that something had affected me enough to wear the tux home. One more thing about the tux, it wasn't uncomfortable and I was surprised that it still looked good after almost 18 hours.

We went for a walk in the park to talk about our 'LS experiences. The WLS is 9 days and the MLS is 10. Some say it's because the women 'get it' quicker. While that may be true, and I'm not one to dispute it, I saw at least one other reason. You'll have to have your own 'LS experience before I will share it with you.

As I reflected on my MLS experience, and what we had achieved as C-68 (my class number), I felt a rush of gratification, and pride in being associated with that group of men. I also began to look at my life in terms of segments of time and other groups of people that give so much meaning to my life. I still think of a synchronicity that was revealed, within that context, after Louisa and I met. While I am 9 years older than her, there are people and places that we shared long before we became aware of it, or each other..

There were the basketball and football games between James Blair High School, for whom I was the radio play-by-play announcer, and Warwick High School, where and when Louisa was a student. We never had an occasion to meet there either. We were sharing space, in close proximity, long before we became aware of it.

When Louisa was at WLS, in late October 2003, she called me on the next to last day there. It hadn't occurred to me earlier, that we each had called one another on the next to the last day of the event. She called because she had an opportunity to register us for the 2004 Principia event. Now that I too was an 'LS graduate, I was eligible to attend Principia. I agreed that we should go.

Principia, we were told, was quite different from any of the other PSI seminars, on or off the ranch. PSI graduates generally refer it to, as "Jane's party." Jane is Jane (J.C.) Willhite, co-founder of PSI Seminars. She has carried the PSI torch for her late husband, Tom, and for more than twenty years since his untimely death. Jane is a powerful, generous woman who shares her passion for helping people live their potential. When I look at what she has done and still does, I see more than PSI Seminars. I see someone who loved her husband immensely and still loves the work they began together.

She serves as a great answer to Tina Turner's question, 'What's love got to do with it?" **(22)**

"YOU USED TO LIVE IN MY HOUSE."

Louisa and I were walking in Washington Park, in July 2004, knowing that we would be going back to the ranch together in October. It held a special significance. It's where our relationship went through a paradigm shift.

We had decided not to go to Powderhorn that summer. Louisa had said that I would come back from MLS so charged up that the peace and quiet of Powderhorn would almost be too much to bear. So, we planned a ten-day road trip to Illinois and Virginia. We would be in the car together a long time again, but also interacting with family and friends at Louisa's high school reunion. We'd also be stopping in Topeka, Kansas where Bob and Betty McKann now live with their daughter and son-in-law, Mary & Wayne Roberts.

My only disappointment about planning that trip was a reminder that I had thought we'd be doing it in the Volvo convertible. It was a goal that I hadn't reached, and as good as my life was at that time, I still felt the pang of losing sight of my goals. One of my lessons from my PLD and MLS experiences was that I often set unrealistic goals, or set them within unrealistic timetables. I know too, that I have set goals based on the expectations of others, or my desire to please them.

Work on another goal got underway just before our trip. I started the confirmation classes through the RCIA program.

Our road trip plans were changed for the better, and made easier that time around. We always enjoy being with Bob and Betty McKann. We like Mary quite a lot and I was eager for the opportunity to get to know her husband Wayne. We stopped at their place in Topeka on the first night.

We arrived in Topeka early enough to have some time to visit with them. Well, it was early enough for me. Bob keeps later hours than I do. I know because he has called us late at night, *and* early in the morning on occasion. In the morning we had breakfast with them and were off to see my mother. We could not have been prepared for what we found on that stop.

Louisa has grown so close with my mother that Mom will sometimes share things with Louisa that she will withhold from me. After I parked the car in the driveway, Louisa went into the house while I picked up the cooler. By the time I got to the front porch she was back outside, saying that something was wrong with Mom. She said that Mom hadn't hugged her and hadn't looked directly at her. I went inside and Mom was sitting on the sofa. She didn't get up to hug me. She looked disheveled. We sat down with her and asked what was going on. She said she had almost called us to tell us not to come by. There were no sheets on the bed that we use, and she said that she didn't have any clean sheets.

I walked outside, ostensibly to get something out of the car. I needed air. I was shaken. While I was outside Louisa had asked her if she wanted to go out to eat. She said, Mom's demeanor suddenly changed. Yes, she'd love to go out to dinner. She spoke of the Mexican food restaurant where we'd taken her before.

Mom stopped me, rather forcefully, when I said that I wanted to go down to the basement to look for sheets for the bed. She had also said that I couldn't use the bathroom because the commode was broken. I recalled that she had said the later to me on one other occasion, when I arrived for Ronnie and Linda Meyer's funeral in 2003.

While she was changing clothes, I went outside to make some calls, to her sister and to my brother Mike. She saw that I was on the phone and asked Louisa who I was calling. She said, he's probably calling Mike, or the McKanns to tell them we made it okay. She explained that we had stayed with Bob and Betty, and their daughter and son-in-law the night before.

I was shaken. I asked my aunt if she or the other sisters

"YOU USED TO LIVE IN MY HOUSE."

had seen Mom recently. The family has always been great about helping her and stopping by to visit with her. Frances explained that she and another sister, June, had been by but Mom wouldn't let them come in. On another occasion, they'd been grocery shopping and she wouldn't let them help her take the groceries into the house. Mom has always been a very private person, but recent events were even more extreme.

Mom's mood and demeanor were as normal as ever at dinner. After we placed our order I went to the Men's Room...to use my cell phone. I called Mike and Frances, and Mom's brother Gary and told them that we needed a family intervention. Mom would have to be moved to an assisted living center. She could no longer live alone. It's wasn't so much that she was 82, she was not taking care of herself. I told them that we were traveling to Virginia for Louisa's class reunion, and we could use Paul's computer once we were there, I would research the best place for her. Gary told me about St. Clare's Villa, in Alton, and named a couple of other places. St. Clare's Villa had opened a couple of years earlier after St. Joseph's Hospital had closed and been remodeled. Gary serves as an alderman and knew the project well.

We always carry our sleeping bags on road trips, and because there were no clean sheets for the bed we slept in them that night.

As we were about to leave the next morning, Mom hugged me with tears in her eyes and apologized for how we'd found things. I reassured her that I was okay and that I love her.

I told her that it wasn't about us. We were concerned for her safety and that we had to know that she would be okay. She told us both that she loved us and we were on our way. I told her that we'd discuss it more on our return trip.

Later that morning, while Louisa was driving, I started

making calls. I also called our friends Charlie and Marilyn Wall who live near Evansville, Indiana. Charlie and I have been friends since high school. We were planning to stay overnight with them on the return trip. I told Charlie about Mom's situation, and even he knew of St. Clare's Villa.

Mike called and said that he and his son Michael would meet us in Alton on our return trip. I had chosen the three people that I believe Mom listens to most often, for the intervention; Mike, Frances and Gary.

When we got near Richmond, Virginia, we encountered torrential rain and wind. It was the tail end Charlie, of one of the hurricanes that had come ashore that month. The rains continued to hurl themselves at the roads through most of Southeast Virginia.

After we unloaded things at Paul's place, I called Mom and told her that we made it safely. She apologized again for how we'd found things.

We were in Virginia for Louisa's high school reunion. Before going to the first night activities we visited with David and Julia Scoggins. Even though Julia had graduated with Louisa, she wasn't going to the reunion activities.

The reunion reception was fun…and I needed that. However, it was lightly attended. The second night of the reunion was held at the Coast Guard Officers' Club near Yorktown. It was a night of more torrential downpours.

I spent a lot of time on Paul's computer and on the phone, researching places for my Mom to live. Of course, she wasn't aware of it, or the family intervention that I had planned. I was calling upon the strengths that I had discovered or revived during my MLS experience. I recall telling our friends David and Julia about what was going on, and that I would need to be every bit the leader that I came to believe myself capable of being, for our efforts to be successful.

We headed back west on Monday morning, and drove as far as Newburgh, Indiana where Charlie and Marilyn live. We visited with them that evening and headed to Alton in the morning.

Mike and Michael arrived in Alton just before we did. Frances and Gary arrived shortly after us. Mom didn't know what to think with all of us descending upon her. We each expressed concern for her well-being. She was initially was strongly, verbally opposed to any type of move. She thought she had cancer and said that she just wanted to die. Mike said, "Mother, this is not a question about whether you should move. We're telling you that it's necessary to move and have you live safely."

She wouldn't go with Mike, Frances and me to look at St. Clare's Villa or any place we might want her to consider. The three of us did go there for a tour. Gary said he would see her the next day. Louisa took Mom to a hair stylist. On the way, Mom told Louisa that it was her worst nightmare. To her, it was the worst day of her life.

We could look back on it and knew that Mom was thinking that we were moving her to a nursing home. It was in a nursing home that her brother Leonard had died in September 2003. It was easy to understand her fear of that.

Mike, Frances and I were impressed with everything about St. Clare's Villa. Still, afterwards, Mike and I drove to another place, near the river. It didn't take long to rule it out.

We asked Mom where she'd like to have lunch. It was Louisa's birthday and she had an idea about where mom wanted to eat. We were surprised when she'd like to go to the Kentucky Fried Chicken. I think she did that because she knew that Mom would like it. Mom did like her idea and suggested the one where my cousin Marie is the Manager. So, KFC, it was. Unfortunately, Marie wasn't there.

After we got back to Mom's house, we decided to go on to Topeka that day. Mom was a little upset that we weren't staying and apologized again for what we had seen the previous week. After hugs, kisses and I love you, we we were on the road again. We drove back to Mary and Wayne's home in Topeka on the 17th. Louisa had spent at least three birthdays on the road, somewhere in Missouri, Kansas and/or Colorado over that past few years.

After a brief visit with Bob and Betty we headed back to Colorado the next morning. I think Wayne was off to work early and that Mary had an early flight that day.

Mike and Gary took mom to St. Clare's Villa on the 18th, and at just the perfect time. Mom saw some of the residents eating cheesecake and drinking coffee in the cafeteria and decided she liked the place after all.

CHAPTER TWELVE
A new fork in the road

I was coming to the end of my term as president of our BNI chapter. At that time the terms were six months long, and renewable for another six months, which I didn't want to do. As it turned out, I couldn't have continued as president anyway. Dawn Margowski, the BNI Area Director, asked me to consider working for and with her as an assistant area director. It was another paid part-time position.

A couple of months earlier, Dr. Ivan Misner, the founder of BNI, had spoken to a gathering of members of various chapters throughout metro Denver. I think it was a combination of that event and my MLS experience that led me to take on another paid part time position. I have a great deal of respect for BNI and of course I was flattered that they asked me to work with Dawn.

At the same time, I was also helping another BNI member Kevin, and his wife Tracy find a home. I really enjoyed working with them and their kids were easy to have along. It rarely took more than a look from either of their parents to settle them down when they became excited about one house or another.

We were still on the go as October arrived. It was back to northern California and the ranch. It would be our first trip for Principia, AKA "Jane's party." It would also be our first trip back to the ranch, together, since PSI-7 in May 2003. So much had happened since that event. Most importantly, our relationship had flourished.

Our assigned room was at the Best Western El Grande Inn in Clear Lake, and we'd be riding the bus to and from the ranch, that PSI Seminars provided. Somehow we were assigned a suite. Principia was already different from our other trips to the ranch.

We went to the ranch for the opening session that evening. As the bus passed through the main gate, we pointed out things and places we'd seen before as though we were confirming that our memories were real.

There is a vibration of high energy on the 1600 plus acres that make up High Valley Ranch. I sense it and I know that many others have expressed feelings about it too. It goes beyond the incredible beauty of the landscape, or the cattle and horses that make it their home. It's a working ranch like so many others in the area. For me, and for many others it is hallowed ground. I say that with no less respect for Gettysburg or Yorktown, places that gave birth to the freedom we enjoy. I gained a freedom here, unlike any sense of the word that I had known before.

The featured speakers included Mary Mannin Morrisey, Mark Victor Hansen and Bob Proctor. However, we were particularly drawn to.... Cherie Carter-Scott...and her husband Mike. If you've read <u>Chicken Soup for the Soul</u>, by Mark Victor Hansen and Jack Canfield, you've seen the contribution of Cherie's "Rules for Life."

However, it was Jane's "surprise event" on the weeklong agenda that provided an opportunity for Louisa and me to experience another paradigm shift in our relationship. It's no secret now that we walked through a "fire walk" under the direction of Bill Bastian. For me, and I think for Louisa also, as big as that was, the exercise that set it up had a bigger impact.

"YOU USED TO LIVE IN MY HOUSE."

Much of what I was "learning" had been taught to me before and some things on more than one occasion.

During Principia there is a "free day." Many people go down to the vineyards or to relax in the hot springs near by. Louisa and I decided to spend the day at High Valley Ranch. We'd been there together for PSI-7 and separately for WLS and MLS. We walked around the ranch re-visiting and sharing experiences.

I sang Karaoke for the first time. It was only symbolic of the changes I allowed myself to experience. I was nervous and changed my mind about doing it several times. It was definitely an 'outside the box' experience for me. I sing well enough that I don't fit the stereotype of karaoke and well enough to fear rejection. After waffling on whether to sing, I sang, "Beginnings," (23) a Robert Lamm song; one of Chicago's big hits. I was genuinely shocked that several people asked me to sing it again the next evening, and I have a big enough ego that I did it. I even sang a second song the second night.

Even the *food* was really over the top…superb. Jane had hired a chef whose credentials included being the chef for Wolfgang Puck's 50th birthday party.

While singing Karaoke was big move for me, Louisa took a giant step when she told Adrienne Willet, then the Advanced Course Manager for PSI Seminars in Denver that she would join the next PLD team.

We didn't stay over in San Francisco on that trip. We'd been traveling so much that year that we were eager to get home and put to use what we had learned. In 2004, we had spent a week in Snowmass, a week on the Big Island of Hawaii, a ten-day road trip to Alton and Newport News, and then the trip to High Valley Ranch for Principia. I had also been away eleven days for my MLS trip, and I had another trip, to Long Beach, scheduled for a BNI conference in November

CHAPTER THIRTEEN
No place for the weak of heart

While I was reveling in what I had just experienced, I knew that my brother Mike had taken on the formidable task of getting Mom moved to St. Clare's Villa. With the travel behind and before me, I needed to spend time with my real estate business and determine where my new clients would be found. Before going to Principia I had begun my work as an Assistant Area Director for BNI Colorado too. I had gone to a meeting of directors in Colorado Springs and had visited three of the four chapters to which I had been assigned.

Mike and I talked almost daily about what he was doing in Alton. I give him kudos for taking on the task, and also for staying there for so long to get it done. I saw him go through changes as he dealt with surprises and obstacles along the way. I gained a new respect and appreciation for my baby brother.

Whereas Bob had initially misunderstood Louisa, and our relationship, Mike never did. He has always shown her respect and affection. He has often talked about how good she and I are for each other, and how our relationship encourages other people.

I felt great about my Principia experiences and about what Mike was accomplishing in Alton. On the other hand, October meant red-October in St. Louis. Oh, there was plenty of Cardinals' red and this year it included red faces as the hometown team was swept into history that the Red Sox were re-writing.

During the World Series I skipped an RCIA class to watch one of the games. It was a class that Fr. Tom would lead. He's from St. Louis and he knew why I had skipped his class. On Sunday, after mass, he said, "I made it to the class Tuesday... missed you, Perry." I don't have any trouble making decisions. However, *living with them* isn't always as easy.

Louisa was supportive of my work for BNI, not only because it would create a little more cash flow. She became a member of our BNI chapter a month before I did, and knows its value. More importantly she saw how it caused me to extend myself beyond my comfort zone.

In addition to our weekly BNI meetings, I was attending meetings at the four chapters that I had been assigned to work with. Two of them were in disarray, having been formed perhaps too soon and apparently without strong leadership or support. There were early indications of déjà vu, relating to some of the things that I had uncovered when I worked with the CHRB four years earlier.

I enjoyed working with the four chapters and was developing some new relationships. I was also struggling with a lack of communication and support from the Executive Director in Colorado Springs. When I went to Long Beach for the annual conference, I was thrust into three days of classes for new directors. I roomed with another new director from Buffalo, NY and we found it easy to share our room and new experiences. There was entirely too much classroom time for me. I felt the training schedule had been poorly planned, with hours and hours of butt time and volumes of information thrown at us. I was reminded of the saying, "The mind can only absorb what the butt can endure." My top and bottom were way out of balance.

"YOU USED TO LIVE IN MY HOUSE."

By the time the classes ended and Ivan was ready to host a social gathering, I was so burned out that I stayed only long enough to eat and visit with a few people, then I left for a walk to the beach. While I met interesting people from all over the world over the next three days, I also knew that deep inside I wasn't connecting with the duties that made up the role of assistant area director. I was drawn to Dawn and Frank Margowski, the area directors for Denver, and the people with whom I'd been working in those four chapters and I thought that would be enough to keep me interested in the work.

I spent my birthday at the conference on a day when I could have been traveling home. There was a miscommunication between the Colorado Executive Director, and me, about the grand finale. So I spent that night in my room watching TV. It hadn't taken very long to learn that she and I had very different business practices and communication skills.

Perhaps it was the amount of travel that I had undertaken that year, or my feelings about the conference, but I was ready to head home on that pre-dawn flight on November 21st. The highlight of that week in Long Beach, was an evening spent talking with our friend Tanya Avedovich over coffee…how else?

The morning I left Long Beach the weather was cool and a rainy. I boarded a plane that was packed and somewhere along the line, because of my attitude about the disappointments of the week, the plane packed with damp clothing, and/or its recycled air, I picked up a cough and chest cold. It was severe enough that I didn't make it to the family Thanksgiving dinner at Chris and Brandy's. It also stayed with me well into December.

The best news during that period was how happy my mother had become with her move to St. Clare's Villa. Mike and others in the family told me that she was like a new person. One of her brothers said that he was sure the move saved her life.

CHAPTER FOURTEEN
Ready for another lap around the sun?

We rang in the New Year quietly as we looked ahead to what 2005 would have to offer.

We had been together, in some fashion, for almost 24 years. I had never been with anyone that long and I had never lived in any one place for as long as we'd been in our home. While I was running on New Year's Day, those were among my rambling thoughts. Judi and I had been married for 18 years. We had lived together for 14 of them. From the time I left home for the Army, in 1961, I had lived in 14 different houses, **not** including the four different barracks I'd stayed in at Fort Leonard Wood and Fort Riley. The 7th house had been *"Louisa's house."*

I thought too, of something a friend had said to me when we were teenagers…that I could get any girl I wanted, but I couldn't hold on to them. Her comment didn't cause my philandering, or anything else I did over the years. However, I know that that thought was always there, somewhere in my subconscious.

I'd been able to "hold on to" Louisa. I often tell people that without the PSI experiences, particularly PSI-7 and the work that we do to make our relationship *work*…there's that word again…it is unlikely that she and I would be together today. That is a scary thought for me, to know that I came close to losing the person who has become my best friend.

Louisa has told me that I think too much. On January 1, 2005, while running around Washington Park, so many thoughts filed my head. It seems that I spend a lot of time reviewing experiences and wondering what lies ahead. I had promised myself, while I was lying in the hospital bed in 2003 that I'd be more vulnerable and act on my impulses more. I hadn't kept that promise. I've always wanted things to be orderly and neat.

By late January I had knew that I had to have a meeting with the BNI Colorado Executive Director (ED). There were things that I had to discuss with her if I was to continue working as an assistant area director. I had discussed them with the Area Director and she had encouraged me to have the meeting with the ED. I made calls and sent emails that went unanswered. I offered to drive to Colorado Springs to meet with her.

She went on a trip to Australia and it wasn't until the middle of March that she called about my earlier messages. She declined my request for a meeting, saying that we could discuss anything on the phone. I unloaded the list of things that I had on my mind.

In April I went to a meeting of area directors in Colorado Springs. It seemed there were fewer attending than I'd met in September. The ED said something about herself, at that meeting that told me that she had no intention of addressing my concerns that I had related to her on the phone in March. I saw enough to know then that I would not renew my contract with her in August. Through all of that, Louisa was supportive even as she watched another exercise in creating additional income, go south.

During the time when I was making every effort to communicate with the BNI Colorado franchise owner, I volunteered to staff the February PSI Basic. I knew that it would pick up my spirits and take my mind off of my own challenges. It was certainly the right choice. The Chiefs were great, giving us quality direction and trust in handling our responsibilities. I know that I was in a different place than I'd been when I staffing March 2004. Having experienced other PSI events, PLD, MLS and Principia, I was better equipped to serve the students. Every time I go back and plug into an event with PSI, I grow more. If that sounds like a commercial, I can accept that. I've shared a lot of the ca-ca that I, and Louisa have gone through, so it's only fair that I share an antidote, too.

CHAPTER FIFTEEN
Shattered...again

I felt my heart break on February 17th. Bill Michaels had asked me to meet him for coffee that morning. When I saw him he looked tired and I mentioned it. He didn't address it until we sat down with our coffee. He had been diagnosed with lung cancer. My close friend, my confidante, who loves his family so deeply, who had run 19 marathons, has cancer. "What can I do for you?" I asked. "Make me laugh," was his reply. And I thought stand-up comedy was tough.

It was a difficult challenge because my heart was already crying. I accepted his challenge and since that day I have watched the most remarkable attitude carry him and those of us who love him. He looks great today, after the chemotherapy, the loss of hair and weight and regaining both. He's enjoying his family and friends, and his life. He's even running again. Bill's living the Tim McGraw song, "Live like you were dying."

I was active in the PSI arena, too. I worked as a volunteer staff member for the PSI Basic in February. We had a great staff, and I had a ball. I think my playfulness that weekend, while I was dealing with the news Bill Michaels had given me, came from the same strength I'd found when I went on-the-air after right after Kevin was born...and I'd been told he probably wouldn't live another day.

Louisa was well into playing PLD on Team 32. She was playing big. She was embracing the challenges with which I had often struggled. I rationalized that the game had changed in the year between our teams. In fact, elements had and the leadership had as well. However, as my friend Dawn says, "People will show you who they are." Louisa's special nurturing qualities and indefatigable enthusiasm won out again. She virtually put her PLD buddy on her back and carried him to ACK Night too. That's not said to diminish the work he did. She has brought out the best in many of us over the years.

Easter came in late March and with it, my confirmation as a member of the Catholic Church. I had already become very comfortable with the liturgy and doctrines. I found many similarities with the Methodist religion to which I had subscribed for many years, and also to the Lutheran services that we had attended after Kelly became a member of that church where she and Pete were married, and Brendan and Riley were baptized

Louisa and I saw the warmth and openness of St. Ignatius Loyola on the first day we visited in August 1999. I didn't know whether that warmth and diversity was unique to Loyola or embodied in the spirit of the Catholic Church.

I still see myself as more of a spiritual person rather than a religious person. I embrace my religion and I enjoy learning about it. Fr. Tom's homilies are works of literary art for me. He puts Jesus and His teachings into a context that I can relate to every day...not in only an historical context. I recall that former, or non-practicing Catholics have on a few occasions told me that they left the church because it/they didn't talk about Jesus. I don't know where they went to mass, but it sure wasn't at Loyola, or for that matter at Mt. Carmel where my father-in-law is a member. Both churches are filled with the spirit and the Word of Jesus.

One particular Sunday Fr. Tom described how the word catholic means 'universal' and it really brought me closer to my new religion. I could then see that the doors of our church are open to all and that still gives me a rush. There are times when, during mass I will look around at the people in the congregation and feel 'goose bumps.' *This is my family.* I recall how many reached out to me in prayer, phone calls and with cards, when I was sick in 2003.

After one of Fr. Tom's homilies on forgiveness, I was moved to call Judi, my ex-wife. I apologized for "being such a shitty husband." She said that she didn't think I had been rather that I'd been a "shitty ex-husband." I said that I could live with that. While she never called me on it, she must have…at some level…known that I'd been unfaithful to her while we were married. We each have our own way of dealing with reality.

Louisa is a spiritual person too. She was raised as a Catholic, Cradle Catholic if you will. Yet she doesn't fit any of the traditional Catholic stereotypes or molds. Perhaps that is, in part, because her Father is a traditional Catholic and her mother was an Episcopalian. Then again, like her mother, she doesn't fit many molds. She's said that if it hadn't been for Vatican II she might not be a practicing Catholic. I'm still working to understand the meaning of that. It could also be because so many of those stereotypes, like many stereotypes, are inaccurate. She has welcomed my joining 'her' religion, and has never pushed or even directed me to it.

About two months after my confirmation, I was elected to serve on the Pastoral Council. It wasn't lost on me that my former nemesis, from my choir experiences, was also elected. I am happily surprised at how well she and I are working together on the council. I told some people that God was telling me to 'get over it.'

CHAPTER SIXTEEN
Work hard, play hard

My first real estate transaction of the year came from a surprising source. Our friends Woody and Siri wanted to sell their house to their daughter Pam, and her fiancé, Mark. I worked as a transaction broker to help them achieve the results they wanted. Then, another member of our BNI chapter had asked me help her find a place for her father, whom she would move to Denver from Texas.

That was followed closely by a call from a woman named Cindy, who said that our friend Katie Langeberg had referred her to me. Whereas Louisa would also put together the mortgages for Pam and Mark, and for Janice, Cindy came along with her own loan officer. Cindy had placed calls to other Realtors before she talked with Katie and was referred to me. Imagine Cindy's surprise when the other agents didn't return her calls.

Cindy's circumstances for her move were tender and I wanted to be very sensitive to her real estate goals. She had recently become a widow. Cindy has a glow about her that hasn't diminished even considering the circumstances she's dealt with.

I had been window-shopping for a new cell phone. I was due for an upgrade with Verizon. In April I walked into their store at the Cherry Creek Shopping Center and met a young salesman named Chad. He took time to explain to me the features of the two or three phones my plan entitled me to have as a free upgrade. I was so impressed with his customer service that when we were wrapping up the sale, I gave him my card and Louisa's. I said, "I really appreciate your customer service. If we can provide you or a friend with the same level of customer service, please let me know." That was way outside of my box. I had seen Louisa do it on many occasions. Chad said, "Actually, I'd like to buy a condo." Louisa and I met with him two days later and after she pre-qualified him, we started searching for a townhouse for him.

We had quickly developed a good rapport. While looking at places, I told him that Louisa and I would be gone for about eight or nine days in May. We were going to High Valley Ranch as volunteer staff for PSI-7. Chad didn't even ask about it. His reply was simply, "Cool. We'll look when you get back."

With that we were off to High Valley Ranch. We staffed PSI-7 in May, two years after own experience on Team 378. It's a very rewarding experience to be on staff, assisting the students and facilitators. Of course, being there as husband and wife, who are happy with each other, added a different perspective for us. We loved it and recommend it to all PSI grads that have the opportunity to do it.

A little more than a month after our return we closed on Chad's townhouse.

It appeared that I was headed for a record year for my real estate business. And, the saying goes things aren't always as they appear. It wouldn't be my best year, but a very nice recovery from 2003 and 2004.

A couple of weeks before the closing for Chad's townhouse, Louisa and I escaped to Powderhorn for our 22nd Anniversary. We actually left on our Anniversary, and we left later than planned because of business activity…*there goes our anniversary again*, drumming up more business for us. We decided to stop at Glenwood Springs for dinner and happened across a very good Cajun food restaurant, the Bayou Cajun Restaurant &

Bar. The food and service was good enough to warrant that commercial. We pulled into Powderhorn close to midnight, unloaded the bikes and baggage as quietly as possible, while enjoying the cool night air.

The nights were typically cool on the Grand Mesa. The days, however, felt warmer than normal to us. We didn't ride bikes or hike on the mesa because they'd had record snows and still had a lot of snow and even more mud on the trails.

We took the bikes to Grand Junction, looking for the trail we'd ridden on our first trip in 1998. The heat was intense. The temperature was 100 degrees or higher. There isn't any foliage there, open space and small gravel that reflect the sun. I had a very difficult time with the heat, to the point that Louisa took my bike ahead for me at times. She would ride ahead then come back for my bike. Note that when she did that she took both bikes up hills. We cut the riding short because of the heat and found refuge in a café in Grand Junction.

Isn't it funny how things can change so quickly? I don't mean humorous funny, but rather ironic funny.

We were getting along great, business was good and I had jumped into the Pastoral Council duties by offering to help with the St. Ignatius Loyola Day picnic. It was a big deal because our parish hadn't had a picnic in the park, even though the church is located across the street from City Park, since being chastised for not having a permit a couple of years ago.

At the council meeting I offered to secure the permit because I had been through the process before. When I called the Denver office of Parks & Recreation, I was told that they weren't issuing permits in City Park for Sundays because of the jazz concert summer series there. We could just have someone at a picnic site early and lay claim to it.

It was easy enough to print a map and have it inserted into the weekly bulletin, showing parishioners where the picnic would take place. I volunteered to be the first person on the scene because I'm up early anyway.

Louisa and I hadn't had a real good fight in ages. So, somehow it came to be on St. Ignatius Loyola Day, or perhaps the day before. And like so many of the past arguments or fights, I don't recall what brought it on. Bring it on though, we did. I went to City Park at 6:30 AM, coffee in hand, setting out directional signs I'd made, and picking up odds and ends of trash, making the site look presentable. Around 7:30 or 8, Richard Ryerson arrived, and he joined me in policing the area. Richard was running errands when Charles Liesering arrived with coolers and other goodies. I bid adieu, saying that we'd be back for the picnic, when I knew that it was unlikely.

Back on the home front, Louisa had swollen and red eyes from crying and I was in no mood to start the debate again. Because of the tools we've grown accustomed to using, even in the worst of times, we were able to talk through it once I gave in to the process. We did get to the picnic at a point that fewer people were there and it was almost time to break camp.

We still know how to push each other's buttons. Maybe it happens we we're tired, or one or both of us is dealing with some stress that we haven't shared with each other. The point is that it still happens. Whether you look at it from the perspective of our having been through so much together, and apart over the years, or our PSI journey or our involvement with our church family, we are finding ways to lessen the turmoil and deal with whatever it is that causes us to be at odds. Now, we work through things in a matter of hours, rather than weeks.

It was about that time that I passed through another transition. I notified the BNI Colorado Executive Director that I would not renew my contract. I played by the rules, giving thirty days notice. Predictably, she dismissed me immediately.

"YOU USED TO LIVE IN MY HOUSE."

My friend Bill Thompson teaches math at Red Rocks Community College. From time to time he had suggested that I teach real estate there also. While I felt flattered by his suggestion, I didn't feel qualified, not having a college degree. He put me in touch with Wendy Bird from the business department who explained that they often hire adjunct teachers who have experience in a given field that balances the lack of degree. I was asked to consider teaching two units for Record Keeping and Escrow Accounts.

Wendy cautioned me that the students, particularly near the end of the semester, would have 'that glazed over look' when it came to those subjects. I replied, 'not to worry. I come from that glazed over look.' I was taught more about record keeping by Louisa, than any real estate course.

I don't minimize the importance of record keeping in the business of real estate. It just isn't a sexy aspect of it. I don't use an escrow account in my business, trusting a title company to hold and disburse monies. I hadn't given it much thought since passing the exam for my broker's license. The new challenge of teaching would cause me to do more homework and of course, learn from teaching.

In September we were heading back to the ranch, and back to Principia. We flew into Sacramento rather than San Francisco so that we could make the connection to get home earlier at the end of the week.

Somewhere along the route between Sacramento and Clear Lake, Louisa was hit with a severe migraine headache. When we arrived on Sunday afternoon, she needed food pretty badly and quickly ate the box lunch that PSI had provided while I handled the registration for both of us. The headache hadn't subsided when it was time to go to the ranch for the opening event and she stayed in bed at the hotel. So many people asked about Louisa, that I could have used a continuous loop recording that night…"Hi, great to see you too. No, she's in bed with a migraine. I think she'll be okay tomorrow. She'll be looking forward to seeing you, too."

Some of the speakers were speakers we'd heard in 2004 and some of them were new to us. Dr. John DiMartini was one of the new speakers. Jane had sent each of the registrants a copy of Dr. DiMartini's book…early enough to have read it before Principia. In a role reversal Louisa buzzed right through it and I got bogged down. I enjoyed his "story," and then I thought he went esoteric on us. Not so in person. If you have the opportunity to attend one of his seminars in less than two days driving, do it. I went back to his book and saw it differently. One of the things I haven't done and must allow myself time to do is to do the exercises in it. Every parent with an under achieving child, or one who has been labeled by a school counselor or teacher as ADD or "slow," would do well to read the book.

Bill Bastian was back with another fire walk and the same set up, but he added something almost unimaginable… something that presented a different *bend* to the cliché about stepping outside the box.

Fortunately the chef returned too, and he went way over the top with the meal for the annual Mardi Gras party on the last night of the event. And speaking of the Mardi Gras party, to some people it is a formal dressy affair with masks, which is what I think Jane has in mind. Louisa had that part covered. She looked elegant and beautiful and not like the type who would go anywhere with my character. I didn't shave after Monday morning, adding a scruffy look to what would be my hippie costume. I borrowed a red wig from our friend and PSI-

7 Team 378 teammate Gretchen, and wore a t-shirt, complete with large butterfly on the back and a cigarette pocket on the front, and bellbottom jeans. I had owned both, and had worn them when I was a DJ in Williamsburg in 1969. I don't know where they got it, but more than a few people called me Willie. Maybe it was the red bandana. Jane had brought in a band, Wall Street, from the Bay Area and they are **HOT!** The lady knows how to throw a party.

The next day we headed home and would have one week to catch up on things before leaving for a long-awaited trip to New England. Our friends David and Julia, from Virginia, would join us mid-week.

We had traded a Powderhorn week for a week at Weir's Beach Resort, New Hampshire. It's popular resort for the New Englanders, and others during the summer but deserted afterwards. We didn't mind that at all.

We discovered that everything we wanted to see in New England is 90 minutes from Weir's Beach.

When we were planning the trip I contacted a couple, Steve and Nancy Innes, whose home I had sold in Denver in 1995 when they moved back to New England. We had known Nancy from 10:30 Catholic Community, and while I didn't know Steve well before the real estate transaction, I enjoyed getting to know him and was fascinated by his work. When they lived in Denver he had a machine shop in his garage, and custom-made lenses for observatory telescopes. We scheduled lunch with them on our second day, meeting them in Portland, Maine.

We'd been through Portland on the first full day of that week. We had decided to visit the Shelter Institute, where we had almost spent our honeymoon. They're in a new location, and still near Bath, Maine.

On the way to Bath, somewhere around Brunswick, I recalled that our friends Bruce and Doris Nieman had moved from Cary, IL to New England, and I thought, to Maine. We had known them initially through the SkiGlo Conference and had hosted each other in our homes. Louisa called the CLS office in Austin and learned where they were living. It was approximately 5 miles from where she made the call.

We were focused on reaching the Shelter Institute, and I was focused on getting back to Weir's Beach before the Cardinals' play-off game. Louisa called, and talked to Doris. We made plans to meet them in Portland after our lunch with Steve and Nancy the next day.

We were back in Portland on Tuesday. We met Steve and Nancy at a restaurant situated on what had been a ferryboat. It had served Tidewater Virginia residents before the long Chesapeake Bay Bridge Tunnel was built that connects Virginia's Eastern Shore to its mainland at Virginia Beach, near Norfolk. It was fun to reconnect with Steve and Nancy.

Not long after lunch we caught up with Bruce and Doris. After walking and talking our way around Portland, we stopped at a small restaurant for dinner, bidding adieu shortly afterwards.

David and Julia arrived in Boston on Wednesday night and we spent the next couple of days catching up with each other, driving to Vermont, Portsmouth and most points north, east and south...hiking and playing tourist. We really enjoyed our time with them.

Louisa and Julia have known each other since childhood. Louisa's known David since he and Julia started dating in high school. I met them shortly after Louisa and I started dating. I have always enjoyed their company, and their friendship. They each thanked me for inviting them to join us. I told them that they were on a very short list of people with whom I felt that I could travel and spend a few days or a week with.

I think we hadn't been back in Denver very long when Louisa was asked to be a coach for PLD Team 36. She waffled, initially saying no and then agreeing to do it. Michelle Fournier, the PLD coordinator, who was on PLD Team 29 with me, had asked me to coach too. It's just not the right time for me to do it. I told her that Louisa would be a great coach. She coaches me everyday. That's not intended to be funny or sarcastic...okay, funny. However, it is true. I discovered a while back that I am blessed to have her in my life and that I am a better human being for it.

CHAPTER SEVENTEEN
Almost a quarter of a century later

Late in 2005 Chris and Brandy declared that they wanted to buy a different house in 2006. They'd mentioned it before, but I heard a decision when they talked about it this time around. Not long after that we learned that Brandy was pregnant, and not long after that we'd have our first granddaughter. When Brandy decides that something will happen, it happens. We call it the 'law of attraction.'

I like their relationship. I believe they have what it will take to work through the challenges that lie ahead. They've been married over six years now, so in terms of marriage years, they've learned how to walk. They're both very excited about the baby they're expecting.

I taught the two units of Record Keeping & Escrow Accounts for Red Rocks Community College. The students were bored and I wasn't effective in my efforts to draw them into the discussions about the topics. Over Christmas break, I decided that I wouldn't return for the spring semester. I think Wendy was disappointed. I know that Bill Thompson had hoped that I would enjoy it. Perhaps if I were to teach a different topic, or give it another chance, I might enjoy it. I felt that my heart wasn't in it. The students and faculty at Red Rocks Community College deserve more than I would have given, had I stayed.

That was the first Christmas that we drew names for exchanging gifts. I recalled that the Coons family had done that when I was a kid. It also ended a trend. The 'kids' had pooled resources the previous two Christmases and purchased big grill for us and a TV for us the following year. My brother Michael was in on it too.

Dave came home in January...*in transit* as the military says. Before leaving for his new duty station, Okinawa, he took a side trip to Utah, to see a friend. He stayed a couple of extra days and was back in Denver long enough to pack before heading to Japan. He had hoped to leave his Australian Cattle Dog, Kota with friends during his tour in Okinawa. As it turns out, we are keeping Kota...much to his surprise and to the surprise of the other young men and women we call our children.

Chris Coons and I planned to go to the Cardinals' Spring Training in March. I had hoped to trade a timeshare week for it. However, it became impossible to find an available unit because Spring Training and Spring Break occur at the same time. One of our friends who'd been in the travel business for years told me that the damage caused by Hurricane Katrina very likely sent more people to Florida than might have gone to New Orleans, making the rooms even harder to find.

As it turned out, Chris did go to Spring Training, in a manner of speaking. The manager he works for in Chicago asked him and a couple of other guys to go to Sunrise, Florida, near Fort Lauderdale, to help train a staff at a new restaurant. He agreed to go, not only because of Spring Training...it was February when he was asked. His three weeks of temporary duty turned into six weeks...great time to be in Fort Lauderdale rather than Chicago for sure, but he spent most of his time at the restaurant or the motel.

"YOU USED TO LIVE IN MY HOUSE."

We put Chris and Brandy's house on the market in February and had an offer submitted by the second person that looked at it.

Our friend Steve Little has called me a hopeless romantic. I think it first happened when I sent out emails with our wedding photos, and current anniversary photos.

Sometimes fate provides the right opportunity to embrace my romantic nature. For the past year I have been the recipient of several Starbucks gift cards. One such occasion was earlier this year. I thought about how hard it is to surprise Louisa, buying anything with our debit card, or God forbid, our credit card. She'll go on-line to check balances on each.

A couple of weeks before Valentine's Day I was in a Starbucks with a client and noticed that they have Passion Tea. Louisa had ordered that at The Cheesecake Factory and really enjoyed it. I was able to surprise her with a box of it, using a current Starbucks gift card…without her knowledge…for Valentine's Day.

As I am writing this story Chris and Brandy are expecting Sienna Jade Harrison to arrive in April. They'll be moving into a new house at the end of this month. Chris Coons is temporarily living in Florida and Dave is in Okinawa. Pete and Kelly are in transition too…as Kelly prepares to start her own business.

It seems that Pete and Kelly have good communication and I believe that they'll be able to face their challenges successfully if they keep it as open as it is. They *do* have challenges that I can relate to. Pete's a great stepfather and yet the boys haven't really let him in completely. They'd like Jeremy to be more of a dad and I don't think he's man enough to be there for them. I told Brendan that God put enough love in his heart for Pete *and* Jeremy. He won't have to love his dad any less to love Pete a little more. I think Riley is more open to Pete. After all, he was a week past his first birthday when Jeremy walked out on Kelly, and ultimately on the boys as well.

I know too well, that when I left Judi, I left Kevin, Kelly and Chris too. It wasn't my intent, but it became my reality. I made an effort to be there for them, and they're in a better place than I, to say whether I succeeded.

Chris and Dave saw their dad walk out too, and have had precious little contact with him since. Chris opened up to me long before David did…but he did. Claude didn't have to miss out on their lives. He chose to. It was his loss, and to some degree, theirs too.

Dave's friend in Utah is a young woman named Jamie. They met over the Internet and "talked" for a year before they met face to face. Dave told us about her after he arrived in Okinawa. Pete and Kelly met over the internet too, and they're approaching a third anniversary of what I see as a good marriage…defined by me as one where the partners are willing to do the work.

While I'm paging through our family album, I'm seeing another transition. It's one that will take some time for me to get used to. In the months ahead my youngest brother will move to Florida, just when I'm getting used to calling by his preferred name, Michael. There are a number of reasons why it's a good move for him. He came to Denver twenty years ago…my baby brother whom I didn't know as an adult. We've developed a strong friendship and I know I'll miss him.

There isn't a full day that goes by that I don't think about Kevin. When I speak of him people will express their sympathy for my loss. I'm quick to say that Kevin was a true blessing and that he gave us more than he ever asked of us. God must hold me in high regard to give me the opportunity to be his father.

"YOU USED TO LIVE IN MY HOUSE."

I asked Chris, Chris, Kelly and Dave to contribute something to this book. When Chris Coons and I were discussing it, I told him that I think I know what Kevin would say about the journey that Louisa and I are on. Chris said he often looked into Kevin's eyes, knowing there were thoughts behind them. I agree. We could almost see Kevin's wheels turning.

Kevin was very expressive when he was happy, making loud squealing sounds or laughing or 'singing'…particularly to the sounds of Crosby, Stills & Nash, the Eagles and Dan Fogelberg. He was equally expressive when any two of us were fighting, and it was easy enough to tell that he didn't like it.

When Kevin was born the doctor said he wouldn't live another day. He lived 21 and a half years. His remarkable courage inspires us to be as strong in our challenges as he was in his.

Louisa hasn't read what I've written, or contributed to writing it…directly. I told her that I would wrap up the story, which is of course a work in progress, on March 6, 2006. That would be 25 years from the evening when she said those seven words, *"You used to live in my house."* On that anniversary, she prepared a terrific meal of scallops and crabmeat. So, 25 years later, we spent a quiet evening enjoying a terrific dinner and each other's company.

We could look at the many instances of synchronicity that are a part of our relationship and believe that we were destined to be together. I've joked about them, saying, "Okay God. I get it. I'm staying." Obviously, I didn't accept it that easily.

Louisa and I both work from home offices. We spend an inordinate amount of time together. Kelly once said to me, "Dad, I love Pete too. But I don't want to spend as much time with *anybody*, as you and Louisa spend together."

My space does feel a little crowded sometimes. However, I am enjoying our relationship more than I could have ever imagined before I came to expect it. We create it everyday.

We have a small chalkboard at the door to our bedroom, ostensibly for notes. After one of our more heated exchanges, Louisa wrote this message on it:

"I pray for understanding, harmony, peace and a relationship where love flourishes."

Louisa

That message will stay there to remind us that prayers are answered.

One more thing...we *are* growing old together and we're excited about it.

AfterWords

For years, I thought about writing short stories, or perhaps a novel. However, three events occurred in recent years that became the impetus for this story.

One occasion occurred in San Francisco, on our way the "Life Success Course,"/"PSI-7" offered by PSI Seminars. (www.psiseminars.com). We were traveling with a friend, Juan Panzardi, whom we'd met in the PSI Basic course a month earlier. After dinner we were walking around Pier 39 and, at one point he said he wished that he and his wife could be as happy as Louisa and me. I laughed, and said, "You don't have a clue. When you get to know us, we should give you hope. If nothing else, we should give you *hope*."

At times I thought we had tried everything to make our marriage work, and yet we weren't happy. For a long time, I didn't understand why we weren't, or why *I* wasn't.

"YOU USED TO LIVE IN MY HOUSE."

It was during the exercises at PSI-7 that I began to see myself as someone who could be happy, who deserves to be happy.

The second came a year after PSI-7 while we were hosting Juan Cedillo, from Guatemala, through the Denver International Program. (www.dipusa.com). One of the other hosts suggested that we meet for dinner with her and her guest, a young woman from Chilé. We had *just been seated* at the restaurant where we met them, when the other host said, "So you have the perfect marriage?" I replied, "If you mean one that's willing to do the work, yes." I don't know what she had heard about us, or from whom. I had previously met her briefly at a meeting, and Louisa had not met her before that day. The other event was a promise that I'd made in 2003, to my PSI-7 Buddy, Courtney Krenz. I told Courtney that I would write a book within the next two years. Completing Surreal Estate in 2005 gave me the confidence that I could write this story.

What Louisa and I have is a marriage, a relationship, and a friendship that is worth the work required to make it successful. We enjoy our relationship. We want to share our happiness and let others see that it's possible to be even happier after more than 23 years together. It does keep getting better and stronger…because we want it to be that way.

It is *my* hope that you will see something in this story that gives you hope for your relationship, or to encourage others. To that end, I have disclosed things that I wouldn't for any other reasons, save Confession.

The love that Louisa and I share today bears little resemblance to the love that precipitated our marriage. It is so much more.

R. Perry Coons

So faith, hope, love remain, these three; but the greatest of these is love.

1 Corinthians 13

"What would the children say?"
Chris Coons
Chicago, IL

Last October, while driving across Michigan, I stopped in a gas station for something to drink and I found myself holding a bottle of Faygo Redpop. It had been roughly 20 years since I had seen one of these sweet red sodas, and probably as long since I had recalled some of the memories that the drink triggered. After buying the drink and getting back into the car I called my dad to share the nostalgia with him for a moment, and then I went on my way back home to Chicago. But my thoughts kept going back across those 20 years and into my early childhood for the rest of the day.

I don't remember the first or last Redpop of my childhood, but I do remember the only time that I downed two bottles of the stuff in a matter of seconds. I was about seven years old and I had just taken my first vitamin that was not shaped like a cartoon character. Now either nobody bothered to tell me, or as usual I didn't bother to listen, but these vitamins weren't meant to be chewed. The resulting battle between the vitamin and the Redpop for the control of my taste buds seemed to go on forever, and in more ways than one it is symbolic of the relationship that I developed with both my father and the rest of my family over the next 15 or so years.

I am still amazed at times by the things that we used to fight about. Food was a common subject of dispute, but if you where to walk in on some of those arguments you'd have thought we were fighting life and death struggles. There were also the expected parent/child fights over the music that I listened to, behavior problems at school, and the friends that I kept. But I also remember heated arguments over drawings on a chalkboard and "aluminum glasses" among other things. All of those arguments however had the same root as most of the disputes that I've come across in my life, and that's simply a lack of communication. One person failing to say what needs be said, either because they're unwilling or they don't know how. And another failing to hear what needs to be heard for the same reasons.

That is not to say that all we did was fight, because I do have plenty of fond memories of my childhood as well and even a few of my adolescence. And sometimes even the arguments were tender in their own way. One summer night in particular I remember sitting on the front steps with my father and my older sister as he went about the unenviable task of explaining our parents' divorce and his subsequent remarriage to our stepmother. My sister and I were probably about 12 and 10 years old respectively, and we couldn't possibly hope to understand the dynamics of the adult relationships that he was trying to explain to us, and which he was probably trying to get a grasp on for himself at the same time. But I remember still the care and effort that was in his voice and in his eyes as he tried to console us and at the same time give us the painful truths the he knew we had to hear.

I don't have many opportunities to sit on those steps any more because I have lived far from home for about 10 years now. And a lot has changed over that time with the relationships that I have with my parents and my siblings. While I can say with gratitude that my parents and I have developed more open and honest relationships, and have begun to get to know one another much better than we ever did before, I have to also admit that the opposite is true with my brothers and sisters. Though we are all close in age and therefore grew up fairly close, we seem to have grown apart over the years. My older sister has a family of her own now and will no doubt have some tough things to explain to her own children in the coming years. My older stepbrother is also married and has a child, and he seems to be doing very well, but I can't say that I talk him often enough to know for sure. And my other stepbrother, whom I shared a room with and was in the same grade with in school, now lives on the other side of the world and I've only seen him 2 or 3 times over the last 10 years.

And my oldest brother passed on 14 years ago, but I can say with complete sincerity and without sentimentality that he is still a big part of my life. Perhaps the one sibling that I can say that I have gotten to know fairly well as an adult is the one that has only recently become one. Through her difficult situations, which she has worked through and even benefited from, I have been able to get to know my younger sister in ways that I do hope to get to know my other brothers and sisters as well.

I honestly don't know exactly how or when that will happen. I do know that those things take effort and don't happen on their own. But I also know that the common excuses of time and distance are much easier to come by at times than the sincere commitment to get to know another person. Perhaps you have to chew the vitamin before you get the motivation to drink the Redpop.

Whatever may come though, I do feel blessed to have these people as my family. The differences that have separated us at times have helped us to broaden ourselves as well. And if there is more of that to come then I welcome it with open arms.

June 9, 2006

Chris Harrison
Thornton, CO

As I start to write this, I think about where I'm at today with myself and my family. The wonderful wife that inspires me to be the best person I can be. Our new beautiful daughter that has started me on my newest journey, and our new home which I love. I think about the people and events that helped me get to this point in my life.

I don't remember the first time I met my stepfather, but I do remember spending time at his A-frame beach house on a Virginia beach. I did like that house and it's view of the ocean. I liked him more than other boyfriends my mother had. I did love the fact that they got married on the beach. I didn't know what to think of his kids from his previous marriage; Chris, Kelly, and Kevin.

I'm not sure when I learned we were moving to Colorado for his job, but it didn't seem to take long for the move to happen. Once we were here our lives sure changed. I remember he seemed so serious and sometimes angry. When he lost his job with the company that moved us out here things seemed worse. He did drink a lot and argued with my mother, none of us got along at times. We all fought and argued, it was a tough situation for all of us. I think the turning point for my dad and I was a large fight we had when I was a teenager. He was arguing with my Mom and I got in between and yelled at him, we wrestled around and had a few punches. After we both settled down we had a small talk but it turned out big. I gained a lot of respect for him shortly after that. I learned he wasn't always so serious; he has a good, dry sense of humor, which I think has worn off on me. I liked the red clown nose he would put on when things seemed to get too serious. As I got older I understood his side of things. He has become such a loving and wonderful man to my mother and our family. He has been there for us every time he has been needed and is always willing to help, even when it meant bailing me out of jail. He has such determination, drive and patience. As I said at the beginning about how happy I am with my life and the person I have become. I think about how I owe a great deal of who I am to him and I thank him.

I love you Dad.

June 9, 2006

Kelly Blood
Arvada, CO

Some people believe that many couples who stay in a marriage forever are not truly happy. Some people say divorce should always be avoided when there are children involved. Some people say staying together just for the sake of the children is a bad idea. Some people think divorce is too easy and people should try harder to make their marriage work. Statistics show discouraging odds when it comes to second marriages, especially when merging two families with children. Wherever you fit into these various belief systems, I can tell you that all of them have elements of truth. Statistically speaking, I suppose our family had little chance of sticking together. After all, are children a motivator in working through a marriage when it comes to stepfamilies? Wouldn't it be easier to walk away if you didn't share biological children? Particularly if the conflicts are often having to do with the children?

Knowing what I know now as an adult, it's almost unbelievable that my dad and stepmother's marriage survived. But what's more impressive is the genuine happiness and contentment I see. To them both, I say thanks for working through all of the factors that contributed to a challenging marriage and family. Our lives as adult siblings are enriched because of your endurance. Having divorced parents was perhaps the only thing we had in common when our families merged. I'm fairly certain as young adolescents we never imagined we would be so close and emotionally healthy as we are today. In particular to my father, I would say your courage and growth as an individual has given us a chance to have a father daughter relationship that I am proud of. And to my stepmother, thanks for all of your love and support over the years, in spite of my often-sarcastic attitude. And to my brothers, my children are lucky to have you as uncles and I am proud of how far each of you has come. Kevin, the fifth sibling who is not here to speak for himself today, would probably be proud as well. He had the gift of seeing the best in all of us.

I am not of the mindset that every marriage should stay intact. I can only imagine how different the lives of us siblings would have been if our biological parents had never divorced in the first place. And quite honestly you two, I don't know what you were thinking when you got married. Didn't you do the math? Five children (one severely disabled) all within five years of each other. I know it was never easy, dare I say difficult and exhausting. And if anyone asks you "was it worth it" you would say absolutely.

June 9, 2006

Dave Harrison
Okinawa, Japan

If there is one thing I've learned from my parents' journey, it would have to be the importance of communication. Along with that, the understanding that developing communication between two people, no matter how strong the love, can and usually will require a huge amount of patience. I remember fights not long after we moved to Denver as simple as one not leaving a note for the other if they left for a while. I thought they were silly at the time. As time passed I noticed less fighting though. I also noticed little notes or messages in random places more often. It sounds very simple, but I watched their communication build from there. The biggest fights can develop from smallest misunderstandings, I know because I was witness to it. Of course I was also often a reason for it. I've mentioned fighting a lot so far. Not something you'd probably think of with two people so happy for over 20 years. That's where the patience comes in.

I couldn't tell you exactly how long it took, but if you looked at my parents the first couple of years, you probably wouldn't be thinking to yourself how much you'd love to be like them. But now, 23 years later I couldn't imagine a better model. I may not have grown to have the same beliefs that they have. In a lot of ways I am probably quite the opposite of both of them. The lessons I learned while watching them learn and grow, will be with me for a lifetime though. I wish I could say that would make it easy for me when I get married, it's funny that way though.

No matter how much I've learned from watching them build the life they have together, I know that chances are I'm going to go through the same building and learning they had to with each other with my wife. Understanding that is the head start I was given by my parents. You can bet that when I am married and making a toast at my anniversary, whether my 1st or my 23rd my parents with be receiving an enormous amount of credit for what they have shown me. The good, the bad and even the ugly.

June 13, 2006

AUTHOR'S NOTE

When I thought of asking the 'kids' to write something that I could include as *their* perspective of our journey, I considered the order in which they would appear. It could have been chronological. They've experienced that all their lives. They appear in the order that I received them.

I am deeply moved by what each of them has had to say.

Of course if Kevin were here, rather than in Heaven, he'd have his say…in his own special way. Perhaps someone would read it to him. I can almost see him, kicking his legs and making those sweet sounds of excitement.

As both Chris Coons and Chris Harrison have noted, we now have a third grandchild. Chris and Brandy Harrison, and all of us in our combined families, proudly welcomed our beautiful granddaughter, Sienna Jade Harrison, to our world on April 27, 2006.

We have also welcomed Jamie Barker Harrison into our family, as she became Dave's wife on January 12, 2007. She read the manuscript before their wedding and still went through with it. She's a keeper.

R. PERRY COONS

June 18, 1983 Perry & Louisa with David, Kevin, Chris C, Kelly and Chris H

"YOU USED TO LIVE IN MY HOUSE."

Wedding Party: Phyllis, Terry, Louisa, Dr. John Harwood, Perry, Dave & Brian

Carol Hunter's Original Drawing of 49 Brandon Road, Newport News, VA 1950

"YOU USED TO LIVE IN MY HOUSE."

Perry & Brian FINISH Philadelphia Independence Marathon 11-29-81

Perry's Parents: Perry and Virginia Coons

"YOU USED TO LIVE IN MY HOUSE."

Louisa's Parents: Paul and Carol Hunter

Kevin Todd Coons 1971-1992

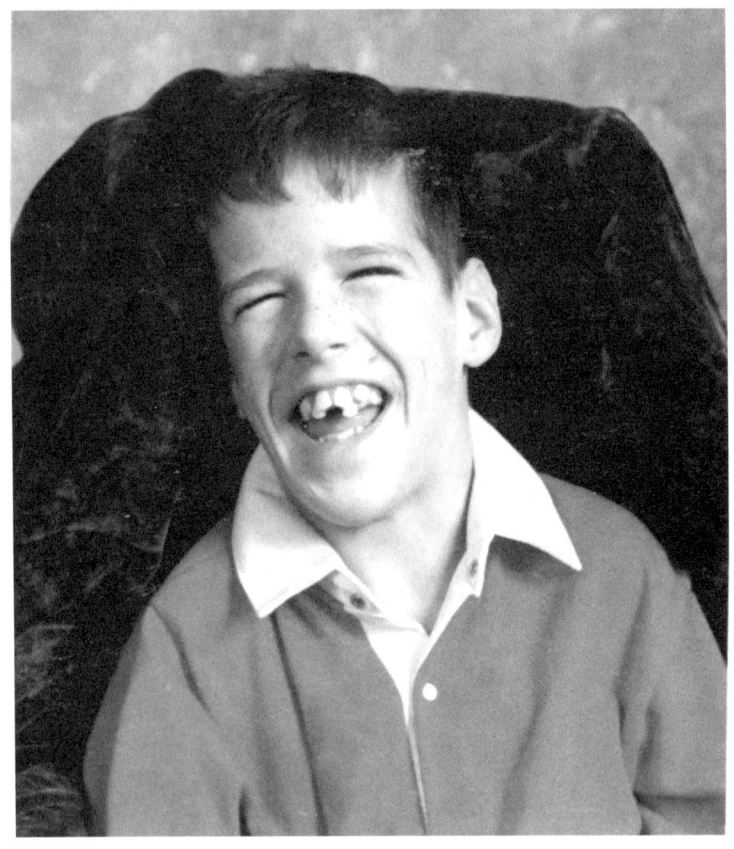

"YOU USED TO LIVE IN MY HOUSE."

Chris and David Harrison, Chris & Kelly Coons July 1985

Perry and Louisa Coons August 1985 Tivoli Denver Grand Opening

"YOU USED TO LIVE IN MY HOUSE."

Perry as Wyoming Statehood Festival Coordinator July 1990

R. PERRY COONS

Perry's Original Computer Art 1991 Christmas Card

"YOU USED TO LIVE IN MY HOUSE."

Perry and Louisa Coons February 1997

Antony Donkor of Weija, Ghana with Perry at Sphinx Park, Colorado 1999

"YOU USED TO LIVE IN MY HOUSE."

Pete and Kelly Blood with Brendan and Riley, July 26, 2003

R. PERRY COONS

Chris Coons, Kelly Blood, Dave Harrison and Chris Harrison, July 26, 2003

"YOU USED TO LIVE IN MY HOUSE."

Louisa with new PSI Basic Grad Juan Cedillo of Nebaj, Guatemala and Perry, May 2004

R. PERRY COONS

Perry surprises Louisa, **arriving in tux** from PSI Men's
Leadership Seminar C-68
July 26, 2004

"YOU USED TO LIVE IN MY HOUSE."

Brandy and Chris Harrison 2006

Louisa with Kota, Dave's Australian Cattle Dog, chasing squirrels in Washington Park, March 2, 2006

"YOU USED TO LIVE IN MY HOUSE."

Perry and Louisa Coons, and the journey continues…

ENDNOTES

1. Synchronicity (Sting) Gordon Sumners, 1983, Magnetic Publishing as performed by The Police, 1983, A & M Records
2. Larry 'Yogi' Berra, (Lawrence Peter Berra & ac Thomas N. Horton, 1989, McGraw-Hill Publishing.
3. What a Fool Believes, Michael McDonald & Kenny Loggins, 1978, Milk Money Music & Snug Music, as performed by The Doobie Brothers.
4. In My World, Justin Hayward, 1981, Warner Brothers Music, Ltd. & Bright Music, Ltd., as performed by The Moody Blues.
5. Changes, David Bowie, 1971 RCA Records
6. Waiting for a girl like you / Michael Jones, Lou Gramm, as performed by Foreigner, Atlantic Records, 1 July 81 Somerset Songs Publishing, Inc, & Evansongs, Ltd.
7. Hard to Say I'm Sorry, Peter Cetera/David Foster, 1982, Double Virgo Music & Foster Freeze Music, Inc., as performed by Chicago.
8. The Boxer, Paul Simon, 1968, as performed by Simon & Garfunkel.
9. Hair, Gerome Ragni, James Rado, pseudonym of James Radomski and Galt MacDermot, March 1, 1968.
10. It's a Big, Old, Goofy World, John Prine, 1991, Weona Music
11. Runaway, 1989, Max Cook & Del Shannon (pseudonym of Charles Westover), as performed by Del Shannon.

12. Tha 2 of Us, 1996, Ralphy MacDonald, William Salter, Bill Withers, Cherry Lane Music Pub, Arista Music, Inc, Bluenig Music, as performed by Bill Withers.
13. Happy Trails, Dale Evans, Paramount-Roy Rogers Music Co., Inc., as performed by Roy Rogers and The Sons of the Pioneers,
14. If Tomorrow Never Comes, Kent Blazy & Garth Brooks, 1988 Major Bob Music, as performed by Garth Brooks.
15. David Crosby, 1970, Crosby, Stills, Nash & Young, "Déjà vu", Atlantic Records
16. My Way, Paul Anka, 1974, BMG Music, as performed by Frank Sinatra.
17. Long Lonesome Highway, George W. Duning. EMI Feist Catalog, Inc. (ASCAP), as performed by Michael Parks.
18. "Where've You Been?", John Vezner, Don Henry, 1988, Wrensong Pub & Cross Keys, as performed by Kathy Mattea.
19. Truckin,' Words by Robert Hunter; music by Garcia, Lesh, Weir January 1971, as performed by The Grateful Dead.
20. Husbands and Wives, w & m, Roger Miller, 18 Jan 66 as performed by Roger Miller.
21. Where Were You When the World Stopped Turnin', Alan Jackson, EMI April Music Inc, Tri Angels Music 2001, as performed by Alan Jackson.
22. What's love got to do with it? By Terry Britten & Graham Lyle, Good Single, Ltd., Myaxe Music, Ltd, Rondor Music, Ltd. 1984, as performed by Tina Turner.
23. Beginnings, Robert Lamm, 26May69, as performed by Chicago.